16-

EUROPEAN POLYPHONY: PERSPECTIVES BEYOND EAST–WEST CONFRONTATION

European Polyphony

Perspectives beyond East–West Confrontation

Edited by
Ole Wæver
Pierre Lemaitre
and
Elzbieta Tromer

Language-editing by Chris Miller

MACMILLAN

First published 1989

Published by
THE MACMILLAN PRESS LTD
Houndmills, Basingstoke, Hampshire RG21 2XS
and London
Companies and representatives
throughout the world

Typeset by Footnote Graphics
Warminster, Wilts

Printed and bound in Great Britain at
The Camelot Press Ltd, Southampton

British Library Cataloguing in Publication Data
European polyphony: perspectives beyond East–West confrontation—(The Centre for Peace and Conflict Research).
1. Western Europe. Foreign relations with Eastern Europe 2. Eastern Europe. Foreign relations with Western Europe
I. Wæver, Ole II. Lemaitre, Pierre III. Tromer, Elzbieta IV. Series
327′094
ISBN 0–333–49611–6 (hardcover)
ISBN 0–333–49612–4 (paperback)

Contents

Notes on the Contributors

Dr Nansen Behar is Bulgarian; he was born in 1940. He teaches at the Institute for Contemporary Social Studies of the Bulgarian Academy of Sciences and is Vice-President of Ecoforum for Peace. His major publications are *Comparative Analysis of Economic Systems* (Sofia, 1985), *Peace and Science* (Sofia, 1985) and *Global Problems and Social Progress* (Sofia, 1988).

Dr Barry Buzan was born in 1946, took his first degree at the University of British Colombia in 1968, and received his doctorate at the London School of Economics in 1973. He is currently Reader in International Studies at the University of Warwick, and Director of the Project on Non-Military Aspects of European Security at the Centre for Peace and Conflict Research in Copenhagen. His principal publications are *People, States and Fear* (Brighton, 1983), and *An Introduction to Strategic Studies* (London, 1987).

Michael Clarke is British; he was born in 1950. He lectures at the University of Newcastle-upon-Tyne and is an Associate Fellow of the Royal Institute of International Affairs. He has been a Guest Scholar at the Brookings Institute, Washington, DC; his principal publication is *The Alternative Defence Debate* (1985).

Dominique David is French; he was born in 1949. He is Secretary General of the Foundation pour les Etudes de Défense Nationale in Paris. He coauthored *Le Désir d'Europe: l'Introuvable Défense Commune* (FEDN, Paris, 1980).

Dr Janet Finkelstein was born in the USA, and has lived in France for the last fifteen years. She works at the Centre National de la Recherche Scientifique in Paris, researching for US and French think-tanks, and undertaking policy analysis for various French political organisations. She is co-author of *La Nouvelle Doctrine de Guerre Américaine et la Sécurité de l'Europe* (Paris, 1983); her *Vers Une Nouvelle Doctrine de l'OTAN aux Etats Unis*, Paris, appeared in 1980, and *L'Initiative de Défense Stratégique: Une Idée qui Fait son Chemin?* (Paris) in 1987.

Dr Helmut Fritzsche is from the GDR; he was born in 1929. He is Dean of the Faculty of Theology at the Wilhelm-Pieck-Universität, Rostock, and Coordinator of the Conference of Systematic Theologians of the Socialist Countries. He is also a member of the Centre for Peace and Dialogue Reseach at the University of Rostock. Among his publications are: *Freiheit und Verantwortung in Liebe und Ehe* (Berlin, 1983), 'Christian–Marxist Cooperation in the German Democratic Republic since 1945', *Occasional Papers on Religion in Eastern Europe* (Philadelphia, 1987), and 'A GDR View of the Christian–Marxist Dialogue referring to Cooperation between Theology, Marxist Philosophy and Scientific Research in the Universities of the GDR', *Reformed World*, Vol. 40, No. 2 (Geneva, 1988).

Dr Marek Grela was born in 1949; he is Polish. A member of the Polish delegation to the CSCE (Helsinki, Geneva, Madrid and Vienna) and to the Conventional Stability Mandate Talks in Vienna, he is currently Senior Research Fellow at the Polish Institute of International Affairs. He was formerly the Scientific Secretary of the Polish Committee on Peace Research (1985–7). 'The Events in Poland and European Security' appeared in the *Polish Yearbook of Political Sciences* (1983). He is the author of two books (in Polish): *Poland's Position in East–West Relations* (Warsaw, 1987), and *Poland and the Development of the International Situation in the Eighties* (forthcoming). He has written on East–West trade, European security and arms control for Polish and other journals.

Pertti Joenniemi is Finnish; he was born in 1942. He works at the Tampere Peace Research Institute, and is Chairman of the Society of Foreign Policy Associations (the Paasikivi Society) and advisory member of the Board of Disarmament Affairs of the Finnish Foreign Ministry. He has published works on Nordic security, Arctic security developments, on neutrality in the theory of foreign relations and on the arms policies of the European neutrals.

Mary Kaldor is British; she is currently Senior Research Fellow at the Science Policy Research Unit at the University of Sussex. She was until recently editor of END Journal. Among her latest publications is *Mad Dogs* (1986). She is co-editor of *Dealignment; A New Foreign Policy Perspective* (Oxford, 1987), and *The New Detente; Rethinking East–West Relations* (forthcoming in 1989).

Dr László J. Kiss is Hungarian; he was born in 1945. He is currently Head of Department at the Hungarian Institute for International Affairs, and Guest Scholar at the Peace Research Institute in Frankfurt am Main. His publications include 'Europäische Sicherheit: Interpretationen, Perzeptionen und Aussenpolitik Ungarns', *Europa Archiv*, 4 (1988), 'Die Rolle Ungarns im europäischen Sicherheitssystem', *HSFK-Report* 9 (1987), and 'Interpretation of Security in the Eighties', *International Security*, a special edition of *Külpolitika/Foreign Policy* (Budapest, 1988).

Dr Berthold Meyer is from the FRG; he was born in 1944, and is Senior Researcher on West German Security Policy and Western Security Cooperation at the Peace Research Institute in Frankfurt. In 1983 he published *Der Bürger und seine Sicherheit*, and in 1985 *Atomwaffenfreie Zonen und Vertrauensbildung in Europa* (Frankfurt am Main and New York).

Erik Noreen is Swedish; he was born in 1951, and lectures at the Department of Peace and Conflict Research of the University of Uppsala, Sweden. He is currently engaged in writing a dissertation on the formation of the post-war security system in Scandinavia. In 1983, he published *The Nordic Balance: A Security Policy Concept in Theory and Practice; Sweden between the Great Power Blocs: Swedish Security Policy 1945–1988* is forthcoming (in Swedish) in 1989.

Pavel Podlesnyi is Russian, Cand. Sc. (Hist.), is sector head at the Institute of US and Canadian Studies, Moscow. A leading specialist in Soviet–American relations, author of monographs such as *USSR–USA: Fifty Years of Diplomatic Relations* (in Russian) (Moscow, Mezhdunarodnyie Otnosheniya, 1983) and, together with G. Trofimenko, *Soviet–American Relations in the Contemporary World* (in Russian) (Moscow, Nauka, 1987). His article 'Confidence Building as a Necessary Element of Détente' appeared in Karl Birnbaum (ed.) *Confidence Building and East–West Relations* (Wien, Austrian Institute for International Affairs, Laxenburg Papers, LP 5 / March 1983).

Dr Ole Karup Pedersen is Danish; he was born in 1929, and has been Professor of International Politics at the Institute of Political Studies of the University of Copenhagen since 1970. He has been a member of the Danish Commission on Security and Disarmament for the last five years and a member of the board of the Centre for Peace and Conflict Research in Copenhagen since 1988. In 1970 he published *Foreign Minister P. Munch's Perception of the Place of Denmark in International Affairs,* and in 1986 co-authored *Naval Strategy and Nordic Security Policy* (both in Danish).

Ole Wæver is Danish; he was born in 1960. He is a researcher at the Centre for Peace and Conflict Research in Copenhagen and lectures at the Institute of Political Science of the University of Aarhus. He co-authored 'European Security – Problems of Research on Non-Military Aspects', *Copenhagen Papers*, No. 1 (1987) with Egbert Jahn and Pierre Lemaitre, and has published works on Nordic security, political theory, peace movements and the arms trade.

Pierre Lemaitre is Danish; he was born in 1946. He is currently a research fellow at the Centre for Peace and Conflict Research at the University of Copenhagen. Prior to this he was researching Soviet military build-up and doctrines at the Slavonic Department of Aarhus University, and wrote (in Danish) a Research Report, *Analysis of the Soviet Naval Build Up: An Introduction to Sources and Methods of Analysis* (Slavonic Institute, Aarhus University, 1983). He was co-author (with Ole Wæver and Egbert Jahn) of 'European Security'. His 'Krise und Reform in den Sozialistischen Staaten und das Europäische Sicherheitssystem' is forthcoming in Christian Wellman (ed.), *Frieden in und mit Osteuropa: Osteuropa in den Neunziger Jahren* (Frankfurt, 1989).

Elzbieta Tromer is Danish; she was born in 1960. She is Candidate in Political Science (Aarhus University) and Master of Letters M.Litt. (Oxon.). Her thesis on Polish economic reform is being prepared for publication. She is currently a research fellow at the Centre for Peace and Conflict Research at the University of Copenhagen.

Acknowledgements

Barry Buzan agreed to be the director of our project group on Non-military Aspects of Security when the book was in its late and hectic phase. His advice on contractual arrangements was very helpful, but we are above all indebted to the perspicacity of his encouragement and criticism.

Professor Egbert Jahn, of the Peace Research Institute, Frankfurt, was the group's first project director. Many of the ideas of the project group, including the theoretical foundation of the conference which led to this publication, were worked out during his stay at the Centre. He guided the research on which our present work is based.

Once the conference was over we entered the dangerous phase of editing papers written by researchers more experienced than ourselves. In that process, we met with great support and encouragement from all the contributors – both when we got behindhand and felt that contributors all over Europe must be meditating publication elsewhere, and also when we were approaching the deadline and papers were being hastily faxed forth and back.

The authors, of different disciplines and national origins, all agreed to write in English. And English proved to be many things. So, we tempted Chris Miller to exchange his native Oxford for the charms of Copenhagen and work with us for a while. The work proved so plentiful and the deadline so close that all he saw of Copenhagen was the red roofs of the city (for which Copenhagen is *also* famous) from his office at the top of Vandkunsten 5. Without his anglicising of the (at least) 16 different versions of English and his supreme ability to grasp and render the authors' ideas the book would have been much less readable – and half as long again.

Finally, we would like to thank the Centre's technical staff under the leadership of Grete Bille for the work of several long evenings and weekends. And we are much indebted to our student assistants, Trine Bie-Olsen, Thomas Dalager and Ib M. C. Nielsen, for their readiness to step in and solve each new problem as it came up.

OLE WÆVER
PIERRE LEMAITRE
ELZBIETA TROMER

Introduction: A New Europe? The Menu

Elzbieta Tromer

Is there a security interest common to both Eastern and Western Europe? And if so, is it compatible with national and alliance security interests? Europeans' perceptions of themselves are changing. The 'old world' is no longer content to be junior partner to the superpowers; it senses in itself a new if unspecified vision, a new confidence in 'European' values, and wishes to build on its cultural heritage.

A consequence of this development is that the terms of the security debate and its orientation around the two superpowers are in the process of changing. Fluctuations in confidence in the respective superpowers have caused fundamental questions to be raised about the bloc system of security. In the past, security has been associated predominantly with the capacity of a nation to defend its borders against military attack, and thus in the European context with the binary model of Europe. Today, new trends can be observed: (i) Attention in security matters is shifting away from the military toward the political, the economic and the ecological. (ii) The traditional identification of national and alliance interests has been partly supplanted by the identification of national and regional interests; these may be all-European or include only a part of the European continent. An example of the latter is the Balkan Peninsula, where regional détente between countries belonging to different military and political alliances was initiated well ahead of the superpower détente. These two trends have created a proliferation of notions of security. The new concepts of security tend to avoid the notion of a bipolar Europe. Instead, they stress the emancipation of the smaller East and West European states from the two superpowers, and the interdependence of all European countries; this is one of the meanings given to the term 'the europeanisation of Europe'.

But is Europe being 'europeanised'? On this point there seem to be two conflicting bodies of opinion: the one refers to the tradition of 'European' culture and perceives a growing awareness of 'things European'. The other points to the equally traditional disunity of

Europe, and suggests that whatever unity currently exists is a product of superpower alignment. On one point there is unanimity; in so far as interrelation depends on physical contiguity, it emphasises European distinctiveness.

A task for peace researchers and other social scientists in the wake of these developments was to search for the existence of security interests common to Eastern and Western Europe. The 'retreat' of the superpowers exposes new patterns of conflict; can these already be discerned? And if common East–West security interests were identifiable, how would they then relate to the national and alliance security interests?

The need was therefore felt to present a broader spectrum of European opinions on security. A first step was the conference arranged by the Centre for Peace and Conflict Research at the University of Copenhagen on 'National Viewpoints on Non-Military Aspects of European Security'. The idea behind the conference was to create a forum for discussion of the changing official and unofficial perspectives on European security of the superpowers, and the major and minor European states. Among the most important topics discussed during the conference were the contrasting views on security of parties in power, parties in opposition and the peace and other alternative movements.[1]

At the conference, no attempt was made to parcel out responsibility for the dangers to European security. Attention was given to the way in which government, opposition and peace movements represent different security interests. The different social forces are mainly relevant in different time perspectives, which means that they are less incompatible than they might at first seem. The daily task of not making war is mainly the job of governments and military men. For the party in power, pragmatic considerations often seem of greater weight than political colour. This security thinking is often short term. The prevention of war is, however, not only a matter for governments, nor are governments free agents. The political opposition, unconstrained by the practical realities of power, can offer medium-term security ideas. And non-governmental organisations and individuals can also directly influence the European security process. Very often their programmes reflect radical, long-term or 'visionary' thinking. It may be that it is a characteristic of periods of large-scale change that these different time-perspectives are no longer so clearly demarcated.

Before discussing national views on European security, it seemed relevant to elicit views as to why the 'first' détente process broke down. Not only because the question is interesting in itself; to understand national positions on Europe's future security structures, it is necessary to understand national views on the reasons for the breakdown of détente. It may be that intra-European détente originally failed or was weakened because détente was perceived as monolithic, and therefore followed the logic of superpower relations. Or it may be that the preconditions for détente did not exist, and that the impression of a détente process was illusory. Other arguments ascribed the breakdown to intra-European factors such as the increasing influence of the conservative parties in Europe, the structural problems affecting East–West trade, and other national and intra-bloc tendencies that surfaced the moment the 'discipline' of external confrontation was slackened during the first détente.

The evaluation of these arguments is central to our understanding of the new process of détente. What are the reasons for the renewed top-level interest in détente? The usual 'peacenik' argument is that peace is the only alternative to war and that all of us, even the top decision-makers, have by now finally realised that we either keep the peace or perish in nuclear catastrophe. However, today there is a greater awareness of the (separate) economic motives underlying both the improvement in US–Soviet relations and the European interest in détente.

The superpowers have been forced to review their short-term security policies in the light of their medium-term economic prospects. On the Soviet side, the new leadership now tends to subordinate foreign to domestic policy goals. A long-term argument for this strategy is that Soviet economic strength is a prerequisite for maintaining Soviet influence in the world. Nuclear war, like ecological catastrophe, cannot be confined to a single country, and the danger they represent emphasises the interdependence of the European states – and, indeed, all states. In recognition of this, the concept of 'peaceful coexistence' has been elevated to the 'highest universal principle' governing relations between states, and 'peaceful competition' is stated to be the *only form* of competition between the capitalist and socialist political systems. On the US side of the Bering Strait the level of deficits does not encourage growth in armaments spending. The threat of recourse to force is no longer considered so useful an instrument of foreign policy. And it is argued in Chapter 5 that Europe no longer has so great a strategic role in US foreign policy.

To a greater extent than the superpowers, the Europeans also adduce economic arguments in favour of détente. Europeans expect to benefit from the expansion of trade with their neighbours, and hope, too, that better contacts will lead to a common effort to combat pollution.

The economic benefits to be expected from the new period of détente are particularly stressed by the East European governments. They take development to be a *sine qua non* of peace. For the East European governments, improvements in East–West relations are widely considered a precondition of successful economic reform. Researchers from Bulgaria, Hungary, and Poland stressed that for their governments this factor is no less important than the atmosphere of *perestroika*. They argue for a ban on all political barriers to economic and technological cooperation between East and West, and refer to the possibility of such bans serving the purposes of an economic cold war. Great stress is laid in the East European contributions on the increasing incidence of economic factors on security. In their view, economic war through discrimination and embargo is currently among the greatest dangers to national and thus to European security. It is economic relations that must lay the basis for a second détente. Should they fail to do so, and growth rate differentials continue to widen, the very foundations of European security will, in the East European view, be undermined. Political, economic and environmental security are central to recent East European security discussion, at both governmental and opposition levels, but for the governments economic security is top of the list.

In the West, military–political security remains the priority. Economic relations between Eastern and Western Europe are seriously hampered by the incompatibilities between the two economic systems. The point is made in Chapter 8, and was frequently referred to in discussion: the economic links between the East and West European blocs are not important enough to have significant consequences for the West, still less are they capable of influencing Western policy toward the East. On the contrary; trade between the two blocs tends to be a function of the political relationship between them; COCOM remains an example of subordination of trade to security interests. Thus, the conclusion from the Western perspective was: economic détente is impossible without thorough reform of the East European economies, with the emphasis on decentralisation and export orientation.

The reformist fractions within the East European communist parties support this view. They hope that contacts with the liberal market economies will have effects that go beyond the economic sphere. Attempts to close the economic gap with the West involve, it is said, a degree of political and cultural identification with the West. Such identification at the political level means to strive towards greater autonomy for civil society. The lower level of economic development in the East could be remedied by introducing market forces. Once a similarity in economic structures and levels of development was achieved, conditions for rational interdependence would exist, and mutual benefits would guarantee economic contacts between East and West.

The supposition of 'mutual benefit' and 'interdependence' seems to be a major problem in this line of argument. The new détente and Soviet *perestroika* have awoken expectations in some West European countries of access to huge Soviet and East European markets. Not everyone is so confident of the trade prospects. Sections of the West European business community see little advantage in expanded trade with the East except access to Soviet raw materials and cheap Eastern European labour. But they are inclined to keep their options open. The goal is uncertain, but the race has started. The limited economic benefits for the Western trading partners are a further argument for Western political leaders, in particular the practitioners of *Realpolitik*, who are uncertain of the benefits of interdependence. Though economic motives for trade are limited, the political leverage that it might offer is regarded in certain quarters as a political inducement for expanding trade with the East. From the East European point of view, trade relations based on exchange of natural resources for technology and manufactured goods are exposed to the same problems as those between the industrialised and developing countries. This kind of interdependence does nothing to create a system of non-military security.

For the East, as for the West, a further factor influencing trade may be the desire to ensure good relations with one state rather than another. The influence of such considerations is however not unique to intra-European trade; they also weigh with the superpowers. But the political criteria that influence the trade decisions of the superpowers are more likely to represent the inflections of their overall policy, and are not determined by the necessity for coexistence felt by countries that share borders.

This is not to say that the alliances do not themselves impose certain limitations on trade. But the degree in which such inhibitions make themselves felt varies and is related to the geostrategic position of the country. Thus for Hungary the priority lies with economic rather than military security, and the possible repercussions of alliance policy on trade are felt as a danger to security. For Hungary, the deterioration of superpower relations was frightening not only because it involved a threat of nuclear war, but because it stood in the way of the integration of the Hungarian with the world economy.

The majority of the non-communist Western peace movements support the demands for economic reforms put forward by the East European oppositional groups. These demands are more radical than those put forward by the reformist fractions within the communist parties; they tend to include complete economic liberalisation accompanied by far-reaching political reform. Also, a good number of the East European oppositional groups have given up hope of constructive cooperation with the East European powerholders. The Western peace movements have not completely decided on this point. An example of this ambivalence is the FRG's Green party, a majority of which maintains contacts only with the oppositional groups in Eastern Europe, while others give priority to contacts with the East European ruling élites.

The focus of the Western peace and ecological movements is however not on economic but on political and ecological issues. The END (European Nuclear Disarmament), CND (Campaign for Nuclear Disarmament) and others, for example the US Freeze campaign, propagate common security. Most of the West European peace movements argue that opposition to nuclear weapons must be based on a policy of promoting political change in Eastern and Western Europe as part of a plentary commitment to non-militarism. They are against West European defence cooperation as all such cooperation is regarded as undermining the cause of peace. On the same lines, movements like the Greens maintain that no security policy which allows the threat or use of military force can be described as a 'peace policy'. The first step toward peaceful security policy would be the demilitarisation of the East–West conflict. The Greens would also like to see the dissolution of the opposing blocs in Europe, and believes this could be facilitated by the FRG leaving NATO.

In contrast with the conservative parties now in power, the social democrats in opposition in Western Europe have taken up some of the views heard in the peace movements. The SPD, Labour, and the other North European social democratic parties fully adopted the concept of 'common security', while the European conservatives reject the concept on the grounds that it requires too great an identification with a basically alien system, and cannot accommodate alliance with the USA. When it is discussed as a policy it is essentially with reference to NATO and its 'managing' of 'cold war'. But the conclusion of the INF agreement indicated a change in the conservative perspective and this change not only contributed to weakening the association of *Ostpolitik* and social democracy, but also took much of the steam out of the 'absolutist' peace movements of the West.

The peace movements in the East were meanwhile thriving on a variety of different oppositional perspectives; disarmament, in their eyes, was not a monolithic issue. The combined influences of détente and *perestroika* enhanced the scope of their actions, and they had behind them the example of Solidarnosc. Until recently, no long-term perspective governed their actions. Their agenda was set by the immediate problems of their countries; their energies were spent on individual cases of infringements of human rights, action in favour of conscientious objection, or to close a polluting plant. They could not collaborate with similar movements in Eastern Europe. There are new trends in the East European peace movements; the theme of a common European heritage and the vision of a 'Common Europe' are increasingly heard.

The Evangelical Churches of the GDR occupy a position apart; in accord with the official peace movement in its recommendations on disarmament, they reach this position from a Christian perspective, and tend to take the logic of peace to its Christian conclusion in conscientious objection. The Churches refuse to refer the threat to world security to one political system and maintain that changes are necessary in both systems for the sake of peace and common security – the latter concept was officially adopted by the Federal Synod of Churches. Instead, the Church concentrates on threats to peace that come from one's own cultural traditions, in which conflictual behaviour and 'friend–enemy' conceptions are implicit. The Churches are careful to avoid all suspicion of being an opposition movement, and do not, for example, concern themselves with economic issues.

Like Hungary, the German Democratic Republic in the early 1980s made strenuous efforts to maintain relations with the West despite the increasingly cool relations between the superpowers. For these and other small and medium-sized European states, the lesson of this period was, that the smaller a country, the more its security depends on international cooperation. And since it is they which suffer particularly from inflections in superpower policy, it has been proposed that the small and medium-sized countries have a special role to play as mediators between the two Europes. For others, however, the role of bridge-building itself offers too many hostages to the binary view of Europe, and it is the common European culture which should now be stressed.

******

The new developments in European security have internal and external sources. One part of this book deals with internal sociopolitical changes that the traditional political structures have not been able to incorporate. A second part deals with another important source of change, the perspectives of the superpowers. There follows a survey of the debate on European security in each of 11 states. The book begins and ends with a theoretical overview.

Barry Buzan (Chapter 1) uses an approach based on the 'Neo-realist' theory of international politics. The global pattern of distribution of power is undergoing a transformation: the system might be changing away from bipolarity towards a new multipolarity. He shows how the new debates in Western Europe take on completely different perspectives when viewed in this context. Analysis of the politico–military divide between Eastern and Western Europe, and of the split in security perceptions between Western Europe and the United States, leads him to the conclusion that Western Europe ought to take greater responsibility for its own security. But he also shows that a precondition for large-scale West European security initiatives is greater cohesion within that region. The present internal disunity of Western Europe is in contrast with its status as a single security entity. The level of cohesion in Western Europe is thus a major variable deciding the future directions of European security.

Buzan's study deals with the state and regional (European) level. The chapters by *Helmut Fritzsche* and *Mary Kaldor* (Chapters 2 and 3) deal with social movements and the changes they initiated within the West and East European states. The peace work of the Evangelical Churches in the GDR is an example of the coordination of apparently disparate perspectives. In Helmut Fritzsche's account the Churches have succeeded in finding common ground between, on the one hand, the political leadership of the GDR and, on the other, their own integrity. By combining the Christian command to love one's enemies with considerations of political practicability, the Evangelical Churches have become distinctive participants in the official peace philosophy. The secular, Western peace movement shares certain preoccupations with its Church-based, East European equivalent: these include the role of the state in modern society, and ethical issues, such as who has the right to make decisions about life and death. Mary Kaldor analyses the nature of the security system and corresponding tactics for the peace movements in the post-zero option era. She concentrates on the new peace movements which arose in the 1980s. They are fuelled by a sense of disillusionment with the conventional political process which stems from experience of social democratic governments during the 1970s.

The views of the superpowers are analysed by *Pavel Podlesnyi* of the Moscow Institute of USA and Canada Studies (Chapter 4) and *Janet Finkelstein*, a US researcher currently working at the Centre National de la Recherche Scientifique, Paris (Chapter 5). Janet Finkelstein's contribution considers the obstacles to the creation of coherent foreign policy in the USA. The strategies of the Reagan administration are examined in association with some of the economic sources of tension between the USA and its European allies. The USA is torn between the need for European approval and the desire for European military–strategic compliance. The USA looks to its European allies to validate its claims that it is defending (e.g., democratic) interests other than its own. The pressure on Europe to increase military expenditure is unlikely to decline now that the USA is realising the economic limits of its power. Its European allies are, paradoxically, among its principal economic rivals, and have recently made economic overtures toward its principal strategic rival.

Pavel Podlesnyi's study sets out the new policies of the Soviet Union. Emphasis is placed on balancing conflicting international interests and, in armament policy, on 'reasonable sufficiency'. The official recognition of the desire for survival as a principal interest of all states, and its corollary, the recognition that all states are prepared to compromise, leads to a new conclusion in Soviet security policy – namely, that security should be considered in a perspective of collaboration rather than emulation. In other words, security problems can be solved by a more generalised policy of active coexistence in which steps taken at the non-military (political, economic and humanitarian) levels contribute to downgrading military tensions. The recognition of the legitimate interests of the 'adversary' leads to a redefinition of the concept of 'peaceful coexistence'. This is combined with an appeal for a more open formulation of Soviet policy.

France and Poland border on 'the German question'. Each is neighbour to a German state with which it is allied and yet the two German states – or perhaps rather a partly imaginary 'Germany' – constitute serious worries for the security policy in both Poland and France. *Dominique David* (Chapter 6) describes the French security position in the aftermath of the INF agreement. In the 1960s, the French deterrent was considered self-sufficient. Today the French and their leaders agree on the necessity for a common European defence perspective in the long run. In the more immediate perspective, it has been acknowledged that French armed forces cannot function independently of NATO in Europe, though they will not come under the NATO integrated military command. In contrast with Janet Finkelstein, David expresses the view that Europe has an essential place in US foreign policy, but questions the US commitment to incur nuclear attack on Europe's behalf. He therefore wishes to see a stronger Western European defence, built on the two axes Paris–London (collaboration on deterrence) and Paris–Bonn. The FRG should show itself a little freer from the 'Atlantic framework'.

In *Marek Grela*'s analysis (Chapter 7), Poland belongs among those states whose national security is particularly sensitive to the influence of external developments. It is, however, also a country whose internal development affects the security of the European region, and it is acknowledged that its internal stability depends on the pace of the political and economic reforms announced. Poland sees itself as having an active rather than a passive role in international politics. Yet its role in Europe is strongly influenced by its geography. Thus, among the state's main security preoccupations we find 'old' topics such as territorial integrity, and new issues such as ecology. A situation particular to Poland and Hungary is that they both have a large emigrée population, which in the case of Poland has been much reinforced of late. This tends to affect the relations of the countries of origin and of destination. In times of détente, the links between the emigrants and home population tend to improve relations between the two countries. (However, it should be said that at other times the effects are quite the opposite; we may cite the pressure exercised on Western governments by the post-Solidarnosc emigration groups.)

France and Poland see their security as closely related to the East–West conflict. This is in contrast with Great Britain, where the security debate seems little affected by East–West relations. In *Michael Clarke*'s analysis (Chapter 8) the British security debate is fairly narrowly focused on arms control, and détente is considered almost exclusively in this context. Visions of new security arrangements in Europe do not figure in the debate. Margaret Thatcher's 'realist' policy favours decision-making at national rather than international level. This is not about to change. True, Labour's unilateralism constitutes a challenge to the traditional conceptions of British defence policy. But the party has experienced some difficulty in convincing the British electorate of the merit of its policies. The self-image of independence seems to persist in British foreign policy, despite Britain's heavy dependence on the special relationship with the USA. Both these factors reinforce its unwillingness to think in terms of closer relations with other European states.

The next four chapters consist of studies of two countries, viewed from within and without. *Laszlo Kiss* (Chapter 9) describes the Hungarian perception of security, that of a small European country whose historical perspective is relevant to its contemporary experience. *Pierre Lemaitre* (Chapter 10), a Danish researcher, analyses the new Hungarian concept of security, with particular emphasis on the changes in the Marxist–Leninist concept of 'peaceful coexistence'. The Hungarian emphasis on interdependence and a European 'identity' is noted by both researchers and ascribed by both to the Hungarian concern to limit the economic damage that can be caused by a decline in superpower relations. The alliances are at such times likely to close ranks, and Hungary therefore tends to assert its historical and trade contacts with countries that are not part of the Warsaw Pact, notably Austria and Yugoslavia. In Hungary, the imposition of the Soviet model is considered as 'East Europeanising', and an implicit parallel is sketched with the orientalisation experienced by parts of Hungary under the Ottomans. Economic and political reform are perceived as Westernisation.

A larger state like the FRG has quite different motives for propagating the 'europeanisation' of Europe. The effects of the particular interests of the FRG – in Eastern policy in general and the GDR in particular – are described in the two chapters on the Federal

Republic. Since 1982, a Conservative–Liberal government has continued along the lines laid down by the socioliberal *Ostpolitik*, while the Social Democrats in their opposition role have reformulated security policies in a way that has proved widely influential in reformist groups all over Europe.

Berthold Meyer (Chapter 11) deals mainly with the views of the political parties on several related topics: nuclear weapons, defence cooperation, 'europeanisation' and 'security partnership' with the East. The background to all of these issues is *Deutschlandpolitik*, or the FRG's concern to avoid definitive foreclosure of the convergence of the two German states. He concludes that since the interests of European détente and disarmament are always compatible with the FRG's efforts to improve relations with the GDR, the suspicions of East and West as to the FRG's intentions can never be wholly alleviated.

Ole Wæver's study (Chapter 12) focuses on the Eastern dimension of West German security. The debate between the political parties in the FRG is analysed at the level of conceptual systems. By searching for *figures* of security thinking and the rhetorical procedures of party discourse, he is able to isolate certain tensions that characterise both the CDU-led government and the CDU itself in its relation to détente, security and social change in Eastern Europe. It is suggested that the FRG – under CDU leadership – is likely to remain a positive but not a leading participant in the processes of détente and europeanisation. In critical periods it might easily 'flip over' into participation in new and inflexible international constellations.

Bulgaria is another small European state concerned with the consequences of East–West tensions. But it is also, in *Nansen Behar*'s account (Chapter 13), a Balkan state and the Balkan, like the Scandinavian countries, have some common interest across the political borders. Bulgaria, though a socialist state and member of the Warsaw Pact, has developed its own Balkan policy by independent security initiatives. The latter include a friendship treaty with NATO-member Greece. Another, more recent initiative is the Bulgarian proposal for a Balkan nuclear weapon-free zone. In recent years Bulgarian security research has increasingly concentrated on non-military aspects, in particular on ecology. This too has a sub-regional flavour as the most important project is to obtain the ecological cooperation of all the states through which the Danube flows. The ecological dimension tends to generate cooperation in sub-regional groups – often reviving historical patterns of cooperation.

Another example of this is cooperation around the Baltic Sea. But the battle against pollution in the Baltic, since it involves high levels of technology and inter-bloc cooperation, is a controversial issue.

The common interest of the Nordic countries in avoiding any tensions in the region has so far been respected by both superpowers. Despite the Nordic countries' common cultural heritage and many other similarities, their security policies are quite diverse: Finland, a neutral, maintains a special relationship with the USSR, Sweden maintains an armed neutrality, and Denmark is a somewhat recalcitrant member of NATO.

Pertti Joenniemi's analysis of Finland (Chapter 14) attempts to discern a pragmatic strain in the history of Finnish security policy and government, a strain he associates with a liberal and non-military oriented outlook on power. In this way he is able to show the Finnish specificity of Finland's neutrality, which is not only much younger than that of Switzerland, but – unlike Swiss neutrality – might seem to be geographically determined. It is, Joennimi suggests, Finland's skilful management of international relations that has allowed it to enjoy the friendship of the West *and* the trust of its local superpower throughout the post-war period. It abstains from idealistic criticism of other countries, and believes that the major powers have sufficient common interests to promote them. But it has abandoned its isolationism of the post-war years, and now tries to promote international stability, not least through the process that bears the name Helsinki.

The concept of 'common security' achieved notoriety on the initiative of neutral Sweden. The Palme Commission wished to replace the concept of 'mutual deterrence' by a security concept that foregrounded mutual understanding and carried in it the promise of long-term demilitarisation. *Erik Noreen*'s study of Sweden (Chapter 15) shows that the 'common security' concept was discussed no less vehemently there than in NATO member states: the philosophy of deterrence was considered by the conservatives, and also by many centrists, the only solid basis for national security policy. Today, Sweden's interest in Europe is reawakening, and the question arises of the compatibility of membership of the EEC with neutrality. Neutrality has till now taken priority.

Denmark, on the other hand, is one of the three Nordic NATO members. But its role in the alliance has generated much debate within the alliance and at home. In contrast with, for example, Great

Britain or Finland, Danish foreign policy is not considered a matter for the experts. On the contrary. *Ole Karup Pedersen* (Chapter 16) explains how during the last six years of conservative–liberal coalition governments a state of institutionalised dissent on foreign and security policies could be observed in Denmark. The discord between parliamentary majority and minority government has been publicly debated by scholars, journalists, Danish military and diplomatic personnel, the Danish peace movement and the general public. This curious institutional deadlock was ended by the April 1988 election, which was called partly for this purpose; one of the parties of the dissenting majority joined the governmental coalition. Ole Karup Pedersen's conclusion is that discussion of Danish foreign and security policy is now likely to continue only within the specialist forums established. He is not confident that the subject any longer generates sufficient interest to remain on the political agenda.

The concluding chapter by *Ole Wæver* (Chapter 17) draws together some of the themes from the individual studies. At the same time it introduces some of the axes of the theoretical work of the project group in Copenhagen, which formed the basis for the conference. The chapter aims to formulate a conceptual apparatus for future research on non-military aspects of European security. The analysis is based on an understanding of the present situation as characterised by 'Europeanisation' – not in the sense of a specific order awaiting intronisation but in the sense that the 'binary' grip on Europe is being loosened. A space is opening up for projects of Europe. However, several contradictory projects compete. This is mirrored in the very idea of 'Europe' where four different geographical images are shown to be in play.

'Europeanisation', then, is not an answer but a new question. In this more complex situation, a fine-tuned conceptual approach, able to grasp security fears and aspirations, is indispensable. Wæver's approach analyses sub-national and trans-national factors in the context of a classical notion of security – that is, one that emphasises sovereignty, national stability and the stability of the international political order. Into this framework are introduced some concepts for the understanding of regional security dynamics (security complex, conflict formation, security regime, security community, non-violent conflict culture, common security, etc.). These are organised in a hierarchy of analytical concepts. They are compared with political concepts and certain further methodological conclusions drawn concerning the study of security processes in Europe.

Notes and References

1. For theoretical considerations behind the conference see Egbert Jahn, Pierre Lemaitre and Ole Wæver, *European Security – Problems of Research on Non-military Aspects*, Research Report from the Centre for Peace and Conflict Research at the University of Copenhagen (Copenhagen, 1987).

1 The Future of Western European Security

Barry Buzan*

1 INTRODUCTION

In recent years, questions of defence and security have moved to the forefront of the political agenda in many Western European countries. Popular dissatisfaction with existing defence policies has led to sustained mass campaigns against nuclear weapons in several countries. Opposition to Western Europe's defence dependence on the United States has become deeper and more widespread since the 1979 triumph of the political right in the USA brought to power a government openly dedicated to military competition with the Soviet Union. The durable nature of the concern about Western Europe's defence dependence on the USA is indicated by the wide variety of its sources. At one extreme the concern is generated by the fear of unwanted or accidental war arising out of superpower rivalry. At the other, it is generated by fears such as those unleashed by the INF agreement, that the United States is loosening its commitment to protect Western Europe. Even the British Foreign Secretary has spoken of the need for Western Europe to play a more independent and self-reliant role in the provision of its own security.[1]

An opinion poll of February 1987 in the four biggest Western European countries revealed large majorities opposed to the basing of US nuclear weapons in Europe (Britain 56 per cent, France 60 per cent, Germany 66 per cent, Italy 78 per cent). This poll also revealed that the Atlantic alliance gets majority approval only in Germany (54 per cent). In Britain, NATO gets a plurality (41 per cent) over alternatives defined as either a European defence alliance (23 per cent) or national self-reliance (26 per cent). In both France and Italy the idea of a European defence alliance is more popular (respectively 35 per cent and 38 per cent) than NATO (respectively 26 per cent and 19 per cent).[2] These figures suggest that the political basis for the current security arrangements in Western Europe is already seriously corroded. In Britain, the party political consensus on the nuclear component of defence, both national and alliance, has collapsed, making security policy an area of electoral competition. Dissatisfaction with the present security arrangements is not confined to Western Europe. Noises from the United States about unequal burden-sharing, and the necessity to reorder the USA's military deployment priorities in the light of its global responsibilities, have been part of what has motivated those like the British Foreign Secretary to speak out.

Under these conditions, it is necessary to think urgently about alternatives to the present arrangements. As one editorial writer reflecting on the opinion poll put it:

> The statistics of the moment show an affair and an alliance cooling fast. As that happens, something else is bound to come; the European defence community that almost 25% of Marplan's respondents already see emerging. If the politicians are still reading and pondering, they have two questions to answer. Can the drift from America be stopped? And if not, when do we begin building what comes next?[3]

To address the question of alternatives requires that one be prepared to think on a large scale. The problem of European security is one of historic proportions. It involves not only a major geographical area, and a huge, complex, and politically and culturally divided society, but also one of the five centres of industrial and organisational power in the international system. The present political and security arrangements in Europe are the principal result of the US and Soviet victories in what almost everyone devoutly hopes will be the last all-out war ever fought amongst the world's major powers. Any fundamental change in the organisation of Western European security would thus have profound implications not only for the social and political organisation of Western Europe, but also for the pattern of power and security relations in the international system as a whole. A shift away from the pattern set by the Second World War would inevitably be an event of historic importance. It cannot be just a local European matter.

This study attempts to set the Western European security problem in a global perspective. In order to achieve some simplicity of vision, the historical perspective used here will itself be structured by some of the insights of the *Neo-realist theory* of international politics. By Neo-realism, I mean the school of thought deriving from Kenneth Waltz, in which the logic of power politics is seen to derive from the political structure of the international system, rather than from either human nature or the domestic political characteristics of states.[4] According to this theory, the pattern of relations amongst the major powers is an important determinant of events in the international system. Among other things, this pattern is strongly influenced by the number of such major powers within the system, with history suggesting a spectrum of possibilities ranging from a minimum of two (e.g. classical Greece, the superpower system since 1947) and a maximum of nine (before the First World War). Neo-realist theory suggests that the impact of great powers on the international system becomes stronger as their number becomes smaller. Changes in the number of major powers in the system mark structural transformations, and are especially important when they involve shifts either into, or out of a small number like two. The Second World War generated a massive transformation of this type by collapsing a system dominated by seven great powers (a *multipolar* system) into one dominated by only two superpowers (a *bipolar* system). The bipolar system that emerged from the ashes of the Second World War has endured for more than four decades.

The Neo-realist approach does not claim to explain all behaviour in the international system, and consequently this study can present only a partial picture. It is particularly insensitive to social and political forces beneath the state level, and if these forces are potent, they may counteract Neo-realist logic. The reason for adopting this perspective here is my belief that the intense focus of power factors and superpower rivalry in Europe, and the strong state structures there, give overwhelming dominance to Neo-realist logic. Because Europe embodies such massive forces, and such deep oppositions, the framework of power politics is exceptionally important to any understanding of European security. This is not to deny that other factors may be in play at the sub-state level. But it is to assert that whatever these factors are, they are doomed to operate in an environment heavily shaped and constrained by state and system level power politics. Because this is so, any soundly-based appreciation of the European security problem must at least start with a Neo-realist analysis.

In Neo-realist terms, the question before us is whether the present upsurge in security consciousness in Western Europe is part of a global transformation away from the bipolarity of the superpowers, and towards a system containing perhaps as many as five great powers (the two superpowers plus China, Western Europe and Japan). If it is, then it is absolutely vital that the debate within

Western Europe take this global factor into account. Not to do so could involve major misunderstandings about the nature of both the problems and the opportunities that confront us. The argument here is that for Western Europeans, the concept of state-centred national security is, by itself, at best nearly meaningless, and at worst, dangerously misleading. Western Europeans have made a history for themselves in which their national securities now have to be subordinated to a larger regional security entity if they are to have any sound basis. In turn, the collective security of Western Europe can be fully understood only if it is placed firmly in the security context of the international system as a whole.

As things now stand in Western Europe, this broader political and historical–structural view is not nearly influential enough in shaping either the way the problem is perceived, or the terms in which it is discussed. The public debate is dominated by arguments about existing military arrangements, and much of it is driven by the tension between pro- and anti-nuclear and/or military opinions. Argument on this level is unquestionably a valid part of the process. But it dominates debate because it is easier both to think of – and to organise politically – than the more constructive, but more demanding, alternatives that stem from a politically focused approach to security.

The public debate is too narrow in at least three dimensions. First, in terms of issues it has short time horizons largely defined by current events such as weapons deployment decisions (cruise and Pershing II, Trident) or arms-control objectives (INF). (ii) Second, in terms of areas of analysis it is too much preoccupied with the military and technological problems of defence at the expense of broader political, historical and structural views of security. (iii) And third, where it does take a longer view, it is usually in terms of moral attitudes towards peace and weapons rather than in terms of the concrete political and security implications for Western Europe and the world of moves away from the post-war system. The only major exception to this last point is the growing section of the peace movement that tries to conceptualise the security problem in terms of Europe as a whole.[5] For reasons that will be developed below, this approach makes the gain of greater political breadth only at the cost of discounting the durable power determinants of the security problem in Europe. The danger of a public debate dominated by narrow anti-militarism and broad, but misleading, idealism, is the same as that raised by revolutionary leftism in an environment ripening for political change: that it will succeed in destroying its target without in the process laying the foundations for a more desirable replacement.

Part of the long-standing academic debate is more broadly-based, though even here the terms are often too narrow. A section of academic opinion has long been rightly aware that changes in the global distribution of power over the last three decades, both within and outside NATO, have been steadily working against the maintenance of the status quo in Europe.[6] This literature is rich in the insight that Western Europe needs to do more in its own defence. But much of it is set within the confines either of the Atlanticist framework of NATO, or the slightly broader framework of Europe between the superpowers. Very seldom is the attempt made to put the situation into the broader historical context of the evolving global power structure as a whole.

Given the intensely parochial nationalist structure of politics and society in Western Europe, the dominance of narrow views within Europe is not surprising. But unless Western Europeans can generate a broader and more coherent political image – not only of their collective future, but to some extent also of their collective past – they will be unable to acquire any constructive leverage on the major determinants of the international security problem whose centre they occupy.

In what follows, section 2 examines the historical origins of the post 1945 security system in both Europe and the world as a whole. Section 3 looks at the resultant security problem for Western Europe. It concentrates on the entanglement of Western European and American security concerns and policies, and on the way in which the global pattern of security defines Western Europe as a single entity in security terms. Section 4 builds on this last point. It makes the case that political cohesion is central to Western European security, and examines this variable in relation to four options for the future of Western European security. Section 5 concludes by assessing these four options in terms of six key objectives for any Western European security policy.

2 THE ORIGINS OF THE POST-1945 SECURITY SYSTEM

The current security position of Western Europe was created by the outcome of the Second World War. That war was itself the second and final round of what can be seen as a civil war marking the breakdown of both the regional balance of power system among the major nations in Europe, and the global balance of power system that was shaped by the primacy of European world power. This history can be seen in terms of the European security complex (a 'security complex' being defined as a set of states whose principal security perceptions and concerns link together sufficiently closely that their national security problems cannot realistically be considered apart from one another).[7] The European security complex was unusual in being composed largely of greater powers, many of which had global reach. Until the First World War, it comprised Europe from the Atlantic to the Urals, and from Turkey to Norway. Its long history of shifting rivalries and intermittent conflict defined not only an intense local pattern of security relations, but one that reached out to dominate patterns of security over much of the rest of the planet. The two World Wars not only broke the global influence of the European complex, they changed its boundaries and shattered its internal autonomy.

This breakdown was triggered by the rise of a powerful and industrialised German state in the heart of Europe during the late nineteenth century. Germany was too large a power to allow the traditional European balance system to function smoothly. It was not strong enough to overawe a European system still composed of highly nationalistic states, but it was too strong to allow its neighbours to live comfortably in its shadow. The competitive, nationalistic atmosphere of the time reflected the culmination of a long history of independent European states, and precluded any durable cooperative, or integrative, pan-European solution to the disruptive impact of Germany. The fact that Germany's power and position meant that it could not avoid threatening the independence and security of the other European states defined what later came to be known as 'the German problem'. The patterns of alliance leading to both World Wars were shaped by this dilemma: for the eight decades leading up to 1945, the German problem dominated Europe's security dynamics.

The European civil war solved the German problem only at the cost of transforming both the internal and external conditions of European security. Rather than, as in the past, either creating a new balance of power or leaving any one European power dominant over the continent, the First and Second World wars resulted in the dismemberment, collapse or exhaustion of almost all of the traditional European great powers. They also pulled a rising outside power, the United States, into a massive, and eventually dominating, involvement in Europe's security affairs. Germany's last bid for superpower status led not only to the geographical truncation of the German nation, and the division of its remaining core into three states, but also to the division of Europe into spheres of superpower influence. The collapse of European power meant that Europe not only ceased to be the organising centre of a multipolar global power structure, but also virtually ceased to function as an autonomous security complex. It became instead the principal object of contention in a bipolar structure of global confrontation between the successor superpowers, the United States and the Soviet Union.

For Europe, the victory over Germany thus did not allow a return to the nineteenth-century balance of power system even on a diminished regional basis. The foundations of the independent European security complex lay in ruins, and after 1945, a radically different system emerged. The struggle against Germany had been very long and very costly. Although it had caused great damage all over Europe, its impact on the distribution of power was highly unequal. In the West, the struggle had obliterated Austria–Hungary as a state, eliminated Germany and Italy as great powers, and greatly debilitated Britain and France. But in the East, the struggle had galvanised previously backward Russia into both political revolution and industrialisation. Although Russia suffered more damage than the Western European powers, it also had the time – and the stimulus – to mobilise its much larger power base. By 1945, the German problem had been solved not only by the dismemberment of Germany, but also by the fact that it was now the Soviet Union, not Germany, that threatened to overawe the independence of the European states. In effect, the German threat to the European balance of power was replaced by a Soviet one that was alarming because it represented an even greater imbalance in the distribution of power within Europe than that created earlier by the rise of Germany.[8]

The situation created by the Second World War left the democratic capitalist countries of Western Europe in a very difficult position. All of them were exhausted and bankrupt. The acute threat from the hostile ideology and power of Nazi Germany had been removed, but only at the cost of destroying the protection that a German great power offered against the rising threat from the hostile ideology and growing military power of the Soviet Union. By 1947 the Western European democracies had good reason to fear both the ideology and the military power of their recent ally. They were too weak to defend themselves against Soviet military and political pressure, and were obliged to cajole an initially reluctant United States into a close defence relationship. In the early post-war environment, the Western European states could not have created a balance of power against the Soviet Union even if they had been able to unify themselves into a single defensive alliance. The Soviet threat to the European balance of power was thus not solvable in the 1940s and 1950s without US intervention. The only alternative to such intervention was to allow the Soviet Union to assume virtually hegemonic status within the old European security complex.

The Soviet Union, heavily damaged by the war, was determined never again to have to fight a Western invasion on its own territory. It had done so once against Napoleon and twice against Germany within the previous century and a half. Defeating Hitler had cost the Soviet Union 20 million dead and the devastation of its major western cities. By the late 1940s, the Soviet Union had become the dominant power in Eastern Europe on the basis of its military occupation of the countries liberated from fascism. The consolidation of Soviet power in Eastern Europe reflected the military imperatives of forward defence, but it was – and is – also deeply connected to the political legitimacy of the Soviet regime itself. This combined commitment is intensified by, but not dependent on, the Soviet rivalry with the United States in Europe. By the late 1940s the United States had become the dominant power in Western Europe, partly on the basis of its occupation role in Western Germany, partly at the invitation of the independent Western European states, and partly in pursuit of its own lessons from the war about the need for forward defence.[9]

The combination of rising Soviet power, collapsed Western European power, and the USA's engagement in Europe, meant that the long history of complex intra-European rivalries was submerged by the overriding power and rival interests of the two superpowers. Like small magnets suddenly locked into the force field of larger ones, the European states lined up according to the terms of the new superpower order. In the case of the Western European states, this subordination was freely undertaken, and based on a genuine harmony of interest with the United States. Nevertheless, Europe no longer danced to its own tune. It ceased to be the main security focus for the Soviet Union, becoming instead only one of several forums (albeit the principal one) in which it confronted the USA as its primary rival. The USA's involvement in European security affairs was likewise only part of a wider global confrontation with the Soviet Union.

This expansion of superpower influence into Europe was paralleled by a similar process in East Asia. The USA extended its military power right across the Pacific during the Second World War, and the Soviet Union gained a windfall from the independently successful communist revolution in China. This process led to subordination of the security complex in Northeast Asia not only to the overriding power and influence of the superpowers, but also to the security imperatives of the global rivalry between them (I use the term 'overlay' to refer to the subordination of a regional security dynamic by the *direct* politico-military presence of external great powers.)[10] In both areas the meeting of the rival superpower spheres of dominance produced sharp geostrategic boundaries that divided both individual countries (Germany, Korea, China), and the regions as a whole, into opposed blocs. Except in Korea, the 'bamboo curtain' in East Asia was somewhat easier to manage than the 'iron curtain' in Europe because most of the dividing line there ran through insulating areas of sea. Over and above the stark structural fact of a bipolar distribution of power, it was this military and ideological overlay by the United States and the Soviet Union of all the world's major centres of power that justified the coining of the term 'superpowers'.

The pattern of global security set by the outcome of the Second World War is still largely with us. The only major political change has been the dramatic, but partial, collapse of superpower overlay in East Asia caused by the defection of China from its alliance with the Soviet Union in the early 1960s. The shift of China from ally to rival of the Soviet Union was the first major move away from the structure of bipolarity. China lacked the industrial, and therefore the military, capacity to assert itself as a third superpower. But it quickly carved a role for itself as an independent variable in relations between the superpowers, and mounted a global-scale ideological challenge to them in the Third World. After the Sino–Soviet split, it became possible to talk about the pattern of global security in terms of tripolarity. Such usage flattered the power of China, which is still more potential than real. But it did accurately capture the importance of the fact that a major centre of power had begun to take a political and military line independent of the superpowers. Although China did not measure up to either Japan or Western Europe in industrial capability, both of them were still voluntarily subordinate to superpower overlay, whereas China was fully in charge of its own house.

By leading the move out of overlay, China began the process of political change away from a bipolar superpower system, and back towards a multipolar great-power one. Elsewhere, the bipolar structure has come under pressure more from changes in the underlying distribution of power that have now seriously eroded all but the military dominance of the superpowers. This overall shift towards a more multipolar world defines the security choices that now confront Western Europe with increasing urgency.

3 THE WESTERN EUROPEAN SECURITY PROBLEM

Despite the loosening of superpower overlay in East Asia, in Europe, the post-war pattern has persisted to the present day. A deep boundary divides Europe – and Germany – into two distinct systems. The character of political life, values, and social and economic organisation on either side of this boundary are sharply different. Notwithstanding the currently congenial image of Gorbachev, the Western Europeans cannot help but be worried by the closed, totalitarian character of the Soviet system, and by its need to use force to maintain political control in Eastern Europe, and in parts of the Third World. The many stylistic echos of 1930s fascism in Soviet life underline this political gulf. The differences between the two systems are so profound that the mere existence of each cannot but permanently threaten the social and political legitimacy of the other. The depth of the political divide between them is illustrated by the fact that their boundary is guaranteed by the largest peacetime concentration of military power the world has ever seen.

The existence of this boundary is the fundamental fact that defines the contemporary security and defence problem of Western Europe. The fact that it reflects not only the geopolitics of superpower rivalry, but also a major political divide between Western Europe and the Soviet bloc, explains why the attempt to define the *whole* of Europe as a single security entity is misconceived. The old European security complex was not only buried by the post-1945 developments, it was also transformed by them. Eastern Europe is now permanently locked into the Soviet sphere. There is no possibility of reviving a multipolar European complex. The choice is between Soviet hegemony over a fragmented Europe, or a bipolar balance between Western Europe and the Soviet Union – with or without the United States.

It is perfectly legitimate to focus on relations between Eastern and Western Europe as a key part of the security problem, and this approach opens interesting and useful possibilities for action at the trans-national level. But the major realities of security in Europe are determined by the state system. On that level, only Western Europe has the degree of power and independence to be even potentially available as a policy-making entity capable of transforming the increasingly unsatisfactory structure of the post-war security system.

The argument here is that action based on a Western European security entity offers the only real possibility for moving the European security problem in desirable directions. Whatever its emotional attractions, action pitched at Europe as a whole will be unable to make more than a minor impact on the dominant power structures that determine the major features of the security problem. In order to improve the security of Europe as a whole, the first step must therefore be for Western Europe to redefine its relationship with the superpowers. The character of that redefinition offers considerable scope for taking into account the security interdependencies between Eastern and Western Europe. But only when the deconstruction of superpower overlay in Europe is well under-way, will scope become available for serious restructuring of relations between the two halves of Europe. Aiming for pan-European action first obscures the need to start with Western Europe. Only by starting with Western Europe can the global elements of Europe's security problem be tackled. This situation is a classic case of the best (but unobtainable) option being the enemy of the good (but possibly attainable) one. The reality of the matter is that Europe has lost its world power, and is therefore not in a position to pursue idealistic visions on the assumption that the interests of the superpowers can be easily discounted or pushed aside.

The existence of a deep and durable politico-military divide between Eastern and Western Europe has two consequences that determine the security and defence options available to Western Europeans. The first is that Western Europe is inescapably caught in a geostrategic nutcracker of superpower rivalry. The dictates of geography and the momentum of history mean that Europe cannot avoid being a decisive factor in both the global balance of power and the ideological contest between the United States and the Soviet Union. Both superpowers define their own military and political security in terms of forward defence – the deployment of their armed forces well outside their national boundaries. The necessity for forward defence was a major lesson for both superpowers from their experience of being attacked during the Second World War. So long as they continue to define their own security in forward defence terms, their interests cannot help but push against each other in the middle of Europe.

The second consequence is that for the countries of Western Europe, concepts like 'defence' and 'security' make sense only in terms of Western Europe as a whole. The extent of the Soviet political and military challenge, the range and destructive power of modern weapons, and the entanglement of the USA's security with Europe's, mean that the individual states of Western Europe can no longer serve as separate, self-contained national bastions for military defence and security. The idea that the individual states of Europe can or should be meaningful units in terms of military and political security belongs to the period now nearly five decades past, when the European states related to each other within a balance of power system dominated by them. The replacement of the German problem by the Russian one, and the rise of great powers outside Europe, means that the European states will never recover a self-contained security complex. For the forseeable future, inescapable conditions of geography and politics bind all of the Western European states into a common security entity whether they recognise it or not.

3.1 Western Europe and US Security

The key fact for Western Europe is that, because of its global rivalry with the Soviet Union, the United States *cannot* disentangle its own security from the fate of Western Europe. Initially, it was Western Europe that needed to draw the United States into NATO in order to offset the proximity of overwhelming Soviet military power. But as the superpower rivalry developed into a global pattern, Western Europe became the keystone of the American security system. For the United States, Western Europe provides not only a forward line of defence, but also a major industrial and ideological asset to the Western camp. The United States did not suffer greatly during the Second World War, but it did learn some durable lessons. Foremost among these were first, that appeasement merely feeds the appetite of expansionist totalitarian states, and second, that a security policy of isolationism like that pursued during the 1930s, simply means that the country takes a grave risk of being drawn into a war at a disadvantage. US security policy in the post-war world can be explained as an attempt to avoid the outcome of the 1930s, with the Soviet Union being seen as an essentially similar type of opponent to the fascist states. The Americans want to ensure that the Soviet Union does not repeat the fascist trick of winning a series of small cheap victories that greatly increase its strength for an eventual showdown with the United States.

The US commitment to Western Europe is a response to both of these lessons from the Second World War. A sustained and robust policy of deterrence is designed to avoid the weaknesses of appeasement, and a durable system of alliances is designed to avoid the dire consequences of isolationism. In pursuit of these goals, the USA has, for nearly four decades, provided a major component of Western European defence through the institution of NATO. US forces make up a substantial percentage of those deployed in Western Europe, and the United States has also extended its nuclear deterrence to include its NATO allies. The costs of this commitment to the US are visible in the higher percentage of GNP it spends on defence compared to the Western European states.[11]

So long as the USA continues to define its security in terms of the ideological and military threat from the Soviet Union, Western Europe will play a crucial role in US defence policy. Over the decades since the Second World War, this US policy has in many ways harmonised with Western European security interests. It has provided a continuous subsidy, which means that the Western Europeans have not had to pay the full cost of the defence strength that they have enjoyed. Through NATO, the United States has provided an organisation that has enabled the major Western European states to coordinate, and to some extent to integrate, their defence policies. Western European governments and societies have been given the luxury of being able to ignore the hard realities of their security and defence problems by transferring overall responsibility for them to the USA. In other words, the dominant position of the USA has both supported Western Europe's need for security *vis à vis* the Soviet Union, and enabled the Western Europeans to avoid the difficult question of how to devise, pay for, and coordinate a coherent defence policy of their own.

For three decades conditions were such as to make this arrangement more or less comfortable for both sides of the Atlantic partnership. During the period from the late 1940s to the early 1960s, Western Europe and the USA shared similar views on the nature and extent of the Soviet threat. At this time, the USA also had a massive superiority in nuclear strength over the Soviet Union. That superiority enabled it to extend its nuclear deterrence to Western

Europe in a way that was easy for, and acceptable to, both sides. Since the Soviet Union could not make a major nuclear attack on the USA itself, a US threat to use nuclear weapons against the Soviet Union in defence of Europe was a simple and solid guarantee to the Europeans.

These advantages, however, now have to be weighed against increasing costs. Western Europeans have given up control over their own security in return for US protection, and this close association with the US makes Western Europe's security and defence highly vulnerable to the evolution of political and military relations between the superpowers. During the 1960s and 1970s, the easy extension of US deterrence to cover Western Europe was rapidly eroded by the growth of a Soviet nuclear arsenal equivalent to that of the USA. Once the US became vulnerable to Soviet nuclear threats, its own threat to use nuclear weapons on behalf of Europe looked increasingly empty. France responded to this development by loosening its ties to NATO and building its own nuclear deterrent. In an attempt to maintain the credibility of extended deterrence, the USA responded by developing ideas like 'flexible response' and 'limited nuclear war'. These two ideas required NATO to strengthen its ability to fight a war with the Soviet Union in Europe. They destroyed the simplicity of deterrence, and stimulated fears in Europe that defence policy might make war more likely. During this period, however, these adverse developments were offset by the reign of détente between the superpowers. Because the USA and the Soviet Union were engaged in a sustained attempt to manage their rivalry, the risk of war appeared low, and therefore the increasing difficulties of extending deterrence to Western Europe did not seem to matter all that much.

But by the end of the 1970s, détente was collapsing, and the USA and the Soviet Union were embarking on a renewed period of political hostility and military rivalry. This development had two effects: first, it brought the accumulated military worries about extended deterrence into sharp focus; and second, it opened a gap between US and European perceptions of the Soviet threat. Under the Reagan Administration, the USA adopted a more bellicose posture towards the Soviet Union. The US government downgraded arms control, pushed the development of new weapons, raised military spending, and talked freely of prevailing over the Soviet Union at all military levels from arms-racing to nuclear war. The US image of the Soviet Union shifted back towards that of the early Cold

War. The Soviets were not to be trusted, and were once again seen in the aggressive totalitarian mould of 1930s fascism.

It is these developments (and others such as SDI and arms control) that have put the question of the future of Western Europe's security and defence back on top of the political agenda. Most Western Europeans do not share the USA's new image of the Soviet threat. They are much more worried by what appears to be an increase in the risk of war, since any war fought with modern weapons, whether nuclear or not, would have a devastating effect on Western Europe. During the 1980s Western Europe's security dependence on the USA has become threatening in two ways. Firstly, because of its position as the major front line of confrontation between the superpowers, Western Europe is inevitably squeezed more tightly when relations between the superpowers become hostile. But because it is so dependent on the USA, Western Europe has almost no latitude for distancing itself from the more bellicose US posture which is not in accord with the mainstream European view. The dependence of Western Europe on the USA thus denies it a significant moderating role when the pendulum of superpower relations swings away from détente. Secondly, because extended deterrence has become more difficult, NATO's deterrence is now based substantially on threats to fight limited wars in Europe. The making of such threats in times of tension does not induce feelings of security in those they are designed to protect. Put simply, the means and doctrines of defence appear more threatening to the wellbeing and existence of the Western Europeans than anything that the Soviet Union seems likely to do.[12]

The split between Western European and the US security perceptions that opened up during the 1980s will not go away. Although superpower relations have already started to drift back towards détente, the USA will never be able to extend deterrence easily to Western Europe as it did during the 1950s. The USA will not be able to reassert military superiority over the Soviet Union, and consequently NATO's policy of extended deterrence will always have to rest on the uncomfortable threat of limited war. So long as it does, Western European security will be highly sensitive to fluctuations in relations between the superpowers.

Under these conditions, the advantages to Western Europe of a close security entanglement with the USA begin to be outweighed by the costs. As the 1987 poll figures indicate, much of the Western European public finds it unacceptable to live under a regime of nuclear threats that are controlled from elsewhere, especially when that outside controller is moved by confrontational policies. In assessing the public reaction to the situation of the 1980s, it is a matter of great significance that public protest has been much more focused on US nuclear weapons than on nuclear weapons in the hands of European states. If there was to be a common Western European defence independent of the USA, only 35 per cent in Britain, and 25 per cent in France, would favour purely conventional defence over national or European nuclear defence.[13] In Britain, Trident is more controversial because of its cost, its capability, and its implication of continued dependence on the USA, than because of its nuclear status. In France, where the national nuclear force is strong, and self-reliant, and where no foreign nuclear weapons are deployed, there is virtually no mass movement against nuclear weapons.[14]

The reasons for Western Europe's dissatisfaction with the security position in which it now finds itself are all too apparent. It is uncomfortably and dangerously squeezed between the rival superpowers. It cannot escape the facts of geography and history, nor can it escape the fact that it is an economic and political prize of such weight that its fate decides the balance between the superpowers. Having generated so many wars themselves, and suffered catastrophe as a result, Western Europeans are now virtually unanimous in their desire for peace. The problem they face is that Europe might become the arena in which two hostile superpowers pursue their rivalry. So long as Western Europe remains dependent on the USA for the backbone of its defence, its security will be at the mercy of political and military relations between the superpowers. Current strategies on both sides pursue deterrence by threatening to fight a war in Europe. Massive armed forces on both sides are deployed for this purpose. If deterrence works all is well. If it fails all is lost. The problem is that the means required for extended deterrence seem to raise the risk that it will fail, either by accident or miscalculation, because the mutual fear and suspicion that such preparations incite will make any crisis between the superpowers difficult to control. Living with deterrence under these conditions can never produce real feelings of security.

3.2 Western Europe as a Single Security Entity

As soon as one tries to think of alternatives to NATO as a means of making Western Europe secure, a second aspect of the Western European problem emerges. There is the gap between, on the one hand, the externally imposed unity of Western Europe as a politico-military security entity lying between the superpowers and, on the other, its internal disunity in terms of political and military cooperation and integration. In terms of the dominant external pressures on it – both the Soviet threat, and the American security interest in forward defence and deterrence – Western Europe is undeniably a single security entity. The threat of Soviet political and military domination, whether in terms of occupation or 'Finlandisation', applies as much to Western Europe as a whole as it does to any single country. Only odd exceptions like Greece and Turkey have other external threats comparable in significance to that from the Soviet Union. Likewise, the threat of unwanted war stemming from extended deterrence applies to all Western European states, whether members of NATO or not.

Even in terms of relations among its component states, Western Europe is in a limited but important sense a single entity. The security of Europe is not, as in the past, determined by military rivalries amongst the European great powers. Western Europeans have perhaps finally learned the lesson of their long history of internecine war, and know that no issues amongst them are worth the destruction wrought by modern war, fought with or without nuclear weapons. Such disputes have also been suppressed by forty years of subordination to the overriding power and interests of the superpowers. Partly because of the common outside pressures on them, and partly as a consequence of their earlier history of violent conflict, the Western European states (with the exception of Greece and Turkey) are able to live together virtually without fear that any of them will use military force in relations with any other. Such a situation is unprecedented in the whole history of Europe. It is rare anywhere in the international system, and usually reflects unusual conditions of geographical isolation and cultural similarity, as between the USA and Canada, or Australia and New Zealand.

Despite the pressures and opportunities for unity, the idea of a United States of Europe, or even a European Community, has failed to develop sufficiently to support a common Western European defence policy. In some economic, legal, social and political ways, the Western European states are much more integrated than they have ever been before. There are few massive differences in the ideological style and range of political life in the countries of Western Europe. Linguistic and cultural differences still run deep along national lines, but less so than in India, which survives as a political union despite enormous problems of development.

But in terms of defence and foreign policy, cooperation is partial and discontinuous, with the individual states jealously preserving their own rights and powers. An attempt to create a European Defence Community in the early 1950s failed.[15] NATO provides an impressive vehicle for military cooperation amongst most of the Western European states, but one that is dependent on US leadership, and deeply associated with existing policies of flexible response and extended deterrence. Several countries are outside the NATO framework altogether (Ireland, Sweden, Austria, Switzerland, Finland) and several others have major restrictions on the degree to which they integrate themselves into NATO's joint military structures (France, Norway, Denmark, Spain, Greece). France has cultivated an independent nuclear force, and Britain also has some nuclear independence, despite the dependence of its nuclear deterrent on US delivery systems and the formal integration of its nuclear forces into the NATO command structure. The Western Europeans have even failed to integrate their arms industries, despite enormous technical and financial pressures to do so. Although there have been some joint projects among some Western European states, such as Tornado, there is still strong resistance to abandoning national military independence within an integrated European arms industry. Consequently each of the major European countries deploys different, and often incompatible weapons systems.

On defence issues, the individual states and peoples of Western Europe still hang on to their national military traditions and styles. They do so despite the fact that the military rivalry amongst them that originally generated these traditions is consigned permanently to the past, and despite the fact that nearly all acknowledge the primacy of the superpower confrontation in defining their security problem. Since their security problem is a common one, the lack of political cohesion amongst the Western European states on defence and security policy is the principal barrier confronting any attempt to devise realistic alternatives to continued dependence on the United States. The security threat from the Soviet Union is real, and given the deep incompatibility between its organising ideology and that of Western Europe, has to be faced as a durable, long-term issue. Greater coordination amongst themselves on defence and security policy to stand off the Soviet challenge is thus the only way in which the Western European states will be able to escape from the dangers and discomforts of their present entanglement in the forward defence policy of the USA.

The Western Europeans could enjoy the luxury of political fragmentation and competitive nationalism only so long as they held the reins of world power. Having lost power through the self-destructiveness of their civil war, they can now find security only in a higher degree of political integration than they have so far been able to achieve.

4 POLITICAL COHESION AND OPTIONS FOR WESTERN EUROPEAN SECURITY

The case that Western Europe is a single security entity, and should therefore be taken as the basic unit on which alternative security policies might be focused, rests on four points.

1. The superpower rivalry defines Western Europe as a single security entity by placing the whole area into a geostrategic nutcracker whose jaws are composed of a politico–military threat on the one side, and a danger of war on the other.
2. Although Eastern Europe shares the common danger of war, its long-term subordination to the Soviet Union, and its consequent political separation from Western Europe, mean that there is no real prospect of common policy at the state level for all of Europe. Only when Western Europe begins to have an appropriate security policy of its own will substantial opportunity arise to coordinate tension-reducing policies between Eastern and Western Europe. The bottom line here is that the requisites of superpower dignity will prevent any significant loosening of the Soviet military grip on Eastern Europe until the USA has begun to withdraw from Western Europe. Even the modest project of 'Finlandising' Eastern Europe, proposed by some,[16] confronts major obstacles.[17]
3. With the exception of Greece and Turkey, Western Europe is unquestionably a security community in its own right. That status almost certainly now exists independently from the common threat defined in 1 above, though it is obviously complemented by it.
4. Only policy options based on Western Europe have any chance of moving away from the current arrangements in ways that will increase the security not only of Western Europe but also of the superpowers. Indeed, because of its key position, Western Europe

will not be able to improve its own security, or that of Eastern Europe, unless it can simultaneously increase the security of both superpowers.

If one accepts the case that Western Europe is the key security entity, then the level of political cohesion within Western Europe becomes central to the whole question of its security options. In dealing with Western Europe as an entity, it is instructive to make parallels with India and China, both of which are similarly large and internally diverse polities. Of these three, Western Europe is considerably the weakest in terms of the degree of overall political cohesion it has achieved. Even chaotic India puts it to shame not only in the crude sense of having more potent centralised political institutions, but also in the more important matter of having a better developed national identity linking its citizens into a common polity. In Western Europe, the parts are still much greater than the political whole in terms of both collective institutions and individual identities.

The importance of political cohesion within the overall equation of security is most clearly shown by the contrast between Western Europe and China, both of which share a similar pattern of threat from the Soviet Union. China is economically and technologically much weaker than Western Europe, and therefore in some important ways militarily weaker as well. Neither does China have the benefit of a strong outside ally. But despite its militarily weaker position against the Soviet Union, there are far fewer doubts about the credibility of its deterrence posture against the Soviet Union than is the case with Western Europe. Nobody doubts that the Soviets would meet a unified and deeply-rooted resistance if they attacked China. In terms of China's overall security position, its political strength thus compensates for its military weakness. In Western Europe, by contrast, political fragmentation – both within Western Europe and between it and the USA – consistently undermines a relatively strong militarily position. The whole history of NATO has been dogged by the problem of credibility, which is just another way of talking about the linkage between political cohesion on the one hand, and military strength on the other. The lesson is one that has echos in cases like South Vietnam, the Chinese Civil War, and South Africa. It is that political cohesion is an essential condition for meaningful national security, and that superficial military strength cannot compensate for underlying political weakness beyond a fairly limited point.

The four major options for Western European security policy can be defined in terms of the degree of political cohesion that they require and/or reflect. In ascending order they are: balkanisation, NATO status quo, 2-pillar NATO, and an independent Western European security entity – call it WETO (Western European Treaty Organisation).[18]

The existing arrangement of the NATO status quo reflects a rather modest level of political cohesion in Western Europe, which is compensated for by large inputs of US military power. Paradoxically, US hegemony both underwrites much of the political and military coordination achieved by Western Europe, and prevents the development of higher levels of Western European cohesion. So long as the USA is prepared to manage and to subsidise Western Europe's security, Western Europeans are spared the stronger external pressures that might increase their own sense of common identity. They can afford the self-indulgence of nationally orientated policies because the US engagement covers all of their security, whether they participate through NATO or not. The NATO status quo thus both reflects and reinforces a low level of political cohesion in Western Europe. It also solves the problem created by the different perceptions of the Soviet threat between Western Europe and the United States. US subsidies ensure that the level of defence in Europe accords more with the generally higher American threat-perceptions of the Soviet Union, than with the often lower European ones.

Balkanisation would mean a move to an even lower level of political cohesion in Western Europe. Such a move is highly unlikely because of the countervailing pressure of inertial momentum in the European Community, and because of the widespread fear of the vulnerability to Soviet power that disunity would bring. There is still nonetheless a considerable constituency in most Western European states favouring nationally-based, usually neutralist, security policies. There is no reason to think that balkanisation in Western Europe would recreate a classical multipolar balance of power, and every reason to think that it would produce results no different from those in much of the Third World. US hegemony would be replaced by superpower rivalry, with both the USA and the Soviet Union competing in political relations within and between the Western European states. From the perspective of the analysis in this study, a move to lower levels of political cohesion would be a disaster not only for European security, but also for the security of the superpowers.

The much mooted idea of a 2-pillar NATO requires a higher level of Western European political cohesion than the status quo. In order for Western Europe to constitute a pillar in its own right, it needs to generate a more cohesive common defence policy, a more integrated military industry, and a more explicit and shared security outlook than it now has. Within a 2-pillar NATO Western Europe would take on more defence responsibilities, allowing the USA to reduce significantly the level of its direct military engagement in Europe. Western Europe would still enjoy the ultimate strategic backup of its alliance with the USA. Like China, its security in relation to the Soviet Union would be enhanced by a more solid political identity than exists at present. A reduction in tensions with the Soviet Union could also become possible once large US forces no longer sat directly on the most sensitive border of the Soviet empire. Achieving such a gain, would, however, require careful management of both military postures and political relations with all of the Warsaw Pact states.

A more robust and self-reliant Western European security posture, but one still closely linked to an Atlantic alliance, would reassure the USA in terms of its forward defence needs, while at the same time easing the credibility and burden-sharing issues that so constantly cloud the horizons of the NATO status quo. There would still be considerable scope for tension if lower European threat perceptions of the Soviet Union led to a defence provision inadequate by US standards. It remains to be seen, however, whether moves away from the high dependence of the NATO status quo would trigger a lowering or a raising of threat-perceptions and defence provision by Western Europe. Within a 2-pillar NATO Western Europe would gain some scope for beginning to transform itself from being the principal front-line of superpower rivalry, to being an insulating buffer between them.

The WETO option could take many forms, but all of them would require a level of political cohesion in Western Europe that would represent a transformation in the existing situation. WETO would need some elements of political structure approaching federalism, though these are perhaps best envisaged in terms of multiple overlapping bodies, in line with existing Western European patterns, rather than as a highly centralised move towards a full federal government. WETO would also need to be based on some sense of collective political identity amongst the population, and here India perhaps serves as a model. Neither of these is likely to develop unless the sense of shared fate and shared responsibility in security terms can be made a more prominent part of Western European political life. WETO could represent anything from an emergent Western European superpower to some kind of semi-neutral zone of disengagement between the superpowers concerned principally with defending itself in ways that would maximise its value as a buffer between them. Given the dictates of ideology and geography, WETO is unlikely to be truly neutral between the USA and the Soviet Union. Western Europe cannot escape from the primacy of the Russian problem in its security outlook, and this will create a long-term common cause with the USA (and also China). Neither can Western Europe escape from the fact that the USA has a deep security interest in its fate, both ideologically and militarily, and an enduring capability to fight limited nuclear war in Europe whether the Europeans wish it to or not.

A Western European superpower does not seem to be either a likely or a desirable prospect. Neither the peace movement nor the pro-status quo streams in public opinion reflect values and priorities that would lead in such a direction even if the requisite degree of political cohesion had been created. If the current trends point anywhere, it is towards some kind of buffer role. A WETO in which a robust, but non-provocative, defence policy is used to loosen the pressure of the superpower nutcracker, could enhance security not only for Europe but for both superpowers as well.

This line of analysis points firmly again to the political component of Western Europe's security problem. Non-provocative defence options cover a wide and controversial range, but the idea does identify an approach that would complement the political objectives of this kind of WETO. Non-provocative defence options, however, require political cohesion of the highest order if they are to be cost-effective. This is especially true for those versions of it that seek to emphasise civilian defence strategies, but a high level of political cohesion is also fundamental to military strategies based on decentralised, militia-based, territorial defence. The countries that have demonstrated territorial defence policies successfully have all enjoyed high levels of political cohesion – Sweden, Switzerland, China. Non-provocative defence strategies can only be credible if they rest on a firm political identity and a strong common sense of what is to be defended.

On this basis, one can conclude that a Western European political identity is a necessary condition for any move towards workable alternative security policies. The cultivation of such an identity therefore has to be a major priority for those looking to find ways out of the current dilemma. Until Western Europeans are much better integrated on the level of their collective social and political perceptions of themselves, no amount of military offset will be able to compensate for the political weakness in their security position. Lack of political cohesion forecloses better security alternatives for Western Europe at all levels, and ensures that Western Europe remains caught in the squeeze that closed in upon it at the end of the Second World War. But although greater political cohesion is a precondition for constructive change, it is also true that a clear vision of desired options is a necessary condition for the creation of greater political cohesion. Unless such a vision is widely shared, there is no hope of meeting its precondition. In my view, that vision has to be Western European in scale. The distance between the present parochialism of Western European politics and the needed broader vision, defines, I think, the major agenda for European idealists in relation not only to their own security problems, but also to those of the planet as a whole.

5 CONCLUSIONS

Given the intractable realities of their historical and geostrategic position, Western Europeans should ideally seek a security policy that would lower the possibility of war by achieving the following:

1. provide a convincing and sustainable deterrent to Soviet military pressure or attack;
2. not threaten, or appear to threaten, the Soviet Union with either first-strike offensive action or political destabilisation;
3. not stimulate an arms race between the Soviet Union and either the United States or Western Europe;
4. reduce tensions between East and West;
5. reassure the USA that Western Europe was secure against political pressure and military threat from the Soviet Union;
6. command a stable political consensus amongst the Western European electorates and their governments.

The NATO status quo achieves only points 1 and 5 to a level that might be called satisfactory. The direct US military presence in Western Europe, and the doctrine of extended deterrence that it requires, are in direct contradiction to points 2, 3 and 4, and since the late 1970s, increasingly against 6. Given the mutually provocative impact of the US presence on superpower relations, there does not seem to be any way in which a mere variation on the present arrangements will achieve all six points. Balkanisation might serve point 2, but would be a disaster on all other counts. A 2-pillar NATO would be an advance over the status quo. It would continue to meet points 1 and 5, and would offer some useful scope for improvement on points 2, 3, 4 and possibly 6.

The Western European superpower version of WETO would meet points 1 and 5, and possibly point 4, but it would not fulfil points 2 and 3, and it is doubtful that it could be made to support point 6. The non-provocative defence–strategic buffer WETO is problematic to assess without detailed specification of what its policies would be. The version that appeals most to me is a WETO based on what might be called a 'high-low' policy: a combination of a Western European minimum nuclear deterrent, and an in-depth, Western-Europe-wide, non-provocatively orientated, policy of territorial defence.[19] If we ignore the difficulties of how such things might be achieved, and simply assume that it could exist, then this option might score well on all six points:

1. The synthesis would deter the Soviet Union by presenting it not only with robust capabilities to resist invasion and respond to nuclear attack, but also with a demonstration of political will to preserve independence. A similar, though militarily weaker, policy has served China quite well, and even without a formal Atlantic Alliance, the Soviet Union cannot assume US passivity in the event of a Soviet attack on Western Europe.
2. Such a policy would not add to the military threats faced by the Soviet Union because nothing in it would give them cause to think that their own vulnerabilities to attack had increased. Indeed, by removing US forces from Western Europe, the policy would take some pressure off the Soviet Union, and invite it to make unilateral reductions in the strength of its own forces in Eastern Europe. To the extent that Soviet forces there are now more a reflection of past momentum and the security dilemma than of aggressive intent, the Soviets might be glad of an opportunity to reduce their numbers. If they did not reduce them, they would be exposed to the world as a militarist and aggressive society, since it could be made obvious to all that the new Western European arrangements were physically incapable of either large-scale invasion or counterforce first strike.

Reassuring the Soviets politically might be more difficult. Although reduced military threats would be welcome, the Soviet government is unlikely to warm to a more cohesive Western Europe, which it might see as a political threat both to its own status, and to its dominance over Eastern Europe. Soviet worries about Western Europe transforming itself into a rival superpower could be effectively addressed through both the rhetoric and the military character of non-provocative defence. Its political insecurities would require delicate handling. A loose political structure for Western Europe would help allay Soviet fears, and maximise opportunity for a multifaceted pursuit of détente. Soviet paranoia about Eastern Europe, and the necessity not to threaten its vulnerability in this unstable area, is one of the most compelling reasons for addressing the security problem first in Western European, rather than in pan-European, terms.

3. The policy would not stimulate 'arms racing' through the mechanism of the security dilemma, and should reverse some of the arms-racing pressures in the present arrangements. The Soviets would have an opportunity to respond to the withdrawal of US nuclear forces by reducing their own theatre nuclear weapons. Nothing in the new Western European policy would require a defensive response from the Soviet Union. The policy would stimulate arms racing only if the Soviets either decided to deploy strategic defences for their cities, or if they adopted a hostile attitude towards Western Europe and increased their military pressure on it. It is conceivable that superpower force reductions in Europe might simply release resources to intensify their rivalry elsewhere. Some in both superpowers might even favour WETO for that reason, and if they became dominant there would be little that Western Europe could do. There is, however, reason to think that the major reconstruction of international security of which WETO would be a part, would tend to discourage that option. In a more multipolar, great power, system, the two declining superpowers would have less opportunity and less reason to confront each other than they do under the intensely focused rivalry of bipolarity.
4. The policy should reduce East–West tensions by inserting a more independent Western Europe between the superpowers. Since Western Europe would pose no aggressive military threat to the Soviet Union, the removal of direct US–Soviet confrontation in Europe should lower tensions. Western European military

self-reliance would also remove the problem of extended deterrence, which has been a prime cause of military rivalry between the superpowers. In global terms, a more independent Western Europe would be part of a general shift away from superpower security policies based on hegemonic control, and towards a more decentralised, great-power, balance system. The objective here would be to give political expression to the diffusion of power away from the superpowers, not least by completing the project begun by China of replacing superpower overlay with self-reliant great powers. Multipolarity would not be achieved by creating new superpowers, but by having rising new powers and declining superpowers meet on the common ground of great power status.

5. Since Western Europe would be providing a robust self-defence, including a nuclear deterrent, the USA should feel secure in withdrawing its direct presence. Such a development would support a longstanding US ambition to encourage greater self-reliance on the part of its European NATO allies. It could either release US military resources for use elsewhere in the USA's global rivalry with the Soviet Union, and by so doing produce a much more comfortable division of labour in relation to the overall security of the West, or it could allow the USA to bring its military expenditure more into line with its economic capacity. The USA would retain the assurance of its own military capability to fight a limited nuclear war in Europe if need be. Because they would have their own nuclear forces, Western Europeans would feel less threatened than they now do by the prospect that American nuclear weapons would or wouldn't be used on their behalf. An interesting question here is how the USA would react to the conspicuous erosion of its superpower status that the winding down of its direct military presence in Europe would signal.
6. Because it contains powerful elements of both the realist and the idealist views, a high-low policy has a better chance than any alternative of restoring a stable consensus within Western Europe on defence and security policy. The realists win a strong defence policy, maintenance of an important role within the Western camp, and support for a high technology arms industry. They stand to gain escape from the current conflict over defence policy, and the re-creation of broad-based support for defence. The idealists win escape from entanglement in what seems a dangerous US nuclear policy, the adoption of a morally sound position of

> non-provocative defence, and a real chance to pursue détente and arms reduction with the Soviet Union on a unilateralist basis. They also gain the possibility of setting an example that, if followed by other major powers, would substantially advance the cause of common security for all of humankind. Both sides would have to face the necessity for greater Western European coordination and integration on defence, and both would have to accept that the additional security of self-reliance in defence has to be paid for. The costs of transition to, and maintenance of, the new policy would in part be offset by economies of scale resulting from a common Western European strategy and weapons procurement. If territorial defence options were pursued, both idealists and realists would, in their different ways, also have to adjust to the mixed blessing of mass participation in defence. The big loss for realists would be the sacrifice of offensive military options. The big loss for anti-nuclear idealists would be the retention of a minimum nuclear deterrent.

This high-low policy of minimum nuclear deterrence and non-provocative conventional defence is not a panacea for the security problems of either Western Europe or the world at large. It would raise difficult problems within Western Europe, most notably about the position and role of West Germany and Turkey. West Germany might welcome a reduction of tensions with the East, and an opportunity for the German *nation* to act as a bridge between the political and economic systems of East and West. But it would occupy an awkward position in the front line of a non-provocative defence policy, and its relationship with a Western European nuclear deterrent would also be problematic. Turkey and Western Europe would have to think harder than at present about the long-term basis and character of their relationship. The policy would require a substantial redefinition of Western European relations with the USA, and to a lesser extent with the Soviet Union.

These problems are not small, and neither are those that would need to be overcome to implement such a policy. They have, however, to be weighed against the costs of continuing with the present dependence on the USA, and the even greater costs of losing both US protection and a cohesive Western-European-scale security policy. The policy outlined above at least measures the distance between where we are and where we might want to be. It also gives a coherent view of the direction in which we might want to move.

This proposal is modest in comparison with some idealist visions – notably those of the disarmers, and those who would like to see *all* of Europe as a neutral buffer between the superpowers. But like these other idealist visions, it would be the work of more than one generation to achieve it. If this is a project for the twenty-first century, then the building of its political foundations needs to be started now. Western Europe does not occupy a remote and quiet corner of the planet. It is – and will remain – one of the major centres of political, social, economic and military power in the world. It cannot afford to indulge in sustained uncertainty and internal discord on the issue of its own security and defence.

Notes and References

* I would like to thank Ole Wæver for his penetrating comments on an earlier draft of this study.

1. The *Guardian Weekly*, 22 March 1987, 1.
2. The *Guardian Weekly*, 22 February 1987, 4.
3. The *Guardian Weekly*, 22 February 1987, 7.
4. Kenneth N. Waltz, *Theory of International Politics* (Reading Mass.: Addison-Wesley, 1979).
5. Jolyon Howorth, 'The Third Way', *Foreign Policy*, 65 (1986–7) 114–34.
6. For example: Hedley Bull, 'European Self-Reliance and the Reform of NATO', *Foreign Affairs*, 61(4) (1983) 874–92; Eliot A. Cohen, 'The Long-Term Crisis of the Alliance', *Foreign Affairs*, 61(2) (1982–3) 325–43; Zbigniew Brezezinski, 'The Future of Yalta,' *Foreign Affairs*, 63(2) (1984–5) 279–302; Earl C. Ravenal, 'The Case for Strategic Disengagement', *Foreign Affairs*, 51(3) (1973) 505–21; Peter Bender, 'The Superpower Squeeze', *Foreign Policy*, 65 (1986–7) 98–113; David Calleo, *Beyond American Hegemony: The Future of the Western Alliance* (New York: Basic Books, 1987).
7. Barry Buzan, 'A Framework for Regional Security Analysis,' in Barry Buzan, Gowher Rizvi *et al.*, *South Asian Insecurity and the Great Powers* (London: Macmillan, 1986), Chapter 1.
8. Bender, 'The Superpower Squeeze' (Note 6) 98–9.
9. Norman Graebner, 'Introduction: The Sources of Postwar Insecurity', in Graebner (ed.), *The National Security: Its Theory and Practice 1945–1960* (New York: Oxford University Press, 1986) 7–27.
10. Buzan, 'A Framework' (Note 7) 24, 26, 30–1.
11. Calleo, *Beyond American Hegemony* (Note 6) especially Chapters 7 and 12.

12. Michael Howard, 'Deterrence, Consensus and Reassurance in the Defence of Europe', in *Defence and Consensus: The Domestic Aspect of Western Security*, Part III, Adelphi Paper, 184 (London: IISS, 1983) 17–26; and Barry Buzan, *An Introduction to Strategic Studies: Military Technology and International Relations* (London: Macmillan, 1987) 182–90.
13. The *Guardian Weekly*, 22 February 1987, 4.
14. Jacques Fontanel, 'An Undeveloped Peace Movement: The Case of France,' *Journal of Peace Research*, 23(2) (1986) 175–82.
15. Edward Furdson, *The European Defence Community* (London: Macmillan, 1979).
16. Bender, 'The Superpower Squeeze' (see Note 6) 106–9.
17. Raimo Väyrynen, 'Neutrality, Dealignment and Political Order in Europe', in Mary Kaldor and Richard Falk (eds), *Dealignment: A New Foreign Policy Perspective* (Oxford: Blackwell, 1987) 178–9.
18. As coined by the *Economist*, 21 March 1987.
19. Barry Buzan, 'Common Security, Non-provocative Defence, and the Future of Western Europe', *Review of International Studies*, 13(4) (1987) 265–79.

2 The Security Debate in the Evangelical Church of the GDR

Helmut Fritzsche

1 INTRODUCTION

In August 1986, the Church and Society Committee of the Federation of Evangelical Churches of the GDR published a study entitled 'New Thinking in the Nuclear Age'[1] for distribution exclusively to Church members. Its first section summarises the course of the Church debate on security issues from the mid-1970s to 1985 with impressive lucidity. The section concludes with a rejection of 'the spirit, logic and practice of deterrence'.

The two remaining sections[2] deal with new scientific, political, and philosophical thought from the East. Professor O. Reinhold's approach to the 'politics of dialogue' is cited, as is Gromyko's reaction to the idea of 'security partnership'. But the bulk of the material is devoted to the position of Gorbachev. His reflections after Chernobyl are quoted, as are his announcement of the unilateral moratorium on nuclear testing and, above all, his speech of 18 August 1986, in which he appealed for 'the new thinking of which today's world stands in so great a need ... a new thinking incompatible with a patronizing approach to people's outlook on the world, whether this be socialistic, capitalistic or other'.

How congruent the views expressed in the Church study with the radical new approach to peace and security evinced in Gorbachev's declarations, each reader must decide for himself. But it is noteworthy that the authors felt it necessary to warn against any complacency of a 'we've been saying that for ages' kind.[3]

Today the Evangelical Church may indeed feel a degree of satisfaction at its unique position in the GDR,[4] at the dialogue it has been allowed to initiate with official doctrine,[5] and at its potential role as a 'pace-setter in new thinking'. But criticism is not lacking. The various Christian peace, environmental, feminist and emancipation associations, whose membership is not confined to Church members, tend to accuse the Federation of Evangelical Churches of 'political irresponsibility', and wish to see the Church take up the classic Christian approach of an unconditional rejection of violence.

Tension between the Church and groups is not as high as it seemed likely to become some years ago.[6] But it is to a background of challenges from these groups that the Church debate on security has unfolded. Though the Western media have often chosen to focus on the more controversial statements such as the 1982 'Berliner Appell' (see note 27), the relations of Church and groups have generally been productive rather than confrontational, and much less attention has been accorded to the Church's not unsuccessful attempts to come to terms with the groups and integrate their challenge as a valuable stimulus.[7]

The integration of the groups is not of course the primary function of the Church security debate. The Evangelical Churches have acquired a very special function in the GDR, that of a forum in which views not necessarily consonant with those of the official peace movement can be publicly debated.

Thus, on 22 October 1983, the 'Neues Deutschland', the official journal of the Central Committee of the Socialist Unity Party (the East German 'Communist Party'), gave its second page over to an open letter from the (Dresden) Loschwitz parish to Erich Honecker on the subject of missile deployment. The letter unconditionally rejects the deployment of new missiles in the West[8] and stresses the dangers arising from any similar counter-measure taken in the East. While expressing its thanks to Honecker for his acceptance of the notion of security partnership, the parish appeals to him to respond not on a tit-for-tat basis, but by unilateral initiatives, these being 'the only way to secure peace'. The letter claims that this approach combines the New Testament injunction to love one's enemies with a political rationale appropriate to our time.

The Loschwitz letter exemplifies some of the more remarkable features of the Church's work for peace in the GDR.

1. The letter is an example of the efforts toward peace made at grassroots level, in the parishes. Though the synods and their theological 'thinktank' have evolved a very sophisticated intellectual approach to peace and security issues, the grassroots level has the most sociopolitical impact; and the two are very closely connected. The grassroots peace movement in the Church began with the 'Swords to Ploughshares' youth movement, whose influence in the parishes was considerable.[9]

2. The Loschwitz letter is at pains to stress the independence of its views, and this is characteristic of statements emanating from the Church. The freedom of thought to which it lays claim is freedom from neither the constraints of political realism nor the need for political commitment. It is simply felt that a forthright stance is the only acceptable one.[10] Heino Falcke wrote on the subject of deployment: 'I think we have to say No in the name of Jesus and on political grounds. I said No in the Federal Republic and I say the same here. This is an issue for faith and conscience. I think the church of Jesus Christ is permitted neither to agree nor to participate' where deployment is concerned.[11]
3. The issues of peace, security and disarmament are not, in the Church debate, associated with questions of East–West rivalry. The confrontation between the two social systems is considered a thing apart, and one which falls outside the scope of the debate on peace, deterrence and détente.[12] The Church debate therefore rejects all attempts to ascribe the threat to world peace to one of the two sides. Neither side is blamed for the danger of war, and both sides are regarded as rational and responsible agents. But the statements of the Church make no bones about the fact that changes are necessary in both systems if peace and security are to be achieved.[13]
4. A thorough grounding in the Bible and a clear political rationale characterise the arguments set out in the Loschwitz letter. The obligation in Christ to love one's enemies is at one with an appreciation of political circumstance. This convergence typifies the arguments of the Church, which assert that Christian duty and political rationality go hand in hand; that the utopian Biblical requirement for a world without weapons is now simply a practical necessity, and though its utopian aspect will remain an inspiration transcending any conceivable practical measure, the direction in which it points is the correct one. In this way utopian ideas translate into practical political measures. The demand to make Christian ideas '*politikfähig*'[14] is one which pervades the totality of the Church debate on security.

Not only does the Church security debate serve to integrate currents of Christian opinion, whether these arise inside or outside the institution of the Church; it also serves as a forum for the discussion of points of view which are at odds with official doctrine. These two functions fulfil real needs in the GDR, and help the Church to achieve a new and distinct identity within socialism.

Whether the Church is so well-equipped to tackle the function previously mentioned – that of a 'pace-setter in new thinking' – is less clear, and is a question to which I will return. What is certain is that the Church's independence is the condition of the influence and integrity of its work for peace. The value of its independence quite transcends the credibility that is conferred by the formal separation of Church and state or by the perceived integrity of its message. Its independence is grounded in the spiritual identity of the Christian in life and word, and this aspect is every bit as important as the meticulous care with which ramifications of the political and social situation are analysed. Churches function as 'moral institutions' in a world in which the credibility of words and ideologies has been sadly undermined,[15] and the guaranteed intellectual integrity of the Churches makes a genuine contribution to the solution of conflict by non-military means.

How much political conviction do the Church's judgements carry? Are they of real service either at grassroots level or to the holders of political office? Do they contribute to the identification and resolution of conflict? To answer these questions, we will study a practical example, that of the reception accorded within the churches to the Palme security concept, in the context of the evolution of the relations of State and Church in the period 1976–86.

2 THE RECEPTION OF THE PALME REPORT WITHIN THE FEDERATION OF EVANGELICAL CHURCHES IN THE GDR

Debate on the subjects of peace, security and strategies for conflict resolution within the Church dates back to the mid-1970s. The initial impulse came less from events in the world than an event in the GDR, the introduction of obligatory paramilitary instruction in schools as a part of the state programme for the inculcation of the communist–socialist personality.[16]

The response of the Church came in the form of a wide-ranging programme of activities and courses of study under the umbrella title 'Education for Peace'; it was introduced in 1978 and is still going strong. An ad hoc committee, the *Friedenserziehung*, (Peace Education) was founded and published a study 'Rahmenkonzept: "Erziehung zum Frieden"' (Conceptual Framework: 'Education to Peace').[17]

The Church peace education courses are intended not only for those still in full-time education but also for adults in their working lives. They draw attention to the fact that threats to peace are very often a consequence of one's own cultural traditions. Techniques of conflict resolution relying on oppression and on the traditional dichotomy friend–foe are among our most deeply entrenched of behaviour patterns. The issue is not the form – psychological, sociological, or physical – taken by oppression; the fields of conflict studied in the course are all but universal, ranging from family life and group behaviour patterns to social and political conflicts and the particular kinds of violence characteristic of these. The alternative propounded is conflict resolution by dialogue, exchange of ideas, identification with the other, proofs of goodwill, unilateral first conciliatory steps and so on.[18]

The theological background of peace education is the Christian faith in the influence of the Holy Spirit, working inside and outside the Christian Churches and other humanistic traditions, and inspiring people to ever more humane and complete resolution of conflictual situations. The millenial cultural tradition of aggression in conflict management should not be considered an invincible obstacle to the transformation of human behaviour. And the social function accomplished by these courses is clear: the context for discussion of conflict resolution in the GDR has almost invariably been that of military conflict rather than conflict arising from internal issues.

In August 1982, some months after the first publication of the 'Palme Report',[19] a 15-page excerpt was published for members of the Church by the Theology Department in Berlin. Some weeks later, at the Synod of Halle, the Federal Synod declared that it was adopting the concept of common security 'as its own';[20] it considered the concept's realisation 'the most important political task for the 1980s', and pledged its support similarly to all endeavours tending toward 'peaceful political alternatives to military deterrence'.[21]

Reference to common security or security partnership is now almost universal in the Church debate. The principle that 'both sides much achieve security, not from the opposing side, but in common with the opposing side' (Egon Bahr) is the cornerstone of the Church's position. The contrast between deterrence and security partnership is another feature common to the Palme Report and the declarations of the Church: 'A doctrine of common security must replace the present expedient of deterrence through armaments' says the Palme Commission, and the point is explicitly taken up again in the statements of the Church: 'Common security instead of deterrence'.[22] The views of the Palme Commission are also reflected in the concrete political proposals of the Church – namely, a nuclear freeze, the establishment of a zone free of tactical nuclear forces in Central Europe, and the use, in common with other confidence building measures, of minor unilateral initiatives to overcome the present deadlock. All of these have featured in the Church's demands.[23] The Church also shares the concern to strengthen the authority of the United Nations Organisation and to give a greater binding force to international law. Thus on the occasion of the Assembly of the World Council of Churches in Vancouver in 1983, the Federal Synod entered a plea for 'an international legal instrument which would outlaw as a crime against humanity the possession as well as the use of nuclear arms'.

The weakness of the Palme Report is the question of motivation. What kinds of consideration would convince politicians and peoples to value the goal of common security over and above that of superiority? How powerful are these considerations relative to the drives that incite man toward an ideology of superiority? Is the motive cited in the Palme Report – that is, the fear of mutual destruction – a sufficiently solid one to form the keystone of a security partnership?[24]

It is at this level that the Church's concept of security seems both broader and more realistic. The Church does not consider deterrence and the arms race as isolated phenomena, but in a social and psychological context that takes account of the profound differences that characterise the two social systems in confrontation. The rivalry of East and West is for the most part stated in material rather than moral terms, and this in itself provides a fertile breeding ground for the mentality of deterrence. The Church, by contrast, affirms that the common security concept cannot be made to work without a thoroughgoing reappraisal of the terms not only of our approach to armaments but indeed of our approach to this world.

The achievement of the Church security debate has been to combine the ideas of security partnership with those of peace education. The product has been an outlook expressed as 'Rejection of the spirit, logic and practice of deterrence' (*Absage an Geist, Logik und Praxis der Abschreckung*). Common security serves in this perspective[25] to formulate an alternative not merely to deterrence as a military strategy but to the forms in which both societies and individuals are accustomed to attend to their own interests.

An impressive feature of the debate is the way in which the 'logic' of deterrence is set against that of common security. The Church here points to the mechanisms governing enemy or partner perception.

The deterrent effect of mass destruction depends on a perceived willingness to use it, at least as a second strike. But any use of weapons of mass destruction is suicidal. The knowledge that universal death will result suggests that only monsters could have recourse to them. The logic of deterrence generates an infinite regress in such perceptions of the enemy, which in turn seems to justify greater and greater efforts in the direction of security through deterrence. The logic of common security stresses quite different aspects of the enemy – namely, his concern for his own survival, his sense of responsibility and his capacity to forge a peaceful and warm coexistence. First moves in this direction will provide an ever growing perception of real security partnership. The dynamic of common security is consistently emphasised in the Church debate.

Security partnership as envisaged by the Church is not underpinned by the advance of trade as it is in the theses of Kant. Kant thought that the *Handelsgeist* (the spirit of trade), in combination with international law, would lead to *ewigen Frieden* (everlasting peace). The Church debate focuses more on the moral and psychological challenges presented by the aspiration to peace. The effect of current policies of mutual deterrence on the 'Third World' and on the environment is particularly stressed.[26]

The security debate is very wide-ranging, and consequently very difficult to summarise; a great many declarations, bulletins, commission reports and theological studies are produced, mostly for church members only. But some of the essential features may be given in brief:

1. The concrete political proposals – and particularly those referring to arms reduction – are not original. They derive for the most part from the Palme Report or the debate to which it gave rise. The Church should not, I think, be reproached for this lack of originality; dilettantism in politics is dangerous.[27] Though Church statements on the subject of arms reduction do at times give an impression of originality, the significant originality of the Church lies elsewhere.
2. Central to the Church debate is the notion of the failure or inadequacy of the individual in his reaction not only to the antagonism inherent in the North–South divide, or to the threats that stem from the rivalry of East and West, but also and above all to those posed by the ambivalence of the nuclear age.

3. The failure of the individual is twofold. On the one hand lies the attitude of moral disengagement in the face of the challenges represented by questions of nuclear energy and the East–West and North–South divides. On the other lie mistrust, feelings of weakness or inadequacy, and the friend – dichotomy; and these too are a source of danger that proceeds from the individual. In relation to this subjective element, the participants in the Church debate appeal to the Gospel, and to the radical rethinking demanded by the Gospel of our concept of self and enemy, and indeed of the goals of mankind.
4. Unilateral and multilateral initiatives are no less appropriate at the level of the individual. Among those initiatives cited as able to change societies in both East and West, and to strengthen the desire for peace, are the renunciation of hostile propaganda, more meetings between individuals of the two German states, and a greater awareness of conflict management at grassroots level, in education as well as public and Church life.[28]
5. The Churches support conscientious objectors, and recommend conscientious objection as a 'clearer witness' (*das deutlichere Zeichen*) in comparison with people manifesting their desire for peace in combination with weapon-carrying service.[28]

3 CONCLUSIONS

3.1 Results of the Security Debate

Has the security debate in the Federation of Evangelical Churches proved an effective way to promote peace? The answer to this question presents three aspects:

1. Amid the tensions that threaten world peace today, the variant of common security put forward by the Church is an illuminating one. The factors highlighted in the Church debate are special ones – notably those that relate to the individual – and this is true of both the causes and the solutions proposed. Despite these relatively specialised concerns, the Church debate has helped people to come to terms with the issue of peace. Its terms of reference are broader than are found in similar debate in the GDR outside the Churches. The debate proved particularly beneficial for Church members at every level.

2. The debate has helped to rationalise a field of conflict in which it had become customary to blame threats to peace on one side only, or to evoke univocal causes. The wider cultural context to which the debate referred the issue improved people's comprehension of and resources for dealing with conflict; the groups' insistence on praxis as well as theory was particularly beneficial.
3. The debate has contributed to elucidate the complexity of the threat to peace. That issues of foreign and domestic policy, the rivalry of capitalism and socialism, the questions of justice raised by the North–South divide, and environmental issues are a single complex whole it has been one of the merits of the debate to point out. The Church statements have been accompanied by more or less symbolic first moves in the direction of engagement with Third World problems and of a lifestyle compatible with a proper respect for the environment. Here again the emphasis on the practical steps provided by the groups has been important, not only in educating people to the multiplicity of the threat to peace, but in overcoming the syndrome of emotional and intellectual helplessness to which it frequently gives rise.

In retrospect, it can be seen that this work went forward in three different social contexts. The first is the Evangelical Church of the GDR. In it, the common security concept provides a means for improved communication between base and leadership and has proved a key notion for the affirmation of Christian identity in sociopolitical issues. There is scarcely any other term or notion of equal potential for transforming Christian ethics in the social sphere.[30]

The second social context is that of the ecumenical movement. The idea of common security, which is very popular in both German states and in their Churches, has not acquired a similar currency in Churches outside Europe. It occupies a very marginal place in the statement of the Methodist bishops of the USA,[31] and is scarcely referred to in the letter of the Catholic bishops of the USA.[32] The special contribution of the Churches of the GDR at the VIth Assembly of the World Council of Churches in Vancouver in 1983 was the proposal to convoke a universal Christian peace council for 1990. The proposal cites the concept of common security as a factor that may help to bridge the gulf that separates the rival social systems.[33] The very wide approval enjoyed by the concept in both East and West give it a unique claim to such a function within the Christian *oecumene*.

The third social context is the relation between Marxists and Christians. The security debate has provided a better and deeper understanding of the Church's concern with social and political issues. Now, not only political but philosophical issues are coming within the horizons of a new dialogue.[34]

For Marxist orthodoxy, the Christian perception of the destructive forces inherent and active in all social systems, and the affirmation of the constructive power of religion, are controversial tenets. Nevertheless, the social functions of religion, the value of the Christian approach to mankind, and the merit of the language of Christianity as an instrument with which to analyse issues of responsibility in a fragile world are some of the themes of a dialogue which, in the GDR, began at the time of the celebrations marking the 400th anniversary of Luther's death. Common security is a concern and a concept which has helped to promote this dialogue.

3.2 A Dilemma of the Security Debate

With its rejection of nuclear war, and of war in general as 'the continuation of politics by other means', and its demand for the possession of nuclear and all other weapons of mass destruction to be outlawed, the Federal Synods went a long way towards an unconditional rejection of the situation relative to armament in which we all of us live. And on all these points, the consensus in the Churches is very general. But what consequences ensue for individuals, groups and parishes? A very thorny dilemma has to be faced, a dilemma with which the Churches of the West are already acquainted. A pacifist Church such as the Quakers, in conformity with its principles, finds itself of necessity rejecting individuals and institutions that directly or indirectly support armament. The argument that the Evangelical Churches should adopt this principle in the GDR is countered by the consideration that in this way the Church would jeopardise its position and thus its capacity to act for peace.[35] Moreover, there is some controversy as to the effects of the Church adopting this line. The Churches hope that ecumenical contacts will help them to clarify this issue.[36] I think the dilemma will remain.

3.3 Open Questions

We began with the question: 'Has the church peace debate acted as a pace-setter in new thinking?' The Churches of the GDR did indeed plead in favour of tolerance rather before this became a commonplace with either philosophers or the political authorities. Since the very first Federal Synod in 1969, the Church has called for fair treatment of people with divergent lifestyles or divergent social or political opinions. Greater freedom to travel East and West, not least as a way of promoting understanding between people living in conflicting social systems; deficiencies in the organisation of society in the GDR, such as the lack of parity between men and women, when the double role of women as mothers and employees is taken into account; these are some of the other issues that have emerged over the course of the Church debate.[37] The authorities in the GDR have increasingly responded to these criticisms.

Does the Churches' role as forerunner derive from its sensitivity to its minority situation in a very secular society, or is it simply an outcome of the essential message of the Church? Only time will tell. For the time being, the openings and developments in the socialist system are challenges that the Church must take up.[38] Crucial to new developments in the GDR and to their acceptance by its citizens is a satisfying combination of the two values of socialism: social justice and individual freedom. World peace and freedom from the burden of armament are the first and primary condition of this. The second is the improvement of individual responses. It is particularly in the second of these two areas that the Church is called upon to show whether it is truly a standard bearer or whether it merely brings up the rear.

Notes and References

1. *Neues Denken im Atomzeitalter*. Arbeitspapier für die Gemeinden. Zusammengestellt im Auftrag der Konferenz der Evangelischen Kirchenleitungen in der DDR vom Ausschuss 'Kirche und Gesellschaft'.
2. *Neues Denken* (Note 1) 25ff.
3. *Neues Denken* (Note 1) 2.
4. See Manfred Becker: '*Und so bietet sich mir das Bild der Kirche am ende des Jahres 1985*: . . . – ihrer ehemaligen Privilegien beraubt, ist sie sich ihrer immerhin vorhandenen gesellschaftspolitischen Einmaligkeit bewusst und nicht unzufrieden mit ihrer Rolle . . .', Kirche des Jahres 1985, *Kirche im Sozialismus*, 1 (1986) 24.
5. For details, see Helmut Fritzsche, *Christian–Marxist cooperation in the GDR since 1945, Occasional Papers on Religion in Eastern Europe* (USA, OPREE) vol. VII, no. 3 (1987) 1–13.

6. Concerning Church-group relations the *Bericht der Kirchenleitung* at the 1986 Federal Synod in Erfurt declared: 'Eine Polarisierung, wie sie noch als möglich erschien, ist nicht eingetreten, *Bericht der Kirchenleitung*, 15.
7. An exemplary approach for accommodation with the groups is that of Heino Falcke, moderator of the Federal committee *Church and Society*, and unofficial theological counsellor to the groups. He asks: Könnte es sein, dass hier die Berufung der Gruppen liegt, unseren Kirche weiterzuhelfen, auf die Sprünge zu helfen, auf dem Wege zur Kirche des Schalom?' 'Unsere Kirche und ihre Gruppen', *Kirche im Sozialismus*, 4 (1985) 147. A concrete case of conflict is tackled in '*Friedenswerkstatt. Offener Brief an die Friedenskreise und Friedensgruppen in Berlin. Berlin 29.9.1986', Kirche im Sozialismus*, 6 (1986) 238.
8. '. . . Die Vorstellung erfüllt uns mit Entsetzen, dass bei der von uns allen verurteilten Stationierung der amerikanischen Atomraketen in Westdeutschland auch auf unserem Territorium entsprechende Gegenmaßnahmen eingeleitet werden, und wir und unsere Kinder unmittelbar mit Atomraketen leben müssen . . . Sie haben auch den Begriff der Sicherheitspartnerschaft aufgenommen . . . Uns scheint, die mit dem vertrauen verbundene Bereitschaft zu einseitigen Vorleistungen, d.h. nicht Gleiches mit Gleichem vergelten zu wollen, könnte heute die einzige Möglichkeit der Friedenssicherung sein. Diese Überzeugung erwächst für uns aus dem Neuen Testament, insbesondere aus der Botschaft Jesu. Wir wissen, dass die Gedanken Jesu, vor allem im Blick auf die Nächsten- und Feindesliebe bisher für politisch undurchführbar, ja, für unvernünftig gehalten worden sind. Im Angesicht einer tödlichen Rüstungsspirale jedoch könnte in ihnen ein Impuls der befreiung entdeckt werden: Vertrauen und schaffen durch Massnahmen, die einer einseitigen Vorleistung gleichkommen, damit der tödliche Automatismus durchbrochen wird', *Neues Deutschland*, 22–23 October 1983, 2.
9. The Swords to Ploughshares movement in the early 1980s was a very spontaneous movement, which surprised both Church and state authorities. Young people gathered and demonstrated in churches, schools and other places for a world without military deterrence. Peace Church services brought together thousands of young people, not all of them members of the Churches. They opposed the planned deployment of the cruise missiles and Pershing II in the West but also the deployment of nuclear missiles in the GDR and other Warsaw Pact countries. The Swords to Ploughshares movement was a broad one with many different groups mostly of emotional rather than rational motivation. When the movement first began, there were fears that it might cause a return to the confrontation of Church and state that had occurred in the 1960s, and mistakes were made on both sides.
10. 'Wir müssen jeweils prüfen, wer (und welche Handlung) eine besondere Gefährdung des friedens darstellt und durch welche Massnahmen Frieden gefördert werden kann. Es ist nicht vertretbar, "auf dem Felde christlicher Verantwortung die Schuld gleichmässig in alle Richtungen" (Halle 1982) zu verteilen', *Neues Denken*, (note 1) 8.

11. Heino Falcke, *Frieden schaffen aus der Kraft der Schwachen*, Theol. Stud. Abt. (1984) 6.
12. The same is now said in the context of New Thinking by the Marxist philosopher Rolf Reissig: 'Die Systemauseinandersetzung ist heute auf das engste verbunden . . . mit . . . der Verhinderung eines nuklearen Weltkrieges . . . mit . . . der weiteren Gestaltung der entwickelten sozialistischen Gesellschaft . . . mit der gesamtheit des revolutionären Weltprozesses. Zugleich besitzt die Systemauseinandersetzung als reale Erscheinung unserer epoche relative Eigenständigkeit', *Deutsche Zeitschrift für Philosophie*, 4 (1986).
13. For example: Heino Falcke: 'Ich bin heute der Meinung, dass es darum geht, die Verantwortung für das Morgen jeweils an dem Ort wahrzunehmen, an dem man lebt. Das ist für uns diese sozialistische Gesellschaft, die anders werden muss, wenn sie sich den Herausforderungen der heutigen Welt wirklich stellt. Genauso wie die westlichen gesellschaften anders werden müssen, wenn sie diese Verantwortung wirklich wahrnehmen', Kirche für andrer in der DDR, *Kirche im Sozialismus,* 2 (1986) 61.
14. See the summary of the debate, in '*Bulletin of the ad hoc Committee "Friedensfragen"*, given at the Federal Synod, Erfurt (1986). Enclosure II: 'Politikfähige Konzepte der Friedenssicherung'.
15. Today a new debate is unfolding which concerns Church membership in the GDR (see Becker, '*Und so bietet*', (note 4) 73). The question most discussed is whether 20 per cent or less Church members is a realistic assessment for the 1990s. My thesis is: The political impact of the current peace and security debate is demonstrably independent of the number of Church members. Besides, in the past the vast majority of Church members rarely attended services together. Today non-members also attend sporadically; sporadic contact can also be influential. The impact of the Church in the 1980s has not been that of a mass movement, but of striking ideas emanating from individuals and small groups.
16. Two further impulses should also be mentioned: The Final Act of Helsinki 1975 and the World Assemblies of the World Council of Churches, particularly the 5th Assembly in Nairobi (1975).
17. Published in *Kirche als Lerngemeinschaft* (Berlin, 1981) ed. by the Secretary of the Federation of Evangelical Churches in the GDR, 266–75.
18. 'Erziehung zum Frieden ist eine Erziehung, die befähigt, ermutigt und anleitet: -zur Austragung und Bewältigung von Streit mit Mitteln des Gesprächs, der Verständigung und des Kompromisses, -zur kritischen Gewaltkontrolle und zum Gewaltverzicht (Druck, Zwang, körperliche Züchtigung) im zwischenmenschlichen bereich, -zur bereitschaft, in einem Konflikt den ersten Schritt zur Lösung zutun, -zur Gewährung von vertrauen und zu vertrauensbildenden Schritten im Zusammenleben . . ., -zur Mitverantwortung für öffentliche, kommunale, betriebliche, schulische Angelegengheiten, -zur kritischen Auseinandersetzung mit ausschliesslich militärischen Sicherheitsvorstellungen und -konzepten, die persönliche entscheidung in der frage des waffendienstes eingeschlossen', *Kirche als herngemeinschaft* (note 17), 274.

19. The Independent Commission on Disarmament and Security Issues introduced its Bulletin '*Common Security. A Blueprint for Survival*' in Stockholm on 25 April 1982.
20. *Bulletin of the ad hoc Committee 'Friedensfragen'* at the Synod in Erfurt (1986) Enclosure II, 1.
21. *Neues Denken* (note 1), 6.
22. In *Bericht der Konferenz der Kirchenleitung (KKL)*, Federal Synod, Erfurt (1986) 25, and in many other places.
23. A complete survey of the Church demands is given in *Bulletin of the ad hoc Committee 'Friedensfragen'*, Erfurt (1986) Enclosure II, 5–6.
24. Berthold Meyer and Peter Schlotter in a comment to the Palme Report: 'The relations between two blocs bristling with arms cannot be characterized as a security partnership if each party hesitates to attack the other only for fear of destroying itself. This is Cold War. Fear of mutual destruction does not constitute a security partnership. This is why a model should be developed that would go beyond the postulate of "common security" in the narrow understanding of the Palme commission', 'Common Security between East and West', Bulletin of Peace Proposals, vol. 14, no. 3 (1983) 220.
25. The concept has been worked out in detail in the debates of the Federal Synods since the 1982 Synod in Halle (the word 'practice' was added 1983 in Potsdam) and – amongst others – in the following studies: *Sicherheitspartnerschaft in Europa*. 1983; *Möglichkeit und Unmöglichkeit einseitiger Abrüstung*, 1984 (both from the Theol. Stud. Abt.), and in the statement: Unsere Kirchen auf dem Wege zum Bekennen in der Friedensfrage, *Bulletin of the ad hoc Committee 'Friedensfragen'*, Erfurt (1986).
26. One example among many: 'Die Aufrüstung geht unvermindert weiter . . . Dabei werden Mittel durch die Rüstung verbraucht, die ausreichen würden, das Elend der armen Länder zu beseitigen. Vierzig Millionen Menschen sterben jährlich an unterlassener Hilfeleistung reicher Länder. Indem sie weiterrüsten und ihre Kräfte für die selbstzerstörung ansammeln, unterlassen sie dringende Nothilfe', *Bericht der Konferenz der Kirchenleitung*, Erfuert (1986) 25.
27. Some statements divergent from the mainstream Church debate have been made by groups inside and outside the Church. One example is the '*Berliner Appell*' of 1982 pleading for 'Wiedervereinigung Deutschlands' and a relatively strong confrontation with the foreign policy of the GDR. Another example is the *Initiative für Blockfreiheit in Europa – aufruf an den Kongress der USA*' (1985) signed among others by Generalsuperintendent G. Krusche. (Text in *Kirche in Sozialismus*, 4 (1985) 162.) These views were not enthusiastically received by the public or Church members.
28. Der Gedanke der gemeinsamen Sicherheit muss deshalb in der Friedenserziehung Gestalt gewinnen. Das bedeutet unter anderem: – innerhalb der politischen Bildung und Erziehung für gewaltfreie Konfliktlösungen einzutreten und sie einzuüben. – Kontakte zwischen Einzelnen und Gemeinden aus den beiden politischen Systemen zu unterstützen, -die besondere Friedensverpflichtung der Deutschen

in Ost und West bewusst zu machen, *Neues Denken*, Federal Synod, Postdam (1983), 7.

29. Tensions between state and Church arose in 1961 with the introduction of compulsory military service. A first move toward the resolution of this conflict came in 1964 with the establishing of *Bausoldat*, a non-weapon-carrying military service for conscientious objectors. On the question of conscientious objection the Federal Synod declared in 1986 in Erfurt: 'Der Frieden der Welt wächst mit der friedensgesinnung vieler einzelner, und der Frieden der Welt braucht die Zeichen der Friedensgesinnung einzelner. Auch weiterhin wird Friedensgesinnung im Verhalten Wehrpflichtiger bezeugt werden. Das geschieht in der Verweigerung jedes militärischen Dienstes. Das geschieht im waffenlosen dienst in den Baueinheiten. Um dieses Zeugnis bemühen sich auch Wehrpflichtige, die Dienst in bewaffenten Einheiten leisten', *Bericht der Konferenz der Kirchenleitungen*, 27.
30. 'Sicherheitspartnerschaft erscheint mehr als ein vernünftiges Gleichnis der Feindesliebe, die in der Liebe Gottes begründet ist', Karl Heinz Dejung, 'Theologische Überlegungen angesichts der Herausforderung zu einer Sicherheitspartnerschaft', *Theol. Studien.* Abt. Referat Friedensfragen (Berlin, 1985).
31. *Defence of Creation*: The Nuclear Crisis and a Just Peace 1986, 78.
32. Challenge of Peace: *God's Promise and Our Response* (1983).
33. 'Wir bitten die Christen, christlichen Krichen und Gruppen, ihre Brückenfunktion im Spannungsfeld verfeindeter Völker und Staaten wahrzunehmen und sich einzusetzen für das friedenspolitische Konzept der "gemeinsamen Sicherheit": Lothar Coenen and Wolfgang Traumüller (eds), *Beiheft zur Ökumenischen Rundschau*, 48 (Vancouver, 1983) 205.
34. See Fritzsche, *Christian–Marxist cooperation* (Note 5).
35. The 1986 Federal Synod in Erfurt stated: 'Die Gliedkirchen des Bundes haben trotz des Minimierungsprozesses volkskirchlichen Charakter behalten und halten die darin einbeschlossene Pluralität und Offenheit bewusst fest. Darum weckt die Herausforderung, in der Frage des Wehrdienstes verbindlich und eindeutig in die Richtung gewaltfreien Friedensdienstes zu weisen, die Sorge, gesetzlich zu werden und einen Teil ihrer Glieder faktisch auszuschliessen und zu verlieren', Unsere Kirchen auf dem Wege zum Bekennen in der Friedensfrage, *Bulletin of the ad hoc Committee 'Friedensfragen'*, Erfurt (1986) Enclosure I, 7.
36. *Bulletin of the ad hoc Committee 'Friedensfragen'* (note 35), 8.
37. An example is the Federal Synod Bulletin 1985, *EPD Dokumentation 43/85: Bericht der Konferenz der Kirchenleitungen*, 5.
38. Ibid.

3 The New Peace Movement and European Security

Mary Kaldor

1 INTRODUCTION

The new peace movement, which emerged in the early 1980s, appeared to be primarily an anti-nuclear movement. Its activities coalesced around the issue of a European nuclear-free zone, and specifically, the non-deployment and later removal of the Euro-missiles. But the underlying concerns were more profound. They had to do with the role of the state in modern society and the issue of national self-determination. The Euro-missile issue, in particular, was about the relationship of the USA to Western Europe, about national sovereignty in security matters, about who has the right to make decisions about life and death.

Most peace activists, moreover, were aware that these were the substantive concerns. Of course it is true that fear of nuclear war was a mobilising factor. On the other hand, fear of nuclear war can also be a demobilising factor. It can lead to psychological suppression, to withdrawal from politics, or indeed it can be used to justify deterrence. The showing of films like *Threads* or *The Day After* seems merely to have entrenched existing positions on deterrence.

Most peace activists saw the peace movement as a new form of political engagement, and this is confirmed, not just by my own political experience, but by sociological studies. Often their activities arose from a disillusion with the conventional political process and especially a loss of confidence in the emancipatory role of social democracy, after the experience of social democracy in power during the 1970s. The term 'control over life and our lives', drawn from the women's movement, is often used. Only some such broader interpretation can explain the mobilising potential of the peace movement, which was able, in the autumn of 1981 and again in 1983, to bring some 5 million people out in the streets of different European capitals. It is difficult to think of an historical precedent.

The zero option does represent a belated, if indirect, victory for the European peace movement. Today, the peace movement is much less visible than in the early 1980s; it does not get the same media attention. Nevertheless, its activities remain widespread. After deployment in 1983, the peace movement entered a phase of doubt – unable to escape from the missile issue, unwilling to accept defeat, and therefore confused about its direction. The zero option finally resolves the issue of the missiles and allows the peace movement to formulate a new post-zero option strategy.

I think it is true to say that, in the post-zero option era, there is general agreement within the peace movement that the issue is European security – or, rather, how to move towards an alternative security system for Europe that does not rest on military confrontation between East and West. But there the agreement ends. There are very different views about the nature of this security system, and about the appropriate tactics. Broadly speaking, it is possible to identify three main differences.

First of all, there are those who continue to put the emphasis on denuclearisation and demilitarisation and those who have a broader approach. Those who emphasise disarmament generally include those who talk about 'common security' or 'security partnership'. They would advocate peace movement campaigns on a whole series of post-INF arms limitation proposals such as alternative defence policies (including opposition to FOFA (Follow-On Forces Attack), AirLand Battle, etc.); nuclear-free zones in Central Europe, the Nordic area and the Balkans; a European chemical weapon-free zone; opposition to independent British and French nuclear weapons; opposition to the arms trade and to military intervention in the Third World.

Others would argue that the military forces are an expression of underlying political conditions and that overcoming the East–West confrontation involves much more than demilitarisation. Arms limitation proposals would, on this view, be regarded as one element of a broader anti-Cold War strategy which also involves internal social and political changes in both East and West, especially democratisation, and greater East–West cooperation and communication. Advocates of this approach talk about the need to build a European civil society, or a new European political culture.

A second set of differences has to do with the relationship to political parties. Broadly speaking, those who emphasise demilitarisation also tend to emphasise access to government and the need to work closely with political parties, especially Socialist, Social Democrat, and (at least in Italy) Communist parties. After a second set of defeats for social democracy in the elections of 1986–7, the view is gaining ground that the peace movement ought to focus on the broader political environment – that what is needed is an improvement in the relations between state and society so that the state is more responsive to public demands rather than an improved ability to capture state power. It is argued that, in any case, Socialist and Social Democrats in power find themselves constrained by the structures of the state, and that their environment is hostile to disarmament. The alternative approach is to create an environment in which even right-wing politicians find themselves forced to take up the peace movement agenda. The zero option, itself, and the new peace-making roles of Thatcher and Gorbachev are perhaps evidence for the success of such an approach.

In Eastern Europe, this kind of approach has been called 'anti-politics' by writers such as Vaclav Havel or George Konrad.[1] Within the West, those who espouse the anti-political approach include those who favour direct action – cutting wires, painting missiles, occupying bunkers, etc. – and those, like myself, who argue that the peace movement should use its ideas to penetrate a wide range of social institutions – Churches, schools, universities, trade unions, theatre, film, etc.

A third set of differences concerns the approach to East–West relations. Those who emphasise demilitarisation also emphasise improvements in relations with official bodies – peace committees, arms control experts, etc. – and the importance of countering right-wing stereotypes of the Eastern bloc by fostering good relations at a governmental level. Those who favour a broader anti-Cold War approach put more emphasis on what is variously known as grass-roots détente, citizens' détente or détente from below. This means fostering a dialogue with what are viewed as the peace movements' 'natural' partners – human rights, green and peace groups, who oppose the militarisation and authoritarianism of their own societies.

I use the word 'emphasis' advisedly. There are hardly any strands in the peace movement that favour exclusive dialogue with officials or alternatively with 'independents'. But managing a dialogue with both ends of the East European political spectrum is extremely difficult precisely because of the extreme difficulties of independent political action in Eastern Europe and the polarity of the domestic political confrontation, although this could well be changing. These problems thus come to bear upon different attitudes within the Western peace movements.

I tend towards the anti-Cold War approach, although I do believe it has to encompass demilitarisation. Likewise, I also favour the anti-political approach and détente from below, although I would be opposed to an exclusive approach to these issues – alliances with social democracy and détente from above are also important. In developing the reasons why I favour such an approach, it is important to start with an analysis of the East–West confrontation and its various phases; Cold War (roughly 1950s and 1960s), Détente (roughly 1970s), and New Cold War (the first half of the 1980s). I shall then discuss the role of social democracy in existing and future European security arrangements; and return to the role of the peace movement in the concluding section.

2 THE NATURE OF THE EAST–WEST CONFLICT

The conventional view of the Cold War is what Isaac Deutscher has termed the 'Great Contest'.[2] It is an inevitable clash of political or social systems. In the orthodox Western view, the contest is between freedom and totalitarianism, and in the orthodox Eastern view, it is between capitalism and socialism. This view of the confrontation is shared both by the hawks, the proponents of confrontational Cold Warist stance, and by those who favour a softening of the confrontation, a détente from above or détente as it was practised in the 1970s.

These views have implications for the way in which the conflict might be resolved. The hawks can see no other solution but the victory of one side or the other – and, therefore, envisage permanent military stand-off. The détente view envisages the removal of the military aspects of the confrontation and the continuation of the conflict by non-military means. This is what is meant by the Soviet term for détente – peaceful coexistence.

It is worth noting that the détente view which underlies the emphasis on demilitarisation appears to miss the link between international politico–military arrangements and domestic social processes. Those who see the European security problem primarily in military terms, tend to see the main danger of the conflict as nuclear war – the holocaust that overrides all other issues. (Again, this view is shared by the hawks who see deterrence as the only way to avoid holocaust.) Those who see the issue of European security in broader terms emphasise the dangers of the continuing confrontation, including military competition, on our own societies – the cost, the secrecy, the erosion of democratic processes, the link with poverty in the Third World, and with ecological problems.

An alternative view of the East–West conflict,[3] which might inform the broader anti-Cold War approach, could be set out as follows. The East–West conflict masks an internal social contest within both 'East' and 'West'. In peace movement parlance, Gorbachev and Reagan are now so friendly they can even agree to explode nuclear devices on each other's territory, so there has to be some other explanation for their slowness in agreeing to demilitarise. The answer is that the cruise missiles are really directed against the women of Greenham Common – as can be seen from the barbed wire, paratroopers, etc. defending the base – and not against the Soviet Union at all, just as Soviet tanks are really directed against the populations of Eastern Europe.

Put in a more abstract way, the argument is that the 'Great Contest' is an ideological tool for disciplining the two sides, for sustaining the hegemony of the USA and the Soviet Union. Fear of the other, fear of war, helps to ensure domestic cohesion. The Cold War was a way of prolonging the benefits of the Second World War – social cohesion, effective economic management, etc. – without the bloodshed. At the same time, it insulated Europe from the real wars in the Third World.

But US and Soviet hegemony should be understood not simply in power terms, but in systemic terms. Moreover, the systemic issue is not a simple issue of capitalism versus socialism, with the USA imposing capitalism and the Soviet Union imposing socialism. Rather it is about varieties of capitalism and socialism. What I am saying – and to develop this argument would require a theoretical treatise – is that specific state forms are an essential component of the social formation, and that different social formations are more variegated than the 'Great Contest' approach would imply. Indeed, the notion of a clash between two homogeneous systems has served to stimulate a diversity of experiments in socialism and democracy.

In the West, in the post-war period, the USA was able, through various mechanisms linked to the US military presence – the free trade regime, the NATO infrastructure, the effects on domestic politics – to shape the direction of European development along lines charted by the USA. In the NATO area, one can talk about a sort of a compromise between the social democratic ideas prevalent in the 1940s and 1950s that reached their fullest expression in Scandinavia, and the US Fordist model of capitalism. (Of course, it was rather different in Southern Europe where the US presence was maintained by force.) In the East, Soviet-style socialism was brutally imposed on the countries of East-Central Europe.

The notion of a 'Great Contest' was effective in the early years of the East–West conflict precisely because the notions of capitalism versus socialism or freedom versus totalitarianism seemed to have resonance in terms of the internal social contest. State versus market, economic justice versus democracy, seemed to reflect domestic political issues. But, in the West as Social Democrats entered government and became part of the institutional elite, the 'Great Contest' idea became less convincing. There are, of course, still important economic issues – unemployment, welfare provision, inflation – but their resolution seems to lie outside the realm of economic management – they have more to do with state structures. Other issues like feminism or the environment seem to cut across or to be irrelevant to the notion of a 'Great Contest' – at any rate, in its conventional form. Indeed, in both East and West, radical social movements share common preoccupations that seem to have little to do with the traditional formulation of state versus market – democracy, the environment, the militarisation of society.

The East–West conflict has passed through three phases – Cold War, Détente, and New Cold War. It is important to distinguish between the superpower détente, which really began with the conclusion of the Vietnam war, and the intra-European détente which began earlier with Willy Brandt's *Ostpolitik*. In Kissinger's conception, détente was a kind of reborn Metternichean Concert – a mutual agreement to preserve spheres of influence. The so-called Sonnenfeldt doctrine was an explicit recognition of this. But, for this very reason, détente was inconsistent and contradictory. In my view – and again I do not have space to expand on this argument – détente failed not because it failed to deal with the military aspects of the confrontation – a dominant Social Democratic view[4] – but because without the discipline of an external confrontation, new and old domestic and intra-bloc tendencies surfaced.

Take economic détente, as an example. There was much enthusiasm for East–West economic cooperation in the early 1970s. But economic cooperation began to decline, well before the onset of the New Cold War. The reason was the structural difficulty for centrally planned economies of participating in the world market – these difficulties were most dramatically exposed in Poland. The experience of East–West cooperation, at least for a while, reinforced traditional centralising tendencies in East European countries – tendencies which tend to be linked to more hawkish political standpoints. Without structural change – decentralisation, export orientation, etc. – in East European economies, an economic détente is very difficult.[5]

I am not, by the way, arguing that détente is linked to internal reform in either East or West. On the contrary, I am arguing that this depends on internal social processes. But I am suggesting that it is difficult to suppress reform processes without external confrontation. Hence the New Cold War *followed*, in many cases, the introduction of represssive measures, like *Berufsverbot* in West Germany, or concerns about the independent behaviour of individual countries. Schmidt's interest in the Euro-missiles, for example, arose from his concern about the drifting apart of the USA and Western Europe.

The New Cold War has to be understood as a restoration of US and Soviet hegemony, in a systemic sense. In the West, the New Cold War was linked to a free trade ideology (monetarism, privatisation, etc.) which actually destroyed the post-war social compromise with social democracy, and increased repressive measures – increased powers for police forces, restrictive legislation on trades unions, etc. The New Cold War seems to have been effective in undermining the economic and political base of social democracy – an anti-socialist crusade conceived in traditional 'Great Contest' terms. But it stimulated the growth of new movements that lay outside the conventional definition of the 'Great Contest' – i.e., peace, green movements.

In the East, the New Cold War was assoçiated with a tightening up process, a reassertion of centralising tendencies, austerity policies, increased repression in several countries. Yet the early 1980s also witnessed the emergence of new autonomous social groups or circles, mainly concerned with peace or green issues, that could not be described as dissident or anti-socialist.

3 THE ROLE OF SOCIAL DEMOCRACY

The current institutional structure of European Socialist and Social Democrat parties can be traced back to the 1940s and 1950s. In order to capture power in the post-war period, these parties had to adapt to what one might describe as the 'Atlanticist' framework. Atlanticism can be said to have meant the acceptance of Cold War ideology – the notion of a 'Great Contest', and the relationship with the USA – combined with a commitment to managed capitalism. This period also witnessed the marginalisation of the neutralist, often statist, left.

Atlanticism was a bipartisan commitment. But, of course, left parties had some room for manoeuvre. They tended to favour détente rather than Cold War, and they were able to push for social objectives like full employment, welfare, and the nationalisation of some industries. Anthony Crosland's book *The Future of Democratic Socialism* remains the clearest statement of this Atlanticist outlook. During the late 1960s and early 1970s, Socialist or Social Democrat parties came to power in most Northern European countries in NATO. They were able to benefit from, and contribute to, the détente process.

The New Cold War of the early 1980s marked the end of the bipartisan consensus. It is worth noting that it was the right who broke this consensus first, by abandoning the commitment to managed capitalism – and, particularly, to full employment.

The Socialist and Social Democrat parties, under pressure from the peace movement, adopted more or less radical proposals for nuclear disarmament, but remained committed to a détentish view – i.e., the accommodation of different systems and the continuation of the competition by other means, which, in effect, means sustaining the systems in their current forms. Most of these parties, for example, now favour increased conventional spending even though most right-wing governments have abandoned NATO's 3 per cent target. The increases in conventional spending are supposed to 'compensate' for nuclear reductions and/or to ensure that the USA retains its commitment to Europe. The contradictory nature of this position is most vividly illustrated in the case of the British Labour Party. The Labour Party adopted an extremely radical policy for the denuclearisation of Britain. At the same time, it insisted on the special relationship between Britain and the USA (resulting in Kinnock's somewhat embarrassing visit to Reagan), favoured increased conventional spending particularly on the Navy, emphasised Britain's role as a global power and, in particular, supported Mrs Thatcher during the Falklands/Malvinas War in 1982.

In Southern Europe, the situation is somewhat different since Socialist parties came to power only during the early 1980s. Although some of the Socialist parties, especially in Spain and Greece, came to power on radical anti-Cold War platforms (out of NATO, and Balkan nuclear-free zones respectively), all of these parties, in government, effectively became agents of the New Cold War. Whether this was because they also faced large Communist parties, on their left, or because the Atlanticist Compromise was never so clearly established historically, or because of their limited room for manoeuvre in the international context cannot be answered without a much more lengthy investigation.

The defeat of social democracy in the 1980s in North NATO Europe (except Norway) has to be understood partly in demographic and sociological terms – the decline of the traditional working class because of the decline in manufacturing employment and in the skill composition of manufacturing, as well as the erosion of trade unions, owing to unemployment and restrictive legislation. But there is also a more political explanation, which is simply that their policies lacked credibility. They seemed to be offering new disarmament policies together with the traditional foreign and domestic policies of an earlier period. Nobody really believed that these policies could be carried out in the current context.

What we now seem to be witnessing is a widespread disillusion with politics – or, rather, party politics – and a loss of the sense of what it means to be a citizen. Because the left parties seem out of touch with predominant social concerns, there is no institutional outlet for new ideas and ideologies. The situation is akin to that described by Gramsci in *State and Civil Society*.

> At a certain point, in their historical lives, social classes become detached from their traditional parties. In other words, the traditional parties in that particular organisational form, with the particular men who constitute, represent, and lead them, are no longer recognised by their class (or fraction of a class) as its expression. When such crises occur, the immediate situation becomes delicate and dangerous, because the field is open for violent solutions, for the activities of unknown forces; represented by charismatic 'men of destiny'.[6]

Perhaps Thatcherism and Reaganism can be understood in these terms.

The point is illustrated by the left's reaction to the elections of 1987, at any rate in the British case. The defeat of the Labour Party in 1983 led to much despair, agonising, and heart-searching. In contrast, the defeat of 1987 passed almost unnoticed. It was accepted with resignation. No one expected anything different – party politics seemed to have become irrelevant. Because of the dominance of traditionalist party structures, social movements have emerged to provide an organisational expression of new issues and ideas. They have the task of mediating between the citizen and the party, of overcoming that sense of resignation, of rebuilding a democratic political culture in which electoral politics are able to express predominant political and social concerns.

4 THE ROLE OF THE PEACE MOVEMENT

My version of the nature of the East–West conflict implies that ending the Cold War has to do with changing society in both 'East' and 'West'. It means that, in place of homogeneous concepts of capitalism and socialism, a pluralism of concepts is allowed to flourish both in theory and in practice. Social tendencies and changes that are currently suppressed by the discipline of external confrontation would be promoted. Essentially, we are talking about how to ensure peaceful democratic change without resort to force as in Eastern Europe, or without the fear of war, as in Western Europe.

These social changes have to do, in the first place, with the changing relationship between state and society, with democracy or the renewal of democracy. They also have to do with the direction of development – reductions in military spending, greater concern for the environment and for poverty. These concerns are similar in both East and West, although there are many different types of solution. In this connection, it is interesting to note that both the Thatcherites (or Reaganites or Kohlites) and the new social reformers share a common commitment to minimise the role of the state and to improve efficiency. An alternative approach shared by many of the new social movements is to change the role of the state and to put more emphasis on equity and the environment.

It is worth noting, parenthetically, that the social basis of the new social movements is drawn from the growing professional middle classes. They tend to come from what are known as the 'caring professions' – doctors, teachers, social workers, lawyers, etc. – who have grown as a result of the welfare state, and the new class of information workers who result from the electronics revolution. These people are very often dependent on the state, as state employees or as beneficiaries of state expenditure, but they are frustrated by their lack of control over the state. They have generally received an elite education which prepares them for political participation and yet they feel excluded from power. This social grouping is quite different from the old petit bourgeoisie which formed the social basis for fascism. They were self-employed shop keepers, artisans, small farmers, etc. In contrast these are highly educated salaried employees. Nevertheless, it should be emphasised that this group remains a narrow stratum of society.

The specific task of the peace movement is to offer an alternative conception of international political arrangements – an alternative European security system – in which these domestic social and political concerns can be realised. As well as emphasising the dangers of the present situation, which is largely what the peace movement has done up till now, it needs to show the link between the international political change and domestic social change. Above all, this involves a move away from concepts of 'East' and 'West', from what might be termed 'blocism'. At a political level, this means a loosening of the relations between the USA and Western Europe and between the Soviet Union and Eastern Europe, as well as increased cooperation between Eastern and Western Europe. It also means that individual European countries should be able to undertake independent initiatives, especially in the security field; this is essentially the significance of unilateralism – being able to depart from the rules and norms of bloc behaviour.

But this political level has a systemic content. These changes in political relations have to be expressed in measures of demilitarisation (the removal of missiles or troops); in democratisation, especially in Eastern Europe; in increased economic, cultural, or ecological cooperation and concomitant structural reforms. Hence one is talking about a process in which demilitarisation interacts with – or, indeed, is one component of – a broader process of social change.

Within the peace movement, there is now talk of creating a 'league of oppositions' East and West – bringing together social movements to challenge Cold War mentality. This arises, in part, from the defeat of social democracy and, in part, from the actual experience of the last eight years. Gorbachev and Reagan seem to have become agents of a peace process – there is no reason to suppose that the left would succeed any better. Therefore the task of the peace movement is to create a peace oriented political environment and this is more effective if it is genuinely trans-national.

There is much in this argument and it is consistent with a broad anti-Cold War approach. Nevertheless, I would end with a note of caution. There is a danger that the new social movements will become a sub-culture – a way of living with the present situation, of disclaiming responsibility for the Cold War and the arms race. To some extent, this is the situation of the peace movement, at present; it is no longer a serious political actor. Essentially, the social movements have to engage in dialogue and debate with the existing institutions, especially the Social Democratic parties. Otherwise, little can be changed.

Notes and References

1. George Konrad, *Anti-Politics* (London: Quartet Books, 1984).
2. Isaac Deutscher, *The Great Contest* (London: Penguin Books, 1960).
3. I have set out the argument at greater length in 'The Concept of Common Security', in Raimo Väyrynen (ed.), *Policies for Common Security* (London: SIPRI, Taylor & Francis, 1985) and 'The Imaginary War', in E. P. Thompson and Dan Smith (eds), *Prospectus for a Habitable Planet* (London: Penguin Books, 1986).
4. See M. Kaldor and R. Falk (eds), *Dealignment: A New Foreign Policy Perspective* (Oxford: Basil Blackwell, 1987), especially the introduction and the Chapters by Alan Wolfe and Ben Lowe.
5. A good example of this kind of thinking is Horst Emke, 'Second phase of detente', *World Policy Journal* (Summer 1987).
6. Andras Köves, 'East–West Economic Cooperation', in G. Holden, M. Kaldor and R. Falk (eds), *A New Détente* (London: Verso, 1989).

4 Non-military Aspects of Security: The View of a Soviet Scholar

Pavel Podlesnyi

1 INTRODUCTORY REMARKS

The subject of this book is both timely and important; throughout the world, the significance of non-military forms of security is increasingly recognised. It is timely also in that it coincides with a fundamental rethinking of foreign and armament policy in the Soviet Union. The discussion of these issues in the Soviet Union is very wide-ranging, and I can do little more than touch on certain of them in a study of this length.

2 THE NEW SOVIET PERSPECTIVE

The Soviet vision of the world has undergone a radical transformation over the last three years. The scope and nature of these changes have been analysed at length in the recent articles of such well-known Soviet authors as A. Bovin and V. Zagladin.[1] For many years we in the Soviet Union perceived the world in terms of the struggle between two hostile camps, the socialist and the capitalist. The direction of world development was predicated on the issue of this struggle, and the tendencies of the two camps were regarded as irreconcilable. This view can no longer be sustained. Over and above differences of ideology and development, one fact is clear: the interdependence of all the nations of this earth. This is true not only of the danger of nuclear catastrophe, but also of the ecological threat, whose effects are scarcely less catastrophic. In common with the pressing need for international cooperation if economic disputes and regional conflicts are to find a peaceful issue, these factors all lead to the same conclusion, and the *de facto* interdependence of the nation states finds its recognition in principles which will come to govern the policies of the Soviet Union in foreign affairs. (i) Survival is the principal goal of all states, to which other interests are necessarily subordinated. (ii) Peaceful coexistence should not be considered merely one of the guises which class war can assume, but as the *highest universal principle governing relations between states*, and in particular states belonging to different systems or alliances. (iii) The contest between socialism and capitalism can take only one form, that of peaceful competition. The emergence of these trends, and the marked historical discontinuity they represent, does of course stress the need in the Soviet Union for democratic institutions capable of designing and formulating foreign policy, institutions which would give their due not only to the relevant experts, but also to the public at large. In the past, the vested interests of the different ministries and organisations have weighed too heavily in foreign policy decisions, and only by throwing the debate open to the public can such pressures be resisted.

This point is all the more important given the change in the image of the Soviet Union effected by *perestroika*. The new political doctrines, the greater transparency in the formulation of foreign and military policy, the democratisation of domestic Soviet politics – and, last but not least, the numerous Soviet initiatives in the fields of arms control and international security – have all contributed to diminish the 'Soviet military threat' in the eyes of the West. It would obviously be satisfactory if the West chose to reciprocate in these fields.

3 SECURITY POLICY AND ECONOMIC CONSTRAINTS

In today's world, security is one and indivisible, and recognition of this point is fundamental to any attempt to create a viable international system of peace and security. It is one of the lessons of the 'détente' of the 1970s that only by adopting a holistic approach and developing cooperation in many different fields simultaneously is it possible to build stable relations between East and West, relations that cannot be changed overnight by political events elsewhere in the world. The new Soviet policy begins with the acknowledgement that the interests of the various protagonists of the international scene are not identical and that each state will attempt to pursue its own interests. It is the task of a resourceful foreign policy to attempt to balance these interests, and the concept of the balance of interests is another extremely important innovation in the Soviet foreign policy of the last few years. But it follows from the interdependence of the world today that no state can guarantee its security unilaterally, whether by military means, political *diktat* or economic pressure. We may cite as proof of this the efforts of the first Reagan administration (1981–4) to restore military superiority over the USSR. This effort, and the concomitant attempt to dictate to the USSR the form of its relations with the USA, failed. The USA was forced to find ways of reducing tensions, and has subsequently resumed cooperation in many fields. But on the same grounds, during the recent conference held by the Soviet Foreign Ministry (July 1988), the views of those scholars and diplomats who held that the USSR was able to sustain any military challenge from the West, or that it should be strong enough to neutralise the threat of any probable coalition of states ranked against it, were rejected out of hand. The ambition of creating forces such as to confront the combined forces of all potential enemies is not only unrealistic, it is also a source of tension in the world, and is, as such, contrary to the interests of the Soviet Union.[2]

Though these views reflect the new Soviet outlook, other pressures are at work. Economic constraints have made themselves felt throughout the world, and the arms race has caused tangible and increasing damage to the economies of the East, the West and the developing countries. Limits to military expenditure are relative, but this is not to say that they do not exist. The build-up of military expenditure begun by the NATO member states during the late 1970s and early 1980s has since ground to a halt. The decision to maintain an annual 3 per cent increase in military expenditure, to which NATO members committed themselves in 1978, has not been observed, and military spending in these countries is on the wane. In some of these countries this process has been compounded by demographic tendencies; in West Germany, for example, the number of persons of an age for military service will fall by half within the next five years. In the USA, a similar trend toward reduced military spending may be noted. The budget deficit forces the USA to halt the increase of military appropriations in 1985, and the difficult passage given by Congress to recent proposals for military expenditure suggests that this trend is irreversible. For the Soviet Union, the relative priorities of domestic and foreign policy are currently the subject of much debate. The USSR faces a tremendous task in improving the efficiency of its economic and political system, and in the process of democratisation in general. The purpose of this effort is precisely to improve the quality of life of the Soviet people, and this choice must be reflected in the allocation of budgetary resources. The standard of living of the Soviet citizen must testify to the superiority of socialism: 'This is the principal national interest of the USSR', Foreign Minister Eduard Shevardnadze has said, 'Only such an approach can and should be applied to the notion of national security taken as a whole'.[3]

4 'REASONABLE SUFFICIENCY'

In military terms, then, the new conception of security taking shape in both East and West is that of *reasonable sufficiency*. The notion of 'reasonable sufficiency' requires some elucidation. It derives in the first place from certain modifications in the Soviet purview. An excess of force, even where intended for exclusively defensive purposes, itself contributes to the tensions it is supposed to defuse. Provision for national security must therefore begin with a realistic appraisal of the intentions and interests of the potential enemy. In the present circumstances, the function of inflicting intolerable damage on a nuclear aggressor could be served by a relatively small percentage of the strategic arsenal of the victim. Security under these circumstances is not reduced by arms reductions, indeed, the contrary is true. The intentions of the potential enemy are not unfathomable, being determined by relatively stable factors such as class, geography, politics and history, and security lies not in matching the forces available to the potential enemy, but in ensuring that these forces are never unleashed. With the recognition that survival is the priority of all states comes the recognition that all states are prepared to compromise. Security should therefore be considered in a perspective of collaboration rather then emulation. *An overestimation of the threat of war is itself a danger to the peace*. The practice of reasonable sufficiency involves the introduction of strictly defensive strategic planning, and the bringing of the armed forces along the NATO–Warsaw Pact fault-line into strict conformity with the officially-proclaimed defensive nature of the doctrines under which they are deployed. It also involves the creation of a politico–psychological atmosphere such that neither side fears a sudden attack. One contribution to this lies with the design of military exercises, which should not be such as to induce suspicion or fear.

For the USSR, the realisation that nuclear and conventional parity are not in themselves conducive to security is an important one, and it suggests that military programmes should derive from a realistic assessment of our strengths, and not simply mirror the programmes and policies of the USA or NATO. In some cases, asymmetrical responses may be more efficient, both strategically and economically, than a reflex imitation of the actions of the West. (The doctrine of reasonable sufficiency implies minimising military expenditure; the selection of political objectives is brought in line with economic potential.) Moreover, the errors of the past are there to tell us that foreign and military policy should arise out of broad and long-term political considerations. Soviet experts have recently admitted that the decision to replace SS4 and SS5 missiles with the more sophisticated SS20 was motivated not by a thorough-going analysis of European and global contexts, but merely by the availability of the relevant technology.[4] And the consequences for Soviet security were in fact negative; a second nuclear front was opened, and the image of the Soviet Union abroad suffered correspondingly. Fortunately, the new Soviet leadership was able to remedy this situation, and its constructive outlook was the decisive factor in the preparation and conclusion of the US–USSR Treaty of 1987. This provides for the elimination of intermediate and short-range nuclear missiles, and constitutes, by contrast, a major contribution to the security of the Soviet Union. Not only does it reduce the US nuclear presence on Soviet borders, but it also strengthens the security of other states. The atmosphere created by the successful negotiations is of course conducive to further progress in the field of disarmament in Europe, while the processes of verification and control that were arrived at are radically new and very far-reaching in their consequences. And the Treaty is exemplary in taking into account – quite rightly – the interests of European and Asian security at large. Perhaps I should add that these negotiations have much to teach us concerning the value of the machinery of arms reductions. 'The Mutually Balanced Force Reductions' talks that began in Vienna in 1973 are an example of all that is worst in this field. It is now clear that the West was never interested in progress in this field, and the Soviet Union should never again allow itself to be dragged into a stalemate of this kind. Immediate proposals for radical reductions in military manpower and conventional arms are one way of avoiding being caught up in such games, and the Warsaw Pact member states put just such proposals in the period 1986–8.

Treaties such as the INF Agreement are one contribution among a panoply of measures that also involves elements of non-military security. In Europe new approaches to peace and disarmament research, the promoting of broad economic, technological, cultural and humanitarian contacts between states and peoples have all contributed to a new and more hopeful atmosphere. A decisive influence in this respect has of course been the emergence in the Soviet Union of *perestroika*. The theory of reasonable sufficiency implies that security problems can be solved not only by military means, but by a more generalised policy of coexistence, in which steps taken at the political, economic and humanitarian levels are rewarded by a downgrading of military tensions. The creation of confidence between states favours security doubly, as it both reduces tensions and lays the basis for further arms reductions. It also serves to change the ossified perceptions of the 'potential enemy' into that of a partner. *Perestroika* has had much to contribute on this front. Contacts with Western Europe have grown more intensive. East and West cooperate as never before. The effect of *perestroika* in the other socialist countries of Eastern Europe has contributed to erode the 'enemy stereotype' and dent the myth of the 'Soviet threat'.

5 'THE COMMON EUROPEAN HOUSE'

The dynamic of peace in Europe is also reinforced by an underlying trend of European integration. The project of a genuinely common market in the EEC for 1992 is one illustration of this. The process of economic integration is already under way, and the questions to which it gives rise relate to its political implications; the dynamic of the economic process is already unstopable. It is vital that the processes of integration at work in the East and West do not result in the creation of new barriers between the two politico–economic alliances. Ideally, both processes should allow for expanded, equitable and mutually beneficial cooperation on an all-European basis.

The process of economic integration is at the root of the growing need felt over the last few years for greater intra-European cooperation in the spheres of transport, ecology, and industry standards. And the economic dynamic is reflected in the greater demand for cultural and sporting exchanges. Both of these processes reflect a new and growing all-European consciousness in both East and West. At the same time, the emergence of popular movements such as the 'Green' parties on both sides of the continent is an indication of the popular pressure toward greater interdependence as a means of improving life on the European continent. These developments call for action, and it is in response to them that the Soviet concept of the 'Common European House' was developed. The concept was given a first airing at the Soviet–Czechoslovakian summit of 10 April 1987. It is intended to take account of the following realities: (i) The objective interdependence, in the spheres of security and ecology, of all European countries, regardless of ideology. (ii) The economic and technological dynamic impelling East and West toward mutually beneficial cooperation. (iii) The historico–cultural unity of Europe, 'from the Atlantic to the Urals', and their common cultural heritage which is the product of all the European nations. (iv) The existence of new threats to that civilisation, threats which are common to both sides of Europe, such as terrorism, organised criminality, drug abuse, and AIDS, and which can be fought only along a common front.

Certain clarifications of the concept are essential. For the Soviet Union, Europe is not simply a scenic background. The USSR is a European power; it is connected with the European continent by a thousand and one ties cultural, historical and emotional. And Western Europe is not the passive object of some historical process, but an active protagonist. But, as Gorbachev has said, 'Reference to the "Common European House" does not mean we want to slam a door in anyone's face. On the contrary, the progress of Europe would allow it to make a still greater contribution to the progress of other parts of the world. Europe should not escape its part in the solution of problems of hunger, debt, underdevelopment and armed conflict'.[5] The Soviet Union has always supported the participation of the non-European countries in the formation of the wider Europe, and the durability of these countries' ties with Western Europe has never been put in doubt. This point is particularly valid as it relates to the place of Europe in the relations of the USSR and the USA. Bad relations between Europe and the USA would have adverse consequences for Soviet security, as the history of the century reminds us. And it is transparently true that the people of Europe are vitally affected by the normalisation of Soviet–US relations. Here the Cold War began, here let it end. For the Soviet Union, one point is already decided: the question 'Europe or the United States?' is a false dilemma. The suggestion that the 'Common European House' notion is intended to drive a wedge between Europe and the USA is absolutely groundless, and is propagated by champions of the old order of international power politics, and by those for whom the lack of a clearly identified enemy is itself disturbing. The Soviet Union is not the enemy of the West, and is not therefore engaged in attempts to split the West. It is simply attempting to normalise the situation in Europe, the continent in which two world wars began, and is the more motivated to do so by the vivid memory of the terrible suffering caused to the Soviet Union by these world wars.

On the other hand, it is undoubtedly true that Western Europe constitutes, in matters of economic, scientific and cultural exchange, an extremely important partner for the Soviet Union, and is likely, as regards trade, to be a more important partner than the USA for the foreseeable future. For Western Europe, the prospects of cooperation with the Soviet Union and the other countries of Eastern Europe are already good and promise to become better still. And in relation to the place of Western Europe in Soviet–US relations, we obviously hope that Europe will cease to be a moat between two fortresses, and become a broad and inviting bridge, a prosperous and peaceful mediator.

In this context, it is only proper to point to the thornier problem that combining political independence with economic integration will pose. This is a very delicate issue. In certain quarters, the integration of Western Europe has already produced the aspiration of commensurate military power, the ambition to create a kind of West European superpower. Such aspirations are at odds with the task of overcoming the contemporary divisions in Europe, and are fraught with dangers for European security as a whole. Yet this political dimension must be faced, and it is well to point out the difficulties from the first. As Gorbachev has said: 'Nations that have for centuries sought, sometimes in bitter struggle, to attain national independence, are hardly likely to acquiesce in some formula of "limited sovereignty". On the other hand, what will the fate of the all-European process be, if the Western part of Europe locks itself rigidly into this formation? How, in that case, are we to build the "Common European House"? All this should be carefully considered, for, regardless of their countries' social systems, political regimes, and so on, the inhabitants of Europe must live together'.[6] Issues of survival and of economic and ecological security are global in their scope, nor are they unique in this, and to that extent we in the Soviet Union can only desire for both ourselves and Western Europe the benefit of reliable partners, just as we desire this for our socialist friends, for China, and for Japan. The world is, after all, indivisible.

The starting point for the realisation of the Common European House is the demilitarisation and humanisation of intra-European politics. For Europe, overburdened as it is with huge stockpiles of nuclear and other arms, there is only one way forward – the avoidance of confrontation, and the promotion of confidence and security by non-military means. To this end interaction within Europe should be coordinated and harnessed. In the political sphere, this means redirecting the Helsinki process from an instrument designed to improve the status quo into a means of transforming the status quo. Though at every step due attention must be paid to ensuring political and military stability, the process of dismantling the two military blocs must be set in motion. The process could proceed simultaneously along several different paths. The two blocs could become less and less military and more and more exclusively political; this could be achieved by the dissolution of the integrated military structures of the two blocs. Above and between the blocs a web of political contacts and institutions of all-European character could be spun, which would push aside the military alliances and supplant them, gradually eroding their influence and evacuating their purpose. The Warsaw Pact and NATO could finally be wholly dismantled – or could survive as non-military political alliances open to change in the manner of other political institutions.

That these proposals can now be made is obviously attributable to the new political purview of the Soviet Union. They are also closely connected with the notion of reasonable sufficiency. Clearly, too, they require the full force of non-military security means to be exerted: confidence building measures of the kind prescribed by the Stockholm CSCE Conference, intensive political contacts throughout Europe, a consolidation of European détente, and so on. But the first priority for the Soviet Union and its allies remains disarmament. Though this applies at all levels, nuclear, chemical, and conventional, top of the agenda in Europe now is the radical reduction of conventional forces. This involves establishing equal but much lower levels in both manpower and major conventional arms. Particular attention should be paid to reducing the offensive arms and capabilities of both sides, so that a characteristic of both sides in the aftermath of the cuts would be a *structural incapacity to mount surprise attacks or major offensive operations*. (The details of this programme were elaborated by the Socialist countries in the period 1986–7, and have since been presented to the West.[7]) A goal for the immediate future would be the reduction of the forces on both sides by 25 per cent. Cuts on this scale would leave both sides incapable of major offensives, and would do much to strengthen trust and confidence. A quantitative measure of this kind could have a qualitative effect on the politico–military situation in Europe. It should, of course, be accompanied by a broadening of verification measures, in particular by on-site challenge inspections (with which compliance would be obligatory), and by greater openness in military matters in general. And it cannot come too soon. To quote a contribution to the July 1988 conference, 'The interests of common security at present require as a matter of urgency the movement toward radical cuts not only in the nuclear but in the conventional sphere. This is particularly important for the European continent, since from the viewpoint of the threat to mankind, the use of conventional weapons in this theatre of battle can also have appalling consequences. What is there to prevent the opposing sides ordering atomic power stations to be targeted by highly accurate conventional weapons? Yet the NATO governments continue to regard conventional weapons as a legitimate component of a policy of military deterrence. By continuing to develop their conventional weapons, they seek to "compensate" for the INF-treaty'.[8]

The attitude of the Soviet Union in these matters has been spelt out by the Soviet Foreign Minister, Mr Shevardnadze: the Soviet Union, he said, was ready 'to reach agreements on the implementing of the principles of sufficiency and non-offensive defence; on giving military doctrines a defensive orientation; liquidating the existing imbalances and asymmetries; making radical numerical cuts in manpower and armaments; and building confidence through structural changes and relocation of forces. We are also ready to discuss all other problems and imbalances that are a source of concern, and to join the search for a mutually acceptable solution. And it would be only fair, if the NATO countries would show themselves equally ready to discuss and solve the issues which cause concern to ourselves, that is, the forward-based systems, maritime forces and confidence building measures in the maritime department'.[9]

If such proposals could be realised in Europe, it would open up the possibility of further cuts in the nuclear arms stationed in Europe – a possibility otherwise remote. It would dramatically change the politico–military status quo, and would strengthen trust to the extent that nuclear and other forces in Europe could be reduced to minimal levels. Then, as trust accumulated, and the political foundations and collective security guarantees of the new Europe gained strength, these weapons would be seen to be obsolescent, and would be phased out altogether.

In the interim, attention should be drawn to a further Soviet proposal, which concerns the creation of an all-European centre for the reduction of military danger. Soviet experts have suggested that a centre of this kind should collect and analyse information about the military situation in Europe, with a view to eliminating the danger of an unexpected strike, and diminishing the tensions which might result from some misunderstanding between East and West. The centre might also coordinate military–political decisions which have been or might in the future be reached in the framework of the Stockholm Conference.[10]

A model for the form that should be taken by future negotiations has been elaborated by academician G. Arbatov in an article in *Pravda*.[11] The heart of his proposals is that agreement should first be reached at the highest possible level, for example by the Foreign Ministers of the states participating. Such agreement or understandings should then be implemented in detail in the form of convention or treaties. The article also calls for broad-based discussion within the Soviet Union as to the position adopted by the USSR in such negotiations, and a forum for debate of this kind is obviously an important item on the current political agenda.[12] This new negotiating model is of clear relevance to the forthcoming negotiations on the reduction of conventional forces in Europe, as the subject there will be even more complicated than that of the MBFR negotiations; there will be more than twenty participants, and geopolitical, geostrategic and other factors of unprecedented complexity will have to be tackled.

Of course, the form of negotiation is only a secondary aspect of the problem of security and arms reductions. The decisive factors are the willingness of a substantial group of European nations to affect radical changes in their policies, to compromise, and to find a median point in the diversity of their interests. And since the issues of security in the military field cannot be disconnected from the other common causes of concern in Europe, it would be a great step forward if the Vienna conference were to issue in substantial progress. This would allow us to envisage convening more than ten all-European forums on politico–military, economic and humanitarian issues, with particular emphasis on ecological security, in which the need for action is ever more urgent. A positive outcome for the Vienna conference would be a first and practical step in the construction of the Common European House.

Notes and References

1. See, for example, *International Affairs* (Moscow, August 1988) 17–27.
2. *International Affairs* (Moscow, September 1988) 18.
3. *International Affairs* (Moscow, September 1988) 16.
4. *International Affairs* (Moscow, February 1988) 37.
5. *Pravda*, 11 April 1987.
6. *Pravda*, 15 October 1988.
7. *International Affairs* (Moscow, September 1988).
8. *International Affairs* (Moscow, October 1988) 26.
9. *Pravda*, 22 September 1988.
10. *Pravda*, 10 October, 1988.
11. G. Arbatov, 'Glasnost, Negotiations, Disarmament', *Pravda*, 17 October 1988.
12. *Pravda*, 17 October 1988.

5 The Pledge of Allegiance and the Test of Alliance

Janet Finkelstein

1 INTRODUCTION

A standard criticism of the US political process is that it is not conducive to the creation and implementation of a coherent foreign policy. This view has frequently been heard, especially during the Reagan administration, and a combination of change in the Soviet Union, new developments in arms control and new US strategic initiatives has created a certain unease in the relations of the USA with its European allies. European economic strength is growing and, contrary to historic example, the allies of the USA rather than its principal 'adversary' are its main economic rivals. But the parameters of military planning are economic, and defence spending at national and international level is a highly politicised issue. US defence and foreign policy have become instruments of economic redistribution, both domestically and internationally. At a time when the deficit largely fuelled by Reagan's defence-led 'New Deal' is overwhelming the world economy, the USA is putting pressure on its allies to take up a larger part of the burden of their defence. The advent of *perestroika* is downgrading European perceptions of the Soviet threat, and enhanced the attractions of the Soviet Union as a potential market. Do these changes put at risk the very existence of the alliance, or are the current tensions merely the latest in a series of transatlantic 'misunderstandings' that have periodically arisen during the history of the alliance? The present study concentrates on the sources of tension that arise within the US political system, and concludes that the USA is likely to remain an uncertain ally in the years to come.

2 THE DOMESTIC PROCESS

Foreign policy decision-making in the USA is peculiarly susceptible to the influence of a very pluralistic public opinion. The forms this takes are both contextual and reactive. Contextual pressures arise from two sources, the political institutions of the country and the nature of nuclear weaponry. Reactive pressures are those set off by the acts and strategies of the administration.

The cycle of congressional and presidential elections constantly reopens the options under review, and makes it difficult for any consensus to become established. Of the four-year presidency, some two years are devoted to primaries and the presidential campaign, and congressional elections run parallel to this. The focus of the 1988 elections was on narrow emotionally and ideologically charged appeals, such as the pledge of allegiance and Willie Horton's furlough, and the dominant mode of communication was 30-second television spots allowing, on average, nine seconds for the candidate's message. This facilitates the creation of an image rather than fostering well-informed debate. Moreover, contest between legislature and executive for control of foreign policy is intense, and while President Bush was being elected on a Republican ticket, the Democrats were extending their majority in Congress. In the wake of Vietnam and Watergate, the President cannot necessarily impose his foreign policy on a hostile congress, and this difficulty exacerbates the confusion of economic and foreign policy; the price to pay for the passage of his bill through an ill-disposed Congress may be the inclusion of quite extraneous measures.

The difficulty of arriving at a consensus when Congress and President are locked in combat is aggravated by the system of presidential appointments and the lack of continuity this implies. This problem did not begin with the Reagan administration. The creation of a homogeneous foreign policy team has been a problem for every president of the last twenty years. Nixon at one point solved the problem of conflict between his National Security Adviser and Secretary of State by appointing Kissinger to both posts, and the period is remembered as one of relatively stable policy and high achievements. Under Carter, arguments between Security Adviser and Secretary of State ended in the resignation of Vance. The situation under Reagan has no parallel in any US presidency; quite apart from the parade of Security Advisers and the continuous feuding between the Secretaries of State and Defense, 'Iran–Contragate' gave the impression that foreign policy was frequently implemented by a parallel but 'privatised' system operating from a White House basement without the knowledge of the Vice President or either of the Secretaries. Such impressions do not predispose the Allies toward an automatic compliance with US foreign policy.

One of the unifying forces in US politics is ideology, symbolised by 'the American way of life' and 'the American dream'. Ideology is also the traditional mainstay of US foreign policy.[1] And the system of political appointees is liable to place ideologues at the controls of the only democratic superpower; their conversion to pragmatism at times alienates the electorate to whom they originally appealed. Such transitions operate over the course of a term of office, and the pragmatists are themselves replaced. Hard-liners such as Shultz and Nitze became converted to a form of neo-détente, and in doing so fell out of step with Reagan's electorate. Reagan came to power on simple messages: on the restoration of American greatness after the humiliations of the Iran hostages affair, and on the rhetoric that later defined the Soviet Union as the 'evil empire'. Only in the second half of his second term of office did Reagan embrace the goals of peace and disarmament. His conversion to disarmament seemed as drastic and simplistic as his initial belligerence, and caused much the same degree of anxiety to the allies of the US. Not only to them. In 1987 Kissinger and Nixon, for the first time since leaving office, coauthored an article, in which they urged Reagan to take a hard line with the USSR on the zero option agreement.[2] The spectacle of the architects of détente and the SALT treaty rebuking the arch-anti-communist for being soft on the Soviet Union is a curious one. But it is indicative of the switchback motives in Reagan's policy-making, the context of which is the fear and awe with which nuclear weapons are imbued.

For the pressure of public opinion is exacerbated by the nature of nuclear weapons. The 'ultimate weapon' has acquired a psycho–symbolic dimension which is intimately linked with the US status as a superpower, and the ideology of 'national greatness'. On the one hand, there is the requirement that the USA maintain parity at least, superiority at best, in the department in which its superpower status was first acquired. On the other, there is the fear elicited by the possibility of its use against the USA in first-strike or retaliation, and this fear itself tends to produce two contrary reactions, that of pressure toward increased arms build-up or toward disarmament. Arms control, if at all possible, thus becomes the ultimate political weapon. The result was the disarmament auction of Reykjavic, which, in the context of the declared intentions of the first Reagan presidency, would seem incomprehensible. Over the nuclear issue, public concern shows the tendencies of a catastrophe graph, flipping over from support for military build-up (American greatness) to a perfectly logical fear of its consequences.

The disproportionate significance attaching to the 'zero option' is an illustration of the irrational priorities that apply in this field. The withdrawal of one or two categories of ground-based nuclear weapons from central Europe or Asian Russia may represent a step forward in détente, but it is of little strategic significance; the ground-based INF weapons are only one of a wide variety of nuclear weapons available for striking at Soviet forces on Soviet territory, submarine and air-launched cruise missiles being others. A military issue of minor strategic importance came to dominate the political agenda.

During the Reagan years, the terms of the nuclear debate shifted. The imbrication of politics and public relations reached new heights during the Reagan presidencies, not least because Reagan's understanding of US public opinion was more advanced, and more attentive, than his grasp of world affairs.[3] It has now been documented that Reagan launched the Star Wars programme against the advice of the Joint Chiefs of Staff and most of his senior advisers. At a White House meeting, Secretary Shultz screamed at one of the advisers favourable to the idea 'You're a lunatic!' and twice pleaded with the President not to make the speech.[4] The SDI debate is revealing of a distortion that permeates the US political system as a whole. It was a mobilising theme for the US psyche. It had a visceral appeal, which pandered to the contradictory public attitudes to nuclear deterrence. It stressed the optimism and dynamism of the USA. It seemed the characteristic product of the USA as the USA sees itself, as a super-superpower, venturing into regions technologial and financial where the USSR could not follow. It was a super-ultimate weapon, since it theoretically disarmed the Soviet deterrent while leaving the US deterrent intact. It was a weapon for peace, since it was 'purely defensive'. It was a 'new frontier', and a 'high frontier', and it put the destiny of the USA back in its own hands. And last but not least – it allowed unprecedented levels of funding for emerging weapons technologies. That the X-ray laser, one of the major components of a system that was supposed to make nuclear weapons obsolete, had to be set off by a nuclear explosion, was a point of little account. The physics of Star Wars are largely imaginary; what made the programme so compelling was its metaphysics.

It was convenient for several scientific, military and political communities not to inform Reagan that his 'Star Wars' goal was not realistic. But technological criteria eventually came to the fore, and the technical questions asked about soft and hardware in the Star Wars project soon overflowed into the issue of their place in deterrence generally. These issues interlocked with others that the Reagan administration had already begun to investigate, of operational planning for the whole spectrum of possible conflicts. The need in any of these eventualities to entrust authority to men and computers outside the President's reach caused some disquiet. Command, control, communication and intelligence (C^3I) networks are not as robust as the nuclear forces they are supposed to control, and raised the spectre of unintended nuclear escalation. The uncertainty attaching to the chain of men and computers that leads from president to ICBM was at once reassuring, in that the ramshackle chain of command scarcely seemed intended for use, and alarming, in that the same qualities seemed to allow of catastrophic nuclear accident. But the need for operational planning, and references to 'limited nuclear war' or the attempt to 'prevail' in nuclear conflict, stirred up some alarm in the public. The prospect of nuclear war was becoming too real in these scenarios. They gave a new impetus to both the US 'freeze' movements, and to the traditional foreign policy establishment, led by R. McNamara, M. Bundy, G. Kennan and G. Smith. The US Catholic hierarchy has called for radical changes in security policies, and the Bishop's Pastoral Letter on War and Peace condemned mutual assured destruction and first strike, drawing attention to 'the political folly of a system which threatens mutual suicide, the psychological damage this does to ordinary people, especially the young, the economic distortion of priorities'.[5] The endless discussions on the size and shape of arsenals have led to a growing consensus, public and specialist, that the halving or doubling of military forces would only marginally affect security. Security has come to be perceived as more than the sum of the statistics of military balance.[6] Of course, this is only one side of the reactive pressures generated in the public. The Reagan administration's later, more conciliatory attitude toward the Soviet Union drew on it the wrath of the neo-conservative constituency to whom Reagan had originally appealed, and this conflict did not confine itself to the media, but was fought out within the White House staff under the relaxed eye of the President himself. Paradoxically, SDI served to answer both pacifists and hard-liners, as well as serving a useful function on the negotiating table.

3 SECURITY POLICY IN THE REAGAN ADMINISTRATION

In 1980, Ronald Reagan pledged to 'restore US supremacy', and four years later he mobilised voters by proclaiming 'America is back!'

These were not empty slogans; there has been an attempt to revise US global strategy fundamentally. The signs of a more assertive US stance, visible at the end of the 1970s, have become the hallmark of Reaganism. The global posture projected by his administration, in so far as a single posture can be detected, was known as the 'Reagan doctrine', a flattering term to apply to a series of declarations proclaiming that the threat was everywhere.[7] Two aspects of this posture should be stressed. The first is that the Reagan administration attempted radically to alter the prevailing relationship between, on the one hand, the threat or use of force and, on the other, foreign policy. This point is behind certain of the tensions with the Western European allies, who generally favoured a more diplomatic approach, when they were asked. The second is the ideological slant, which emphasised the 'unnatural', 'godless' and terroristic ideology of the adversary, the Soviet Union. There is no impugning Reagan's sincerity on this point, but beneath the rhetoric, a stance emerged that gave absolute priority to US interests.

'We must stand by all our democratic allies. And we must not break faith with those who are risking their lives on every continent, . . . to defy Soviet-supported aggression and secure rights which have been ours from birth.'[8] Stanley Hoffman summarised his thorough analysis of this doctrine of global interventionism with the remark: 'More of everything is not a policy'.[9] And the lack of a strategy made itself felt. Kennedy's 'long, twilight struggle with communism' at times seemed likely to degenerate into a series of OK Corrals, presented under the blazing lights of the media. Ethnic, tribal and religious conflicts were interpreted through the prism of East–West confrontation, and international incidents chosen for their potential as demonstrations both of US invincibility and its chosen role as the protagonist of virtue. Grenada was seen in the USA as exemplary of this kind of intervention, whereas the short embroilment in the affairs of Lebanon showed that casual, ill-informed intervention for symbolic purposes is unlikely to survive the first reverses. This series ('policy') of piecemeal interventions was at odds with the views of the traditional East Coast Establishment, which had traditionally contributed to shape the US side of the debate on Atlantic security. In the Establishment's view, a major power's survival as such depends on its respecting two principles: first, that it avoid the decline of its technological and economic base, second, that it ensure a balance between defence commitments and the means to sustain them. A classic exponent of the second view is Walter Lippman. In this view, the 'Reagan doctrine' might result in short-term advantages, but was likely to have damaging effects in the long term. Seeking a smoother relationship with European allies, the traditional Establishment criticised the moral crusade against communism for its failure to distinguish between vital and peripheral issues, especially at a time of budgetary constraint. Former Ambassador George Kennan referred to 'the histrionics of moralism' at the expense of substance in foreign policy.[10] To these might be added, in the wake of the 1988 election, the 'histrionics of patriotism'; histrionics perhaps form part of the Reagan legacy.

Elements of a new global strategy can be inferred from Defence Secretary Caspar Weinberger's remarks in 1981 about 'a new geography of conflicts'. The changing geography of conflict was a reflection of changing global economic geography, and the emergence of a new set of economies on the Pacific Rim. Hong Kong, Singapore, Taiwan and South Korea have joined Japan as centres of rapid economic growth. Europe has traditionally been seen as the cornerstone of US foreign policy, and Weinberger's announcement went some way toward suggesting that this emphasis would change. If such change was intended, it took the rather odd form of Europe gaining part-responsibility for US interests in 'out of area conflicts'. The justification for the attribution of responsibility in this area was the 1974 Ottawa Declaration on Atlantic Relations. This states that the common interest of the Allies 'can be affected by events in other areas of the world'. This doctrine has been at the root of some of the more overt conflicts between the Reagan administration and its European allies, a point that will become clearer after the examination of the economic rivalry dividing the States from its European allies.

One attempt has been made to formulate an 'integrated' and 'long-term' US strategy for the twenty-first century. This is the report of a bipartisan committee of thirteen experts in defence and international affairs.[11] It criticises the present US posture for placing too much emphasis on the two most 'extreme threats' – a Warsaw Pact conventional attack on the NATO central front and a US–Soviet strategic nuclear exchange. More probable are considered 'Low Intensity Operations' (Central America, the Persian Gulf, NATO's southern flank). For the defence of Western Europe a new mix of conventional and nuclear weapon systems is proposed, along with enhanced offensive capacities for the NATO armies. Preference is given to the implementation in weaponry of the most advanced technologies, such as 'black' aeronautical designs ('Stealth' technology). This latter point relates to the theory of 'competitive strategies', the attempt to 'force the Kremlin's military investment into areas of comparative disadvantage, and reduce Moscow's flexibility to redirect defence resources rapidly to counter new developments by NATO'.[12] 'Competitive strategies' encapsulates in a single notion the intricate relations of economic and military parameters, and President Bush made support for them a (minor) part of his electoral campaign.

'Discriminate deterrence' is intended as an overview of American grand strategy for the next century. But though extensive cover is given to ballistic missile defence, C^3I, and emerging technologies, little space is devoted to politico–diplomatic considerations. The technological edge is the priority. Little heed is given to recent developments in arms control and non-military security in Europe.

4 ECONOMIC DECLINE, SUPERPOWER EXPANSIONISM

The USA has for long been the motor of Western capitalism, its most unflagging economy and its paradigm of entrepreneurial dynamism. Clearly, the USA remains an immensely powerful economy. But the signs of decline are there for all to see. The world economy has been evolving rapidly, and the USA now faces new competitors in many of the fields in which it was previously dominant. US industrial and agricultural produce have declined as a proportion of global production. The USA has changed from a creditor to the largest debtor nation in history. The country to whose standards of productivity the rest of the world aspired has fallen disastrously behind the productivity rates of Europe and Japan. In 1986, the trade deficit for the first time included high technology products as well. Reagan's economic legacy is a poisoned chalice. It is recognisable in President Bush's commitment not to raise taxes. It is also recognisable in the budget deficit, and the existing military programmes. The scale of the spending cuts necessary if tax increases are to be avoided is illustrated by the consequences for Reagan's procurement jamboree. Shortly after the recent election, Michael Moodie wrote: 'Over the next five years planned forces would be as much as 25–30 per cent larger than the planned budgets can sustain. Defence, therefore, will have to be cut more than $300 billion relative to planned outlays, if the conventional wisdom about flat growth in the defence budget proves to be correct'.[13] It is therefore not surprising that General Brent Scowcroft had no sooner been appointed National Security Adviser than he began to talk of 'burden-sharing'. The USA currently sustains some 50 per cent of NATO spending at a time when the dollar is low against both the yen and the European currencies.[14]

Though burden-sharing may seem, on these grounds, irreproachable, it is not unambiguous. The economies of Europe are buoyant, and carried forward by the impetus of 1992. They constitute an economic nexus that has its own security interests, which must also be defined in economic terms. The constitution of a genuine common market has already caused fears that it will, by definition, be protectionist toward the outside world. The crisis in the US defence budget coincides with the opening salvoes of a prospective trade war over meat products between the USA and EEC, the opening of the latest round of GATT negotiations, and advent of *perestroika*. Europe's perspective on the Soviet threat has changed more than that of the USA, and further defence spending will be hard to justify to a West European public well aware of these changes and of Soviet disarmament overtures. Despite the claims of the latest NATO documents on the strength of Soviet conventional forces,[15] there is little political will toward higher military spending in Western Europe. But at a time when the Europeans are demanding that action be taken over the US deficit, demands that US rather than European taxes be raised may not be sympathetically received.

Higher military spending in NATO is, on the other hand, a politically divisive issue, and the cohesion of the alliance cannot be taken for granted. A 1976 study on NATO concluded that the alliance was basically becoming a collection of bilateral and multilateral agreements.[16] The recent emphasis on out-of-area responsibilities has accelerated this trend. Economic summits have become the occasion for major declarations on Western security. Bilateral consultations, *binômes*, mini-summits and capital-to-capital axes seem to be the rule in Europe. The USA has to take the coherence of the alliance into consideration even when applying pressure for greater expenditure, and this concern may or may not be at odds with US fears over the united European market of 1992. The US *paterfamilias* encourages its children, but is not without envy of their achievements.

The security issue therefore has behind it a political and economic rivalry, in which the long-term status of the USA as superpower is at stake. Paradoxically, only by imposing its political will on its allies, and thus sharing the military burden of the West, can the USA conserve the economic basis of its power. This was already the case during the Reagan era, when military, political and economic pressure was exerted on the allies. The doctrine of 'out-of-area conflicts' was at the source of much of the tension between the USA and Western Europe, and since it made exorbitant demands in terms of resources, forms the background of the current conflicts. It emphasised the degree in which the USA depended on the logistics of its allies to fulfil its global role, while ultimately weakening the USA in the very course of its attempt to reassert itself globally; the Reagan administration overreached the resources on which its military power was based.[17]

Examples of unilateral initiatives for which the USA sought a joint allied front were numerous. We may cite the Siberian pipeline, Libya, Achille-Lauro, the Middle East peacekeeping forces and the reflagging of the Gulf tankers. The view that NATO necessarily shared the US position on Soviet-inspired global terrorism found its clearest exponent in Congressman R. Garcia (Democrat, New York), member of the House Foreign Affairs Committee and chairman of the Civilian Affairs Committee of the North Atlantic Assembly, who raised the possibility of an anti-terrorist commando force under NATO control, and wrote: 'NATO is after all primarily a political organization'.[18] Where resistance or criticism was heard, the allies were accused of disloyalty. In the case of the bombing of Tripoli and Benghazi, the connections with the terrorist outrage to which it was supposed to be a response were afterwards the subject of considerable doubt. But in the view of the USA, loyalty to the alliance should have been decisive, and the *New York Times* editorial noted: 'Only Prime Minister Thatcher of Britain passed the test of Alliance this week'.[19]

Such reactions are characteristic of US public and expert opinion. Anecdotal, but indicative is the advertisement taken out in the summer of 1987 by multimillionaire developer Donald J. Trump in three papers concurrently: the *Boston Globe*, the *Washington Post* and the *New York Times*.[20] In this open letter to the American people on why 'America should stop paying to defend countries that can afford to defend themselves', he suggested that the USA present the bill for its efforts to safeguard the oiltankers' passage through the Gulf to the Europeans and Japanese. It becomes less anecdotal and more indicative when compared with the statement of ex-Security Adviser Zbigniew Brzezinski:[21] 'In an ideal world, the US forces patrolling the Gulf would be joined by French, British, Italian,

Belgian and Dutch forces, all financed by Japan. That would be a perfect solution. But if that is not possible, it does not follow that America should do nothing. The United States, after all, is a world power; its allies are simply regional powers.' The latter part of his remark echoes those made by Henry Kissinger in an earlier US onslaught on NATO in 1973; the problem is not a new one. Kissinger himself has called for a high-level group under NATO to study out-of-area threats, and further suggested that redeployment of US forces in Europe might include the F-111s stationed in Great Britain, as the USA might not be able to count on this ally again in similar circumstances. Acquiescence is apparently not enough. The leading neo-conservative critics, I. Kristol and J. Kirkpatrick, have denounced the 'entangling alliance' with Europeans who do not support the USA.

This attitude finds its reflection in the attempts to influence European policy. The US embargo on the sales of high technology to the Eastern bloc has often caused conflict with European states, most recently eliciting a strongly worded protest from the UK, on the subject of infringement of national sovereignty. This is the more striking as the UK is considered the most loyal of the European allies. Examples of interference in the political affairs of the allies have also occurred. In December 1986, Richard Perle announced that the Federal Republic of Germany could make a greater contribution to NATO if it made less of a contribution to the Democratic Republic of Germany. And during the last British elections, it was let slip that a victory for Labour's unilateral disarmament policy would lead to a crisis in NATO.

The attitudes expressed here elicit the question: why is Western Europe important for the USA? If it is merely a collection of disloyal allies who could afford to defend themselves, why does the USA continue to disburse for their defence? One part of this question may have to be altered in the light of the probable policies of the Bush régime. It seems likely that the allies will have to fund a larger part of their own defence hereafter. But US public opinion, though evincing a certain exasperation with the recalcitrance of its allies, nevertheless continues to express strong support for the alliance.

5 THE USA AND EUROPE: 'FATAL ATTRACTION'?

The USA has some of the characteristics of a great power in decline, and it seems possible to understand the reassertiveness of the Reagan era as the prelude to a period in which the economic limitations of US power begin to take practical effect. It is characteristic of a great power to act as policeman to its sphere of interest, and the behaviour of the USA shows some analogies with the British Empire at its height, performing the role of global policeman according to a code of law with which the imperial interests of the great power have somehow become confused. This confusion is important; the USA has tended to suppose that as a democracy it necessarily represents democracy. The great power inevitably wishes to be perceived as policing according to a just and judicious code of values, and this desire is the more pressing where another superpower with a radically different code is in global competition. The justice of the US outlook has indeed been more readily acknowledged in the states which are in the front line of this ideological confrontation than, for example, by those in the 'US backyard'.

In this perspective, the need for Western Europe is not merely as the front line in a theatre of confrontation whose stage is one of the world's most industrialised areas. The allies are both Western and democratic, and as such, can be expected to share with the USA the values on which its superpower policing functions are based. The critical judgements of Europe are not, in theory, vitiated by their coming, for example, from a tyrannical elite, or from an ideological background with which the USA is completely at odds. The criticism, when it comes, is therefore the more damning, and the USA is inclined to *paterfamilias* reactions of the order of 'he who pays the piper calls the tune'. *The USA claims that its global strategy represents something other than its own interest, and in the view of the US, the only authority competent to validate this claim is Western Europe.* But such 'authority' is resented. It is characteristic of the form of society that the USA seeks to represent that its opinions cannot be controlled; the possibility therefore remains that Western European critics distinguish between what is just or even wise and what the USA actually does. The USA may in retrospect be seen to have made a last effort in the Reagan era to maintain global influence in the face of a perceived or real foreign policy offensive by the Soviet Union, and to have succeeded in doing this at some cost to its own future prosperity.[22] The period of this effort was characterised by a certain disregard for the views of its allies, but was not without idealism. The analogy of Athens and Sparta, and of Athenian treatment of its allies, is sometimes evoked in this context.

The USA of President Bush may be expected to limit its global obligations and attempt to economise in security matters, at least relative to the Reagan era; this may not lighten the allies' burden. The US capacity to deal with 'out-of-area conflicts' will inevitably decline, and the pressure for Europe to assist will presumably not decrease. The realisation of the economic limits of US power will prompt cuts in overseas commitment, and a larger share of the European burden is likely to prove expensive for the European allies. The forces of isolationism and protectionism in the USA are growing, and will grow further if the dollar declines, the deficit causes higher inflation, and the European allies are seen to be prosperous and friendly toward the new and more acceptable Soviet Union. The weight of trade with the Pacific Rim can only grow, and the Japan–US axis be confirmed in its importance. Europe has behaved like the superego of the USA, both critical and relatively powerless, but able to give it a hard time. President Bush campaigned on a theme of 'peace and prosperity', and their ideological analogue, national greatness. A Republican executive and a Democratic legislature will be examining whether a status quo of this description can be maintained. It is this rather than any regional security issue which today preoccupies the American public. One contribution to both US prosperity and European security would undoubtedly be that Western Europe play a larger role in its own defence.

Notes and References

1. Michael H. Hunt, *Ideology and US Foreign Policy* (New Haven: Yale University Press, 1987).
2. *Los Angeles Times*, 26 April 1987.
3. In this respect, the persistence with supply-side economics testifies to a clear recognition that both military build-up and reduced taxation were popular, a point on which he has been proven correct. To point out that they were incompatible was to lose an election, in 1984 and 1988.
4. Hedrick Smith, *The Power Game: How Washington Really Works* (New York: Random House, 1988).
5. 'The Challenge of Peace: God's Promise and Our Response', *National Catholic News Service* (Washington, 1983).
6. G.T. Allison, A. Carnesale and J.S. Nye, *Fateful Visions*, (Cambridge, Mass.: Ballinger, 1988).
7. For an analysis of global strategy, see Janet Finkelstein and Gulliver

Depetre, 'La Nouvelle Doctrine de Guerre Americaine et la Securite de l'Europe', *Cahiers d'Etudes Strategiques* (Paris, June 1983).

8. President Reagan (February 1985).
9. Stanley Hoffman, 'Reagan Abroad', *New York Review of Books*, 4 February 1982.
10. G. Kennan, 'Morality and Foreign Policy', *Foreign Affairs* (Winter 1986).
11. *Discriminate Deterrence: Report of the Commission on Integrated Long-Term Strategy*, co-chaired by Fred C. Iklé and Albert Wohlsetter (Washington, D.C.: US GPO, 1988).
12. Michael Moodie, 'Bush's National Security Challenge', *Jane's Defence Weekly*, vol. 10, no. 20 (19 November 1988).
13. Moodie, 'Bush's National Security Challenge' (see Note 12).
14. Hella Pick, 'A Testing Time for Europe', The *Guardian*, 25 November 1988.
15. 'The Soviet Union has more than half of all the weapons in Europe in many categories ... This would mean that the Soviet arsenals – for tanks, armoured cars and artillery – are larger than the combined forces in Europe of all 16 NATO countries and the Soviet Union's six allies in the Warsaw Pact', Joseph Fitchett, 'NATO Issues East–West Force Data', *International Herald Tribune*, 26–7 November 1988.
16. Janet Finkelstein, *Vers Une Nouvelle Politique de l'OTAN aux Etats Unis*, Fondation pour les Etudes de Défense Nationale (Paris, 1976).
17. See J. Gaddis, *Strategies of Containment, A Critical Appraisal* (New York: Oxford University Press, 1982).
18. 'For a NATO Committee on Countering Terrorism', *International Herald Tribune*, 10–11 May 1986.
19. 'Allies Divided by Terror', *International Herald Tribune*, 18 April 1986.
20. *Washington Post*, 2 September 1987.
21. *International Herald Tribune*, 9 June 1987.
22. See Paul Kennedy, *The Rise and Fall of the Great Powers* (New York: Random House, 1987).

6 A French View of European Security

Dominique David

1 INTRODUCTION

France's role in Europe is defined by the geographical situation of France, the consistency of its defence policy, and the very broad consensus enjoyed by the strategy on which this policy is based.

The current discussions on European security, and on US/Soviet nuclear arms reductions in particular, are evaluated on the basis of this policy. Its mainstays are: (i) a strategy whose principal component is a nuclear deterrent; (ii) political and military cooperation with a collective security institution: the Atlantic Alliance.

I shall confine myself to raising certain questions, and relating them to the distinctive French outlook on European security.

2 'COUPLING' AND COMMITMENT

The surprise is no real surprise. Warnings of the imminent withdrawal from Europe of US troops have been with us for some forty years now. For nearly thirty years we have faced, now the prospect of US nuclear weapons being withdrawn, now the restriction of the conditions under which they could be used. These warnings have fallen on deaf ears and complacent attitudes, and this alone explains the 'surprise' and helplessness which recent events have elicited.

What changes would follow were US withdrawal, conventional or nuclear, large or small-scale, to occur?

Europe is at peace today because nobody knows what chain of violence would follow from that first and fatal shot. This uncertainty is the sum of our knowledge. The magma of arms conventional and nuclear that is Europe today threatens any and every military act with apocalyptic consequences, and armed conflict within it cannot therefore be grounded in reason.

This is the perspective to which we have become accustomed during the forty years of the nuclear epoch; the gravity of danger brings forth peace, and the uncertainty with which no strategist can deal is the complexity of Europe itself.

The military strategies that have evolved over the last forty years have all been aimed at reinforcing the uncertainty of the opponent's strategic calculation. No military strategist envisages combat without the prospect of a positive outcome. The presence of nuclear weapons, and thus of apocalyptic threat, eliminates any potentially positive endgame, and the military experts can envisage nothing – nothing but the need to refrain.

French political leaders are, on the whole, in agreement as to this fundamental diagnosis. For them, the strategic problem is clear: to what extent do current changes – political, military, and technological – increase the adversary's uncertainty?

The essential data of European security today are threefold. One is geopolitical: Europe is the contact area of the two largest military alliances in the world. The second is military: all over Europe, weapons nuclear and non-nuclear confront one another. The third is political; the well-known 'coupling' that unites the two sides of the Atlantic.

It is on everyone's tongue. Attitudes towards it are multifarious. But, when the cards are down, what is this US–European coupling but the political decision of the US president to commit his country to defend Europe when Europe is under threat? The word is 'political'. We should not delude ourselves that, at a time of grave – nuclear – danger, the USA would allow itself, without premeditation, to get involved in a conflict anywhere in the world, simply because it had previously deployed upon the battlefield this or that type of weapon.

American men and arms deployed in Europe do not guarantee that commitment. This is an illusion to which Europe stubbornly clings, believing that every new deployment of weaponry further commits the USA to the defence of Europe. The arms deployed in Europe, whether nuclear or conventional, offer the merest presumption of commitment, the merest shadow of a proof.

Well, the shadow of a proof is better than no proof at all. To be clear about the value of US deployments in Europe, means: (i) knowing they are no automatic assurance that the USA is willing to stand up for us all the way to Armageddon; (ii) knowing that these deployments are in any case valuable because they increase the risk of any military move on our continent – a continent bristling with the weapons of four out of the five members of the nuclear club; sufficient, depend upon it, to deter the strongest invader.

Coupling does not absolutely depend on the quantity of armaments deployed, nor vary with their quantity. But there is probably a threshold of credibility. Thus one question for Europe is: what quantity and types of US nuclear weapon must be stationed in Europe if the presumption of coupling is to be maintained, and with it the uncertainty of the adversary?

The French nuclear armament cannot on its own assume the deterrent role played by the 'mix' of US weapons, conventional and nuclear, and European nuclear weapons. In the 1960s, several French leaders viewed the French forces as 'self-sufficient'; that view has changed. The way in which the French nuclear forces participate in European deterrence depends largely on other forces – in particular on US forces. All French leaders today agree that the French armed forces cannot function in Europe independently of the alliance forces.

3 THE FUTURE OF THE ATLANTIC ALLIANCE

In my view, one hypothesis can be discarded: the hypothesis of total US political and military withdrawal from Europe. Like it or not, Europe has an essential place in the planetary *imperium* of America. Whatever the political ups and downs, there is no such thing as an isolationist superpower. If the term 'superpower', as is likely, implies a worldwide vocation, then, for the USA, Europe is central; it is the frontier where any retreat implies a gain for the challenger. To yield on indirect or outlying fields of confrontation is one thing; to retreat from one vested with geographical, psychological, political, and economic symbolism, is quite another. The USA has interests in the Pacific; its *essential* interests lie in Europe.

A second hypothesis is the withdrawal of troops and conventional arms. For financial reasons, were there no other, this withdrawal is more likely today than in the past. The USA may indeed withdraw troops. But it cannot withdraw many *and* maintain significant nuclear deployment. This would be the worst possible strategy in Europe; a weaker conventional shield, and a nuclear threat wielded of necessity early in the conflict. If the USA is not to undermine the logic of its present position – that it is indivisible from its European allies, but also wishes to minimise the risk of any nuclear escalation that might put US territory at risk – then troop withdrawals may be significant, but they will be limited.

A third hypothesis, which may overlap with the second, is a withdrawal of nuclear weapons. One of the most consistent achievements of US policy has been the care taken to minimise the risk of aiding Europe in the event of crisis. To find this scandalous is simply perverse: put yourself in their place. In this regard, nothing has changed since the McNamara speeches in the early 1960s. Do Europeans really believe they can turn the clock back twenty years, to the period before flexible response? Whether they do or not, Washington's priority today is to withdraw from Europe those medium-range missiles which were supposed to bind it to the future of the old continent. Diplomatic and strategic logic are here perfectly at one.

The logic is very clear. The impetus towards the present US–Soviet agreement began with the Pershing II, for the simple reason that the Pershings, targeted on the Soviet Union from Europe, indirectly put US territory at stake. The selfsame reason that makes these weapons the ultimate accomplishment of coupling in European eyes makes them a deadly risk for the USA. We must repeat: those who consider coupling in terms of its technical components are missing the point. The US decision is a political one.

When, in the early 1980s, Washington deployed a new generation of euro-missiles, it was for reasons related to technological change (the replacement of outmoded weapons) and to European political pressures. Some US leaders may have believed that these two elements could be incorporated into a new strategic analysis. This was a mistake. Contrary to what whole battalions of demonstrators in the streets of Europe claimed, the deployment of the Pershings did not serve the interests of the USA. It served a European interest, that of testifying to the reality of coupling.

It did not take long for strategy to prevail. The more numerous the US nuclear weapons in Europe, and the greater the number of them targeted on the Soviet Union, the greater the nuclear threat to the USA, and this is not in the interest of any transatlantic arbiter.

However close on alliance may be, and US ties with Europe are not in question, it does not eradicate the individual interests of either partner, and in the nuclear age, these interests may quickly become 'vital'. It is in Europe's interest to involve the USA as quickly and as deeply as possible; the interest of the USA, on the other hand, is to modulate its commitment so as always to avoid the unacceptable risk constituted by the involvement of US territory. These interests are mutually contradictory.

All things considered, the most likely outcome is the following: Washington will agree to a limited conventional withdrawal, combined with the withdrawal of those nuclear weapons felt to constitute the greatest danger to the USA during a crisis in Europe. First among these are the medium-range missiles. This would by no means leave Europe defenceless. It would still be home to many nuclear weapons. But the situation would be sufficiently alarming to force upon the attention of the allies a situation that they have been pretending to ignore for the last thirty years.

4 THE AFTERMATH

4.1 France

In the immediate present, Western Europe is in danger of succumbing to three delusions. First: it might be devoting its energies to the wrong goal, and fighting a last-ditch battle against the effect (the withdrawal) rather than the cause (the long-term change of attitude of the USA).

In other words, Europe would be wrong to think that the problem raised by the withdrawal of INF is primarily military, implying military solutions (new deployment, rapid modernisation). The US decision is strategic, and relates to the fundamental interests of the United States.

The two other delusions concern the immediate alternatives. Research on anti-missile defences should be pursued, but, given the polyvalence of the threat, the geographical position of Europe, and its financial resources, no-one should be under any illusion that antimissile defences could constitute any real protection for Western Europe. Secondly, the immediate extension to their neighbours of the French and British nuclear umbrella, and the creation of an exclusively conventional defence of Europe, are neither of them credible alternatives. To improve the existing conventional defences – a goal both practicable and desirable – is one thing, to render the European armies adequate to conventional deterrence is quite another; we have only to consider the enormous financial problems this choice would involve for all West European states. Both these scenarios have their attractions. But they cannot realistically be thought of as a way out of the current predicament.

In the long term, the only conceivable answer is the creation of a European destiny, for which one can today do no more than clear the approach-routes.

The analysis presented has some hope of carrying the day in Europe, or at least in France. There is already a wide consensus in France on the premiss (the classical–nuclear duality is the only guarantee of deterrence in Europe), and the conclusion (the present situation requires the construction of the new Europe, at least in the long term). Analyses have, however, diverged on the problem of how to react to the Washington Treaty itself. It was well received by the Communist and Socialist Parties, but sharply criticised by prominent members of the two rightist parties (l'Union pour la Démocratie Française, and the neo-Gaullist Rassemblement pour la République).

In this respect, a paradox of the French political situation should be noted. It is often difficult to define the positions of French political parties on security matters; the only guide is the series of outline studies ('Livres Blancs'). Few are still in print, and they are not of uniform quality. The leader of the RPR can be assumed to be somewhat hostile to the Treaty of Washington; his views may not coincide with those of the defence experts of the RPR. The response of the UDF in general was muted, in contrast with that of the (UDF) Minister of Defence, André Giraud, who, in the name of the nation, referred to a 'European Munich'.

These divergences are in any case of little account, given the opinion of the President, which is paramount in these matters. François Mitterrand clearly approved of the nuclear weapons being withdrawn from Europe, and highlighted the theme of disarmament during the presidential campaign of 1988.

The French 'defence community' has reservations about the treaty. But the community is a small one, without any influential 'think tanks', and plays, paradoxically, a very limited role in the debate on French defence.

But over and beyond these divergences, the French and their leaders have agreed on the need for a common European perspective on defence, at least in the long run. This fact requires some explanation.

During the 1960s, the French nuclear deterrent symbolised France's rediscovered independence and national strength. It was created in the teeth of opposition from all the Atlantic partners, and could not, therefore, be considered in the context of a common European defence. It, and the new strategy that went with it, had to be imposed on politicians, the armed forces, and a general public who wanted nothing to do with it; to do this, it was necessary to stress the gain in national power that it represented. The objections were financial, military, and psychological, and the task of overcoming them was too great for the European debate to be equally stressed, especially as at that time it primarily concerned conventional arms.

Talk of Europe in the context of the French deterrent therefore had to await the deterrent's acceptance by the political parties. The commitment of the *centristes* came between 1969 and 1974, that of the Communists and Socialists in 1977. The European dimension of French defence was first made an issue during the term of office of Giscard d'Estaing, and has, since the early 1980s, been fully acknowledged by President Mitterrand, as witness the Bundestag speech, the creation of the Rapid Action Force, and so on.

Relations between France and the military and political structures of the alliance have not really changed. But the need for such relations has somehow impressed itself upon the French perception. The reintegration of French forces into the NATO military command structure has been officially rejected by all the French parties. But the need for military and political relations with the alliance is no longer disputed by anyone. The exception is the (marginal) Communist Party, which was the only party not to vote in favour of the recent law on military provision.

Two speeches have vigorously reaffirmed this need: those of Jacques Chirac, then Prime Minister (December 1987), and François Mitterrand (October 1988) at the Institut des Hautes Etudes de Défense Nationale. Fifteen years ago, such unanimity could not have been taken for granted.

Common to the declarations of leading French political figures are now the independence of the French deterrent, and the need for closer cooperation on defence with our neighbours – this refers particularly to the Franco–German *binôme*. Only the Communists dissent on these points, though differences of opinion remain. There is no consensus on the deployment of conventional or nuclear prestrategic forces or on the degree of cooperation with the integrated forces of the alliance.

4.2 Western Europe

What does this imply for the future?

Europe cannot avoid the inevitable, but it can assume responsibility for it. First by making its voice heard in future negotiations, even when not participating. Europe should show that it is nobody's fool. The numerous forces encouraging the denuclearisation of Europe today should no longer be ignored. Given the undeniable conventional superiority of the Soviet Union, these voices promote the interests of Moscow and, since the USA wishes to limit the scale of any outbreak of hostilities in Europe, they promote Washington's interest too. Western Europe, on the other hand, is well aware that denuclearisation would merely be an elaborate swindle. Safety from nuclear weapons is not to be obtained by denuclearising Western Europe, since nuclear weapons will remain in quite sufficient number to destroy it. Europe would, in this way, simply exchange the status of actor for that of victim.

European countries know there is no point in arguing about thresholds of warfare; warfare must be avoided, no war in Europe is survivable. For this reason, there is no way round a deterrent mix of conventional defence and potential nuclear retaliation. Only the conventional–nuclear combination can ensure European security over the coming decades.

To say this is to contradict the anti-nuclear ideology that has grown up around the self-interested advice of the Soviets, the political spin-off of Star Wars, and the tendencies of the European peace movements. The European conventional and nuclear forces may be criticised, modified, or adapted – but the nuclear–conventional principle must be maintained. This implies that nuclear weapons owned by three military powers – the USA, Great Britain and France – remain in Europe. The present negotiations concern only the *proportions* of the conventional–nuclear combination; it is imperative that both elements remain. Should the European countries prove unable to agree on the importance of nuclear weapons in Europe for the conservation of peace, then no transition to a future European security system will ever be possible.

Any future system will have to accord priority to two axes of cooperation: Bonn–Paris and London–Paris. There is still much to do in the first of these cases, but much has already been done. Of late, Bonn has shown a more mature attitude in its relations with the USA. Nobody wants West Germany to betray its friendship with the USA, but the psychological and political ties between the two should not be allowed to inhibit the aspiration toward intra-European cooperation. For some years France has given obvious signs of its solidarity. West Germany too must go beyond its current lip-service to the ideal of Europe (its reactions to SDI or Eureka are examples of this irritating tendency).

There is hardly any debate in France concerning the priority accorded to Franco–German relations: in the past ten years, the latter have become the kingpin of the French project of European defence. Debate in France focuses on the form and not the principle of collaboration with West Germany, and the subjects are familiar ones: strategic and prestrategic weapons, and tactics for forward-based conventional forces. Here it is not the parties that disagree, but the experts. The 1987 and 1988 debate on the new law on military provision articulated the implications for Franco–German strategy of the pre-strategic nuclear programme, and in particular of the Hades missile.

The paradox of Franco–German relations today is that the French, who were at one time averse to the notion of European military cooperation, now feel they are 'leaders' in this area, and that they must gently initiate the bashful Germans who are afraid of anything that might jeopardise the transatlantic relationship.

Beyond the indisputable goodwill on both sides, the problem is: must Franco–German debate remain resolutely within the straitjacket of the Atlantic alliance? Obviously the latter is a point of reference. But the 'overall concept' (*Gesamtkonzept*) of European security, so desired by the Germans, must surely be European in essence, if it is to be adequate to the problems of the post-Washington era.

The London–Paris axis is both unexpected and obvious. Whatever their political complexion, the French and British deterrent forces work on similar principles.

France and Great Britain can, if they so choose, be among the principal 'purveyors' of deterrence in Europe. Their geographical positions are similar. Maintaining the credibility of their forces will present them with similar technical problems. Preserving the conventional–nuclear mix in Europe is a concern for both. Decades of misunderstandings could be put behind them, and cooperation ensue. Paris and London could form the hard core of a European 'declarative strategy', refusing to give up nuclear deterrence, and making common strategic cause. But this would be of little value in itself, unless they also cooperated in the construction of weapons. Franco–British cooperation in the field of deterrence is a suggestion no-one would have taken seriously fifteen years ago, but which has now become urgent.

For years, the Paris–London axis has seemed both necessary and unattainable. Numerous efforts have been expended over the last few years in the hope of renewing this dialogue, which ended ten years ago. Cooperation over the development of weapons seems unlikely to occur in the short term. Exchange of views on strategic concepts, and the adoption of common positions in international forums would be a starting point.

5 CONCLUSIONS

Paris, London and Bonn cannot build the new European defence on their own. But Western European countries should agree on the following principles:

1. Maintaining, in one form or another, the conventional–nuclear mix in Europe.
2. Political and technological cooperation in defence matters.
3. Establishing of a common global security concept, including negotiations on arms control and attitudes towards Eastern Europe.

The post-Washington situation is not militarily threatening in itself, but could become so in either of these two cases:

1. If the Washington agreement was the preamble to a total withdrawal of nuclear weapons from Europe. This would jeopardise the world security system. Whatever we think of the intentions and the goodwill of the Soviets, the fact remains that the Second World War radically shifted the balance of power in Europe. Europe contains on the one hand, a superpower, the Soviet Union, and on the other, countries which are not willing or able to enter a race for conventional parity. This situation simply cannot be modified in the near future. An overall security system therefore remains a necessity, politically and militarily.
2. If the Washington agreement leads Western Europeans to believe not only that it is possible to replace military by political security, but also that it is best to achieve political security individually, by means of bilateral negotiations. If it should prove necessary to elaborate a politico–military concept of security with the Soviet Union, the West European countries must do this together, in the framework of the alliance, taking care always to maintain a specifically European perspective on the future.

The tragedy is that, for Western Europe, a détente and overall security concept of this kind has to be arrived at amid several different structures: NATO, WEU, EPC, and so on. In the short term, Western Europe must do its best to manage within this diversity. But however diverse the 'means of production', the product must be unitary. A difficult transition will be facilitated if Western Europe can speak with one voice. This began to be the case with the WEU, in December 1987. On the basis of a 'European Harmel Report', it could perhaps be the case again.

6 MAXIMS FOR THE EUROPE OF TOMORROW

The questions raised by the Washington agreement, and its effects on the security of the Western European countries, are of two kinds: military and political.

The military question is important, as without a stable system of military security, deterrence could not be maintained. But it is ultimately a dead end, as it relies on US intervention in Europe, and on this point, US and European interests conflict.

What is the Europe of the future? Security means two things: military and political provision. But there can be no such provision without a common West European strategy applied to a unique strategic zone: Western Europe.

For Europe, therefore, the most urgent questions are strategic ones: what does Western Europe want, what can it do, and how can it accomplish its goals?

These questions cannot be answered by analyses of the goodwill of the Kremlin. The emergence of a West European identity is not at odds with détente and the effort to transcend the blocs: a divided Western Europe will not be able to gain the respect of others in a 'common European house', nor will it be able to help the development of Eastern Europe.

Western Europe must choose whether it wants to make its own history – or walk away from it.

7 The Debate on European Security in Poland

Marek Grela

1 INTRODUCTORY REMARKS

Since the Second World War, the issue of European security has been central to Polish political debate and policy decisions. Fundamental to both theory and practice has been a thesis whose cogency the history of Poland underlines: the security of Poland cannot be dissociated from that of Europe as a whole.

States may be divided into two categories: those whose security policy is determined by purely national considerations, and those which, though able to assure their national security, are particularly sensitive to the influence of external developments. Poland clearly belongs to the second category, and the prominence given in Poland to issues of European security largely derives from this fact.

Since the Second World War, Polish policy has had two main thrusts; on the one hand, to strengthen the alliance with the Soviet Union and the other Warsaw Pact countries, on the other to promote whole-European solutions and oppose the division of Europe into two hostile blocs.[1] The second of these two emphases was reflected in the concepts of collective security voiced in Poland previous to the Cold War, the Rapacki Plan to create a nuclear-free zone in Central Europe, the 1963 proposal for an arms freeze in the same area, the 1964 proposal to convene a conference on European security, which contributed to the initiation of the Helsinki process, and in the policy of promoting bilateral and multilateral cooperation during the period of détente of the 1970s.

The continuity of Polish foreign policy in Europe is thus clear, but changes in priority have nevertheless occurred. They relate to two factors, the evolution of East–West relations, and developments within Poland.

2 THE SECURITY DEBATE IN THE 1980S

2.1 Changes of Approach

The 1980s have seen some radically new departures in the Polish security debate. Today the approach is more comprehensive; the notion of security is widely taken to embrace the economic, technological, social, cultural, ecological and moral aspects of international relations.[2] And since domestic instability may translate into international tension, the creation within a society of conditions that allow its aims, values and aspirations to be realised, and its conflicts to be resolved, also falls within the ambit of the security debate.

The greater interest manifested in the security debate for issues moral, ecological and humanitarian can be put down to several factors. First and foremost, it is no longer believed that security is reducible to the military sphere or to the politics of bipolar international relations. Secondly, the failure to achieve substantial arms cuts has increased interest in security at large, and the attention of the public has turned in on itself; reasons for the failure are sought in the moral sphere. Changes within Poland have contributed to the new interest in humanitarian issues. Internal security cannot be dissociated from such issues as freedoms of information and travel and respect for human rights in general, nor are these without incidence on external relations. As regards ecology, the Chernobyl disaster and other European ecological catastrophes have aroused considerable interest in the environment, and this awareness forms a significant element in the perception of security in Poland. Poland faces very grave ecological problems, and various groups have grown up whose aims is to end pollution, to prevent the construction of nuclear power stations, and close those factories that are most noxious to the environment. These groups also put forward political projects, and given their ambition to change the internal political order, their stance may be described as oppositional.

An illustration of this more comprehensive approach is supplied by a work published in 1986 in Warsaw on the 'The International Factors in Poland's Security',[3] in which a broad range of issues is discussed. Among them are the relation of internal to external security, the incidence of the international situation on national security policy, and the main areas – military, legal, economic, technological and ecological – of Polish security. The contributors include not only members of the scientific community – a sociologist, an expert on international security, a professor of law, an economist, and experts on the environment – but also a group of military experts from the General Staff Academy.

2.2 The Participants

A further distinctive feature of the current debate is the broader range of participants involved, which reflects the renewed interest in international affairs after a period in the early 1980s when internal matters, sometimes too narrowly considered as such, constituted the main preoccupation of Polish society. The activities of governmental bodies and the initiatives of the Polish government at the international level are the object of lively discussion in the academic community, in various social and religious associations, in particular those linked with the Catholic church, and in groups that do not necessarily share the official viewpoint. In addition to the existing centres for international studies, certain new bodies have been created, such as the Committee for Peace Studies of the Polish Academy of Sciences, the Council for Peace Research, and the Centre for Peace Research of the Catholic Association PAX, while other groups stepped up their activities, contributing to and influencing the debate.

It is important that this recrudescence of interest in international policy issues be seen in perspective. The 'Centre for Public Opinion Studies', a government body, has shown that the Polish public's interest in international affairs during the second half of the 1980s conformed to the European average. It is significantly lower than in the years of political revival 1980–1 but higher than for the years 1982–4. Though interest in international affairs and thus in European security is not uniform across the political and social spectrum, all groups are aware of the significance for Polish security interests of East–West relations. In the early 1980s, when the increasing East–West tensions were a source of considerable anxiety in Poland, a part of Polish society was strongly pro–USA, and occasionally expressed support for the policies of President Reagan. Such sympathies were often accompanied by anti-communist sentiments which in many cases have not been abandoned.[4]

2.3 Reasons Why Interest Has Grown

No single factor seems adequately to explain the increased interest in security matters. Among the most significant factors are the following:

1. A reaction to the worsening of East–West relations, and fears of a new Cold War, which were particularly strong in the first half of

the 1980s, and stemmed mainly from the unfavourable developments in the military situation in Europe. The view that East–West tensions are detrimental to the very fabric of Polish security elicits a unanimity that spans the entire political spectrum.

2. The Polish crisis of the early 1980s made it clear that international relations are not without consequence for internal affairs, and that they may indeed act against internal security. At the same time, the crisis had a catalytic effect, and many categories and values were reassessed, not least in the field of security.
3. The increased aspiration of professional and social groups to participate in the shaping of internal and foreign policy. Military issues are discussed, but there is also a widespread concern about the economic, technological and environmental dimensions of Polish security.
4. The influence of Gorbachev's 'new thinking' on international security and the related proposals made by the Soviet Union, Poland's closest ally. The climate of *glasnost* and the democratisation of the Soviet Union have strengthened the reform-minded forces in Poland, and favour new approaches.
5. The efforts of the Polish government to regain Poland's international standing, and its role as a country traditionally active in the debate on European security problems. The 1987 Plan for arms cuts and confidence building in Central Europe is an example of this.
6. Last, but not least, the influence of the East–West dialogue on security matters. Matters that had hitherto been debated only on one or the other side have now become common topics.

3 THE MAIN TOPICS OF THE DEBATE

The concepts of European security that are discussed in Poland take account of the interests of all the participants in the Helsinki process. Security in Europe cannot be dissociated from the issues of global security raised by East–West relations. Polish concern has traditionally focused on the reaffirmation of the territorial and political status quo in Central Europe. This concern is an evident one in view of the new territorial and political shape acquired by Poland after the Second World War, and of its position on the East–West demarcation line.

Poles did (and do) view attempts to undermine the Polish political and territorial position in Europe as the main threat to the security of their country. Prior to 1970, the problem was the lack of universal recognition of Poland's western border. Territorial integrity was guaranteed by the alliance with the Soviet Union and the other Warsaw Pact countries. The GDR recognised the Oder–Neisse border in 1950. The Polish–FRG Agreement of 1970 further confirmed the inviolability of the present frontiers: in it, both states 'declare that they have no territorial claims on each other and will not raise such claims in the future'.[5] The government's policy in consolidating Poland's frontiers, and in particular its attention to the 'German dimension' in foreign policy, were supported by a broad national consensus.

The Helsinki Final Act embodied a multilateral acceptance of the post-war territorial status quo, and opened up new prospects for East–West cooperation. For Poland, the Declaration of Principles of the Helsinki Final Act was of particular importance as reaffirming the territorial integrity of signatory states; the potential of the Process for diminishing the military component of East–West relations is also appreciated.

In the current debate, particular attention is paid to the interdependence of the internal situation and the security of the whole region, a concern imparted by Poland's experiences during the crisis of the 1980s, when Polish internal events became a potential source of destabilisation in Europe. The crisis also drew attention to the weakness of a concept of security based on fear, mistrust and mutual deterrence. The instrumental approach, that is, attempted by the USA and its allies to exploit the situation in Poland and undermine Soviet security interests, followed by the policy of isolating Poland, the imposition of economic sanctions, and a recurrence on the part of certain Western politicians to questions of a territorial order, define one side of this coin. Official circles in Poland have little confidence that Western approval of internal reform would ever take the form of economic incentives such as credits. They point to the reluctance of the West to come to Poland's aid even when, in 1980–1, the turn of events in Poland met with Western favour. They do however expect that moves toward a market economy will dispose Poland's creditors to help the country overcome its economic problems. The national debt is now over 40 billion dollars. (It is worth noting that economic sanctions are officially estimated to have cost Poland 15 billion dollars.) In the context of such international repercussions, but also of the current internal reforms and the experience of the early 1980s, a further question necessarily arises: how is the need for internal change to be reconciled with the need to preserve equilibrium and stability in Europe? To what extent can internal reform be pursued without threatening the security of the entire region?

Poland's reaction to external threats and their relation to the crisis has been vindicated by events. It is threefold:

1. to regain internal stability through domestic reforms, democratisation and the development of 'socialist pluralism', thus indirectly contributing to European stability;
2. to strengthen Poland's position in the community of the socialist states and develop ties with the USSR;
3. to pursue a national security policy designed to promote mutual tolerance and mutual confidence.

In the light of internal developments it has been widely recognised in Poland that Polish influence on European security will depend above all on internal stabilisation and thus on the pace of reform and democratisation; the latter are essential if the current acute problems of economic and sociopolitical development are to be overcome.[6] There is no unanimity in Poland as to the nature and scope of reforms or the progress made so far. Favourable external circumstances are a condition of successful reform, and to this extent the improvement in East–West relations, the reforms initiated in the Soviet Union, and the atmosphere of *perestroika* create a new situation. What will be the impact of these new developments on the security policy of the West?

That internal developments should influence security is not a uniquely Polish phenomenon. A Hungarian scholar has written: 'military security as an external factor remains the guarantee of survival of the socialist system in the (often hostile) international environment; and as an internal factor, a guarantee of maintaining power. But because the direct military threat is declining, and because the realistic prospect of a new arms control agreement is increasing, the most important aspects of security are now the stability and prosperity of the socialist system'.[7]

During the early 1980s, the decline in Soviet–US tensions, and the deterioration in East–West relations generally, weakened security in Europe, and concern grew at the consequent danger of nuclear conflict in Europe. This led to a renewal of interest in détente. The reasons for the weakening of détente were several. Détente in Europe had tended to follow the logic of US–Soviet relations, the logic of a bipolar world. Though American policy – and, in particular the attempt to attain military superiority – had been responsible for the weakening of détente, purely European factors also contributed. Among them were the increasing influence of the conservative parties in Western Europe, structural problems affecting East–West trade, and the reciprocal misconstrual of the goals of détente, thus: 'détente as an instrument of the East to disarm and neutralise Western Europe' and 'détente as an instrument of the NATO countries to generate centrifugal processes in the socialist countries and disintegrate the socialist community'. Although superpower rivalry in the Third World contributed to the breakdown in détente, it was probably less significant than another factor, the diversification that the Third World itself was undergoing. The bipolar model was no longer adequate to these transformations, but the superpowers ascribed their failure to reach their goals in the Third World not to the changing realities but each to the activities of the other, and mutual animosity resulted.

Despite these tensions, which were particularly strong during the period 1980–4, détente remained a reality in Europe. The Helsinki Process continued, the results of the Madrid meeting were surprisingly substantial, and there were positive results from the Stockholm Conference on disarmament and confidence- and security-building measures. Such developments are appreciated in Poland, where détente is considered the norm and Cold War postures abnormal and dangerous. The current situation is neither one thing nor the other. Internal factors have a greater influence than in the past; areas of common European interest are more widely recognised; ecological issues are beginning to come to the fore; and the question of technology is becoming more urgent as the growing East–West technological gap promotes East–West divisions, while the political obstacles to the flow of technology are liable to lead to rival or non-complementary technological solutions.

The detrimental effects of East–West tensions are felt at two levels in Poland. First, those which endanger European and international security; in this area, confidence-building measures and arms reductions, along with the creation of a 'danger-of-war-free-zone' in Central Europe are considered essential. At a second level, East–West tensions inhibit political, economic, scientific and cultural cooperation, and limit individual contacts. For Poland, a medium-sized economy with a huge foreign debt, it is vital to preserve its relatively diversified trade structure, both in order to regain credibility in the international finance market and to realise its own economic reforms. Individual contacts and cultural exchanges are also very important to Poland, and the Polish foreign minister has gone on record as saying that the province of cultural cooperation will increasingly serve as that in which national identity is expressed.[8] The Polish emigré population is huge and has recently grown still further; for this, and for historical and cultural reasons, Poland is and seeks to remain a relatively open country, for which cultural relations with other European countries are of great significance, not least in the context of mutual security.

In the process of improving East–West relations, the role of the small and medium-sized countries is increasingly important. In the early 1980s, relations between certain Eastern countries and the West continued unabated despite superpower tensions. Such relations can also influence the security of Europe, and though they cannot replace the role of superpower relations, should be encouraged.

4 NEW IDEAS AND PROPOSALS

The Polish plan for arms reductions and confidence building in Europe was announced by W. Jaruzelski in May 1987. An innovatory aspect is what Egon Bahr, in an interview with the weekly *Polityka*, called its 'fascinating imprecision'. The plan provides for the denuclearisation of Europe, the progressive elimination of offensive military tactics, and the development of confidence-building measures. Reduction of nuclear weapons, it is emphasised, should not be allowed to lead to a conventional-arms race.[9] The importance of verification procedures is also stressed. The plan is not a detailed programme but rather an invitation to East and West to establish an agenda and start negotiations; the June 1987 version of the plan takes account of some important suggestions made by the West, for example the issues arising from inequalities in a particular category of weapon.[10]

In the debate, a significant emphasis is placed on the *strengthening of European identity; on the consolidation of the common cultural heritage and the creation of new Europe-wide institutions*. This is consonant with the notion of the 'europeanisation of Europe' mentioned in rather general terms by some leading Polish politicians.

A security concept much debated now in Poland is the issue of confidence-building measures in the economic field. Internal economic security has decreased in both East and West over the last few years, as political and economic relations have grown more intensive; this has been described as the 'politicisation of economics' or the 'economisation of politics'. But the latter term is misleading. Experience has shown that the incidence of economics on politics is minimal, and that increasing economic cooperation is not necessarily followed by improved political relations.[11] In contrast, it has been a feature of the 1980s that political tension has had a rapid and dramatic effect on economic cooperation, and this has resulted not only in serious economic disadvantage (for example, to Poland) but in the erosion of an important part of the détente process and, in short, to rather negative attitudes on all sides. The 1982 Polish proposal on economic confidence-building measures was mainly intended to protect East–West relations against the deteriorating international environment, by establishing as unlawful the use of economic levers for the application of political pressure, and guaranteeing, more especially to the small and medium-sized states, the right to independent and sovereign conduct of economic activity within their borders, as also of foreign trade.[12] The concept of economic confidence-building is intended as a counterweight to autarchy at a national or sub-regional scale. A first step would be to ban all new barriers of political kind to economic and technological cooperation between East and West, to be followed by the progressive elimination of those already in existence. Finally 'negative interventionism', that is, the imposition of barriers, should be replaced by 'promotional interventionism', which would involve the creation of a favourable institutional framework for East–West trade.

The link between ecology and security in Europe has recently come to prominence in Poland. The government, experts and grassroots movements have all expressed their concern at the existing situation. Both at national and European level, the awareness of ecological risk has intensified, partly under the stimulus of ecological accidents in Europe over the past few years. Both at the national and the international levels, decisive action has been lacking, and new international frameworks are required to overcome the limited scope for action of individual countries and to promote the universal application of ecologically acceptable technologies. Here, a paradox should be underlined. While Europe as a whole is the victim of an unlimited exchange of pollution and pollutants, the exchange of technologies, equipment and know-how in the field of pollution abatement and remedy is often restricted and certainly inadequate even to the most immediately pressing needs. In this regard, the Polish initiative on facilitating the exchange of technologies related to environmental protection, which was put forward at the United Nations in 1985 and at the Helsinki Meeting in Vienna, is worthy of note.

Other concepts debated recently in Poland – in particular within the Catholic Church and religious associations – include *the ethical and moral aspects of nuclear deterrence, a Christian conception of peace,*[13] *and the relation holding between on the one hand internal peace and domestic respect for human rights and on the other international and in particular European security*. The latter concern is not confined to Catholic circles but is characteristic of oppositional circles and indeed of Polish society as a whole. It is reflected in the government's declarations and actions, and in its goal of bringing about the democratisation of public life and of creating new political forums in which the diversity of opinions and approaches may be expressed. The significance of humanitarian concerns, the 'human dimension' in East–West relations, has recently been to the fore, and the Polish government is happy to associate its own efforts with this trend.

Notes and References

1. *Conference on Security and Co-operation in Europe. A Polish view* (Warsaw, 1976) 15.
2. *Study on Concepts of Security*, Report of the Secretary General of the United Nations (New York, 1985).
3. A. D. Rotfeld (ed.), *Międzynarodowe czynniki bezpieczeństwa Polski* (The International Factors in Poland's Security) (Warszawa: Państwowe Wydawnictwo Naukowe, 1986).
4. Wladyslaw Marniewicz, 'Wplyw Sytuacji Wewnetrznej na Międzynarodowa Pozycje i Bezpieczeństwo Polski (The effects of the domestic situation on Poland's economy), in Rotfeld (ed.), *Międzynarodowe czynniki* (Note 3) 44.
5. Polska Rzeczpospolita Ludowa-Republika Federalna Niemiec Bilans stosunków wzajemnych. Problemy i perspektywy normalizacji (Warszawa, 1979) 318.
6. M. Grela, 'European Security and the Events in Poland', *Yearbook of the Polish Political Science*, vol. XIII (1983) 256.
7. P. Hardi, 'Short and mid-term perspectives on East–West relations',

paper presented at the II Annual IEWSS Alumni Conference (Talloires, France, 4–6 September 1987) 5.

8. R. W. Tucker, *The Purposes of American Power* (New York, 1981) 10–11.
9. *Verbatim Records of the CSCE stage I* (Helsinki, 3–7 July 1973) 35.
10. Statement of the Polish representative at the CSCE Vienna Meeting (29 August 1987).
11. S. Michałowski, 'Economic Security in East–West Relations', *International Relations* (Studies of the PISM), vol. I, no. 2 (1984) 76.
12. J. M. Toczek, 'Confidence Building in International Economic Relations', *International Relations* (Studies of the PISM), vol. I, no. 2 (1984) 87.
13. 'Philosophical and Religious Premises of the New Peace Movement', *Dialectics and Humanism, The Polish Philosophical Quarterly*, vol. IX, no. 4 (1982).

8 The Debate on European Security in the United Kingdom

Michael Clarke

1 INTRODUCTION

British discussions about European security are very ambiguous. There is no single debate over European security, but rather a series of confusing and overlapping arguments about defence policy, defence industries, Britain's role in the world, and the future of political parties. Insofar as we can amalgamate these different debates into some sort of British 'approach' to European security, several contradictory trends are apparent. On the one hand, British approaches to thinking about the whole issue of European security reflect a good deal of historical continuity and are generally conservative. On the other hand, where some degree of change *has* occurred, it has been radical, polarised, and politically vehement. So Britain approaches the 1990s with an intuition that the European security debate is reaching a crucial stage as East–West, and West–West, politics are in process of rapid change. Yet beyond this, there is no very clear understanding as to what the debate is really about and what is at stake. Neither the British intellectual establishment – and still less the political establishment – are well-equipped to face the policy choices that the next few years are likely to present. Above all, Britain approaches the issue of European security with a curious degree of parochialism.

2 THE CONSERVATISM OF THE BRITISH PERSPECTIVE

Britain's essential conservatism in security matters is not difficult to understand in the light of its history. Prior to 1979, defence issues traditionally had little salience in domestic political debates, either in day-to-day politics or even in general elections. Till then, foreign affairs had been thought to affect a general election only once; in

1955, when the reputation of Eden as 'a peacemaker' figured in the campaign. The Labour Party's brief flirtation with nuclear unilateralism in 1959 had no perceptible electoral impact thereafter, and since 1964, Britain's economic fortunes had taken centre stage at election time. Only a little over 5 per cent of the British public regard defence or foreign affairs as among the most important issues facing the country.[1] Nor has there been a strong tradition of pacifist dissent in Britain. Pacifism has always been on the fringes of British politics and even in the light of the disarmament debate of the 1980s, only 10 per cent of the population, at most, could be described as holding essentially pacifist views.[2]

In the absence of any significant radical challenge to the conventional wisdoms of foreign and defence policy, there has been an inevitable tendency towards highly centralised policy-making in Britain. This has fostered a powerful deference in the mentality of the British public and a strong predisposition to leave defence matters to the experts.

The result of all this is that British public and élite attitudes to defence have always tended toward a curious disregard for the international context. On the one hand, Britain shouldered a great number of global responsibilities after 1945. As an ex-imperial power, it had commitments all over the world. Britain was pivotal in the formation of NATO and a prominent power in the early diplomacy of the Cold War. To uphold all these commitments, Britain relied essentially on the 'special relationship' with the USA. It was this relationship which effectively augmented British diplomatic power and without it, British foreign and defence policy would simply have lacked coherence.[3] On the other hand, Britain was slow to accept the interdependence which such commitments implied. Britain was always very wary of any European entanglements outside the defence field and once NATO was firmly established, policy-makers preferred to concentrate on colonial and global relations. In a curious way, the process of decolonisation and the special relationship with the USA created a self-image of independence in British defence policy which reinforced its unwillingness to think in terms of closer relationships with other European states.

In the 1950s, Britain saw itself as a genuinely global actor, with the Commonwealth, a strong position in world production and trade, the Sterling Area to reinforce the role of the pound in international finance, and a uniquely close relationship with Washington, through which it became a junior partner in the business of global security management. In these respects, 'defence' was a matter of national interests being defended on a world-wide rather than a European scale.[4] NATO and the structures of European security were a crucial part of that policy, but by no means an overwhelming consideration in it. As time went on, Britain found it impossible to maintain this level of global independence, but the Commonwealth and the Anglo–US relationship served to hold open Britain's defence options for longer than Britain's own power could alone have done. It also created a powerful vocabulary of independence, which in some respects was as important as the reality. The British nuclear deterrent – the Polaris submarine force – provides a prime example of this perception of independence so prevalent through the 1960s and 1970s. Polaris is 'independent' in a technical sense, in that it is capable of being used independently. Only in extremis, however, could its independent use even be contemplated. For all contingencies but the most extreme – and for the totality of its existence so far – the deterrent has, in fact, been an example of strategic interdependence. The missiles are supplied and serviced by the USA. Plans for their use are integrated into the Single Integrated Operational Plan (SIOP), which is the USA's and NATO's joint nuclear targeting system, operated from Omaha. For all peacetime purposes, and almost every conceivable wartime purpose, the technical independence of Polaris is simply irrelevant. It is extraordinarily difficult to conceive of any possible circumstances where Britain would contemplate taking the missiles out of the SIOP network and programming them for a purely independent, separate launch. Though this is technically possible, it is politically inconceivable. Yet debate about Polaris in Britain has always been in terms of its 'independence'. Questions about its costs, its role and its dangers, are all debated on the basis of its existence as a national defence system. In practice its symbolic presence as an independent system has always loomed much larger than its real military role, which is highly interdependent.

Such perceptions of independence owed a greater debt to the Anglo–US 'special relationship' than to almost anything else. This has been so basic to all British diplomacy that even a shift to a more Euro-centred Atlanticism – in reality, only a shift of emphasis – becomes a major reappraisal for British defence policy. With one exception, between 1970 and 1974, British political leaders since 1940 have been determined to assert the power of the special relationship. Neither the public nor the political parties have ever wavered in their essential identity with US cultural and democratic values, whatever their doubts have been over particular US policies. The political and economic evolution of Western Europe, and now the growing change in the trends underlying Euro–US relations, thus pose some acute problems for Britain's conception of itself and its view of the nature of the Western world order. In a sense, Britain has invested so much in its own version of Atlanticism that change comes very hard to the political establishment. The reactions of the British government towards the European Community, the INF debate, the revival of the Western European Union, the Strategic Defence Initiative; not to mention specific events such as the Libyan raid of 1986, or the tanker war in the Gulf in 1987, all indicate either an instinctive willingness on Britain's part to support the USA, or else a reluctance to engage in diplomacy that could be portrayed in Washington as being anti-US.

3 DISCONTINUITIES IN THE BRITISH PERSPECTIVE

Despite the essential conservatism in British perspectives on matters of security and a history that has created a self-image of independence, there have been some startling discontinuities in the perspective since 1979. Certain key aspects of security matters have become the focus of party political debates. And where the party debate has touched the security issue, it has polarised it in a way which is uniquely radical in British politics.

Some time after 1979 the Labour Party, and to a lesser extent the then Liberal Party, latched onto a groundswell of radical public opinion which predated the 1979 general election and which involved the Churches, some trade unions and many single-issue campaigning groups. In the wake of its electoral defeat of 1979, the Labour Party began to channel and mobilise what had previously been a relatively unstructured band of anti-nuclear opinion, noted more for its lack of cohesion or identifiable sub-groups than anything else.[5] In adversity, the Labour Party moved towards its left wing, and began to embrace some of the anti-nuclear policies that were to be found there. The more activist Labour supporters in the constituencies gained some power within the party. The trade union movement had also devolved power away from the more centrist union leaders of the 1960s, towards active members of the union rank and file who were instinctively more left wing. Above all, the swing towards left-wing policies found national leadership among the party executive, ex-cabinet ministers and emergent leaders from the party's back benches. Some centre-right MPs within the Labour Party left it to help found the new Social Democratic Party in an attempt to inject some new life into the centre of British party politics.

A shift to the left whilst in opposition was not unexpected, though the vehemence of the arguments was somewhat surprising. The anti-nuclear platform was used as a weapon by the left of the party to try to capture control of the whole, as indeed it had been in the late 1950s. In that earlier period, however, the issue subsided with the end of the power struggle. In the present case, the successes of the Labour left have been turned against them and the centre-right is back in control of the party having used the novel constitutional weapons that the left had invented. Left-wing activism in the constituencies and the trade unions can find little national expression and no credible parliamentary leaders around whom to coalesce. Certainly, it is clear that the power struggle of the 1980s is over. Yet the anti-nuclear issue is not. As the party moved back towards the centre in 1987–9, the non-nuclear defence issue remained a major problem for it, and whatever the personal feelings of the new leadership, it was clear that the party's commitment to a radical defence policy could not be ditched without incurring a major internal split. The Labour Party, as a party, has committed itself to a non-nuclear defence policy. That commitment first won a majority at the party conference in 1980 and has been reaffirmed at six successive party conferences; since the first such victory in 1982, it has won the two-thirds majority which elevates it to official policy at five out of six conferences. There is little prospect that the non-nuclear issue will disappear from the agenda of the opposition in British politics, even in an era of arms control.[6]

So in some respects the debate over European security has become highly polarised in Britain; but only in some respects. For all its vehemence, the party political debate has concentrated on a very few visible issues, such as the independent nuclear deterrent, US reactions to a change in British defence policy, and in particular, the deployment of cruise missiles in Britain. Other issues have been neglected and a series of important assumptions are left vague and unspoken. And many vital implications of the party debates that are taking place – on essential European security concerns – are simply not addressed. The defence debate at British general elections over the last decade has been at once an exciting and a profoundly depressing spectacle. Those issues which have been swept into the party political arena have been subjected to some very radical critiques and are unlikely ever to be quite the same again. But those issues which the party debate has not touched remain essentially unmoved: symbols of reactive thinking, complacency, and a curiously British insularity on both the right and the left.

4 CONCEPTIONS OF EUROPEAN AND COMMON SECURITY

There is virtually no debate in Britain in either official or unofficial circles on the nature of European security, as such. There is any amount of debate about NATO and about East–West relations; both of which are, of course, vital components of any discussion concerning Europe. But it is very hard to find opinions – let alone an exchange of them – on the nature of a security system that would embrace, as a first order objective, the security of East and West Europe.

The London-based organisation, European Nuclear Disarmament, argues strongly that the problems of dealing with nuclear weapons must be based on a policy of promoting political change in the relations between East and West in Europe and a commitment to non-militarism on a global scale.[7] In this respect it chimes in with the most recent directions taken by the US Freeze campaign, which has a vigorous British counterpart based in Bristol.[8] This line is also consistent with contemporary thinking among the leadership of the Campaign for Nuclear Disarmament, although as a national, single-issue pressure group, CND has some trouble in encompassing such diverse concerns as those represented by END and Freeze. There are also some informal British and American intellectual groups, such as the Common Security Programme and Just Defence, which articulate common security ideas reminiscent of the general thinking behind the Palme Commission Report, in an attempt to influence élite opinion in Britain and NATO.[9] None of this, however, constitutes mainstream argument. END (and to a lesser extent, CND and Freeze) are identified with the political far left in Britain. And common security programmes are as yet too low key to be capable of having a major impact on defence debates. In the British context, 'European security', 'common security', still more 'world order' or 'international security', are all discussed essentially with reference to NATO and how the Western alliance 'handles' the Cold War.

It is surprisingly, for instance, how little the Soviet Union is directly analysed in Britain. Neither in public or in official opinion does the Soviet Union have much direct impact, despite its obvious importance. There is an inevitable curiosity over the progress and the implications of *perestroika*, but even so, the Soviet Union is still seen less as a country and more as a component of the context in which essentially Atlanticist debates take place.[10] The same is true of Eastern Europe, though since 1984 the Thatcher government has shown an interest in bilateral diplomacy with Eastern Europe and is now prepared to see the states of Eastern Europe as something more than an appendage of the Soviet Union. Meanwhile, public opinion in Britain shows little real interest in the Soviet Union and maintains an essentially hostile view of it, though the public increasingly sees less and less to choose between particular Soviet and US policies.[11]

The Conservative government and the Conservative Party hold to a vague but powerful notion of the essentially threatening nature of the Eastern bloc, which is almost never spelt out in detail; indeed it seldom has to be. 'Soviet blackmail' or 'Soviet intimidation' have served as sufficient justifications for important policy decisions, and no further specification has either been sought or offered. This attitude is reinforced by the more sceptical view of international diplomacy that is characteristic of Mrs Thatcher's governments. Before she became Prime Minister, Mrs Thatcher made a series of tough statements about the Soviet Union and of her view of the nature of the threat and the appropriate Western response to it. This went hand in hand with a rooted conviction of the tendency of international diplomacy to compromise national interests, and a clear reluctance to embrace the consequences of growing interdependence.[12] There is no question that the first Thatcher government (1979–83) was not very internationalist in its outlook and was, in any case, preoccupied with domestic economic and social issues.[13] Mrs Thatcher was not at all affronted to be known as the 'iron lady', or even as a 'cold warrior'.

During the second Thatcher government (1983–7), however, this stance began to change. Mrs Thatcher grew in experience and stature; she was accorded a good deal of respect by both US and Soviet leaders, and she began to style herself as the senior diplomatist of the Western world. In this guise, the British government took a series of initiatives to improve relations with the states of Eastern Europe, and Mrs Thatcher has played a personal role in helping to improve détente between the superpowers. She presents herself as a tough-talking Conservative who can 'deal' with the Soviet Union in much the way that Winston Churchill was able to do forty years ago.

This has not, however, resulted in any discernable change in the way that European security issues are viewed through the prism of Atlantic relations, or the way that defence is felt to be something that must remain essentially national. For Mrs Thatcher's diplomacy is still not, in its nature, the diplomacy of interdependence; it is rather an exercise in *Realpolitik*. She still regards interdependence as a problem rather than an opportunity; she remains suspicious of international organisations, and like all practitioners of *Realpolitik*, she believes in the essential legitimacy of making decisions at the national level rather than at the international, or even the sub-national, level.[14]

In matters of European security this translates into an attitude which acknowledges that major changes may be in process, but which sees no reason to look for alternatives to NATO or major changes in the structures of the alliances. Thatcherite conservatives are sceptical about Soviet arms control proposals and do not see unlimited benefits in arms control, particularly if that would threaten the existence of nuclear deterrence. They are sceptical, too, about the chances of Gorbachev being able to reform the Soviet system sufficiently to require them to reassess the threat; and wary of creating any more institutions in the European arena. New institutions can become merely talking shops for insidious propaganda, they fear, and the structures that have seen us this far through the Cold War should be sufficient for the future.[15]

The Labour Party has been no less insular in its approach to European security. Though ideologically more prepared to take a sympathetic view of Soviet motivations and a more internationalist view of the problems of security, it has spent infinitely more time talking about the USA than about the Soviet Union and almost no time at all thinking about innovations in the structures of European security. All of the great defence debates in the party since 1945 have been about the independence of a socialist Britain within the western world; not about the international politics of a socialist Europe. Labour Party statements have always paid lip service to its internationalist visions, but in truth, the nearest it has come to a discussion of the specifics of internationalism was occasioned by the debate over entry into the European Community during 1970–5, and that was not notable either for its consistency or vision.[16] The problem for the Labour Party is that it has not been able to rise above the immediate concerns of policy to elaborate a vision of common security in Europe that could command any broad electoral support. There is a general consensus on the value of Britain's Atlanticism both within the parliamentary party and in the broader Labour movement. But any attempts at more internationalist thinking become identified with ideological struggles for the soul of the party, so the leadership, not unnaturally, takes refuge in compromise policy positions. The party's international conscience is strongly identified with a domestic ideological stance.

Meanwhile, British officialdom proceeds with caution. Its policy towards the Soviet Union and Eastern Europe is reactive rather than initiatory, notwithstanding the more open diplomacy of the second Thatcher government. It is concerned, above all, with Western unity as a prerequisite for any dealings with the Eastern bloc.

The Conference on Security and Cooperation in Europe (CSCE) is a prime example of this attitude in practice. Britain has been highly instrumental in the success that the CSCE has enjoyed. But the success of the CSCE is measured in largely Western terms, in which Britain had a large influence. To begin with, there was widespread official scepticism in Britain about the value of the CSCE process when it seemed, in the late 1960s, to be little more than a Soviet propaganda vehicle. There was barely disguised suspicion that the Western alliance might be being drawn into a Soviet diplomatic ploy, or even worse, a Soviet grand design for European security that would legitimise the regimes of Eastern Europe and weaken the NATO allies. On the basis of such scepticism, the Western powers demanded a high price for their participation in the CSCE. In the event, the Soviet Union was willing to pay it, and in 1973 serious negotiations began, which led to the signing of the Final Act in 1975 and then the succession of review conferences in Belgrade, Madrid and Vienna. Throughout more than a decade and a half since the CSCE came into existence, two considerations have grown in importance for the British officials who have to deal with it. One is that, if the CSCE was a Soviet diplomatic ploy, then it has rebounded back on the Soviet Union, for the CSCE excited more demands for reform inside the Eastern bloc and has become a lever by which the Western powers can put pressure on Moscow. For this reason, the United States became significantly more interested in the CSCE after 1977 as its effects on the Soviet Union were beginning to be perceived. Secondly, British officials are convinced that the CSCE can be a diplomatic success for the Western powers only if there is unity among both NATO and EEC members. So the CSCE process has become a powerful vehicle for the development of allied unity. Indeed, British officials have observed that its chief benefit was not primarily that it opened a dialogue to the Soviet bloc, but rather that it had become an object of European Political Cooperation.[17]

In this respect, the official attitude to European security issues is very clear. On the face of it, the CSCE process provides a starting point for discussions between East and West on the future shape of European security. The official British view, however, is never less than practical: the CSCE must be built on the existing premises of East–West security; it should not try to change them, only to make them work better; and any further proposals that could usefully be made must be detailed and practical; at best, the CSCE can be a useful adjunct to the existing structures of East–West diplomacy. Insofar as the CSCE was a diplomatic contest between the Eastern and Western blocs, then the West has clearly got the better of it. This gain can be maintained, in the British view, as long as the French do not persist in making vague and visionary proposals, as long as the neutral states agree with most of our positions, and, above all, as long as the unity of the Atlantic alliance is preserved in the UK negotiating positions. In this respect, no one in official British circles feels that there is an interest in using the CSCE as the basis for any alternative thinking about security.

5 UNOFFICIAL AND ECONOMIC LINKS BETWEEN BRITAIN AND EASTERN EUROPE

Just as conceptions of European security are dominated by existing structures and preconceptions, so in the economic and social sphere there is a similar phenomenon. There are economic links between Britain and the Eastern bloc, and there are a number of non-governmental organisation (NGO) contacts. None of these, however, are important enough to have significant consequences, still less are they capable of changing East–West political structures.

British trade with the Soviet Union and Eastern Europe represents far and away the least valuable geographical sector of British trade. Within the twelve Centrally Planned Economies that are grouped together for statistical purposes, Britain's trade with the Soviet Union represents about 44 per cent of the total, but even that is well short of £1 billion per year in value terms. Though trade between the East and the OECD countries seems set to rise, Britain's share of Soviet trade as compared with its OECD competitors has been in steady decline. It is not composed of high-technology products but rather of more basic goods and manufactures and in all, Anglo–Soviet trade accounts for little more than 1 per cent of total British trade.[18]

More to the point, whether British economic relations with the Eastern bloc are in a state of growth or decline, they are almost entirely structured by the incompatibilities between the two blocs. The operations of COCOM are only the most obvious example of the subordination of trade to security interests. But even outside the COCOM framework, the sheer structural differences in the economies of Eastern and Western countries act as a severe constraint on the scope for mutual trade. The Eastern states lack hard currency; Western states are ill-equipped to deal with socialist foreign trade organisations; the West is obsessed with the security implications of high-technology trade; the East with secrecy and party control over the running of the economy. Trade between the blocs, in other words, tends to be a function of the political relationships between them. Economic relations have little independent existence; they are structured by, and symptomatic of, political relations.[19]

This picture is repeated when we consider NGO contacts. Eastern European students make up less than 1 per cent of the total number of foreign students in Britain. The British Council, whose function is to foster cultural relations between Britain and the outside world, spends about 1.5 per cent of its total budget on Anglo–Soviet relations.[20] If we ignore official government efforts to foster contact and look instead at more individual initiatives, a number of events could be mentioned: educational schemes, friendship societies, cultural exchanges and parliamentary exchanges and visits. But the intensity of all this activity is not great. A more telling statistic is that passenger transits between Britain and the Eastern bloc, in both directions, constitute just 0.5 per cent of total passenger transits to and from Britain in any one year.[21] The reality of NGO contact, therefore, is that it is a series of highly specific, very structured meetings between particular organisations. There is very little informal contact between Britain and the states of Eastern Europe, and as with economic relations, the prospects for growth are highly dependent on the state of political relations at any given time.

None of this is necessarily the fault directly of the British government. Soviet and Eastern European governments have proved in the past to be extraordinarily difficult to deal with, as many other

OECD states have discovered. Nevertheless, as a matter of dispassionate observation, it is clear that no change is likely to be generated in East–West relations by British economic and NGO activity. Nor does any of this activity serve as an alternative intellectual force of any significance. In a sense, both Labour and Conservative governments have accurately reflected, over the years, the fact that there is a lack of any significant domestic pressure-groups who would benefit from a reappraisal of East–West relations. There is simply no real perception of an immediate community of economic, social or cultural interests among NGOs, sufficient to create a pressure for political change.

6 CONCEPTIONS OF DÉTENTE AND CHANGE IN EAST–WEST RELATIONS

Whilst the party political debate has not significantly touched general conceptions of security or economic and cultural relations, the issue of détente – narrowly defined as the sum of deliberate policies labelled as 'détente' – has been brought into the party arena. For this reason there is some sign of initiatory, rather than reactive, thinking on the contribution of détente to European security.

Détente was not the subject of party politics at all before the Thatcher era. But in 1975 when Mrs Thatcher became leader of the Conservative Party she immediately began to reflect the views of the 'new right' of which she was a part. And when she came into office in 1979 she soon found herself sharing the stage with a 'new right' American president, Ronald Reagan.[22] For the politicians of the new right, détente had been a sham; Soviet behaviour had not improved, the Soviet Union had cheated on arms control, and liberals in the West had been deceived by détente and had mistaken appearances for substance. The events of the early 1980s in Europe posed many acute choices for the British government and the unity of NATO was severely tested. With the confirmed Atlanticism of the Thatcher government, British diplomacy consistently moved away from détente as a way of helping to preserve NATO unity. Though the British government certainly did not always agree with US policies, if forced to choose, it would always back the assertive Reagan administration rather than pursue the more nuanced response that was characteristic of its European partners.

In reaction to this, the opposition parties in Britain began to rediscover the advantages of European détente. Mrs Thatcher was criticised for her unhelpful assertiveness and she was portrayed by all of the opposition parties as the henchwoman of a dangerous US president. Since the support which was given to détente in this way was a reaction to government policy, no particularly clear vision ever emerged of what détente might comprise. Certainly, there was no reassessment of the Soviet threat, beyond a realist assertion that Soviet leaders were pragmatic enough to see the advantages to themselves of less tension and lower levels of defence spending. On the left of the Labour Party there was some element of genuinely alternative thinking about the nature of the Soviet Union; but the Labour left had, for too long, appeared to be an apologist for Soviet policies, and certainly did not represent mainstream thinking even within the Labour movement. And the Soviet Union, undergoing the post-Brezhnev succession, was hardly reassuring in this respect and tended to confirm all the traditional fears of Western conservatives. The leadership of the Labour Party and mainstream thinking in the Liberal Party and the SDP was essentially of one mind; that the Soviet Union was certainly a genuine threat to Britain, but only under certain circumstances. Above all, it was not the 'evil empire' portrayed by President Reagan, apparently with Mrs Thatcher's support.

In practice, the politicisation of détente has been a reaction to the attitude of the opposition parties to the problems of arms control. As the Reagan administration seemed, for the majority of its term of office, to be determined to sacrifice arms control, so arms control became a prime objective for the opposition. And the ultimate rationale of arms control is that it promotes détente and political change. The way in which the Reagan administration blundered into its stance on the Strategic Defence Initiative, for instance, ensured that the whole world saw the issues essentially as a choice between SDI on one side and arms control and détente on the other. Until 1986, therefore, there was a neat dichotomy between hawks and doves in the political establishment which certainly kept détente, however loosely defined, on the agenda.

Since 1987, however, an ironic shift has occurred. Arms control is now moving forwards at an astonishing pace and now it is everyone's policy. Both government and opposition parties in Britain claim fully to support the efforts of the superpowers to reach an historic agreement. In practice, however, they support the endeavour for quite specific and different reasons: reasons which reveal how narrowly defined are British conceptions of détente and how closely détente is tied to the specifics of arms control. For the Conservative government, the successful conclusion of arms control agreements offers clear proof that there is no realistic alternative to multilateral negotiations from a position of strength. The 'iron lady' has been vindicated; the Soviet Union *will* negotiate if we keep our nerve. Our strength and resolve has put the Soviet Union into a position where détente is now possible. This position has been facilitated partly by the respect that Mrs Thatcher won on her visit to Moscow in 1987 and the talks she had with Mr Gorbachev in December of that year, when he stopped over on his way to the USA to sign the INF agreement. The INF agreement was signed proof of the success of a bold conservative policy of strength and rapprochement.

For the opposition parties, however, the INF agreement proved the contrary. It was long overdue and could have been concluded earlier. For the Labour and Liberal parties, it exposed the lie of so many previous hawkish statements. For the SDP, it proved that strength worked, but that it could have worked earlier and more effectively. It seemed to show that the Soviet Union *did* want to develop détente and that there *was* a margin of superfluous nuclear weapons in Europe that could be bargained away. More importantly, for the Labour Party, arms control was seen as a proof that a non-nuclear defence policy was possible. The INF agreement, it was hoped, had begun a multilateral disarmament process that the Labour Party (and, to a lesser extent, the Liberal Party) would have pursued unilaterally. It showed that disarmament was possible, however it was achieved. Moreover, if it helped to initiate a meaningful détente then Europe would be more receptive to new approaches to defence policy. Though their views on the question of unilateralism varied, all of the opposition parties interpreted the success of arms control as proof that their alternative versions of British defence policy were more realistic than that of the Conservatives.

Arms control means different things, therefore, to different shades of opinion in Britain. Some new thinking has taken place as a result of the surprising developments in arms control over recent years, and as the Labour Party contemplates its future in 1989 and the early 1990s, there has been some effort to integrate conceptions of 'common security' into its official stance on defence and arms control.[23] It would, however, be wrong to overstate the importance of such developments. It is still very preliminary; the Conservative government still effectively sets the agenda in any discussions on détente; and the Labour Party's interest in common security is essentially as a device to build internal unity over defence affairs. More to the point, though arms control and détente are on the agenda again, and though the vocabulary of common security has become more familiar, neither the government nor the opposition parties seem to have any new ideas about the nature of arms control, détente, or political change in Europe. Their commitment to these concepts is essentially a function of their need to justify their own particular defence policies in the party arena. A more penetrating look at détente would require a much more careful analysis of the Soviet Union, and this has been noticeably lacking in the political debate so far.

7 CONCEPTIONS OF DEFENCE POLICY

On the specifics of the defence debate, major changes have clearly taken place and it is safe to say that defence issues will never be the same again. The Labour Party has fought two elections on a non-nuclear defence policy, and the Liberal–SDP Alliance and now the divorced Liberal–Democrats and the SDP, embody degrees of defence reformism in their policies. All three parties are attempting to draw upon the substantial minority of around 40 per cent of the British public who are sympathetic to some forms of anti-nuclearism.[24] In this respect, the traditional consensus on defence matters in Britain has clearly broken down.

The Labour Party's defence policy draws its inspiration from non-nuclear studies from several academic schools; the Bradford School of Peace Studies, the Oxford Research Group, the Cambridge Disarmament Seminar, and the party's own research teams. The policy has been based upon a commitment to abandon the Polaris nuclear submarine force, cancel its replacement Trident, to phase out Britain's other nuclear roles, with particular reference to air-delivered nuclear weapons and tactical nuclear devices in service with British forces in Germany. This will be accompanied by a greater commitment to conventional forces, so as to demonstrate the depth of a Labour government's commitment to NATO. The party also advocates a transarmament process; nuclear-free zones, a no-first-use policy, the development of defensive barriers in Europe, the building-up of reserve forces, and the development of appropriate new technologies. It is against gold-plating for defence systems and would reorientate air and sea functions towards a less offensive posture. It applauds European collaboration as a way to produce more appropriate defence systems.[25]

For more than six years, the Labour Party's policy has represented a clear challenge to all traditional conceptions of British defence policy. Whether the Labour Party is electable on this basis, however, is a matter of fierce debate. In 1987 some 43 per cent of those polled by Gallup said that Labour's defence policy made them less likely to vote Labour.[26] Nor was it ever clear how much of this policy a Labour government would be willing – or able – to carry out, given the sort of opposition it would inevitably encounter. Nevertheless, the very policy has served as a potent challenge to the status quo. The same trends that created this challenge have drawn the other opposition parties some way along the same road, though there is evidence that they have shrunk back from some of their more radical positions in the light of so overwhelming an election defeat as they suffered. For the moment, there is an agonised reappraisal in the defence policies of the Liberal–Democrats, while those of the SDP are essentially driven by the personal commitment of its leader, David Owen, who has always taken a pro-nuclear stance and is convinced of the need for an independent British nuclear deterrent.[27]

On the face of it, such challenges have evoked equally vehement and clear responses from the government. The argument is polarised, at least on the surface. Yet though the rhetorical, inter-party argument is between the status quo and a vigorous challenge to it, the underlying argument has become more subtle. For the government is facing a series of pressures which demand more flexible thinking and a reorientation of defence roles. US pressure for arms control in Europe and the pressures from a substantial minority of public opinion which now expects some progress, put government defence policies under a microscope. The government can still win all of the defence arguments, but it is in danger of having to fight hard for every one of them. More immediately, it is facing a difficult financial squeeze. Despite all the government's protestations that it will not introduce a defence review, almost all defence analysts expect there to be one, whether overtly, or by stealth. And when it is undertaken, all the unpalatable choices of the last review in 1981 will recur with all the old dilemmas. The government has little choice but to pursue greater European collaboration for the production of major new weapon systems, excessive gold-plating must be curbed and British forces must rationalise some of their wide distribution of roles within

NATO.[28] The Government's stance, in other words, remains traditional, but it is not stationary, and it is entirely possible that the present government may in effect alter Britain's defence posture – for its own conservative reasons – more radically than any previous Labour government.

Some radical thinking on British defence policy now stems from sources not normally associated with the academic and political left. On the specifics of defence policy, there are now quite a number of intellectual bridges between the 'traditionalists' and the 'reformers'; though the obstacles between them tend to be of a more fundamental nature regarding the role of nuclear retaliation in defence policy. At the very least, however, a polarised defence debate, and the changing context of the international environment, are forcing the political and academic establishment to address some of the less visible, second-order questions. There is, of course, any amount of scope for further fudging via the sort of manoeuvring that characterises party politics. But a series of detailed defence issues are now on the political agenda. The major problem is really whether the public chooses to believe that radical changes in defence policy are possible. After the 1987 election, for instance, around 60 per cent of the public appeared to believe that the new Conservative government would spend more on defence and that the Labour Party, if it had been elected, would have spent less.[29] This belief, however, was directly at variance with the facts. The Conservative government was already spending less on defence, and the Labour Party repeatedly pledged itself to maintain overall spending and to increase it in some specific areas. The Labour Party's problem is not only to establish a viable alternative defence policy, but also to win the credence of a sceptical public. The apparently immutable expectations entertained by the public as to the defence policies of either party do much to reinforce the conservatism of British defence policy in general.

8 CONCLUSION

It may seem strange that the British debate shows such movement and vigour over some of the specifics of defence policy and yet is so little affected in the more fundamental areas of East–West security policy. In one sense, this is to be expected, since the debate is now driven by party political arguments, and they are by nature myopic. And perhaps this party political debate can be regarded as a first intellectual step along a more constructive and innovative road.

There is, however, something more fundamental in the nature of British conservatism in defence matters which suggests that the debate will remain anomalous. The defence policy debate is narrowly focussed; the debate about arms control and détente is a function of it, and wider debates, on the nature of common security or visions of a European future, are predominantly absent. It is as if the British were mesmerised by the existence of the superpowers in Europe. For the British realist, this was an inescapable fact of political life for over thirty years, and absolutely true at that. But if the role of the superpowers is now changing, and Europe is in transition, the realists seem to find it hard to readjust their thinking in an innovative way. We are left instead with a series of political reactions.

It would be foolish to advocate change for its own sake, of course, and conservative thinking may turn out to be prudent. But if we decide to be essentially reactive to our security environment then it should be a clear choice rather than the result of neglect. In order to make choices we need a clearer view of what East–West relations, European relations, and international relations might look like in the future. In the USA, intrinsically more conservative in defence matters, there is no reserve in the attempts that are made to articulate future alternative scenarios. Some of these are trivial, others are highly impressive and have a demonstrable impact on official thinking. Yet in Britain we seem to have neither the intellectual or political inclination – and perhaps not even the means – to examine, *as mainstream political arguments*, visions of possible new security relations. Perhaps in this respect we get the governments we deserve.

Notes and References

1. David Capitanchik and Richard Eichenberg, *Defence and Public Opinion* (London: Routledge & Kegan Paul and Royal Institute of International Affairs, 1983) 18. See also, Philip Sabin, 'Assessing a "Peace Offensive": The Impact of Gorbachev on British Public Opinion about Defence', RUSI and Brassey's, *Defence Yearbook 1987–88* (London: Brassey's, 1987).
2. Ivor Crewe, 'Britain: Two and a Half Cheers for the Atlantic Alliance', in Gregory Flynn and Hans Rattinger (eds), *The Public and Atlantic Defense* (London: Croom Helm, 1985) 29.

3. Ritchie Ovendale, *The English Speaking Alliance* (London: George Allen & Unwin, 1985) 273–8.
4. See John Baylis, *Anglo–American Defence Relations 1939–1984* (London: Macmillan, 1984).
5. Crewe, 'Britain', 47–65. See also, Peter Byrd, 'The Development of the Peace Movement in Britain', in Werner Kaltefleiter and Robert L. Pfaltzgraff (eds), *The Peace Movements in Europe and the United States* (London: Croom Helm, 1985) 63–103.
6. See Labour Party, *Defence and Security for Britain* (London: Labour Party, 1984); Mike Gapes, 'The Evolution of Labour's Defence and Security Policy', in Gordon Burt (ed.), *Alternative Defence Policy* (London: Croom Helm, 1988) 82–105.
7. See, for example, Mary Kaldor, 'Labour and the East', *END, Journal of European Nuclear Disarmament*, 24 (October–November 1986) 1, 24.
8. See Randall Forsberg, 'The Freeze and Beyond: Confining the Military to Defense as a Route to Disarmament', *World Policy Journal*, 1 (2) (1984) 285–318.
9. Common Security Programme, The Rookery, Adderbury, Banbury, Oxon, OX17 3NA; *Common Security: A Programme for Disarmament* (Palme Report) (London: Pan Books, 1982).
10. See Michael Clarke, 'Anglo–Soviet Relations', in Gregory Flynn (ed.), *Domestic Sources of Western Policy Towards the Soviet Union* (Washington, D.C.: Carnegie Endowment, 1989).
11. Clarke, 'Anglo–Soviet Relations' (Note 10) Tables 3 and 4.
12. See Peter Riddell, *The Thatcher Government* (Oxford: Basil Blackwell, 1985) 206–9: Hugo Young and Anne Sloman, *The Thatcher Phenomenon* (London: BBC, 1986) 98–9.
13. Helen Wallace and William Wallace, 'Reversing the Ratchet in Foreign Policy: Will the World Let You Change Your Mind?', Public Administration Conference (1986); Robert Putnam and Nicholas Bayne, *Hanging Together: Cooperation and Conflict in the Seven-Power Summits*, 2nd edn (London: Sage, 1987) 227–34.
14. See Peter Byrd (ed.), *Foreign Policy Under Thatcher* (London: Butterworths, 1988).
15. Michael Clarke, 'The Defence Debate in Britain', in John Roper and Karl Kaiser (eds), *British–German Defence Cooperation* (London: Jane's, 1987).
16. One notable exception, apparently ignored, was Hugh Thomas, *The Socialist Challenge* (London: Fontana, 1974).
17. Michael Clarke, 'The Implementation of Britain's CSCE Policy, 1975–84', in Steve Smith and Michael Clarke (eds), *Foreign Policy Implementation* (London: Allen & Unwin, 1985).
18. Second report from the Foreign Affairs Committee, 1985–86, *UK–Soviet Relations, vol. II, Minutes of Evidence and Appendices*, HC 28-II, 277–87.
19. Clarke, 'Anglo–Soviet Relations' (Note 10).
20. British Council Resource Allocation Working Group, *Activity review, British Council Scholarships, Courses and Visitors* (April 1984) para.

4.3, 4.4.; Second Report from the Foreign Affairs Committee, 1985–86; *UK–Soviet Relations, vol. I, Report*, HC 28-I, 1–11.

21. Central Statistical Office, *Annual Abstract of Statistics 1985* (London: HMSO, 1986) Tables 10.36, 10.37, 215–16.
22. Dennis Kavanagh, *Thatcherism and British Politics: The End of Consensus?* (Oxford: Oxford University Press, 1987) 108–9.
23. In 1988 the Labour leadership began to make an attempt to draw upon the ideas of organisations such as Just Defence. There were fringe meetings at the 1988 party conference on the issues raised by common security.
24. Crewe, 'Britain' (Note 5) 32.
25. See Labour Party, *The Power to Defend Our Country* (London: Labour Party, December 1986) also, *Defence and Security for Britain* (London: Labour Party, 1987). For commentary, see Report for the Subcommittee on Europe and the Middle East, House of Representatives, Committee on Foreign Affairs, *Challenges to NATO's Consensus: West European Attitudes and US Policy* (Washington, D.C.: Congressional Research Service, 1987) 39–44.
26. *Gallup Political Index*, 322 (June 1987) (London: Gallup Organisation) 29.
27. See Liberal Party, *Defence and Disarmament* (London: Liberal Party, June 1986).
28. See Philip Sabin (ed.), *The Future of UK Air Power* (London: Jane's 1988).
29. *Gallup Political Index*, 318, (February 1987) 11; *Gallup Political Index*, 323 (July 1987) 12 (London: Gallup Organisation).

9 European Security: Hungarian Interpretations, Perceptions and Foreign Policy

László J. Kiss

1 INTRODUCTION

In Hungary, debate on the forms and substance of European security; on questions of alliance; on international security; and on the distinctions between 'common', 'mutual', 'equal', and 'cooperative' security, is effectively non-existent, whilst alternative notions such as non-offensive defence have yet to acquire real intellectual currency. Nor is there public discussion by the various social or political groups of alternative security policies. It is nonetheless possible to piece together a specifically Hungarian approach to European security, and to security in general, from the history of Hungary's relation to Europe, from the shifting perception revealed by opinion polls of the image of the adversary, and not least from Hungarian foreign policy itself, in which considerations of security are paramount. Clearly, the homogenising effect of systems of alliance is felt predominantly in the military sphere. The specificity of the Hungarian approach to European security is thus best sought in the non-military sphere.

The object of this study is to consider the meaning for Hungary of notions of security, European and general, from a non-military perspective. Three main areas are distinguished:

1. The implications for Hungary's position in Europe of (a) Hungarian history and (b) the Helsinki process.
2. The specificity of the Hungarian perception of security (changes in the image of the adversary, the excessive influence of economic considerations in matters of security, systemic identity and security, etc.).
3. European security and Hungarian foreign policy.

2 DEPENDENCE ON EUROPE

The subject of European security as such is not discussed in Hungary. But since the late 1970s much has been published concerning (i) the relation to Europe implied by Hungary's past and (ii) the meaning of the notion: 'Europe'. How many 'Europes' go to make up Europe? What are the different roles of these partial Europes relative to Europe as a whole? Is there a true European identity – and, if so, in what does it consist? Why has the economic development of Hungary fallen behind that of the West? Is this to be explained by a 'psychosis of belated development', or as a consequence of Hungary's marginal and subordinate role in the world economy? That these questions are integral to the Hungarian perception of security the events of the early 1980s have made clear.[1]

2.1 Mutual Dependence in a Nuclear Age

Nuclear weapons have, since 1983, faded from the political agenda, and the direct nuclear threat to both parts of Europe has in consequence attained a new level of concreteness and generality. Small to medium-sized European countries, though vulnerable to outside pressure, cannot help but perceive in the threat of nuclear war an enhancement of mutual dependence, and with it the need to foster and maintain international contacts. The growing danger of nuclear war, and the perception of it as the 'common enemy', has had a 'moderating' effect. This has issued in policies of 'damage limitation', which, though not exclusive of loyalty to a particular alliance, have transcended the bloc systems. The relations of the small and medium-sized countries in the two halves of Europe have not conformed to the shifts in the relations of the two superpowers, and Hungary's foreign policy has been a spectacular example of this. The need for a new conceptual model adequate to the nuclear era has been as influential a factor in the creation of this policy as more immediately practical considerations.[2]

At the same time, the Chernobyl disaster served to illustrate the reality of mutual dependence in the nuclear age – that is, that people and societies in both parts of Europe are in equal measure exposed to the dangers implicit in a new technology. It highlighted issues of *ecological, or environmental security*; nuclear war could now be seen as the ultimate ecological catastrophe.

For Hungary, this new emphasis on *European interdependence* is associated with the effects of the technological revolution, which, subsequent to the oil crisis of the 1970s, dramatically accelerated the redistribution of political and economic power in the world. That revolution coincided with the depletion of Hungarian natural resources, the perceived failure of the earlier East European development model, and thus with the need for a radically new development paradigm. For Hungary, to 'stay European' was not only not to lag behind, it was also (and even predominantly) not to repeat a developmental deviation such as occurred in the sixteenth century.[3] The widening economic differentials between the different regions of Europe (the deepening of economic and technological divisions, the increasing danger of the marginalisation of Eastern Europe and of East–West economic relations, etc.) came to be seen as a threat not merely to the security of Hungary, but to that of Europe as a whole.

This is no coincidence. The relevance of the history of Hungarian development to contemporary perceptions of European and Hungarian security is clear. A distinctive feature of Hungary's development has been the geopolitically determined, historically changing, peripheral status of the country, a pattern we shall refer to as 'two-way determinism'. Throughout its development, Hungary has exhibited features characteristic of the periphery of now Eastern, now Western development models.[4]

The creation of the Hungarian state, and its incorporation, into the feudal states of Europe implied a 'Westernised' development model. Hungary's development deviated from this path in the sixteenth century, when the country was divided into three parts, and the 150-year Ottoman occupation of a large part of its territory began. This deviation may be described as a process of 'Orientalisation'. From the end of the seventeenth century, Hungarian development under the Habsburg hegemony was Middle-European, exhibiting features characteristic of regions both East and West of the Elbe. The historical determinants at work in this process were two-way: bourgeois-capitalist development occurred, but occurred under political structures that were fundamentally feudal, nor did modernisation result in a qualitative breakthrough.[5]

Though the new political and territorial status quo that emerged after the Second World War created clear divisions in Europe, the effects of dual peripheral status or two-way determinism remained perceptible in Hungary. From the end of the 1940s, Hungarian development was mechanically copied from the Soviet model. National differences took second place to this priority. From the early 1960s, there was a gradual return to a policy taking national differences into account, and in 1968 Hungary implemented the sole economic reform programme attempted in Eastern Europe at that time. Internal economic reform and accelerating integration into the world economy during détente made further adaptation necessary. The historical legacy of two-way determinism became more marked during the shifts in the world economy of the 1970s and 1980s; in this regard, the political causes of Hungary's failure to adapt to the new conditions are exemplary. Though a member of the Warsaw Pact and of Comecon, Hungary became increasingly involved with the international monetary and trade systems. The goals of simultaneously adapting to Comecon, the world economy, and prevailing conditions in Hungary, were, if not mutually exclusive, extremely disparate. And this has been the task facing Hungarian foreign and security policies: to coordinate Hungary's integration into the world economy, and particularly its 'eurocentric' East–West economic relations, with a position within the political, economic and military alliance led by the Soviet Union. Hungarian interests have remained 'eurocentric' even in a world not centred on Europe. It follows that Hungary has a particular interest in the success of the Helsinki Process, since the latter is intended to create institutional frameworks for confidence and security-building within Europe. It may moreover prove instrumental in promoting the historically determined two-way adaptation of structures in Hungary, while defusing the tensions to which they give rise.

2.2 European Identity

Reference to 'European solidarity' or a 'European identity' calls forth several interrelated aspects of the Hungarian perception. On the one hand, clearly, in this era of interdependence and globalisation, it is both possible and necessary to speak of unity between the two parts of Europe. On the other, it is equally clear that Europe has always comprised a variety of regions of different levels of political, social and economic development, and not simply a geopolitical, geostrategic and geoeconomic unit.[6]

The emphasis on 'European identity' in Hungarian policy, particularly in the face of the growing nuclear threat of the early 1980s, called attention to the fact that European countries, regardless of their political system or their treaty obligations, faced the same threat of annihilation. At the same time, the 'Europeanisation' of Hungarian foreign policy witnessed to the perceived need for national security to be sought in the context of an active policy of East–West coexistence.

For Hungary, the notion of 'European identity' expresses an awareness of Europe as the 'common cultural homeland', of the fact that Europe is, despite its political division, a single cultural whole, with a diversity of links that even the Cold War years could not wholly dissever. And in the maintenance of East–West relations, the relative autonomy of culture has a major role to play. Culture expresses the interests of Europe as a whole, and its subordination to politics is intolerable. This is so even if culture is not merely a form of liaison beween societies but a means by which the values arising from different social systems can be transmitted.[7] 'European identity' also evokes for Hungarians a revival of local identities within Europe, of both historical traditions and models of sub-regional cooperation (we may cite Hungaro–Austrian cooperation), insofar as these contribute to European security.

A similar paradox governs modernisation in the Central European context. Modernisation in response to external challenges has, in Central and Eastern Europe, been carried out by the state. By increasing its already preponderant role, the state 'East-Europeanises' the society, yet the process of modernisation is intended to have the opposite effect – that is, the promotion of structures and models of 'Western' kind, which extend the autonomy of civil society. An example of such modernisation occurred after 1945, when 'external models' were adopted (socialist modernisation) and the role of the state was enlarged. The attempt to close the gap between Eastern Europe and the West did not merely involve transplanting Western cultural models; it also involved a degree of identification with the West. Yet for East European countries, a part of the purpose of modernisation was precisely to protect their own identity, and to protect it *vis-à-vis* the West. The contradiction is clear, and this conflict between fundamentalism and modernisation remains a feature of today's Europe.[8]

3 THREATS TO HUNGARIAN SECURITY

Images of the adversary – that is, answers to questions such as 'Who is the enemy?' and 'Where does the danger lie?' – have a paramount role in the construction of security policy. It is in precisely this area, in the disparity between traditional images of the adversary and politico–economic realities, that changes in the Hungarian perception of security have occurred, as successive opinion polls have shown.[9]

The imminence of nuclear threat in Europe not only enhanced the sense of the interdependence of small countries; it also gave to the threat of nuclear holocaust the status of 'common enemy', and this had a considerable impact on the role and efficacy of the traditional (Cold War) images of the politico–ideological enemy. In Hungary, the term 'small country' evoked, rather than any acknowledgement of socio–ideological differences, a sense of the threat hanging over Europe as a whole – the sense of being a target.

In the period termed 'after-arming', the Hungarian media spoke concurrently (i) of the condemnation evoked by the deployment of US missiles in Western Europe (a traditional image of the adversary as a multiple alliance), (ii) of the tension-reducing effects of intensifying political, economic and cultural relations between Hungary and the West, with particular reference to Western Europe, and (iii) of bilateral attempts to maintain the East–West dialogue, and the contribution these had made to the amelioration of European security. When in 1984 Soviet–US and Soviet–West German relations were at rock bottom, there was no corresponding deterioration in Hungarian–US or Hungarian–West German relations. The situation was perceived not only in terms of the increasing threat of nuclear war in Europe, but in relation to the integration of the Hungarian economy into the world economy. The maintenance and development of East–West political and economic relations were thus indissociable from Hungary's own domestic stability, and the pursuit of an active policy of East–West coexistence was clearly in the national interest.

The heritage of détente was also a significant influence at this juncture. The Cold War 'enemy', to become a 'partner' in the process of détente, had metamorphosed into nothing more threatening than a 'political adversary'.[10] And particularly for the small countries, a trading partner could not overnight resume the status of an ideological and political 'enemy'. Genuine détente means a transformation or elimination for both sides of the image of the adversary, *and not simply an updating of that image*. Relinquishing the monolithic images of the adversary born of the Cold War, and making them relative to particular situations or goals, had a further effect – that of focusing attention on the need for a new conceptual model adequate to the nuclear age, and in particular, on the need to evolve *a tradition of non-military conflict management valid for Europe as a whole*.

A corollary of the shifts in the image of the adversary is the weight assumed in the Hungarian perception of security by economic factors, indeed an overemphasis on this aspect and a sense of economic threat. Hungary is not in the central strategic zone of Europe, and her neighbourly relations with neutral Austria and non-aligned Yugoslavia are a source of particular satisfaction. The nuclear threat is a real one, but the overriding fear is of the economic threat to European security, along with the destabilising effect of the current system of alliances. A glance at the relevant Hungarian literature confirms this. According to one Hungarian author, the losses ensuing from the belated reaction of the Hungarian economy to changes in the world economy in the period 1974–84 were equivalent to those suffered during the Second World War.[11] Other authors have pointed out that the imbrication of economic and political processes, and the ever higher degree of interdependence that follows from the international division of labour, have created conditions favourable to non-military power politics being practised. They speak of 'economic deterrence' and 'economic cold war'.[12] Another Hungarian writer has declared that action against the 'economic cold war' cannot fail to form part of the broader strategy of the peace movement.[13]

Throughout the world, economic factors have an increasing incidence on security, but the reasons that govern the perhaps excessive influence they exert in the Hungarian perception of security are other and more specific.

The open structure and extreme sensitivity of the world economy have meant that the proportion of external economic input in Hungarian security and foreign policies is excessive. History nevertheless suggests that a foreign policy determined largely by economic considerations is perfectly able to promote international confidence-building, to formulate long-term objectives based on mutual benefit, and to defend national interests. Long-term economic relations exert a stabilising influence relative to the fluctuations that superpower and East–West relations periodically undergo.

It follows that one of the greatest dangers for European security consists in the effects of economic restructuring, of 'economic war' waged through discrimination and embargo. Thus during the 1970s, the principal levers of the East–West division of labour were oil prices and the availability of Western credit. These have been of less account during the 1980s, and have not been replaced. It is, moreover, anomalous that trade in processed industrial goods should have fallen away at a time of scientific and technological advance. The problems common to the two parts of Europe have increased, while the framework of the international division of labour has narrowed. The conclusion is clear: if economic relations cannot lay the foundations for a 'second détente', if the marginalisation of East–West trade relations continues, and if as a result the political and techno–economic divisions of Europe, with the consequent widening of growth-rate differentials, are reinforced, then the very foundations of European security will be undermined. Improved economic relations are not necessarily a concomitant of an improvement in the political climate, but instability in the economic field cannot help but infect political relations and thus security.[14]

This gives added point to the Hungarian contention that the Helsinki Process should be supplemented by treaties regulating the relations between EEC and Comecon countries. An institutional framework of this kind, involving continuous assessment of the efficacy of East European policy toward the West and towards Europe as a whole, would eliminate short-term variations and would reinforce the security-promoting effect of an active policy of coexistence.

The situation in Hungary is further complicated by the fact that though the primary thrust of the reforms of 1968 was economic, questions not specifically economic typically assume economic guise, and in particular Hungarian interests expressive of national peculiarities. And it is precisely these interests that, along with the Hungarian economy, indeed the system as a whole, have been jeopardized by the transformation of the world economy over the last decade – and by Hungary's failure to react promptly or efficiently thereto. As a result, it became something of an ideological tenet to exaggerate the implications for security of economic considerations, and this attitude was reflected in security policy. Hungary's loss of status in the world economy was thus initially ascribed on the Hungarian side to the negative impact of the change in the world economic environment. It was said that 'external world economic insecurity' was threatening 'internal economic security'. This took no account of the fact that economic security can exist only in a context of potential economic insecurity, and that the latter could be mitigated by adopting the relevant internal economic measures.

Hungarian writings on the subject of *political* security tend to distinguish external or international from internal or societal security. The latter is taken to include economic security, not merely that of the society as a whole, but of individuals and families. Internal and external security, like national and international security, or the security of adversaries and allies, cannot be considered in isolation.[15]

For Hungary, it is of interest to consider the extent to which 'systemic identity' depends on external factors, and how internal or societal security can be influenced by disorders of systemic identity. Some authors refer to the possibility of internally motivated 'disorders of identity' becoming internationalised either spontaneously or through outside pressure. It is vital to strengthen societal security, as it constitutes the principal determinant of the international security of a country.[16]

The notion of systemic identity is central here. On the one hand, as the authors point out, that a country should belong to the network of international relations or to a sub-system thereof would not in itself constitute a motive for wanting to change its systemic identity, that is 'the essential identity of its social system'.[17] On the other, spontaneous internal change cannot be dissociated from the issue of systemic identity. The identity of a society is subject to change; 'the dynamic movement of the social status quo is an integral part of societal security', nor can 'recognition of the political and societal status quo, that is, détente, rule out social movement or change deriving from internal causes'.[18] Debate in Hungary has tended to suggest a relationship between 'systemic security' and international interdependence. To the extent that security depends on international cooperation, international interdependence is the concept that governs more and more aspects of security, and this is particularly true for small countries which depend heavily on the international division of labour. Shifts in the traditional image of socialism also shed new light on the question of systemic identity.

4 SMALL-STATE FOREIGN POLICY DOCTRINE

The Hungarian perception of security has manifested itself in Hungarian foreign policy, and in particular in the concept it has embodied of the role of small countries (the 'small-state doctrine', as we might call it). This policy, in which security considerations obviously weigh heavily, is based on the following ideas:

1. For Hungary, a policy of active coexistence between East and West is in the national interest, and as such also constitutes a form

of cooperative security policy. This form of limited East–West cooperation (détente) is the most effective way of compensating the disadvantages, and thus meeting the security needs, of an open and highly vulnerable country possessed of few geoeconomic endowments and a sensitive geopolitical situation. It is not a matter of chance that, even at the height of East–West tension, Hungarian politicians continued to use the word 'détente' and spoke or at least wrote of a 'cooling-off period in detente'.[19]

2. Two processes continue simultaneously in the international arena. On the one hand, the superpowers play a genuinely dominant role. On the other, the small and medium-sized countries assume a greater role in fostering East–West dialogue, seeking mutually acceptable compromises, and encouraging diplomatic activity that transcends the bloc purview. Damage limitation and the development of East–West relations are the goals in view. The smaller countries in this way come to have a share of responsibility regardless of their size, and a motivation to assume that responsibility in inverse proportion to their size, for, the smaller the country, the greater the extent to which its security depends on international cooperation.[20]
3. Formerly, socialist countries would subordinate their national interests to common goals and shared interests, but this subordination ceased in the 1980s and is likely to recur only in 'emergency situations'. The relative merits of shared and national interests can now be decided on an empirical basis. Moreover, historical and other connections may facilitate the development of relations between socialist and capitalist countries, even where this runs temporarily counter to the general trend of international relations. The attempt to evaluate relations with Western countries exclusively through the prism of Soviet–US relations is now recognised as simplistic.[21]
4. Though military threats are not today conditional on physical proximity, the European (and more particularly the Central European) regions are those most closely identified with Hungary's security. The 'whole-Europe consciousness' and the phraseology of 'Europe-wide cooperation' testify to a 'Europeanisation' of Hungarian foreign policy which is at one with the interests of both Hungary and its allies. They also suggest how 'Europe-wide' – East–West cooperative interests are, in the long term, integrated into and explicitly formulated in Hungarian foreign policy. During the Cold War, the policies of Eastern bloc countries towards the

West conformed to the politics of the bloc. The early 1980s proved a watermark in this regard, and thereafter to the interests of nation and alliance were added the European – that is, 'whole-Europe' – interests which, transcending bloc interests, contribute to European security by expressing national interests without detriment to alliance interests.

5. For Hungary, the cause of 'whole-Europeanisation' as against 'partial-Europeanisation' (the European Community, Comecon, the North Atlantic Treaty Organisation, the Warsaw Pact) is best represented by the Helsinki Process. By its agency, the discords at the root of the East–West conflict can perhaps be articulated in terms of a sort of 'whole-European domestic policy', a culture of conflict management be evolved with the aid and participation of the two superpowers and, last but not least, the multidirectional adaptation of the policies and economy of Hungary be facilitated.
6. The dynamic of the Helsinki Process creates favourable opportunities for multilateral attention to the national interests of individual countries and, in the Hungarian view, for promotion of the cultures of the minority peoples of Europe, for fuller enjoyment by minorities or nationalities of their rights, and for the better regulation of East–West economic exchanges. Moreover, the Helsinki Agreement, and particularly its Final Act, legitimate the cultivation of cross-bloc relations even in periods of superpower tension. In 1976–9 and again in 1986, Hungary reviewed Hungarian implementation of the Final Act and formulated proposals for further improving relations, such as the abolition of visas. The Helsinki Process reaffirmed not only the status quo in Europe, but also the fact that the blocs belonged together in Europe. For Hungary, it has also played a major role in reviving historical traditions of confidence and security-building. The Hungaro–Austrian sub-regional cooperation could not have attained its current dynamism without the Helsinki Process. Lastly, the Process has had a beneficial effect on Hungarian domestic policy, for example in the implementation of economic and financial reforms, of joint economic ventures, and in the improved working conditions accorded to foreign correspondents.

Notes and References

1. See Zsigmond Pál Pach, *A nemzettudatról napjainkban* (On National Identity Today), Társadalmi Szemle (January 1986) 28; Elemér Hankiss, *A megkésett ipari forradalom kényszerpályája* (Pressures of a Belated Industrial Revolution), in Elemér Hankiss, *Diagnózisok 2* (Diagnoses II) (Budapest: Magvető, 1986) 360–4; Iván T. Berend, *Felzárkózás vagy lemaradás* (Catching up or Lagging Behind), in Iván T. Berend, *Szocializmus és reform* (Socialism and Reform) (Budapest: Akadémiai Kiadó, 1986). 140; Péter Hanák, *Gab es eine mitteleuropäische Identität in der Geschichte?*, *Europäische Rundschau*, no. 3 (1986) 115–25.
2. Gyula Horn, *Társadalmi-politikai tendenciák Európában és hatásuk a nemzetközi kapcsolatokra* (Socio–Political Trends in Europe and Their Impact on International Relations), *Külpolitika*, no. 3 (1984) 34. As early as 1984 the author made the point that the duel of the two opposing social systems was impossible to decide by weapons and hence the concept of 'just war' stopped being meaningful.
3. Berend, *Szocialismus és reform*, 140; Pach, *A nemzettudatról napjainkban*, 28.
4. See Jenő Szücs *Európa három történeti régiójá-ról* (On the Three Historical Regions of Europe), *Történelmi Szemle*, no. 3 (1981) 313–60.
5. Ivan T. Berend, *Kitörési pontok. Dilemmák a gazdaságról* (Points of Sally. Dilemmas about the Economy), *Magyar Nemzet*, 24 December 1984.
6. See Mihály Simai, *Az európai béke ötödik évtizede* (The Fifth Decade of Peace in Europe), *Valóság*, no. 12 (1985) p. 7.
7. See T. Csaba Szanki, *Gondolatok a kelet-nyugati kulturális kapcsolatokról* (Reflections about East–West Cultural Relations), *Külpolitika*, no. 2 (1986) p. 19; Béla Köpeczi, *Magyarország és Európa a kulturális együttmüködés folyamatában* (Hungary and Europe in the Process of Cultural Cooperation), *Külpolitika*, no. 3 (1984) p. 62; József Bényi, *Európa és a Kulturális Fórum* (Europe and the Cultural Forum), *Külpolitika*, no. 2 (1986) p. 3.
8. See Iván Vitányi, *Az 'Európa-paradigma'* (The 'Europe Paradigm') (Budapest: Magvető, 1986) 83; Kálmán Kulcsár, *A modernizáció és a magyar társadalom* (Modernization and Hungarian Society) (Budapest: Magvető, 1986).
9. See Guy Lázár, *Foreign Policy Information and Peace*, in *Studies on Peace Research*, Centre for Peace Research Coordination of the Hungarian Academy of Sciences (Budapest, 1986) 223–4.
10. See Peter Bender, *Das Ende des ideologischen Zeitalters. Die Europäisierung Europas* (Berlin: Siedler, 1981) 114.
11. Ivan T. Berend, *Felzárkózás vagy lemaradás* (Note 1) 135–6.
12. See Tibor Palánkai, *A gazdasági háboru néhány kérdése* (Some Questions of the Economic War), *Külpolitika*, no. 1 (1985) 59–81; Béla Kádár, *Gazdasági-müszaki fejlődés és stratégiai gondolkodás* (Economic–Technological Development and Strategic Thinking), *Külpolitika*, no. 4 (1981) 36–65.

13. Palánkai, *A gazdasági háboru néhány kérdése* (Note 12) 71–2.
14. See András-Nötzold Inotai and Klaus Jürgen-Schröder, *Szakaszhatár vagy fordulópont a keletnyugati gazdasági kapcsolatainkban?* (End of Stage or Turning Point in Our East–West Economic Relations?), *Külpolitika*, no. 2 (1987) 34–65.
15. József Balázs, *A biztonság értelmezéséről* (On the Perception of Security), *Külpolitika*, no. 5 (1983) 7–8.
16. János Berecz, *A nemzetközi biztonság kérdései napjainkban* (Questions of International Security Today), *Külpolitika*, no. 1 (1982) 13.
17. Balázs, *A biztonság értelmézéseről* (note 15) 8.
18. Balázs, *A biztonság értelmézeséről* (Note 15) 8.
19. Gyula Horn, *Enyhülés és konfrontáció a kelet-nyugati kapcsolatokban* (Détente and Confrontation in East–West Relations), *Külpolitika*, no. 1 (1986) 8.
20. See Mátyás Szürös, *A magyar külpolitika a nyolcvanas évek közepén* (Hungarian Foreign Policy in the Mid-1980s), *Külpolitika*, no. 4 (1985) 10; Gyula Horn, *A békés együttélés uj dimenziói* (New Dimensions of Peaceful Coexistence), *Külpolitika*, no. 1 (1987) 12.
21. Mátyás Szürös, *Interaction of National and International Interests in Hungarian Foreign Policy*, in *Studies on Peace Research*, Centre for Peace Research Coordination of the Hungarian Academy of Sciences (1986) 10.

10 A Hungarian Concept of Security

Pierre Lemaitre

1 INTRODUCTION

Of all the socialist states, it is Hungary that has adopted most elements of the Western politico–economic system; it has indeed developed a new concept of socialism. These facts are widely recognised. What is less well known is that even before Gorbachev came to power in the Soviet Union, and as early as the first half of the 1980s, a new outlook on international security was discernable in official Hungarian articles. This new outlook was presented alongside the traditional Marxist–Leninist discourse on war, peace and peaceful coexistence. The new concept stresses, for example, that the Warsaw Pact *and NATO* are peace-keeping forces – quite a novelty, given that traditional Marxist–Leninist thinking defines the military forces of capitalist states as aggressive; they are considered the instrument of a social system inherently prone to war. According to the new Hungarian concept, 'the socialist community is invariably . . . in favour of world political stability',[1] and also favours stable economic development in the capitalist states. From the perspective of traditional doctrine, this is wishful thinking; capitalism is crisis-ridden and 'moribund'.[2]

Another paradox is that the new Hungarian concept surfaced at a time of extreme tension between the two superpowers, when President Reagan had designated the Soviet Union the 'evil empire', and the Soviet Union had compared the USA with Nazi Germany and warned about the growing danger of a Third World War. At such a time, public disagreement among allies is unexpected. Why did a radical new concept of security surface in official Hungarian articles at this point? Was the new thinking fundamental or just a variety of 'peaceful coexistence'? What processes led to the inception of so radically different an outlook? Did it have anything to do with the fact that Hungary was the socialist state that had adopted most elements of the capitalist system? Was it a uniquely Hungarian phenomenon, or was it an early expression of trends also at work in other socialist countries? The significance attaching to these questions at a time when other socialist countries are embarking on reform processes similar to that which has taken place in Hungary is at the root of the current author's attempt to identify the different elements of the new Hungarian security concept, the social forces and structures upholding it, and the societal processes and international dynamics that explain the development of the concept.[3] An analysis of the new Hungarian security concept is presented here, and in the final section (Section 6) there is a preliminary conclusion regarding the relationship between the Hungarian reform process and the development of thinking on security. A fuller study will be published at a later date.[4]

A first point is to determine whether the new Hungarian concept is a fundamental rethinking of international security or merely a tinkering with old concepts. For this purpose, an article representative of the new thinking, written by the leading security expert, József Balázs,[5] has been analysed and compared with Marxist–Leninist thinking of the late Brezhnev era. Entitled 'A Note on the Interpretation of Security', it was published in 1983 in Hungarian and in English in 1985.[6] Dr Balazs was at that time head of department at the Hungarian Institute of International Relations, a research institute under the authority of the Minister of Foreign Affairs.

2 WAR, PEACE AND PEACEFUL COEXISTENCE: THE BREZHNEV DISCOURSE

A key issue in the traditional Marxist–Leninist analysis of the international situation is war and pace.[7] The analysis was founded on the differences between the two social systems, the capitalist and the socialist, the one basically aggressive, the other basically peaceful. According to Lenin, when capitalism entered the stage of imperialism, large- as well as small-scale wars became 'inevitable'. The analysis of the Brezhnev period denies this, stating that when the socialist states attained approximate military parity with the capitalist states in the early 1970s, it became *possible* to avoid a Third World War. The attainment of parity had produced a number of 'realistic' people in the capitalist states, who, it was thought, perceived that a major war would gravely endanger the capitalist states too. The combined efforts of the socialist states and the 'realistic people' might succeed in countering the aggressive inclinations of the capitalist states. 'Security' was not a key theoretical concept within this discourse. When used, it referred mainly to the security of the socialist states, the only true forces for peace. Though a Third World War was not inevitable, it could not be excluded. The socialist states therefore prepared to fight such a war. It was considered possible to avoid it escalating to nuclear level by capturing Western Europe in a *blitzkrieg* operation. This would present the USA with a *fait accompli* and the impossible task of reconquering Europe.[8] The strategy called for huge conventional and nuclear forces on the part of the Warsaw Pact states. The military build-up was also considered a means of forcing the capitalist states to adopt détente and peaceful cooperation. The immediate task of the socialist states was to avoid a new war. But it was also considered important to work towards the elimination of the danger of war. As the capitalist system was considered fundamentally aggressive and the communist system fundamentally peaceful, this could only be done by changing the correlation of forces between the two systems – i.e., working for communism, a society of 'universal prosperity and enduring peace'.[9] The huge military build-up in Europe made it too dangerous to try to change the situation there; but the Third World was thought of as an area where the socialist countries could promote the cause of socialism. In the 1970s, the use of armed force, direct or indirect, was increasingly considered a legitimate means of effecting the necessary transformations.[10]

Peaceful coexistence between the two systems was regarded of vital importance considering the apocalyptic nature of nuclear war. An important element in 'peaceful coexistence' was economic, scientific and technological cooperation between the two systems. However, the view that market forces were a threat to the socialist system proved a major hurdle to such cooperation. The aim of technological and scientific self-sufficiency, dictated by security motives, limited cooperation in these fields too. It was also limited by the 'COCOM list', the list of products whose export to the East was prohibited on security grounds. This embargo was deemed necessary because in the West the socialist states were perceived as aggressive. The Western countries, judging the socialist states by their deeds rather than their words, found Eastern preparations for war a serious stumbling block to peaceful cooperation. It was hard to attach much credence to 'peaceful coexistence', when the reality was, for example, the invasion of Afghanistan. From the perspective of the socialist states, on the other hand, NATO military build-up and the use by some of the Western powers of military force to suppress uprisings in the

Third World, simply confirmed the traditional Marxist–Leninist perception of the aggressive nature of the capitalist states. Thus, while the Marxist–Leninist ruling elites' *desire* for peaceful coexistence was probably sincere,[11] the conceptual discourse in which it was imbedded was a major stumbling block to its realisation. The dynamic generated between the concept of socialism, the socialist discourse on war and peace, and between the two systems, tended to give a *very large role to military aspects of security and a very small one to the non-military aspects*. The question arises, whether the new Hungarian security concept offers better prospects.

3 INTERDEPENDENCE ENHANCING SECURITY

For the new Hungarian security concept, the point of departure was the establishment of the military balance between the capitalist and the socialist countries in the early 1970s. According to Balázs, a new and 'contradictory situation' has arisen in international security.[12] On the one hand, there is 'antagonistic confrontation' between the two systems, on the other, 'unification'. This 'unification' is brought about by several factors:

> the rapid development of the means of land, sea and air transport, the diffusion of the mass media have brought far-away continents close to one another. . . . The intensive economic and cultural links of the peoples, their constant political contacts and cooperation, . . . have turned the immense masses of people . . . into direct or indirect participants of the small and big events of the life of humanity. Even such destructive potentials of modern civilization as the thermonuclear weapons, . . . make everybody feel how closely his individual life is connected with humanity as a whole. Never has such a close relationship and mutual dependence developed among the most different social phenomena and processes, between the objective and subjective side of man's existence, between the international and the national, between the social and the individual as we can experience today. All this goes to show that humanity has reached a certain degree of historic community of interests only in our age.[13]

This is significantly different from the traditional Marxist–Leninist analysis. First, because *many* processes are discerned which promote 'unification' between the two systems. Not only are both sides threatened by nuclear weapons, but improved communication and economic, political and cultural links promote the 'community of interests' of humanity. Second, to the extent that the capitalist states interact with the socialist states, *the capitalist states, too, get a key, dynamic role in the peace-promoting process*.

4 FEWER CONCEPTUAL BARRIERS TO PEACEFUL COEXISTENCE

In the traditional Marxist–Leninist discourse on war and peace, the positive features were bestowed on the socialist, and the negative on the capitalist states. Analysis of the international situation was thus divided into two parts, one for the capitalist, the other for the socialist, states. Moreover, it was necessary to use different yardsticks for the different systems. The Soviet Union could thus accuse the USA of harming the cause of peace by direct and indirect military action against Nicaragua. On the other hand, the Soviet invasion of Afghanistan could be presented as serving the cause of peace, since it was intended to avoid a deterioration of the international balance of forces.

According to József Balázs, the important thing for the long-term peace perspective is to expand cooperation and interaction into many areas as a means of transforming both systems into agents of peace. In order to do so, it is necessary to apply the *same yardstick to the two systems*. This is possible despite the initial inequality of merits. The point of departure is a rough mutual balance of forces and a working mutual deterrence.[14] It is implicit in the following analysis that the *differences observable at the outset of the process become of less and less importance, as the process develops and transforms the two participants*. This view leads one to think in terms of the security of *both* systems. The application of the same yardstick (by and large – in the concrete examples, the yardstick serves mainly as something with which to beat the West) is an integral part of Dr Balázs's theoretical framework. It is especially noteworthy in the section on military security, if we keep in mind the traditional Marxist–Leninist analysis of NATO. Surveying 'the major dimensions of military security', Balázs refers to:

> The defence of peace, which is the very first task of the military sector. It is not immaterial if this function is performed through

> negotiations based on 'mutual deterrence', or on realities mutually tolerating the parties' interests and is kept at a low level of armaments.[15]

The threat to peace is thus not the armed forces of the capitalist states *as such* nor, for that matter, the arms of the socialist states. The threat is the arms dynamic – for which the socialist states too bear some responsibility.

Another barrier to the realisation of 'peaceful coexistence' was the preparation of the socialist states for fighting a war. As Dr Balázs holds that cooperation between the two systems transforms their relationship to a peaceful one, it is implicit that *at some stage preparation for war ceases to be necessary*, as the possibility of war between the two systems can be excluded. In recent articles the notion that increased interdependence leads to enhanced international security has been spelled out even more clearly. Thus, Gyula Horn, State Secretary in the Ministry of Foreign Affairs and a member of the Central Committee, writes;

> The best interests of the West and the need to strengthen its own security require that the situation on the opposing side should be balanced. . . . the development of economic, scientific and technical relations with the socialist countries, if based on equality and mutual benefits, promotes convergence of interests and ways of thinking along with the creation of a safer world. Creating unhampered economic contacts helps to break the bounds of geo-strategic confrontation.[16]

The question is whether cooperation between the two systems has reached a stage where war is excluded, and there is no further need to prepare for it. Or, whether any preparation beyond minimum deterrence is senseless anyway, because a European war between the two systems will destroy the continent anyway. Balázs's article is not clear on either of these issues, despite the importance for the dynamic between the systems (see section 2 above). If the answer to either of these crucial questions is affirmative, we might expect a Hungarian critique of Warsaw Pact strategy to follow. So far, few such critiques have been heard of in the West.

What is certain is that developments in the first half of the 1980s were, from the point of view of Hungarian concept of security, very threatening. The freeze in superpower relations, the militarisation of the international atmosphere, and the decision to deploy SS20s on the one hand, and cruise and Pershing II on the other, seemed likely to severe the economic, political, technological and scientific ties between East and West. It seemed that a retreat to the two-bloc system was imminent, foreclosing the processes conducive to peaceful relations between the two systems. This called for a Hungarian critique of both superpowers, if the Hungarian security concept was a serious one. And there *is* such a criticism in Balázs's article: 'It is unnecessary to put the other side, or ourselves, into an unjustified threat situation'.[17] This critique applies not only to the policy of the Reagan administration, but also to the foreign policy of the late Brezhnev era. In a traditional Marxist–Leninist discourse it is unthinkable to speak of unjustified threats to the other side, since the socialist system is inherently peaceful. Moreover, high-ranking security experts from more than one socialist country have, in interviews with the author, expressed the opinion that, due to the aging of the political leadership and the absence of any procedure of succession, the Soviet military had, to a very large extent, taken over the framing of Soviet security policy. Security was therefore conceived in military terms: more arms, more security. A further security goal was the expansion of the community of socialist states by military means in the Third World. In this context, Balázs's further statement: 'Military security has to be subordinated to politics'[18] ascribes to the Soviet Union, too, a measure of blame for increased international tension and for fuelling the arms race. It is characteristic of Balázs's discourse to criticise a notion of security defined in terms of armament. Balázs states that 'military security' is the 'most conspicuous factor', but the majority of his article is given over to non-military aspects of security. Even when he deals with military matters, it is mostly their non-military implications, for both East and West, that are discussed. It is the *development of non-military aspects of security that constitutes the dynamic element in Hungarian thinking on security*.

5 DOMESTIC DEVELOPMENTS AS THREATS TO SECURITY

Cooperation between the two systems is a key element in the new Hungarian concept of security. But how is cooperation to be established between two 'antagonistic' systems? According to Dr Balázs, it is wrong to try to 'dictate . . . internal conditions' to the other system. 'Internal forces' are the only acceptable agents of domestic change. However, this does not solve the problem, since *all* interaction between the two systems has an element of interference. The question is rather: what kind of interference is acceptable, what kind is unacceptable? This question is the more important as it stresses that international security is closely linked with the internal security of either social system. No clear distinction is made in the article between acceptable cooperation and unacceptable interference, but there are some indications:

> The social *status quo* in our days is beneficial to upholding social and international security. But the social *status quo* cannot remain unchanged for good as it would contradict the objective laws of historical development. Therefore – in accordance with the peoples' right to self-determination – the dynamic movement of the social *status quo* must be regarded as an integral part of social security.[19]

Noteworthy in this statement is the fact that threats to security do not only derive from internal developments and crisis in the capitalist countries. Internal developments in socialist countries can also threaten security. The crisis in Poland in 1980 is cited as an example of this.[20] The 'peoples' right to 'self-determination' also refers to the peoples of the socialist countries. It is acknowledged that certain models for building socialism can, *as such*, be a cause of revolt. In this way internal developments in the socialist states can be a threat to international security. It is further said that the function of 'internal security' is 'to ensure the political and economic power of a given ruling class, or survival of the given social system and an adequate degree of public security'[21] (a statement which refers to the socialist states too!). And, 'no state or country wishes to change its own social system merely because it wants to take an active part in a system or a sub-system of international relations'. It follows from this that cooperation between the two systems must not be a threat to the ruling elites or the social system, but should make the social system more secure. What makes the ruling elite or the social system secure, according to the Hungarian analysis? A factor explicitly named is 'economic security'. According to Balázs, 'the most important dimensions of economic security' are:

(1) The internal social and economic situation of a given country.
(2) The conditions, possibilities and level of participation in the

international division of labour. (3) The capacity of the given economy to satisfy not only its internal demands, but also the extent to which it can bear, tolerate and avert external pressure. (4) The renewing capability of the given economy.[22]

The surprising thing about this quotation is that the world market is considered not as a threat to the socialist system, but as a means of combating economic stagnation and social insecurity. The same goes for extensive scientific and technological cooperation. The *usefulness of both close links with the world market and scientific and technological cooperation with the West is now acknowledged, and this is causing the removal of yet further of the barriers which have hitherto limited the scope of peaceful coexistence.*

To sum up: the new Hungarian security concept represents a radically new outlook on security. The traditional Marxist–Leninist vocabulary is not eschewed; on the contrary, the concept is articulated largely by redefinitions and changes of emphasis. But the framework of analysis is completely new. The almost exclusive emphasis on military security that prevailed during the Brezhnev era has been supplanted by a concern with cooperation with the West. The same yardstick applies to the actions of both East and West. The starting point is military balance, but thereafter the priority is on non-military aspects of security. The capitalist states are accorded an important role in the promotion of peace.

6 THE CONCEPT OF SECURITY AND THE HUNGARIAN REFORM PROCESS

The preliminary conclusion of a study of the relationship between Hungarian societal development and the new thinking on security is that the new thinking is primarily to be explained by the dynamics of the Hungarian reform process.[23] The revolt in 1956 forced the communist party under the leadership of János Kádár fundamentally to rethink the concept of socialism. The reform process started out as a domestic reform, but as the process evolved it acquired more and more foreign policy implications.

The economic reform process began in 1968. In the industrial sector there were attempts at decentralisation and cooperation with the West. Like other socialist countries, Hungary obtained big loans from the West in order to import Western technology and consumer goods. During the late 1970s and early 1980s this policy ran into grave problems. Many of the loans had been squandered on unproductive projects, and because of the recession in the Western economies it became difficult to export, and thus to service the debt. However, the basic problem was the half-hearted nature of the reforms. These had left the political structure underlying the industrial sector intact and able to thwart attempts at economic reform. Therefore, unlike the reform in the agriculture and service sectors, the attempts at reforming the decisive industrial sector did not lead to a marked increase in the production of high-quality goods. These problems were exacerbated by a steep decline in the Hungarian terms of trade, leading to very serious balance of payments deficit in the early 1980s. This made it difficult to pay for Western spare parts, royalties for patents, imports of new machinery, etc. all of which had acquired a crucial importance for the dynamic sectors of Hungarian industry. The standard of living of large parts of the population was stagnating or declining. To get out of the impasse there seemed no alternative but to get huge loans from the West and launch a thorough economic reform; this included the introduction of market forces and of close integration with the world market. This was necessary not only for economic reasons, but also because these economic mechanisms could be used as a means of bypassing the political sabotage conducted by the old economic administration. Close economic relations to the West were thus vital. But the same was true of economic ties to the Soviet Union, as Hungary was dependent on the Soviet Union for import of oil and as a market for the export of low-quality goods.

Politically, too, the social system was suspended between East and West. Soviet tanks installed Kádár in power and have remained in Hungary ever since. Most of the Hungarian ruling elite was ideologically tied to the Soviet Communist Party. But the experience of the 1956 revolt and the ensuing reform process steadily moved Hungary towards a stronger leaning to the West and the Western political system. One of the lessons learned from the revolt was that the policy pursued during the Stalinist period, 'those who are not with us are against us' was wrong. Instead Kádár launched the national alliance policy: 'those who are not against us are with us'.[24] This policy was also motivated by the decimation of party membership after 1956. For that reason alone it was impossible for the Communist Party to retain a leading role in all areas of society. The ruling elite was dependent on expert advice, increasingly so as the society became more complex. The price set by the intellectuals for this alliance was political and human rights. Since 1962, there has been a slow but steady improvement in this field. Hungary was the first among the socialist states to allow several candidates to stand for a single post. The movement towards a Western-style, pluralist democracy has been fomented by other groups strengthened by the economic reform process: peasants, small entrepreneurs, doctors, artists, etc.

A factor which has strengthened Hungary's orientation towards the West is the fate of the Hungarian minorities in the surrounding countries. This is an issue on which feelings in Hungary run high. The Western powers' insistence on human rights has proved important in this respect, as it puts international pressure on Romania and Czechoslovakia in a situation where the socialist community has proved ineffective in securing the rights of the Hungarian minorities. Moreover, among the Hungarian population in general there is a very positive attitude towards the West, and a correspondingly negative one towards the socialist countries.

Because of the excesses of the Stalinist period and because the effects of the economic reforms were rather mixed, the ruling élite did not enjoy the support of the working class. The groups that benefited from the economic reform process considered the social system in Hungary the best among the socialist states, but their real ideal was the Western system. Consequently, though Janos Kádár enjoyed popular support and the social system was accepted, there was no positive backing for it. The social stability in the 1960s and the 1970s had to a high degree been secured through increased incomes, political reform and a steady opening to the West. But even the combination of domestic economic crisis and the freezing of East–West relations was not enough to persuade the Party leadership (against the will of the aging Kádár) to take steps towards political reform.

During the détente period in the 1970s Hungarian foreign and security policy was not distinctive. Hungary favoured a low profile in these areas, and the trend of international affairs seemed favourable, so no clear statement was called for. But the breakdown of détente seemed likely to mean an end to East–West cooperation, and went directly against the notion of security that had been developed in Hungary. It also held the prospect of a still narrower foreign policy space for Hungary.[25] The interplay between the domestic and the international crisis made the situation in Hungary critical. Vital interests were at stake for the Hungarian ruling elite. It was crucial to signal to the international community that Hungary had a standpoint of its own regarding the international situation, and was determined to continue the policy of good relations with both East and West. The signals were of three kinds. Visits to Hungary by the heads of state of all the major Western powers. Support for the standpoint of the GDR and Poland against Czechoslovakia and the Soviet Union concerning the right of the smaller socialist states to formulate a foreign policy according to their own national interests.[26] And, the floating of a *new concept of security*.

If this analysis of the relationship between the Hungarian reform process and the development of a new concept of security is correct it gives added significance to the statements in Dr Balázs's article on security. The premise that East–West cooperation is vital influences thinking on security policy in the direction of defusing the conflict between the two antagonistic systems. Dr Balázs states that 'the socialist community is invariably ... in favour of world political stability' and of creating 'an international climate which exerts a positive impact on all elements of security'.[27] He argues in favour of confidence-building measures and political rather than military resolution of conflicts.[28] And he expresses deep concern about the health of the capitalist economies.[29] He regrets the decline of the détente process, which 'brings benefits' to 'all people' – its demise, he says, is undermining 'political contacts between states and the development of mutually beneficial economic and cultural relations'.[30] These statements are consistent with the new Hungarian discourse on security. But their consonance with the situation of Hungary in the early 1980s, when the dependence of the Hungarian social system on the Western economies would have led to a serious domestic crisis if East–West relations had broken down, is even more striking.

Notes and References

1. József Balázs, 'A Note on the Interpretation of Security', *Development and Peace*, vol. 6 (Budapest, Spring 1985) 145.
2. G. Ziborov, 'Ideological and Political Aspects of War and Peace', *International Affairs*, no. 1 (Moscow, January 1983) 93.
3. This study forms part of the research project, Non-Military Aspects of European Security, at the Centre for Peace and Conflict Research, Copenhagen. The theoretical framework for this article is partly the

one developed by the project: Egbert Jahn, Pierre Lemaitre, Ole Wæver, 'European Security – Problems of Research on Non-Military Aspects', *Copenhagen Papers*, no. 1 (Copenhagen, 1987), and partly by the current author, Pierre Lemaitre, 'A Model For Analyzing The Development Of The Soviet Concept of Security And Arms Build Up' (forthcoming). I am indebted to my colleagues for comments on earlier drafts for this article.

4. Pierre Lemaitre, 'The Hungarian Reform Process and the new Thinking on Security' (forthcoming). This research project is now being expanded by a cooperation with Dr Pál Dunay.
5. I am indebted to Egbert Jahn for drawing my attention to this article. The representativity of the article has been checked by (a) comparing the analysis in the article used with articles on the same subject from that period, (b) asking top party officials and foreign civil servants, (c) asking well informed scholars and dissidents. For the new Hungarian security concept, see also the analysis by Pál Dunay, *Hungary's Security Policy*, Hamburger Beiträge, Heft 17 (Hamburg, 1987) and the study by László Kiss (Chapter 9) in this volume. And *Külpolitika*, 'International Security' (Budapest, 1988) special issue on international security, especially the articles by Gyula Horn, László Kiss and László Valki.
6. Regarding the English version, see Note 1 above. The version in Hungarian appeared in *Külpolitika*, No. 3 (1983). I want to express my thanks to the Hungarian Foreign Policy Institute and especially Dr László Kiss and Dr Magdolna Toth for having arranged interviews with a wide range of Hungarian experts on security. The interviews referred to in this article are not only the two which the author made with Dr József Balázs, but also interviews with other foreign policy experts.
7. P. H. Vigor, *The Soviet View of War, Peace and Neutrality* (London: Routledge & Kegan Paul, 1975). Egbert Jahn, 'Die Einfluss der Ideologie auf die Sowjetische Aussen- und Rustungspolitik', *Osteuropa* (May, June and July 1986). David Holloway, *The Soviet Union and the Arms Race* (New Haven and London: Yale University Press, 1984). Ziborov, 'Ideological and Political Aspects' (Note 2).
8. Alexei Arbatov: 'Military Doctrines', in USSR Academy of Sciences & Institute of World Economy and International Relations (ed.), *Disarmament and Security. Yearbook 1987* (Moscow: Novosti Press Agency, 1988). P.H. Vigor, *Soviet Blitzkrieg Theory* (London: Macmillan, 1983). James McConnell, 'The Irrelevance Today of Sokolovskiy's Book, Military Strategy', *Defense Analysis*, vol. 1, no. 4 1985, 243–54. Michael MccGwire, *Military Objectives in Soviet Foreign Policy* (Washington D.C.: Brookings, 1987).
9. Ziborov, 'Ideological and Political Aspects', 89, who is citing Lenin, *Collected Works*, vol. 27, p. 159.
10. Mark N. Katz, *The Third World in Soviet Military Thought* (London: Croom Helm, 1982).
11. It is the opinion of the present author that the concern about a Third World War of the ruling Soviet elite was sincere – among other things because of the suffering experienced during the Second World War.

12. Balázs (Note 1) 143ff.
13. Balázs (Note 1) 144.
14. Balázs (Note 1) 144.
15. Balázs (Note 1) 149.
16. Gyula Horn, 'Détente and Confrontation in East–West Relations', *The New Hungarian Quarterly*, Budapest, vol. XXVII, no. 102 (Summer 1986) 38.
17. Balázs (Note 1) 149.
18. Balázs (Note 1) 150.
19. Balázs (Note 1) 146.
20. Balázs (Note 1) 146ff.
21. Balázs (Note 1) 146.
22. Balázs (Note 1) 148.
23. Balázs (Note 4.)
24. Népszabadság, 21 January 1962.
25. 'Foreign policy space' is defined as the economic, political (including security) opportunities for a given state opened up by a certain trend in international affairs. For states heavily dependent on economic, scientific and political relations with other states, a narrowing (or broadening) of the foreign policy space will have wide-ranging domestic implications. Usually, for longish periods, the foreign policy space of smaller and medium-sized states is dictated by a certain constellation of the major powers/superpowers, certain patterns of international alliances, etc. Smaller and medium-sized powers will have to adapt to this space, and can have only marginal influence on international developments. However, at certain turns of history, the international situation is characterised by flux, leaving the smaller and medium-sized states, too, with the possibility of influencing the major trend emerging after the period of flux. This leaves the smaller and medium-sized states with a significant *choice* among different, possible, future development trends.
26. Ronald D. Asmus, 'East Berlin and Moscow: The Documentation of a Dispute', *Radio Free Europe Research Release,* RAD Background Report, 158 (Munich, 25 August 1984).
27. Balázs (Note 1) 145.
28. Balázs (Note 1) 149ff.
29. Balázs (Note 1) 148.
30. Balázs (Note 1) 145.

11 Common Security Versus Western Security Cooperation? The Debate on European Security in the Federal Republic of Germany

Berthold Meyer

1 'SECURITY': FROM A NARROWER TO A BROADER SENSE OF THE TERM

The West German debate on European security in the 1980s takes place at several levels; within the government, between the political parties, between military and scientific experts, and in the mass media. This breadth is a relatively new phenomenon. For a long time questions of international security were the preserve of military experts. Among the causes of this wider interest was the debate on the modernisation of INF weapons, which began with NATO's double track decision of 1979 and led to the emergence of a new peace movement. The following study concentrates on the role of the political parties and their representatives in government and parliament. This is because the parties play a central role in the political system of the Federal Republic of Germany.

Before embarking on a description of the debate, some observations about the word '*Sicherheit*' are in order. It has a far more comprehensive meaning than the equivalent expressions in English (security, safety, certainty) and French (*securité, sureté, garantié*). Its 'seemingly evident and unmistakable character which at the same time leaves its denotative content vague' imparts an 'emotionally appealing quality',[1] making it the 'crystallization point of widely differing associations'.[2] Public relations agencies and politicians exploit this in their demagogical approach to the security needs of the ordinary man.

It is, then, no mere accident that the two major political parties of the Federal Republic of Germany, the CDU/CSU and SPD, have, since 1957, based a number of election campaigns on appeals for security. The postwar struggles had by then been overcome, and many people who had striven to attain modest possessions had no wish to lose them. This was a significant factor in establishing the priority then accorded to security, a priority which for most people it has never lost. As a rule, the desire for economic security is placed higher on the personal scale of values than the wish to avert an external threat,[3] which must become fairly acute before displacing the priority accorded to economic security.[4]

The expression '*Sicherheitspolitik*' (security policy) has, in contrast to '*Sicherheit*' always referred to external security. (The term '*Sicherheit*' is used in a variety of other political contexts, notably in relation to securities social, economic and internal). '*Sicherheitspolitik*' (security policy) was originally used as a synonym for defence policy. It referred to military security – i.e., the arrangements necessary to protect the country against military attack or to construct a defence strategy. In this respect, the outlook of the early post-war period retained a decisive role for several decades. From the military point of view, Germany had been annihilated, and the FRG alone could not assert itself against a highly armed and – in the first few years after the war – openly expansionist Soviet Union. It was consequently dependent on an alliance with the USA and its West European neighbours. The Soviet Union was perceived in terms of its acts (expansionism) rather than its motives, even where these included a fear of a remilitarised Germany. The FRG thus acquired the habit of considering its security arrangements as purely reactive, and dictated by external threat. Security, like charity, began at home. Integration into NATO and the ensuing dependence on the US secret service for an estimation of the potential threat merely confirmed the FRG in its perception of its own passivity.

This conception of security can still be found in conservative circles. But in the 1960s other points of view began to emerge. The arms escalation was understood as the product of a vicious circle; the threat constituted by one side's deterrent called for the creation of a counter-deterrent which was in its turn perceived as a threat. Under this view, the desire to break out of the circle gained impetus. Moreover, with the events of the Cuban crisis came the realisation that neither party could emerge victorious from a nuclear war. In the West, this caused a security policy rethink which, on the one hand resulted in the NATO strategy of 'flexible response' and, on the other, in a political strategy based on the Harmel formula, 'defence + détente = security'. This broader understanding of the word 'security' created space for a wide range of non-military approaches – that is, means of settling conflict without recourse to war or the threat of force. A central aim is the creation of a network of various forms of interaction and international cooperation, the benefit of whose existence is greater for both sides than that accruing to either side from its destruction. This point of view determined the new '*Ostpolitik*' of the Social Democratic–Liberal coalition government of the FRG. The '*Ostverträge*' (bilateral treaties with different Warsaw Pact countries) negotiated in this spirit from 1970 onwards were crucial to the initiation of the CSCE process in 1972.

Last but not least, East–West talks bore another fruit; the recognition that the 'enemy' no less legitimately desired *his* security, and that this should be taken into account in one's own security arrangements. These attitudes took shape in sentiments such as 'One's own security also depends on the security needs of the other' and 'there is no security at the expense of the other'.[5] The philosophy expressed in these terms in the mid-1970s by the Liberals had its Social Democratic parallel in expressions such as 'security partnership'[6] and 'common security'.[7]

These approaches to security do not define the outer limits of the debate in the FRG. Sections of the Peace Movement and, in particular, the Green Party, assert that only policies that exclude the threat and use of force are peace policies. If peace is to be achieved, they believe, the East–West conflict must first be demilitarised.

2 THE DIFFERENT VIEWS IN THE DEBATE ON 'EUROPEANISATION'

When we speak of European security, which 'Europe' is meant? Apart from the geographical Europe which covers the continental region from the west of the Urals to the islands, security terminology admits several other senses:

1. The 'Europeanisation of security policies' generally refers to the strengthening of the defence capacities of the Western European bloc.

2. The 'Europeanisation of Europe' refers to the emancipation of the smaller Western and Eastern European states from the tutelage of the two superpowers.
3. Lastly, there is talk of a 'All-European Peace Order' which would include the two superpowers and which could quite possibly be achieved by deepening and furthering the CSCE process.

2.1 Security Policy Cooperation in Western Europe and NATO Membership

Two goals have governed the security policy of the Federal Republic of Germany: to secure the protection of the USA and at the same time to establish close cooperation with its Western European neighbours.[8] 'The West European Union' (WEU) was founded on the basis of the '1948 Mutual Assistance Pact of Brussels' after the collapse of the first 'West European Defence Community' (EDC). But it was always overshadowed by the transatlantic alliance (NATO), into which the FRG was integrated immediately after gaining sovereignty in 1955.

The policy of the first Chancellor of the FRG, Adenauer, was a dual bond to the West, to NATO and to the EEC. This was almost unanimously supported by his own party, the CDU. Both the Chancellor and a strong majority of his party at this time maintained that military strength gained through the Western alliance was a prerequisite for German reunification, and they denied that integration into the West would consolidate partition. To date there has been no substantial change as regards these tenets on the part of the Christian Parties, the CDU/CSU.[9] In the current debate on strengthening West European defence cooperation, the CDU/CSU favours reinforcing the European pillar of NATO as a means of strengthening the Alliance. A greater awareness of the conventional superiority of the Warsaw Pact Countries has contributed to this policy. Soviet expansion, where it concerns parts of the world from which the FRG imports raw materials or to which it exports goods, is also considered dangerous. In this context, strengthening the European pillar of NATO will lighten the European burden of the USA, and thus free it to act in the common interest of the West in other parts of the world. It would also obviate a criticism frequently heard in the USA, that the West European countries do not contribute enough to their own defence, and thus avert the danger of the USA withdrawing large numbers of troops from the FRG out of disappointment or anger. This is the line taken by the current CDU-led government.[10]

During the 1950s, the Social Democrats favoured a Western orientation, but opposed any permanent bond to the West as this endangered the reunification of Germany. The SPD has supported NATO since 1960, but seeks to reduce bloc confrontation to an extent that would eventually make the two blocs superfluous. When the SPD took over the chancellorship in 1969, this line determined the position of the Social Democrats on both *Ostpolitik* and closer Western European cooperation on security policies. Europe should be able to assert itself, and in questions of security, speak with one voice to the USA. This would prevent NATO serving as a cover for US global interests while enabling Western Europe to maintain a policy of détente in times of confrontation between the superpowers.[11]

The third political party, the FDP (Liberals), has been represented in the Bundestag since 1949. Its reservations on the subject of a Western alliance are similar to those of the SPD. The FDP was in favour of rearming and approved membership of the EDC and later of NATO, but opposed equipping the Bundeswehr (W. German Army) with nuclear weapons. Very early in its life, the FDP adopted 'détente' policies aimed at overcoming the division of Europe. In the current debate on Western Europeanisation, the Liberals, whose image is as 'the party of the foreign minister',[12] give a higher priority to the political development of the EEC towards a European Union (which would then be authorised to deal in security matters), than to the reinforcement of the European pillar of NATO.

The Green Party line on NATO differs radically from that of the other parties; it considers itself part of the peace movement and was first elected to the Bundestag in 1983. It would like to see the dissolution of the blocs in Europe and believes this would be facilitated by the FRG leaving NATO. It is consequently against all efforts in the direction of closer defence cooperation, and opposes handing over security policy authority to the EEC or a European Union. It perceives both these tendencies as reinforcing the militarisation of Europe and intensifying the East–West conflict.[13]

2.2 Nuclear Weapons and Partnership Priorities

A closer examination of the line of the three parties which favour both NATO and the reinforcement of its European pillar reveals several significant differences. These principally concern nuclear arms, the military presence of the USA in Western Europe, and the development of Franco–German relations on security policies.

According to the CDU/CSU, security can be guaranteed only by nuclear deterrence, at least until a strategic defence system purpose-designed for Europe-specific threats is installed.[14] Moreover, the majority consider that only the USA can provide this guarantee. There are, however, some well-known Christian Democrats who dream of a European nuclear force. Their endeavours are directed toward the FRG having a greater say in discussions on nuclear defence planning.[15] This became apparent in the spring of 1987, during a clash of opinions within the government on the 'zero-zero option' at the INF talks. Although these politicians managed to obtain US consent to the Bundeswehr's Pershing IA missiles being excluded from negotiations,[16] they were unable to prevent Chancellor Kohl – under pressure from Foreign Minister Genscher and majority public opinion – declaring that these weapons would be scrapped in 1992, when the INF disarmament process comes to an end.

The SPD and the FDP also consider nuclear deterrence necessary, at least for the time being. But both have long felt that the number of nuclear weapons deployed in Central Europe poses a problem, and the 'NATO Double Track Resolution', achieved during their coalition government, was intended to reduce this threat via arms control negotiations. While the majority of the SPD rescinded their support for this agreement in 1982, wanting to abandon INF 'rearmament',[17] in 1983 the FDP and CDU/CSU agreed to the deployment of Pershing II missiles. But when, in 1987, Gorbachev accepted the zero-zero option, the FDP endorsed it wholeheartedly, in marked contrast with its coalition partners.[18] At this stage the SPD introduced the idea of a 'nuclear-free corridor' in central Europe – an idea it had worked out jointly with the East German Socialist Unity ('Communist') Party. If this idea were implemented, it would eliminate the threat posed to the two German states by the shortest-range nuclear weapons.[19] That the FRG and GDR should alone be exposed to this category of weapon seems to the coalition partners unacceptable, but neither was prepared to support the corridor concept nor a third zero option for short-range missiles and nuclear artillery.[20] The Greens have scarcely been involved in this debate. Their aim remains the 'denuclearisation' of the whole of Europe.[21]

The continued presence of the US forces in Europe is closely related to the question of nuclear deterrence. More than any other party, the Christian Democrats fear that the Soviet Union might utilise its conventional superiority if the military balance in Europe tilted further toward the East. They would therefore oppose any reduction in the US forces even if the European pillar of NATO were strengthened. The other side of this coin is the fear that the reduction of nuclear forces in Europe might lead the US to rethink its commitment. This train of thought has been expressed by the leader of the parliamentary party of the CDU/CSU, Dregger, who has called for a 'European Security Union' in which France would play 'a leading role'.[22]

The SPD's thoughts on the need for Europe to assert itself include the possibility of a partial withdrawal of US troops, but this is not meant as a suggestion. In 1985, a draft programme for the long-term future drawn up by the SPD politician von Bülow excited lively public discussion in West Germany. Contrary to the allegations of the CDU/CSU, it did not propose the unilateral withdrawal of US troops. It suggested that around the year 2000, a withdrawal of Soviet troops to their country could be followed by a gradual withdrawal of US troops 'leaving a somewhat more symbolic force, in particular in West Berlin'.[23] The demand made by the SPD politician, Lafontaine, in the same context, that the FRG withdraw from the military integration of NATO, was retracted in early 1987.[24]

In FDP circles the presence of US troops is not an issue. The party favours the step by step creation of conventional balance through a 'Mutually Balanced Force Reduction Treaty'.[25] The Greens, by contrast, consider the withdrawal of all foreign troops from European states essential for peace in Europe.[26]

Progress in Western European non-military unity often depends on France and the FRG pulling together, and the Paris–Bonn axis is beginning to have a similar importance for West European security cooperation. Politicians of all shades who favour NATO participation for the FRG without exception favour stronger ties with France. This is not only in the context of the 'Western European Defence Union' and the 'Elysée Treaties', Franco–German treaties signed in 1963, but also with a view to France becoming a more reliable ally of NATO. There is less consensus on the subject of how to get France out of her self-chosen isolation. The 'Franco–German Tandem'[27] proposed by ex-chancellor Schmidt in 1984 was better received in the CDU/CSU than in his own party.[28] Chancellor Kohl in particular has made great efforts to strengthen the partnership with France. His proposal for a 'Franco–German Brigade'[29] has been accepted by the French government. Moreover, early in 1988, he and President Mitterrand signed an amendment to the Elysée Treaties creating a common Defense and Security Council.[30] Lastly, the two countries came to an agreement on building a common military helicopter.[31] The FDP has no detailed proposals on security policy cooperation with France, while the Greens are against strengthening relations on the grounds that the FRG could in this way gain access to nuclear arms.[32]

2.3 'Europeanisation of Europe' as Emancipation from the Superpowers

Strengthening the European pillar of NATO is not a new subject for the Bundestag but it was not termed the 'Europeanisation of Security Policies' until the revival of the WEU in 1984. As previously stated, the Greens will have nothing to do with this idea. They call instead for a 'Europeanisation of Europe'; this means, in the definition given by the peace movement, the 'emancipation of the East and West European States from their respective superpowers in order to overcome bloc confrontation in Europe and create a non-allied, new, European, demilitarized peace order'. They accuse the two governing parties and the SPD of limiting Europeanisation to the 'economic, political and military integration of Western Europe', and in so doing of hijacking the expression and depriving it of its original sense. They further maintain that it is a matter of indifference whether 'the process of "Europeanisation" remains an integral part of US global military policy or Western Europe develops into a third super power. Both would have extremely negative effects for peace'.[33]

The Greens also oppose formulae such as 'Europe for the Europeans' or 'the self-assertion of Europe'. These solutions appeal to patriotic sentiments. 'Europeanisation' of this type, they claim, often serves to mask the goal of 'attaining increased economic, political and military strength', which, in combination with new technologies, is intended to make Europe competitive even in the space race.[34]

In the opinion of the Greens, the EEC should remain a civil power, and should not, even in the long term, be given any authority in security matters. And they recommend that both Western and Eastern European states align themselves with the smaller neutral states rather than the superpowers.[35] The Greens' attitude toward the military blocs to a large extent mirrors the ideas of the peace movement of the early 1980s concerning a non-allied, nuclear-free Europe stretching from 'Poland to Portugal'.[36]

2.4 A European Peace Order with the Participation of the two Superpowers

Of ideas relating to the 'future of security in Europe',[37] the goal of overcoming bloc confrontation is the most widely shared. But, apart from the Greens and sections of the peace movement, most of those participating in the debate assume that the superpower 'spheres of interest' in Europe would remain intact, and that the superpowers themselves would play a leading role in reducing military tension.

Relatively high hopes are placed in the development of the CSCE process. Although there were and are party political differences on this point, the gap between the CDU/CSU on the one hand and the SPD and the FDP on the other has narrowed appreciably since 1975.

The Final Act of the Helsinki CSCE, negotiated between 1973 and 1975, was rejected, as the bilateral treaties between the FRG and the Warsaw Pact countries had been, by the CDU/CSU opposition of the time. Their criticism of the SDP/FDP détente policy principally concerned the FRG's recognition of the territorial status quo, for which no equivalent gesture on human rights or freedom of movement was required.[38] It found an echo in criticism vented on later governments for not insisting that the GDR and the Soviet Union comply with the principles laid down in the Final Act. However, now that they are in power, the CDU/CSU are apparently prepared to make constructive use of the opportunities offered by the CSCE process.[39]

Between 1970 and 1982, the SPD and the FDP used their 'new *Ostpolitik*' to negotiate the *Ostverträge* (Bilateral Treaties with countries of the WTO) which paved the way for the CSCE. The social–liberal coalition broke up in 1982, but both parties have remained loyal to the policy of détente and do what they can to carry this policy over into a new phase.[40] The consonance of the SDP and FDP on *Ostpolitik* was criticised during the 1986–7 election campaign, in particular by the late Chairman of the CSU, Strauss. But Strauss himself had somewhat surprised the German public by his willingness to condone cooperation with the East and especially the GDR.[41]

The Greens have made notable attempts to improve their image in détente matters at the expense of the SPD. They supported the SPD in its recognition of the territorial status quo and efforts to obtain a deal on disarmament in Europe. But they criticised the SPD for limiting their talks with Eastern Europe to 'discussions with governing elites' and for not seeking talks with representatives of 'independent democratic groups'. In the view of the Greens, this was to accept the military, political and economic status quo in Eastern Europe.[42] The Greens followed this up with a list of demands under the heading 'democratisation and denationalisation of foreign policy', including measures such as: 'individuals, non-governmental organizations and movements ... to get together through travel and town twinning'. Though some of these measures form part of the third 'basket' of the Helsinki Act and others are in theory already provided for, a greater practical emphasis is a relevant demand. But they can scarcely be said to distinguish the Greens from the other parties, and in their catalogue of 'Grassroots détente policies'/'Détente from below' the Greens present only one original contribution: that of creating a 'network' of 'personal peace treaties'.[43]

Within the CSCE process the Conference on Confidence and Security-Building Measures and Disarmament in Europe (CDE) plays a most important role. The first phase was concluded in 1986 when a set of complementary confidence and security-building measures were approved. The results of the conference were greeted with approval by all the parties of the Bundestag.[44] But in the euphoria, further steps of the same kind were not debated, nor was the question of an agenda for the next phase of CDE addressed.[45] Moreover, a majority in the Bundestag accepted the NATO proposals of 11 December 1986 that negotiations should henceforth take place in two forums: confidence- and security-building measures would be discussed by all 35 CSCE states, while disarmament would be negotiated in a Conference on Conventional Stability in Europe from the Atlantic to the Urals, from which the neutral and non-aligned states would be excluded.

The attitude of its delegations will determine whether these conferences are successful in the estimation of the FRG. For at issue are some of the more controversial expressions used in discussions on détente: 'security partnership' or 'common security' and '*strukturelle Angriffsunfähigkeit*' (structural non-provocative defence). The divisions within the FRG concerning the validity of these ideas are considerable.

It was Chancellor Schmidt who, in 1978, first used the expression 'security partnership' to refer to East–West relations. The CDU/CSU, however, insists that it should be used only of NATO partners, and affirms that 'there is no better expression for political neutralism than "security partnership" when applied both to our Eastern and Western policies'.[46] It should, however, be said that for the Christian Democrats the merest hint of the FRG holding a position equidistant between the two superpowers is anathema, and has in the past given rise to vehement attacks on the SPD, the Greens and the peace movement.[47] For the SPD, no implication of equidistance or neutralism is conveyed. The expression simply summarised the fundamental Social Democratic line on détente and arms control. It emphasises the point that in the nuclear age security is no longer a matter for individual states but can only be achieved through partnership.[48] The Christian Democrats, in their polemic against this expression, have tended to dangle before the electorate the old enemy image of a totalitarian dictatorship in the East.[49]

The Liberals, who accept the concept of 'security partnership' and in the 1970s had themselves developed similar ideas,[50] remain loyal to the idea, but out of consideration for their coalition partners have adopted different terminology: 'The will to find a common solution to these *arms control* problems can be found in the area of cooperative solutions between East and West; the FDP maintains that the only way of guaranteeing a lasting peace in the nuclear age is through disarmament and a build-up of confidence'.[51]

The expression 'structural non-provocative defence' first appeared in 1983, in the final statement of the Mayence congress on '*Verantwortung für den Frieden*' (Responsibility for Peace). The statement continues: 'We can either continue to make nuclear war feasible . . . or, to increase stability, we can take what may well be a historically unique opportunity for a bilateral conversion of arms to "structural non-provocative defence"'.[52] The expression was adopted by the SPD in 1984; the final report of the Essen party conference states: 'Any new security policy concept must lead away from nuclear deterrence to the gradual creation of a defensive structure such that structural non-provocative defence is eventually attained'.[53]

Against this the governing parties and the armed forces argue that NATO is, in any case, a purely defensive alliance and does not possess offensive capacity. Thus the emphasis would be on the Warsaw Pact countries giving up their offensive strategy and modifying their military structure.[54]

Nevertheless, the FDP takes the line that an important step towards ending the arms race would be 'an agreement intended to impart a defensive character to the military structures of both sides and in this way reduce the mutual fear of military threat'.[55] In his after-dinner speech at the Kremlin on the 6 July 1987 the President of the FRG, Richard von Weizsäcker, originally a CDU politician, said: 'If security can be guaranteed by each sincerely acknowledging the other's desire for it, then most problems can be solved. Security includes reducing existing threats. Important factors are a balanced defence without offensive capacity, the elimination of the possibility of surprise attacks, increased insight into the interdependence of security, and increased willingness to cooperate in finding solutions, not least in outer space. In this spirit, the Federal Republic of Germany will continue to use ... every means at its disposal, as a steadfast and reliable member of the Atlantic Alliance, to assist progress towards disarmament'.[56]

If the Christian Democrats could bring themselves to support these words, then fairly widespread agreement could be reached on questions of common security and non-offensive capability. This would perhaps leave the Greens and the peace movement in an isolated position in so far as they alone believe that unilateral disarmament is the only way to avert the danger of war.

3 CORRELATIONS BETWEEN EUROPEANISATION AND DEUTSCHLANDPOLITIK

The controversy of the 1950s on whether the integration of the FRG into the West would inhibit or enhance the process of reunification has already been mentioned. Two decades later this controversy recurred in the context of the debates on the '*Ostverträge*' (Bilateral Treaties) and the CSCE Final Act. The Christian Parties complained bitterly that the Socio–Liberal Government was giving up certain rights in agreeing to accept the existing European boundaries. Clearly, both the early 'West Europeanisation' and the first steps towards an All-European Peace Order included a '*Deutschlandpolitik*' dimension, a fact recognised not only by the opposition but also by the government of the time.[57]

The '*Ostverträge*' and the CSCE Final Act were intended to lay to rest certain contentious issues arising from the aftermath of the Second World War. They failed to do so. The 1980s have seen a reawakening of discussion of the 'German Question' (reunification).[58] The return to power of the CDU/CSU, and the fact that several members of the government, including the Chancellor, have spoken at 'Meetings of Displaced Persons' ('displaced', that is, from pre-1945 German territories) have added fuel to the debate.[59] Moreover, high-level discussions are being held between politicians of the FRG and the GDR, and tourism between the two German states has increased.[60] All this is being watched attentively and with some apprehension by neighbouring states.[61] The concern is summed up in the question: are the efforts of the FRG to achieve an All-European Peace Order in fact directed toward reunification?

Wolfram Hanrieder has described the dilemma of the West German '*Ostpolitik*' very aptly: as the immediate goals of *Ostpolitik* – better relations between the FRG and its Eastern neighbours, freer travel between the two Germanies, and the intensification of détente – are consonant with the long-term goal of reunification, no FRG government can completely allay the suspicion that it seeks a change in the status quo, such as neutrality or 'self-finlandisation'. Short-term opportunism consistent with long-term strategy is the basis of all realist foreign policy, and does not merit attention 'except in cases like the "German Question" where the problems involved actually affect all parts of Eastern and Western Europe'.[62] 'The contradiction inherent in an energetic German "Ostpolitik" (and in Deutschlandpolitik in particular) lies . . . and always has done, in the fact that the greater the success – i.e. the greater the effort to intensify inter-German relations or improve relations with the East – the greater the probability that Moscow, and not only Moscow, react by setting limits'.[63]

Hanrieder's analysis dates from 1981, the period of the Social–Liberal coalition. It shows how limited are the chances of success for a policy of détente suspected of concealing other aims. The analysis applies perfectly to the present government, which both reiterates its commitment to the existing boundaries and goes further than any previous government in waving the banner of reunification. Thus when the leader of the main governmental party commissions a study in which the government is invited to 'introduce the reunification of the Germans into the security concept of the current disarmament negotiations in Geneva' and to have it entered on the agenda of the next summit meeting between Reagan and Gorbachev,[64] there is no call for surprise if alarm bells ring in Paris and still further proposals for Franco–German security cooperation are forthcoming.[65]

Perhaps, then, the question should be put the other way round: How can *Deutschlandpolitik* help create an All-European Peace Order? And where does the policy of 'Western Europeanisation' stand in relation to this? The idea sounds tempting: to promote détente by eliminating the division of Germany as a cause of East–West tensions (*a* cause, and not, as the CDU M.P. Friedmann alleges, the main cause). But this is a very German point of view on the delicate balance of power in Europe, nor does it answer the question of how to alleviate the fears and tensions to which reunification would give rise.

It follows that, as in the past, progress in alleviating the results of division is more important than progress toward reunification. 'Agreement with the GDR has priority over unification . . . it is of prime importance that a process be set in motion or furthered, which takes the edge off the political division, makes the differences more bearable, and promises more freedom to the peoples of the Eastern bloc. This road leads via disarmament, economic cooperation, flexibility at the borders, and, in short, détente. We have to give history a chance to modify the coordinates gradually. This may indeed be the only way of achieving reunification in the end. On the other hand, reunification might never be necessary – it could become obsolete like the Anschluss of Austria'.[66] The perspective adumbrated here by the political writer Theo Sommer remains a distant hope, but it suggests the character that an All-European Peace Order might wear for German eyes.

In accordance with the joint statement made by Chancellor Kohl and General Secretary Honecker, 'Never again may German territory be used to initiate war, German territory must be used to initiate peace',[67] the two German states should strive to promote détente and arms reductions within their respective spheres of influence (the alliances). This, and not the standardisation of armament, should be the focal point of West European security cooperation for the FRG. And at the CSCE, the CDE and the forthcoming first Conference on Conventional Stability and Disarmament in Europe, the two German states can initiate an exchange of information on each other's perception of threat. This exchange is necessary if progress is to be made on both sides in achieving a non-provocative defence strategy. The two German States on whose territory so very many engines of war are deployed have a crucial role to play in discussions on conversion to non-provocative defence within their respective alliances. The fact that the *Deutschland-politik* and All- and Western European interests overlap in these areas need no longer arouse fear in the neighbouring European states.

Notes and References

1. Franz-Xaver Kaufmann, *Sicherheit als soziologisches und sozialpolitisches Problem*, 2nd edn (Stuttgart: Ferdinand Enke, 1973) 32.
2. Daniel Frei, *Sicherheit. Grundfragen der Weltpolitik* (Stuttgart, Berlin, Köln and Mainz: Kohlhammer, 1977) 13ff.
3. See Klaus Arzberger *et al.*, *Der Bürger. Bedürfnisse, Einstellungen, Verhalten. Sozialwissenschaftliche Studien zur Stadt und Regionalpolitik*, Bd. 14 (Königstein/Ts, 1979); Manfred Murck, *Soziologie der Öffentlichen Sicherheit* (Frankfurt/M., New York: Campus Verlag, 1980).
4. See Berthold Meyer, *Der Bürger und seine Sicherheit* (Frankfurt/M., New York: Campus Verlag, 1983) 160ff.
5. Friedrich Naumann-Stiftung (ed.), 'Das sicherheitspolitische Konzept der Liberalen', *Für eine Politik der Friedenssicherung*, Documentation, vol. 1 (Bonn, 1983) 93.
6. See Dieter S. Lutz, 'Sicherheit ist "gemeinsame Sicherheit". Zur Idee und Entstehung einer neuen sicherheitspolitischen Konzeption', *Mediatus*, 7 (1987) 3.
7. See Egon Bahr, 'Gemeinsame Sicherheit', *Vierteljahresschrift für Sicherheit und Frieden* (*S+F*), vol. 3 (April 1985) 200.
8. See the more detailed report on this debate prior to 1986, in Berthold Meyer, 'Die Parteien in der Bundesrepublik Deutschland und die sicherheitspolitische Zusammenarbeit in Westeuropa', *HSFK Report* (1987/2) (Frankfurt/M., 1987); for the whole complex of concepts and problems of West-Europeanisation see also Lothar Brock and Mathias Jopp (eds), *Sicherheitspolitische Zusammenarbeit und Kooperation der Rüstungswirtschaft in Westeuropa* (Baden-Baden: Nomos Verlag, 1986).
9. The 'Christlich Demokratische Union Deutschlands' and the 'Christlich Soziale Union Bayerns' are two separate political parties, but as they are working together in a common parliamentary party in the Deutscher Bundestag they are also cited together in this paper.
10. See the speech of Chancellor Kohl at the Internationale Wehrkundebegegnung (1985), 'Presse- und Informationsamt der Bundesregierung', *Bulletin*, no. 19 (14 February 1985) 161. See also the draft for a new programme for CDU foreign and security policy, 'Unsere Verantwortung in der Welt. Christlich-Demokratische Perspektiven zur Aussen-, Sicherheits-, Europa- und Deutschlandpolitik', *CDU-Dokumentation* No. 1, 1988, 3, 10.
11. See Horst Ehmke, 'Überlegungen zur Selbstbehauptung Europas. Ein Diskussionspapier', *Politik. Aktuelle Informationen der Sozialdemokratischen Partei Deutschlands* no. 1 (1984); also 'The draft for a new basic program for the SPD' (Irsee, June 1986) 20ff.
12. See Meyer,'Die Parteien in der Bundesrepublik, (Note 8) 39ff.
13. See Die Grünen, 'Bundestagswahlprogramm 1987' (Bonn, 1986) 26.
14. See the position of CDU/CSU on SDI; Meyer, 'Die Parteien in der Bundesrepublik (Note 8) 19ff.
15. Particularly Franz Josef Strauss and Jürgen Todenhöfer contemplated

a West European nuclear force a long time before the debate on the double-zero option, see Meyer, 'Die Parteien in der Bundesrepublik' (Note 8) 16ff.

16. *Frankfurter Rundschau*, 6 May 1987 and 2 June 1987.
17. See SPD-Parteitag 19–23 April 1982 (München). '*Dokumente, Beschlüsse zur Aussen- Friedens-, und Sicherheitspolitik*', Initiativantrag 19. The SPD's rejection of the NATO double track decision was one of the reasons given by the FDP for dissolving the Social–Liberal coalition in Autumn 1982, see the letter of Hans Dietrich Genscher to the party members of FDP, 1 October 1982, *Die neue Bonner Depesche*, no. 10 (October 1982) 8.
18. *Süddeutsche Zeitung*, 5 March 1987; see also Helmut Schafer, 'Für beide Null-Lösungen', *Die neue Bonner Depesche*, no. 6 (June 1987) 24ff.
19. *Süddeutsche Zeitung*, 8 May 1987; see also Egon Bahr, 'Null Lösung und atomwaffenfreier Korridor', *Blätter für deutsche und internationale Politik* (June 1987) 718ff.
20. See *Frankfurter Rundschau*, 22 October 1986.
21. There was an internal debate in the Green Party as to whether the adoption of the double-zero option would be compatible with the party's stand on unilateral disarmament, see *Frankfurter Rundschau*, 1 June 1987.
22. See *Frankfurter Allgemeine Zeitung*, 19 June 1987.
23. See *Frankfurter Rundschau*, Dokumentation, 14 September 1985, 12.
24. Oskar Lafontaine had claimed this in his book *Angst vor den Freunden. Die Atomwaffenstrategie zerstört die Bündnisse* (Hamburg: Rowohlt-Spiegel Verlag, 1983) 43. But some days after the elections for the Bundestag in January 1987 he changed his mind, see *Frankfurter Rundschau,* 6 February 1987.
25. See 'Schwerpunkte liberaler Aussen-, Deutschland-, Sicherheits-, Europa- und Entwicklungspolitik', resolution of the FDP federal congress in Hannover 1986, *Die neue Bonner Depesche* (June 1986) Dokumentation, 50.
26. See *Wahlprogramm der Alternativen Liste Berlin* (1985) 305.
27. 'Speech of deputy Helmut Schmidt MdB on 28.6.1984', *Deutscher Bundestag, Stenogr. Berichte, 10. Wahlperiode*, 5603.
28. See the criticism of Hermann Scheer MdB, *Der Spiegel,* No. 8, 18 February 1985, 112 ff. and *Die Neue Gesellschaft/Frankfurter Hefte*, Heft 8/1985, 732 ff.; and the favourable response of CDU minister Alois Mertes', *Süddeutsche Zeitung*, 4 July 1984.
29. See Helmut Schmidt, 'Deutsch–französische Zusammenarbeit in der Sicherheitspolitik', *Europa-Archiv*, 11 (1987) 303ff; Schmidt's initiative received a favourable response from the former French prime minister Fabius, see *Frankfurter Allgemeine Zeitung*, 19 June 1987.
30. See *Süddeutsche Zeitung*, 23 June 1987.
31. See *Frankfurter Allgemeine Zeitung*, 30 June 1987.
32. See Volker Böge *et al.*, 'Europäisierung der Sicherheitspolitik als Antwort auf die "Krise der NATO" ', Die Grünen (ed.), *Euromilitaris-*

mus. Zur Bedeutung der Europäisierung der Sicherheitspolitik (Köln–Bonn, 1985) 23ff.

33. Die Grünen (ed.), *Militärmacht Westeuropa?* (Bonn, 1985) 3, 25.
34. Die Grünen (ed.), *Für Blockfreiheit und Menschenrechte! Position der Grünen zur Ost–West-Politik. Für ein friedensfähiges Europa!*, Folder for the Bundestag elections of 1987.
35. *Für Blockfreiheit und Menschenrechte!* (Note 34).
36. See Appeal of the Russell-Peace-Foundation for a nuclear weapon-free Europe, in: Arbeitskreis Atomwaffenfreies Europa (ed.), *Alternativen Europäischer Friedenspolitik* (Berlin, 1981) 16. A nuclear-free Europe is also the aim of two of the traditional parties but in their case it is not linked with non-alliance. The 1986 SPD/SED 'corridor concept' can be traced back to a proposal made by the Palme Commission in 1982, in which the SPD politician Bahr proposed that the nuclear arms deployed in Central Europe be returned to storage in their countries of origin. In this way, a relatively large nuclear-free zone could be created in Europe. However, Bahr was unable to have this idea adopted by the commission. Also in 1982, the FDP stated that they were in favour of a nuclear-free Europe but with the proviso of 'creating a conventional balance on as low a level as possible (throughout Europe)'. This whole idea was dropped in later programmes, quite probably because the party recognised that it could not be realised within the present coalition.
37. See Lothar Brock/Berthold Meyer (eds), *Die Zukunft der Sicherheit in Europa* (Baden-Baden: Nomos Verlag, 1984).
38. See Christian Hacke, 'Parlamentarische Opposition und Entspannungspolitik – Die Position der CDU/CSU zur KSZE', in Helga Haftendorn *et al.* (eds), *Verwaltete Aussenpolitik. Sicherheits- und entspannungspolitische Entscheidungsprozesse in Bonn* (Köln: Verlag Wissenschaft und Politik, 1978) 263ff.
39. See 'the Governmental Addresses of Chancellor Kohl' on 13 October 1982 and 4 May 1983, Auswärtiges Amt (ed.), *Sicherheit und Zusammenarbeit in Europa, Dokumentation zum KSZE-Prozess 1984*, 6th edn, 248 ff., and 'the Governmental Address' on 18 March 1987, *Frankfurter Rundschau*, Dokumentation, 19 March 1987.
40. See *Blätter für deutsche und internationale Politik*, Heft 10/1986, 1269 ff; and 'Schwerpunkte liberaler Aussen-' (Note 25) 50.
41. For example, the essential role played by Franz Josef Strauss in the guarantee given by the Federal government for a credit of 1 billion marks granted to the GDR in 1983.
42. See *Für Blockfreiheit und Menschenrechte!* (Note 34).
43. *Für Blockfreiheit und Menschenrechte!* (Note 34).
44. See the debate of the Deutscher Bundestag on the results of the CDE on 2 October 1986, *Deutscher Bundestag, stenogr. Bericht, 10. Wahlperiode*, 18167 ff.
45. For the prospects for CDE, Berthold Meyer, 'Stockholm brachte Fortschritte – aber auch für die Vertrauensbildung?', *HSFK Friedensforschung Aktuell*, no. 16 (Frankfurt/M., Winter 1986/87).
46. Alois Mertes, 'Friedenserhaltung – Friedensgestaltung. Zur Diskussion für "Sicherheitspartnerschaft"', *Europa-Archiv*, 7 (1983) 190.

47. See *The Program of CDU and CSU for the Federal Elections 1987*, 7.
48. See Lutz, 'Sicherheit', (Note 6) 3.
49. See *The Program of CDU/CSU* (Note 47) 7.
50. 'Das sicherheitspolitische Konzept' (Note 5).
51. Resolution of the Bundeshauptausschuss of the FDP on 1 June 1985 on 'Security policy and SDI', *Die neue Bonner Depesche*, Liberale Dokumente, 7 (1985) 2.
52. In the Editorial of *Vierteljahresschrift für Sicherheit und Frieden* (*S+F*), vol. 5 (1987) 1.
53. *Vierteljahresschrift für Sicherheit und Frieden* (Note 52).
54. See Wolfgang Brost, 'Strukturelle Nichtangriffsfähigkeit – ein irreführendes Schlagwort in der sicherheitspolitischen Debatte', *S+F*, note 52, 12ff.
55. 'Schwerpunkte liberaler Aussen' (Note 25), 50.
56. See Richard von Weizsäcker, 'Vom Denken in Blöcken entfernen', after-dinner speech of the Federal President in the Kremlin, *Süddeutsche Zeitung*, 7 July 1987, 7.
57. See Gottfried Niedhart, 'Konrad Adenauer und die aussenpolitischen Anfänge der Bundesrepublik Deutschland im Lichte neuer Quellen', *Die deutsche Frage in der Weltpolitik, Neue Politische Literatur*: Beihefte, 3 (Stuttgart, 1986) 170.
58. See Jürgen C. Hess, 'Westdeutsche Suche nach nationaler Identität' und Eckehart Jesse, 'Die (Pseudo-)/Aktualität der deutschen Frage – ein publizistisches, kein politisches Problem', *Die deutsche Frage in der Weltpolitik* (Note 57) 9ff. and 51ff.
59. This refers to the debate prior to Chancellor Kohl's speech to the Meeting of Silesians which, as originally planned, was to be given under a banner proclaiming 'Schlesien bleibt unser' (Silesia remains ours).
60. See Norbert Ropers, *Tourismus zwischen West und Ost. Ein Beitrag zum Frieden?* (Frankfurt/M. and New York, 1986) 211ff.
61. See Rupert Cornwell, 'West Germany – a giant hesitates', *Financial Times*, 28 October 1985; Brigitte Sauzay, 'Deutsche Alptraume. Die Angst der Französen vor Friedrich Barbarossa', *Die Zeit*, 17 May 1985, 56.
62. Wolfram Hanrieder, *Fragmente der Macht. Die Aussenpolitik der Bundesrepublik* (Munchen: R. Pipet Cop., 1981) 154.
63. Hanrieder, *Fragmente der Macht* (Note 62) 155.
64. Working paper of the CDU–MdB Friedmann, in *Frankfurter Allgemeine Zeitung*, 20 May 1987.
65. For the French trauma related to Germany, see Mathias Jopp, Berthold Meyer, Norbert Ropers and Peter Schlotter, 'Militärstrategien und verteidigungspolitische Interessen in Westeuropa als Rahmenbedingungen einer europäischen Sicherheitspolitik', in Reimund Seidelmann (ed.), *Auf dem Weg zu einer europäisierten Sicherheitspolitik* (Baden-Baden: Nomos Verlag, forthcoming).
66. Theo Sommer, 'Hausieren mit einem alten Hut. Zur Bonner Geisterdiskussion über die Wiedervereinigung', *Die Zeit*, no. 23, 29 May 1987.
67. Common declaration of Erich Honecker and Helmut Kohl on 13 March 1985 in Moscow, *Deutschland-Archiv*, 4 (1985) 446.

12 Conceptions of Détente and Change: Some Non-military Aspects of Security Thinking in the FRG

Ole Wæver

1 QUESTIONS TO BE ANSWERED

One of the basic questions for this study is whether Theo Sommer of *Die Zeit* is correct in concluding after Chancellor Kohl's 1988 visit to Moscow: 'They are all Genscherists now'.[1]

The core of the analysis is an attempt (sections 4 and 5) to discover the logic in the changes in 1987–8: to what extent did the different parties change their basic stances, thereby opening new options for themselves (and for Germany); and to what extent (and how) did they act to *avoid* such revisions? What are the effects of actions of the second type?

For this kind of analysis it is necessary to present the underlying structure of the thinking of the different parties (section 2) and the detail of its logic at some crucial points (section 3). Before this, an outline history (1978–88) will be offered in 1.1. The questions are then listed in 1.2, and the theory and methodology presented in 1.3.

'Non-military Aspects of Security Thinking in the FRG' implies: first, the exclusion of strictly military questions and second, a focus on security *thinking* – the concepts rather than the positions. The period covered is approximately 1982–8. It is divided into two periods: a period in which the political constellation reflected the debates about INF deployment (1982–7) and a second period (1987–8) where this fixed landscape starts to break up, mainly because of the debates about the INF (withdrawal) agreement. In the present study a structural analysis of the 1982–7 texts serves to answer certain questions about the change of the last few years, and the *matériel* for policy formulation in the FRG during the years to come.

1.1 West German Security Policy in the 1980s

First, a selective historical overview.

Following the 1979 INF double track decision, criticism at first came mainly from outside the established political parties, but a groundswell of critical opinion was also felt within the SPD. With the change of government in 1982, West Germany witnessed a growing polarisation between right and left wings (as the SPD no longer had the function of controlling the controversy but could now instrumentalise it), culminating in the deployment debate in the Bundestag on 21–2 November 1983. For a while, the debate *seemed* to be between a 'Red–Green' (Social-Democratic and Green) *critical* position versus an FDP–CDU position on which the coalition government was based.

In 1987 the CSU and parts of the CDU fought against the INF withdrawal. Positions on this issue did not map onto the coalition constellation. This is one of the theses of the present analysis: the lack of unity within 'the two camps' – government and opposition. The controversies within the SPD and CDU were not adventitious, but derived from fundamentally different understandings of the nature of European security.

Throughout the different phases of the discussion on zero and double zero (Spring and Summer 1987), the right wing tried to block the agreement. It is unusual to find the Minister of Foreign Affairs opposed *in the allied capitals* by the Ministry of Defence and the leader (and deputy) of the parliamentary representatives of the main coalition party (Dregger and Rühe). Commentators stigmatised these events using the term coined by CDU people to criticise the independent activities of the SPD: '*nebenaussenpolitik*' (another foreign policy alongside the official one).

The infighting between the 'Genscherists' and the radical right in the CDU and CSU (*Stahlhelm*-fraction) was, at times, merciless, especially when one considers that this took place within a coalition government. The right wing was ultimately humiliated both by the outcome and more especially by its failure to win the support of the Western allies.

This battle, and its upshot, the decision of Chancellor Kohl to go over to the position of his Foreign Minister, have weakened the right wing of the CDU.[2] At the same time pressures are building up internationally for East–West cooperation in Europe, and, as these combine with improved relations between the Soviet Union and Western Europe, it seems that the FRG is called upon to play its – by now – traditional role as an activist of détente. A new move towards the centre in the SPD, combining with a tendency toward greater consensus with the government, would reinforce the Genscherite line in government policy. Overall consensus can occur only after a definite decision in the CDU (read: by Kohl) to opt for a Genscherite line, and thus after a genuine showdown with the right wing. As the Liberal–Conservative government has also (from its formation in 1982) in most important respects continued the Eastern and Germany policy of the previous government (against the wish of many of its supporters), it would be easy to conclude that from 1987 on, they have all been Genscherists. This is what is postulated by Theo Sommer, and he is wrong.

1.2 West German Security Policy in the 1990s

These are the main questions in analysing the post-INF political constellation in the Federal Republic of Germany:

1. *Does 1987 constitute a decisive rupture in the security thinking of the CDU?* There *was* a collapse of the right wing. Did it lead to a stable centre-right consensus pursuing an (almost) Social Democratic Policy? Or did the right wing only temporarily lose prestige – which is to say: the more or less nationalistic right wing is a basic structural ingredient of the CDU, and the tribute to be paid to it is still a limitation on party policy. From this follows the question:
2. Is a new consensus regarding security in the process of forming, a consensus which would cover the SPD as well as the CDU (and whose centre would of course be Genscher)? Or is a Red–Green constellation more likely? This is basically the question of *what the SPD takes its own position to be*.
3. Is the most general one – based on the two preceding questions – about possible and likely *directions of development for the security policy of the FRG*: which roads are logically open domestically and internationally? What concepts are available that could coherently solve the most immediate policy problems?

1.3 Methods – Material – Theory

The theoretical foundations of the paper are threefold:

1. the understanding of 'Non-military Aspects of European Security' developed by the eponymous project group at the Copenhagen

Centre for Peace and Conflict Research.[3] This understanding will be applied mainly in section 3. It focuses on the various *concepts* of security, 'Europe' and détente – on the political concepts and the way they are linked to domestic politics, and on the non-military conduct of the East–West conflict – that is, on trans-national politics (see the concluding chapter (Chapter 17) of this volume).

2. Foreign policy theory, and especially the tendency to place ever greater stress on the role of the 'cognitive factors' – or, to put it differently, on the role of ideology and 'action theories', perceptions and analogies. Basic orientations in the foreign policy of a country tend to be marked by a certain inertia, so that it will conform to a basic 'code' for a period – and usually not change gradually but following some 'traumatic injection from the outside'.[4]

The third and most basic inspiration comes from:

3. Theories and methodologies dealing with structures of meaning. The primary inspiration is here from discourse analysis and post-structuralist text theory, with its interest in the discoursive construction of meaning, in the internal correlation of concepts and systems and in the ways basic figures control larger fields.[5]

Large parts of the political process are played out at the conceptual levels where the political space is structured by different projects seeking to fix the meaning of the social and meaning in the social by integrating them into their discoursive chains.[6] Here it is primarily a question of the relationship of key-concepts to each other – the whole creation of a political language in which the social is given meaning. In the deepest sense, this does not happen by settling the relationship between concepts on the one side and specific phenomena on the other. Instead it happens by the construction of concepts in relation to each other. In the last instance language is relational – a system of differences.

Analysis should therefore focus on the textual operations that both construct meaning and regulate possible and impossible statements in that particular discourse. Meaning is created by a *closure*. This creates the possibility of meaningful speech in the field, at the same time as preventing talk about that which in reality makes closure impossible (the 'blind spot' of the text).

Analysis is, then, a constant asking about what texts do, and especially how they do it. Important is not only what they on the face of it say, when they speak, but also what they *do* to the general understanding of security and its premisses – and what they thereby do in the direction of regulating possible future thinking and politics. No less interesting is what the texts do *not* say – what they do not talk about. And what they say – while talking – at different levels.

Closure is necessary to make an argument powerful. The force of an argument comes from its ability to *direct* the flow of meaning – and that direction is created by fencing off other possibilities. A specific political discourse is thus constituted by the exclusion of certain perspectives. This does not, of course, mean that a political discourse is totally static. For the purposes of a structural analysis of change, a particular security '*thinking*' might be presented as *layered*. At the deepest level of structured political discourse, one finds some basic narrative which it is extremely difficult to change. You cannot just remove it or stop talking according to its rules, because with it goes the *meaning* of your politics – the answer to 'what is it all about' and 'where does it take us'. Sometimes some elements have been weakened or – more commonly – it becomes necessary to include certain elements that have previously been fenced out. Then one can either place this case in a sort of quarantine – stress the peculiar aspects that isolate it from the general logic, hoping that it will thus cease to disarray the overall discourse;[7] or one can reroute the general structure, so that it ends up more or less in the same place – by the use of different operations. The challenge can thus be handled by deeper or more superficial incisions in the rhetorical structure. When deeper changes are made, there will be effects in various areas. These are likely to be opposed. Dilemmas of this kind are the focus of the present study.

The aim is to analyse the cases where pressure is building up on some of the essential links in the discoursive chains. Section 4 lists the major (political) novelties of 1987–8; by comparing them with the analysis in section 3 of the four key questions of European security, it is possible to see if any deep change did happen in that period, whether any is now about to happen, and even to get some indication of the likely effects of change.

In this context, security thinking does not mean how the actors *think*, which would be rather difficult to uncover – and not all that interesting. What is up for discussion here is how and what they think *aloud*. That is, the thinking they contribute to the public debate/political process: 'public logic'. What we investigate is the *political* process – not the isolated, individual formation of ideas that are afterwards put into the political interplay. The various positions are already part of the totality when they are created. Politics always antedates the political ideas – the figuration is there before the individual actors. We are interested in the thinking of *political* bodies, not personal ones. Accordingly 'West German Security Thinking' means societal thinking – what is (to a certain extent, what *can be*) thought in society.

Regarding *sources*, priority is given to texts 'at work', not negotiated 'positions' (such as party programmes, and other reflections of power balances at party congresses and the like). Preference is given to statements by ministers, books issuing from the debate, and especially debates in Parliament. The best sources are statements made in critical situations where there is a need to mobilise logical and rhetorical power. There the structure of the discourse will be exhibited in its relation to the specific case.

Statements made in a few major debates of the Bundestag will be considered in depth: e.g., the deployment debate of November 1983 and the debates around zero- and double-zero solutions in April to June 1987. Why such relatively military debates? This is to emphasise the concept of non-military aspects that is used in this study. These are seen neither as some 'appendix' to security questions 'proper', nor as some special 'alternative security' to replace the military one. They are a crucial part of considerations about security as such. Therefore the role of these non-military questions will be examined in debates generally viewed as crucial to 'security' (see also the concluding chapter, Chapter 17).

2 BASIC SECURITY NARRATIVES IN WEST GERMANY

This section deals with the period from the 1970s to the early 1980s. It contains a presentation of: (i) the main policy line of the CDU and CSU; (ii) the dominant line in the SPD in the period 1960 to 1982, with the FDP and President Richard von Weizsäcker (CDU); (iii) a few words on the search in the SPD after 1982 for new concepts and an analysis of the structure of the 'victorious' concept, 'common security'. Finally (iv) the Green view will be presented.

1. In large parts of the CDU/CSU, the basic idea of security reflects a degree of continuity with Adenauer's policies, in that both 'Eastern' and 'Germany' policies (*Ostpolitik* and *Deutschlandpolitik*) are

based on 'a policy of strength'. Strength does not necessarily mean military strength. But on this view, reunification or progress for freedom in the East is best served by the moral, political and economic strengthening of the Western states, for example, through the development of the European Community.

The *basic security problem* is the expansionism and repressiveness of the East. Thus the *immediate form of the security problem* is Eastern power – to be *countered by* Western strength. In the *long run* such strength, manifested in the fruitlessness of the East's attempts at policy intimidation, could lead to an exit from the present situation, issuing on greater freedom for the East, or perhaps even the 'normalisation' of the Soviet Union and a consequent new phase of 'ordinary' politics. Change by military might is ruled out – all parties in the FRG support the renunciation of force.

Implicitly or explicitly, it is here assumed that the stronger the West, the better, and this distinguishes the CDU/CSU project from the Harmel-based *Social–Liberal Eastern and Détente Policy*:

2. The traditional SPD *Ostpolitik* is a combination of Schmidt's 'politico–military equilibrium' and Brandt's dynamic '*Ostpolitik*'. The different political temperament of the two politicians notwithstanding, their security logics are closely related, at least as regards their respective periods as Bundeskanzler. Brandt strongly emphasised equilibrium and the necessity of West–West links. And it was Schmidt who, in the 1960s and early 1970s, formulated important parts of the *Ostpolitik* at party conferences and in Parliament. In contrast to, for example, American presentations that suggest that what little sense there was in the SPD was the influence of Schmidt, it must be emphasised that there is in the party tradition a closely integrated conception covering détente, Germany, security and Eastern politics. Certainly, this remains part of the horizon for people like Bahr, Vogel and Ehmke. (To them, however, the centre of gravity has shifted to a different point, thereby making the basic *figure* different; see below.)

For this pre-1982 SPD (1960–82), the fulcrum was *equilibrium*. The justification was the danger of war *or* political repression arising if equilibrium was *not* maintained. Equilibrium is in principle a symmetrical concept without privilege for either side. This is because imbalance as such is seen as destabilising, whoever benefits therefrom. This follows not least from the Harmel logic.

Balance is in fact not just a defensive aim – it is also the foundation for détente and 'mobility'. The détente process creates the better conditions and more freedom for the East Europeans. The superiority of either side blocks détente and thus progress towards freedom.[8] Western inferiority could even endanger freedom in the West. The main security problem is lack of freedom in the East, though war prevention is of course a necessary component of security policy. The view of détente as a movement, as a dynamic policy in the last instance leading beyond the status quo is distinctively German. This can be seen in contrast to Danish security thinking, for example, where détente is viewed simply as an improvement of the security situation. In a perspective of mobility – learnt from the policies of the first post-war decades which were in principle hyper-dynamic but in reality frozen – the *Ostpolitik* was precisely a formula for changes based on balance, absence of pressure, absence of destabilisation. Therefore the aim is to attain the *point of balance* at which the situation again becomes mobile.

The basic problem is the reality in the East and danger for the West of lack of freedom. The *immediate form of the security problem* is imbalance and the consequent policy of strength. This is to be *countered by* one's own policy of *détente* (*Ostpolitik*, securing the status quo and thereby achieving gradual change in the status quo). In the *long run*, this could lead to a *transcendence* of the present situation towards *a European Peace-order*.[9]

The FDP, mainly represented by Foreign Minister Genscher, and some important CDU members – especially Federal President von Weizsäcker have similar notions. Von Weizsäcker has an interesting and original way of arguing this position on geopolitical and historical (German history) premisses, but at the level of basic figures of security thinking the similarity to the presentation above is more or less complete.

3. The post-1982 SPD is marked by the existence of competing new logics. Pressure for 'new thinking' in the party continued to grow up to the moment when the party lost power. At that point – suddenly – the critical line was somehow the party line. The specific position on INF deployment of course had to change gradually, but it was clear to everyone that the basic thinking had shifted. The principles of pragmatism and gradualism were replaced by a general sense of *urgency*. The situation is viewed as *dangerous*. Security policy is no longer something that should just

'continue' (compare the election slogan of the CDU in 1986–7: 'Weiter So!') – it is something that should counteract *negative trends*. There were changes in the position taken by the party on several issues (see the chapter by Berthold Meyer, Chapter 11 in this volume), but no new unifying 'narrative'. Positions differed from group to group, and leading figures continued to propose rival concepts, not least for career reasons. A more critical position was taken, and more *activity* to *change* the military situation was demanded. No new party doctrine was designed to incorporate these positions. Few things were certain, but among them was this: the policy had to be 'new' – as the general understanding was that there had been too much 'traditional security thinking'. Not 'new' in relation to the SPD – there, of course, continuity is often stressed – but new in relation to the kind of 'traditional national security' that is blamed for the present dangerous situation.

The concept of 'common security' seems to have won the *terminological* competition. At the party congress in Münster (Autumn 1988), this term ruled uncontested. However, this does not imply that Egon Bahr's *logic* of security thinking permeates the SPD. Some consider the conflict of the systems in terms of a contest of substantive social and ideological differences, and try to formulate a policy of détente (or 'common security') from this standpoint (Eppler, Meyer). Others (for example, Konrad Gilges) are closer to the Greens and worry about the militarisation of Western Europe and French nuclear weapons. Others again (for example, Voigt) try to formulate positions more acceptable to the Western strategic and political community (Atlantic as well as Western European).

These different conceptions overlap with each other and – to varying degrees and at varying points – with the 'old' SPD security policy. However they also possess distinctive logics. Their political location is almost identical, and party leader Vogel is easily able to use components of all of them in presenting the party position. All these positions relate to a more disarmament-oriented version of *Ostpolitik*, tending towards an active, German policy of détente.

The concept of *common security* and in general the thinking of Egon Bahr seem at present to be highly influential in the party. Other leading personalities, like Vogel, Rau and Ehmke seem essentially to present watered-down versions of Bahr's thinking. For a more detailed presentation of this concept in relation to the competing ones, see section 3.3. This outlook on security is basically different from the equilibrium thinking presented above. The basic problem is the danger of war. Thus *the immediate form of the security problem* is the doctrine of deterrence – and generally 'old thinking' about security *against* the opponent. This is to be *countered by* one's own concept and policy of 'common security', more concretely implying economic, political and military *stabilisation* and an active policy of disarmament. In the long run this is expected to lead to a *transcendence* of the present situation leading towards real security and a lasting European peace.

At first sight, there seems to be some similarity with the basic *structure* of the arguments of the Left. And probably that is no coincidence. The SPD needed a language that would appeal to the peace movements and other dissentient groups. However, on concrete issues, the new Social Democrat often comes to conclusions that could have been reached by the old and more moderate logic. This distances him from the Greens. The change in Social Democratic thinking essentially tends toward a more closed system which, once accepted, leaves less room for the influence of external factors; more questions are settled within the model. This kind of model is a stronger instrument of persuasion. It is less ambiguous. It can, however, be more difficult to get this kind of thinking accepted. Thus, in relation to the Right, the Social Democrats have moved the main debate one step up the ladder of abstraction, to a question of principles. Disagreement on practical questions may not have changed so very much. For the party this brings a further advantage: the new model is a more satisfactory alternative to the grand schemes of the party's left-wing rivals.

4. For the Greens and other radical groups *the basic problem* is the danger of war; thus *the immediate form of the security problem* is policies of confrontation and armament. This is to be *countered by* the party's peace concept (there are different emphases within the party: dissolution of the blocs, the curbing of military–industrial forces, combatting all the specific decisions of NATO, etc.). In the long run this could lead to a *transcendence* of the present situation leading towards peace. Distinctive to the Green conception is the construction of an opposition between, on the one hand, almost all aspects of the present development and, on the other, the positive forces that are to conquer the former, forces that would, in so doing, create a totally new order.

It is important that all these concepts one way or the other coordinate a Europe policy, a Germany policy and a perspective on the Atlantic alliance. It is a necessary condition for a security policy in West Germany that it contains *some* answer to a question about the perspective for the German nation. These may be only an affirmation of principle or an image of policies contributing to mobility. This is an area watched closely by certain groups in both the CDU/CSU and the SPD. It is indispensable for a security outlook that the narrative on Germany be neither weakened nor defined out.[10] *How* the links between the three areas are made will be spelled out in more detail in section 5.

3 FOUR NON-MILITARY KEY QUESTIONS, 1982–7

This section begins with an analysis of the causes to which the principal actors of the early 1980s attributed the crisis of détente, and the subsequent increase in security problems. There follows a more general interpretation of the East–West conflict – is it an ideological conflict, a 'security dilemma', a life-and-death power struggle, or what? The third sub-section deals with the more practical political question of possibilities and preconditions for a new period of détente. Section 3.4 analyses the concepts of peaceful social change involved in such a process of détente. Of these, the most important are questions of interference/non-interference and their consequences for stabilisation, destabilisation and evolution. At the end of the section (as section 3.5) a brief summary will indicate the implicit relationship between détente, future security, social and international change, gradualism versus breakthrough/down – and especially *political* promises and threats to the East.

3.1 Reasons for the Crisis of Détente

One explanation of the crisis of détente is often heard from the Union parties: that the policy of détente was based on an overly optimistic assessment of the situation, and thus represented wishful thinking on the part of the West.[11] It is implicit in this argument that there was no basis for détente either initially or when it was supposed to be at its height. For instance, in the Bundestag debate on deployment, Theodor Waigel (CSU) spoke of the policy of détente having failed during the second half of the 1970s. The argument took the form: a Western policy *proved* defective.[12]

The argument about détente (as such) being 'ill-conceived' and 'delusive' has formed part of a (more or less consequent) CDU-policy only since 1980. Previously, criticism had taken the form that the Social–Liberal government had negotiated a bad bargain for the FRG (it had not *received* enough and it had *conceded* too much in the negotiations). This implied that the principle of détente was not at fault, but that the relationship between human rights and détente had been misunderstood (see below). The Union parties, originally in favour of 'détente', moved gradually toward the demand for *realistic* détente. This culminated during the election campaign of 1980 with criticism of 'socialist détente policy', which was contrasted with their own 'realistic peace policy'.[13]

This kind of criticism implies that the defects (Afghanistan, Angola, the military dynamics, the psychology of United States, etc.) are not *extrinsic*. They are to be found in the concept of détente itself. Consequently, there is no foundation for a new détente until completely new international conditions prevail, which in practice means a new Soviet Union. Until then détente would be wrong. The basic premiss of this is – as will be shown in section 4.3 – that any kind of *transformation* of the basic conflict is impossible.

Richard von Weizsäcker, too, ascribes the responsibility for the crisis of détente to the East. However, he does so in a way that keeps open the possibility of détente. The nature of the Soviet Union was not such as to exclude the possibility of détente. The mistakes made were specific Soviet *acts* such as the continued build-up of arms in the 1970s.[14] There is a similar logic to the claim of FDP Foreign Minister Genscher that détente broke down because the US failed to match Soviet arms spending. Neither of these causes would constitute a structural defect in *détente*.[15]

The liberal–conservative coalition could agree on nothing more than the compromise 'yes to détente – but a realistic one, free of delusions'. That this is an empty compromise[16] is seen from the fact that the Right uses the term 'realistic détente' as a critique of the previous détente, whereas Genscher says, 'The government of the Federal Republic of Germany has from the very outset pursued a realistic policy of détente'.[17]

The conservative criticism is the exact opposite of the view often heard from the Left, that détente collapsed because it failed to gain control over armaments.

Bahr and other common security thinkers strongly emphasise the lack of *military détente* in the 1970s. This is seen as the main reason for the crisis of détente. It suggests defects in the concept of détente, and thus points to the need for new concepts which would, in contrast with the 1970s view, postulate an intrinsic connection between things military and political. The view that new concepts were necessary was not unexpected from a group which consistently advanced such concepts (common security, security partnership, 'agreed' security, structural offensive incapacity). For all that, we are not dealing here with a *new* understanding of détente. The need is for détente to be *expanded* into the military field.

The lack of military détente was presented in the 1970s as a 'leftist' critique of détente; it was heard from peace researchers, amongst others.[18] That was before détente came under pressure (mainly in and from the US). Subsequently, the 'leftist' critics of détente became very active supporters of détente, on the same grounds, a line one might call 'détente-plus'.

There is a consensus at the political centre that the causes of the crisis of détente were extrinsic. Détente is seen as a basically correct approach to the relationship towards the opponent. Setbacks are only to be expected, and the point is then to *learn* from these, and improve the policy of détente in the relevant areas. The causes of the setbacks may be the armaments of one of the two sides, or Soviet–Cuban interference in Angola, or domestic developments in the USA. None of these shows structural defects in the concept of détente. The conclusion therefore is: a more skilful implementation of the same concept will eliminate interruptions to détente.[19]

In the eyes of the Greens, the Soviet Union is able to change gradually, while NATO is not.[20] Using this optical outfit, détente becomes possible – provided that drastic changes be made on *our* side. Nothing prevents us from conducting a policy of détente. The crisis of détente is brought on by a policy change in the West – so the answer is basically for us to change back – insofar as détente is relevant at all. The Greens too are associated with the 1970s' 'critical peace research' critique of détente, that détente was just the continuation of Cold War by different means, since it did nothing to end the bloc system and the arms race. The view is not without its drawbacks, and the Greens have found it difficult to criticise 'new Cold War' while presenting the period before 'new Cold War' as – 'Cold War'. The term détente is now used with a positive connotation, but refers to matters in any case integrated into the Greens' conception of politics.

3.2 Understanding of the East–West Conflict – Duel, Security Dilemma, or Historical Condition?

All the parties agree that the relations of East and West are conflictual, but there are divergent understandings of this conflict, and especially of its perspectives.

Certain events of March 1986 form an instructive example of this. One of the main speakers at the annual 'Wehrkunde' conference in Münich was Fred Iklé, American Under Secretary of Defense. He delivered a speech in which he rejected stability as a sufficient aim in the relationship with the Soviet Union. Continuing competition was stressed as absolutely necessary for winning the 'long-term global struggle between democracy and Leninism'. 'We cannot compete effectively by pursuing an ideal of stability'.[21] Foreign Minister Genscher reacted by sending a letter to his NATO colleagues urging them to reject such an approach and suggested that US Secretary of Defense Weinberger ask Iklé for a retraction.[22] This instance demonstrates that the form in which the conflict is conceived is not an abstract or academic concern. It is seen by high-ranking politicians as of real political importance.

Genscher's own account of the East–West relationship can be summarised as: conflict but not duel. In the early and mid-1980s von Weizsäcker and Genscher both stressed that Good and Evil are not divisible by West and East without remainder.[23] Many of Genscher's statements warn more or less directly against the duel conception.

To one side of Genscher's view, which is probably the most common, one finds a hard, conflict-oriented understanding, and on the other a more optimistic, transformation oriented one. Most politicians from the Union parties (Wörner, Dregger, Waigel, Kohl) have stressed that the East–West 'relationship' will 'for the foreseeable future' be a *political conflict*.[24] Thus: The *relationship* as such *is* a conflict. Cooperative dimensions are clearly secondary. No-one speculates about desirable transformations of the expression of this conflict; such it is and such it will remain. To what extent this concept coincides with Iklé's vision of zero-sum conflict, it is not clear. But that such talk conveys the impression of a duel-style conflict is no accident. If the conflict cannot be transformed, it is, in whatever mode, military or not, a conflict to the bitter end, and if this is the case, then it is logical to think in terms of relative gains. In this way, détente policy almost becomes a *tactic* of conflict.[25]

On the other side of the Genscherite consensus is the new

SPD-thinking and the Green policies, where less *static* interpretations of the East–West relationship are found. Some present the issue rather unconcernedly as just a matter of putting an end to 'confrontation policy' – that would solve the problem. Some sections of the peace movements, with their emphasis on psychology and 'friend–foe' dichotomies, took the line that there was no East–West conflict. In this perspective, it was enough to remove certain 'external' obstacles to peace – arms, for example. This assumption was obviously not well equipped to deal with the conflict if it did exist.

An interesting question is then whether we can find other development-oriented perspectives, where the premisses are not a denial of the existence of the conflict?

From Spring 1987, Egon Bahr offered some new perspectives: mainly due to the changes in the Soviet system and policy, *a situation with the peaceful competition of the systems and ideologies* is presented as *relatively close at hand*. To attain it, it is essential to stabilise the conventional military situation in Europe. (The problem of nuclear arms is the responsibility of the superpowers.) To this should be added some economic cooperation. Then it will be possible to achieve a qualitative breakthrough and open a new chapter in the history of post-war Europe.[26] These are high hopes. Bahr believes we could reach a point where the danger of war is *excluded*[27] – and isn't that what the word 'peace' should be used for?[28]

Only a minority of the right wing of the CDU continued to stress the danger involved in any contact at all with the East ('because they behave so totally differently from ourselves; we, after all, keep to the rules'). The very broad West German political centre was of the opinion that we should make our views known to the East – i.e., should not be afraid to do so. Another premiss, that something might come of contacts – that is to say, that 'communism' itself is not wholly immutable – seemed viable to some. To others the argument *in favour* of contacts was precisely that there was a competition between the two systems and one ought to participate in it. This sounds like Iklé logic, but is not conceived in those war-like forms. In the FRG, nothing closer to Iklé logic is to be found than certain statements by Minister of Defence Manfred Wörner, along the lines of: the threat is primarily military, but we also have to 'wage the political and ideological struggle with "Communism"'.[29]

Regarding the Greens, it need be said only that they stress conflicts on other levels, within individual societies and inside the blocs. In this way, the 'East–West Conflict' itself is relativised, or becomes a superstructure astride a more complex constellation. This often leads to arguments that altogether deny the relevance of classic security problems, and which instead stress the need to put an end to the military–industrial complexes and thus the arms race.

3.3 Possibilities, Conditions for and Forms of a New Détente

The most articulate formulations of a *new* détente have come from the SPD in the form of ideas about common security, security partnership and a second phase in détente policy. A rather complex discourse has developed around these formulations, and a satisfactory treatment of even the similarities and differences between the concepts of Bahr, Eppler and Voigt, for example, would require a full-length study.[30] The reduction of their views to basic figures will consequently remain in outline here.

In the SPD of 1982–7, the general tendency is for concepts intended to promote a further stabilisation of the *security* situation, that is, to alleviate fears about both military and abrupt political threats to the existing systems. The aim is to avoid threatening military developments and to create – in the longer term – a new dynamic in the East–West relationship (including German–German relations). The concept of common security in particular has this orientation towards the social status quo, at least in the medium to long term. This is linked to the claim that 'common security' is based on a 'strong logic' – that it is not so much a political choice among many as a *necessity* for security.

The two main problems with this approach seem to be,[31] (i) that its stress on security *with* the other means that its relationship to deterrence in the short and medium term is obscure;[32] (ii) that the categorical imperative not to decrease the security of the adversary makes it difficult to go through with moves criticised by the adversary regimes – even where these moves might enhance security in the long run (see section 3.4).

These problems clearly result from the attempt to base a 'strong logic' in 'objective' conditions. The basis of the argument is the military 'reality'. From this is deduced a doctrine that claims to treat of security in general. In the light of this criticism, another initiative of the SPD wears the air of an alternative to common security (since its logic runs rather from the non-military to the military): the dialogue with the SED (the East German 'Communist Party') that in

1987 led to the common paper on 'ideological strife and common security'. In fact, the motives as well as the immediate conclusions of the two approaches are similar. The common paper itself is a rather successful *combination* of common security thinking and a different logic based on the role of ideologies.

This is not the occasion to record the process of meetings between the 'basic values commission' of the SPD and the 'Academy of Social Science' of the SED (Socialist Unity Party – GDR),[33] though certain SPD thinkers and politicians – especially Thomas Meyer and Erhard Eppler – have, in this context, tended toward an interesting and novel emphasis on the social and ideological dimensions of détente policy.[34] The common approach developed in collaboration with the SED suggests that antagonist thinking in the conflict can be overcome if the process of détente is more than the continuation of cold war by different means: if, for example, it is linked to the perspective that 'both systems will change – each on its own basis'. Progress in détente is thus related to a continuous development of thinking – or 'ideology' – on both sides, regarding history, war and politics, the peace potential of the other side, etc. The task is then to formulate a policy of détente which makes the ideologies on both sides peace-furthering, 'without either of them having to give up itself or its basic legitimation'.[35] Ideological rethinking is required of both sides. At these meetings, the East Germans have also shown the will and ability to make important ideological reinterpretations – for example, around the concept of 'peaceful coexistence'.[36] That both sides need fundamental internal reforms to be able to handle current problems – and that both are capable of making such reforms, does not amount to a theory of convergence. This perspective is – according to Eppler – decisive to the possibilities for détente, because it takes one beyond any long term 'either you or I'; if *one* of the systems eventually 'won' the competition it would no longer be either of the two we know today![37]

Eppler's statement will serve to define a rift that runs through the coalition government in Bonn. For instance one could take two statements from 1983–4 by Genscher and Kohl.

Chancellor Kohl, 12 December 1983: 'The situation of Berlin shows us again and again, that walls and barbed wire, that closed borders are the major obstacle to peace and understanding. The more the peoples can meet with one another, the more unlikely a war, the more secure peace and freedom. This is the great experience, that we in the free part of Europe – and particularly in the EEC – have been able to make and which we hope one day all of Europe can take a share in. With the opening of our borders we have made a concrete contribution to understanding among the peoples'.[38]

Genscher, Minister of Foreign Affairs, 9 August 1984: 'It does not advance matters that both sides reciprocally ascribe to the opponent the blame for the worsened situation and demand a change in the behavior of the other side as a precondition for its own contribution . . . The correct approach to finding a way out of the predicament is a search for common interests and commonly accepted principles . . . At the end of this development a European peace order must be constructed. In it states with different social systems – under strict obligation to respect the terms of the Helsinki Final Act – will live together peacefully in mutual confidence and without fear'.[39]

For Kohl, the East is the problem. The solution for *them* is what *we* already have, or more precisely: *are* today. Genscher on the contrary asks for changes on both sides and envisages a goal where the societies are still different. Genscher has even emphasised that through détente both societies will find it easier to solve their own problems and therefore develop in a more positive direction. This statement makes clear the connection between concepts of détente and the dynamics in the two societies.

This is closely related to the question of acknowledging the existence of failings and lacunae, in relation to human rights and quality of life, of either society. In this regard, von Weizsäcker always strikes a rather modest tone, whereas most of the CDU emphasises the perfection of the FRG in relation to the East.

The CDU, and most energetically Manfred Wörner, then Minister of Defence, criticised terms like 'common security' or 'European house'. As long as the Soviets continue to bid for ascendancy,[40] and the Soviet Union will always attempt to dominate Western Europe,[41] these terms are, he affirms, dangerous to Western security. But he can find it in himself to support 'cooperative security policy'.[42]

Genscher, by contrast, uses several expressions which resemble common security. He avoids the *term* 'common security'; using it would anyway attract heavy criticism from the Union parties, and weaken the image of the FDP as being somehow above party politics and therefore the natural organ of foreign policy continuity.

Genscher has never ceased to demand a continuation of the previous détente and Eastern policy, for example, by referring to the Helsinki Final Act as 'shaping the course for a European peace order'. This reaffirms the picture of a peace based on different systems, and where the goal is peaceful competition without fear.[43] This is in very direct contrast with the controversy in the CDU/CSU during 1983–5 about total avoidance of the term détente, and the explicit denial of any attempt to return to détente or present it as a *long-term* aim.[44] It might be thought to follow naturally from the policy of the CDU that it formulate criticism of the ideology of the Soviet Union, not with a view to fundamental change but to the modification of specific points that hinder détente and/or are perceived as threatening. Such specific requests are not found in the traditional CDU discourse. They are the preserve of completely different politicians: Bahr has pointed out that the Soviet Union must give up the sentence about the inability of imperialism to embrace peace.[45] This would be a logical adjustment of ideology to policy and the remark corresponds to SPD criticism of the 'Evil Empire' rhetoric of the Reagan administration. Eppler too has pointed to the importance of a revision of this kind.

The right wing of the CDU has *not* made any such demands or criticisms. The most likely explanation is that they do not regard such change as possible, or that they do not regard it as relevant even if possible. The limits that the Brezhnev version of 'Peaceful Coexistence' place on a détente process are reiterated, and said to show the naïveté of Western supporters of détente.[46] It was not expected that under the impetus of political developments, and perhaps indeed of Western criticism, 'Peaceful existence' might begin to evolve. But there are signs that under Gorbachev the concept admits of new emphases, and the GDR has explicitly revised its thinking.[47] Significantly, *Genscher* believes that the concept has indeed been revised.[48] And that this change is important.

The *Harmel principle* is central to all these concepts of détente policy. All significant political forces in the FRG profess the Harmel doctrine about the compatibility of defence capacity with a policy of détente. (This combination was defined in 1967 as NATO's dual purpose.) A detailed analysis is not possible here, but the Harmel principle is a privileged point for reading out the whole set of connections in perceptions of security. The Right presents détente as a luxury that can be afforded when the military leg of Harmel has created security – i.e., it is possible to create your security yourself. This is, of course, the mirror-image of common security. The radical Left, by contrast, wants détente thought into the defence policy – that is the logic of the détente leg shall be valid for the defence leg as well. The political centre points out, in the abstract and on several specific issues, that neither leg can exist without the other.[49]

3.4 Peaceful Change (Interference/Non-interference, Stabilisation/Pressure)

All parties are unequivocally committed to the *renunciation of force*, a principle which has been argued with ever greater conviction since the early 1950s.[50] The considerations below regarding changes in the East have to be seen in this perspective. In the case of the Eastern Treaties this renunciation was strengthened by being specified in relation to the relevant states East of the FRG. And it is repeated in the CSCE final act.

Richard von Weizsäcker has spoken of taking the renunciation of force still further. It should be a living principle, a more general reassurance.[51] This serves to introduce our question whether we can – and whether we should – exert our strength to promote change in the East.

The Social–Liberal *Ostpolitik* was born of the recognition that maintaining certain threats, making all-or-nothing demands, and keeping Western strength up would not in fact lead to changes in the East. The breakthrough in the West came with the realisation that the only possible changes are those acceptable to the regimes over there, meaning that not merely the interests of the GDR, but also those of Moscow had to be taken into account.[52] What came to be the fundamental idea of the *Ostpolitik* was thus confirming the status quo in order to change it: to recognise borders and work for social evolution.[53]

The Union parties basically picture this the other way round. For instance, Wörner often says it is a precondition for more far-reaching development that Soviet policy changes 'in ihrem Wesen' (in their essentials).[54] This is in sharp contrast wih the emphasis placed on stability by certain Social Democrats, in whose terminology 'stability' is scarcely distinguishable from maintenance of the status quo.[55]

An important variation of this theme is the question of how to relate to different social forces in the Eastern European societies. Paradoxically this subject has been debated in relation to peace and security policy only by the SPD: 'Paradoxically', because the SPD has been criticised for overlooking an important question here – and for conducting an immoral policy over the heads of Polish shipyard workers. Possibly because the bourgeois government did not take over until after the climax of the crisis in Poland, its own sentiments on how to deal with the very real dilemmas involved are unknown. The caution of the SPD regarding relations to oppositional groups in the East has been criticised. And the coalition has (as shown above) in varying degree accepted a policy of maintaining the status quo as the price of constructive relations with the regimes in the East.

It has already been said that Kohl and others present human rights in the East as a *precondition* for better relations. But there is no comment on the potential *conflict* between this and all the pious hopes for improved relations. In the view of the CDU right wing the formula 'realistic détente' enshrines the principle of the precedence of human rights over détente. But it is hard to find any instance of the promotion of human rights and thus of realistic détente. Genscher, by contrast, stresses that détente advances reform and facilitates the existence of critical movements.[56]

Kohl and most other CDU politicians place particular emphasis on *the right* to say exactly what one thinks of the situation in the East.[57] The denunciation of human rights abuses is not even considered in terms of its consequences for security, despite the commitment to stability. Kohl says that he does not want *destabilisation*. But he is not so clear on this issue as Genscher.[58] In a general review of the Eastern policy of the Federal Republic on 10 November 1984, the section on Poland, after a clear confirmation of the agreements with Poland and the wish for continuing reconciliation, ends with the 'wish for a stable, economically sound Poland, which can show its own unmistakable profile in the European process of security and cooperation'. And referring to the domestic affairs of Poland there is just: 'Our desire for our neighbour is that it may, independently, through dialogue and national reconciliation, find a way out of its difficult predicament'.[59] This is the kind of regime-friendly statement for which the SPD were heavily criticised in the period 1981–2. We may summarise by saying that Kohl's policy is to demand the right to express one's opinion, but only in fact to exercise this right where it forms part of the critique of détente (as shown above). The policy is in practical essentials oriented toward the maintenance of stability, which the critical points are not used to undermine.

The most representative and detailed account of the SPD view is presented in the article 'Peace and Freedom as the Goals of the Policy of Détente' by Horst Ehmke.[60] Ehmke presents a critique of certain peace movements' policy of 'détente from below' and warns against a policy of destabilisation towards Eastern Europe which will in practice cost détente dear. Détente policy should be neither 'stabilisation' nor 'destabilisation', but 'reform'. Thereafter he argues that the Eastern regimes do have the capacity to reform themselves, and that they are best at doing so in a relaxed atmosphere. The Western policy of détente has been conducive to reform because it has given increased legitimacy to the regimes. Ehmke presents this as a combination of 'détente from above' and 'détente from below'. But, as a Polish critique of Ehmke's article pointed out,[61] the result is 'détente from above'; reforms in the East come about as a result of the latitude created by détente. (For Ehmke 'détente from below' is primarily a German peace movement supporting the policy of the SPD.) And in this way the credit and responsibility goes to the political leadership – not to the social movements. In Ehmke's perspective the latter receive moral 'pats on the back', but have no role to play. In Horst Ehmke's view, developments in Eastern Europe are *not* a product of the interplay of reform-oriented regimes and reformist critics.

The trend in the European peace movements to ascribe considerable importance to the critical movements in the East is supported by many Greens. These Green politicians clearly accord a higher priority to contacts with critical groups in the East than to good relations with the Eastern elites. This is détente from below. Other Greens tacitly conduct a policy based on the hope of constructive interplay with Eastern powerholders. This is especially the case, where questions of disarmament are considered in relative isolation. And within the Green Party there have been interesting debates on how to conceive and coordinate these two levels and processes.[62] But till now no clear-cut contributions to the West German security debate have come out of these debates, nor any visionary new détente concepts, in which the various types of oppositional groups in the East are taken as material for a policy of détente.

3.5 Summary: Détente, Change and Security

The CDU sees a different order ahead. One component of the present order will have to change dramatically: the systems in the East. No concept of a *process* is offered, nor is there any indication of a policy that could be implemented prior to such change. Thus the goal is implicitly assumed not to follow from any *gradual* process. There is a certain willingness to perform individual acts that 'improve' the situation.[63] However as these are not presented as part of a process leading step by step to a different order, the fundamental hope must be for some kind of *breakthrough*.

There is no 'double policy' which might allow the CDU to spell out to official and oppositional circles the roles it allocates to each, thus sending signals to both parties in the East of the necessity of mutual accommodation. And so it creates insecurity in *both* groups – the oppositional groups to whom it pays scant attention, and the power-holders who fear the prospect of sudden change.

The SPD believes in *reform* – in international and domestic politics.[64] In the East–West context, this means processes like disarmament, which change the character of the conflict toward peaceful competition. The SPD too feels the need for a policy that deals with the dilemmas presented by the political processes of the East. It supposes that the Eastern elites are viable interlocutors for détente purposes. However its policy is constructed without any assistance from reality. The argument runs as follows: peace is possible only if both systems are in theory capable of peace and reform. To deny that the other side is capable of peace is thus to deny the possibility of peace, so it is best to assume that the other side *is* capable of peace.

The goal of SPD policy has changed somewhat, and the policy of dynamisation via stabilisation has become one of stabilisation *tout court*. The dynamics of the previous policy were supposed to stem partly from the enhanced possibilities of reform that resulted from the greater stability of the Eastern regimes, and partly from the dynamism of one's own policy, with its own values and goals, and the ultimate prospect of an all-European political landscape. Now the talk is more of a process whose motor is the reform efforts of the Eastern countries which benefit most from détente. The priority is to improve the security–political situation, via second détente, common security and so on. Reform will follow, accomplishing in due course the changes necessary for a European Peace Order to be established.

The position of the centre (FDP and 'old' SPD *à la* Schmidt) is built on a balance of several of these components, and argued more from particular instances than from first principles. The discourse is therefore less closed. The gradualist and qualitative process seen by the CDU as impossible and the 'new' SPD as necessary is seen by the centre as *possible*, if not probable. One should therefore act to improve the chances of it occurring, and not deduce its possibility from its necessity. This group accordingly assumes that *it is possible to live with the present situation* too.

The Left, the Greens, and the like also think in terms of a *break* with the 'bloc system' or directly with NATO.

We can thus formalise the relations of Détente, Change and Security for each party:

1. *CDU*: We are to build our *security* on our own. If we do this well it might help in stimulating far-reaching change in the East; this would lead to a change in the European order. (Then it might be possible to talk about détente.)
2. *Post-1982 SPD*: A second *détente*[65] is to help reform processes in East and West, and partly in this way, partly directly, détente will lead to a change in the East–West relationship, of which the upshot will be a new order that promises real *security*. (In this new order, the systems will still be different from each other – but also different from their former selves.)
3. *The political centre*: A careful combination of self-help security and détente policies may create a mutually reinforcing interplay with social change. However the possibility of change at the international level is not linked much to the domestic changes – it is mainly a *learning process* in international politics leading to the erection of all-European structures between two still competing systems.

4 NOVELTIES, 1987–8

Of the stances presented in section 3.1, one is under pressure: the conservative picture of an immutable Soviet Union. The stance has not changed. But as public perception of the Soviet system as *reforming itself* grows, the union parties tend to place less stress on the external motives for change in Soviet policy. This does not amount to a retraction, it is simply that responsibility for change is no longer automatically credited to the West, but simply passed over in silence. Dispute centres on whether the reform process in the Soviet Union has changed anything in its foreign policy other than the rhetoric; for the Greens and SPD there has been substantive change, for the CDU there have been proposals for change, but the security situation remains more or less the same.

Genscher very early on[66] began to stress that it would be wise for the West to support the process of change in the Soviet Union. What immediate changes could be expected in foreign and security policies even he did not attempt to specify. But before the October 1988 trip to Moscow he wrote about 'the general improvement in the

West–East relationship' that 'an important new development is the policy of reform in domestic and foreign policy ... pursued by General Secretary Gorbachev over the last 3 years ... The withdrawal from Afghanistan, the INF-agreement, the acceptance of on-site verification, show that deeds are following words'.[67] This statement was intended to counter the CDU line that the only positive acts of Gorbachev in foreign policy have been those to which Western or economic pressures have driven him.

Few similar statements by his CDU collegues can be found. But there have been changes of outlook. Just prior to the same trip to Moscow, Minister of Defence Scholz wrote that a mutation of East–West relations was possible, and that the cause was the reorientation of Soviet domestic and foreign policy. Though emphasising that 'words and deeds are still far apart',[68] he went on to speculate that the Soviet Union might in the long term cease to be a danger to the West. This does not mean that some 'overall CDU position' has changed, but it does point to the dilemma that will arise if the conservatives are forced to acknowledge that the Soviet Union is capable of spontaneous change. The goal, 'a reorganisation of European security toward a permanent, just and free order of peace'[69] is still presented as conditional on major change in the East; no attempt is made to evaluate the current changes in this light; talk about positive relations – with particular reference to trade – is more often heard. But the nature of the conflict is not discussed, and this silence is symptomatic of tension. The issue is not being faced.

The reforms in the Soviet Union are of course emphasised by the SPD. The CDU and FDP statements in the special section of *Die Welt* were accompanied by an SPD statement by Vogel. He stressed the chances of all but immediate qualitative change, and spoke of 'de-militarisation and de-enemisation of the power- and systems-conflict'.[70] It was possible *now*, he said, to enter 'a new political phase', in which the form of the competition between the systems would allow (NB) *both sides* to concentrate on domestic reform.

Genscher was among the first outside the SPD to emphasise that the greater openness domestic and external of the Soviet Union was necessarily in the interest of the West too.[71] From 1988 on, CDU politicians also started to state this quite clearly.

Regarding section 3.3, we note that Genscher's 'cooperative security structures' have gained a more precise sense, which refers to the reorganisation of the military systems of both sides in hypothetical all-European institutions.[72] Moreover he talks about European values and European identity in a very dramatic way, as if to indicate that these are in themselves imparting a certain direction to developments. 'European values' in his parlance is not wholly unambiguous, and tends to shade into 'West European values'; this may indicate a retreat from his previous view that both sides needed to change. In this optic, the changes in the East, by promoting Western values, are returning to a European tradition that the West has never lost sight of.

The new Minister of Defence, Scholz, highlights the concept of 'mutual security'. In relation to the Soviet Union, it seems to contain the same implicit requirements of reform as common security. In relation to the West, it similarly implies the falsity of the view that the East–West conflict is a duel, or that superiority of armament is an advantage to either side. What is missing, relative to common security, is the notion of commonality, a notion whose function is nothing less than the implantation of a new perspective on the East–West conflict as a whole.

Lastly, von Weizsäcker came up wih the term 'system-opening cooperation'. Wörner and others have subsequently used the term, but it was mostly taken up by the FDP and SPD.

The conservatives are thus under pressure to develop explanations and structures adequate to the current events in the East.

In the SPD, conflict over one issue is now more acute. That is the issue, described in section 3.4, of détente from above or below. This is one of the two main controversies in the party at the moment. The other is the relationship to Western European security cooperation, French nuclear weapons, etc.: are the 'moral' (anti-nuclear) stances of the early 1980s to be applied to French nuclear weapons and therefore to German security cooperation in Western Europe, or should the SPD take a more 'realist' line and concentrate on coming to an agreement with France in order to promote the cause of West European security?

The SPD is frequently criticised for its attempts to develop new concepts and readjust policies in the direction of fresh initiatives towards the East. Paradoxically the SED–SPD common ideology paper is considered much more problematic than, for example, common security. The paper tries to further the cause of freedom and democracy (and is much less status quo oriented than common security) but is vulnerable to criticism because it formulates certain aspects of the 'unchangeable' status quo explicitly. The same is true of the SPD's attempt to update its Germany policy by defining limited goals and accepting the status quo somewhat more. This is much more controversial than any foreign policy *acts*, the visit to Bonn of Honecker not excepted.

The leaders of the CDU, and Kohl in particular, empty the CDU political discourse, by leaving familiar positions behind, but failing to replace them with new concepts or positions. This is a short-term necessity if the coalition is to be held together. It is not a long-term policy.

5 COGNITIVE TENSIONS AND RHETORICAL DAMAGE LIMITATION

We have seen that the years 1987–8 did not bring with them any novelties in the security thinking of the CDU or Kohl. Genscher's position shifted somewhat – especially as regards all-europeanism. Given that Kohl did not change his outlook on the basic issues, how did he (and the CDU in general) get away with visiting Moscow and doing so, what is more, with a general air of satisfaction?

5.1 1988: Kohl Meets Gorbachev – and Speaks Kindly Words

Kohl has done his bit for a more constructive East–West policy. The visit to Moscow was important. The impression created – that it is possible to cooperate with the Soviet Union – is one that Kohl is criticised for, and may increase public support for the policy the CDU hesitates to conduct. A similar (and similarly inarticulate) positive impression was generated by Honecker's visit to the FRG. This was generally seen as containing a lot of two-state symbolism, but it is important that few changes in attitude were verbally articulated. Furthermore, the Honecker visit was, in the discoursive system, isolated from the general foreign policy question by attributing the positive aspects of the visit to specifically *German* factors, in particular the 'community of responsibility' (see section 5.2).

For this reason, the Kohl visit to Moscow is a better case to investigate. Kohl's discourse did not change. There was no mention of 'détente'. He argued in favour of 'cooperation', which commits him only to potential economic gain. The only other major cooperation concerned the Germans living in the Soviet Union, and this received a rather surprising degree of emphasis.

The aims of the visit were presented as: (i) Cooperation, (ii) 'Good neighbourly relations', (iii) 'Gradually building up confidence'. (See press statement and the after-dinner speech in Moscow.)

(i) This means cooperation for the sake of individual gains – which says nothing about the *nature* of the relationship.
(ii) 'Good neighbourly relations' is a rather vague term. In the East it must clearly be seen as less than détente. And in relation to the West it is far from ideal: It might have awkward geopolitical connotations ('Rapallo'). Its use can be explained only by the desire to avoid 'détente' and other expressions implying process.
(iii) This refers mainly to understanding among the peoples – a kind of détente from below? It is unclear whether it is a familiar and all but threatening Western policy or a hint of greater foreign policy coordination between the two states. It is exceedingly unclear how this 'confidence' is supposed to impinge on the *political* relationship between the states.

Compare the remarks of Genscher on the same occasion: what we are doing now *is* building the European future, the 'common European house'. In this formulation, the present activities are presented as *part* of a process transforming the East–West conflict. This is not implied in the way Kohl speaks about the rationale of the visit to Moscow.

'They are all Genscherists now'? No, we have not seen anything like sufficient change in foreign policy conceptions. There were some interesting elements in Kohl's speech to the *Bundestag* reporting on the trip to Moscow (*FAZ*, 11 November 1988). But if this was the new line why not use it *in* Moscow? The answer must be that this *is* a dangerous direction for the CDU. These elements were invoked in Parliament merely to enhance the importance of the Kohl trip. In November 1988, the leading personalities of the CDU were hesitating on the brink. They were flirting with the prospect of détente, but the change could never have been an easy and inexpensive conversion to the language of détente. The CDU has in many individual cases the same foreign *policy* as Genscher, but its foreign policy conception remains very different.

The rhetoric of the CDU has established itself as a way of covering up the rifts in the party. But this is not done merely by paying occasional tribute to hardliners. It has developed into a moderately coherent CDU conception. Thus it is – as we have seen – hard to change. It is possible here and there to say or do different things. But whenever the attempt is made to alter principles, it sets off a reaction in some of the influential circles in and around the party.

Attempting an analysis at a completely different level – more the level of current political conflicts and general developments in East–West relations – Christiane Rix reaches a similar conclusion: 'there are severe challenges to the West German government about the exact goal of its security policy'.[73] There is a close connection between goals and conceptual thinking. But it is medium-term perspectives that most clearly illuminate policy concepts. Regarding the distant future, the presentation of agreeable prospects unconnected with present processes is easy; it is medium-term goals that are supposed to follow with some likelihood from the actions of today. The most problematic medium-term goals are those of German policy.

5.2 Policies on Germany – Strength, Weakness or Europe?

The present government argues that it has been very successful in its policy towards the GDR. This is confusing; after all, it has basically continued the Social–Liberal policy. And no new rationale has been forthcoming for the few changes there have been. The only argument is that this government is 'tougher' and more Atlanticist. The CDU overtly attributes its successes to a combination of firmness plus flexibility – or to put it slightly less paradoxically: tough and realistic bargaining.[74] The basis is: *they* know where we stand, they can have no illusions about fooling us onto a slippery slope of concessions leading away from the alliance. On this basis, the CDU claims to be better at German politics than the SPD.[75] The SPD does of course recognise the need to rule out the slippery slope hypothesis, it just does not make a policy out of doing so.

For Kohl the dilemma is therefore not *what* to do in relation to the GDR (that is a practical matter with a dynamic of its own), but *how* to integrate this into a general foreign and security policy. Either (i) he stays with *NATO loyalty*, combined with community of responsibility,[76] as the explanation for his successes, *or* (ii) he moves to a perspective where progress in relation to the GDR follows from a *general improvement of East–West relations* and (more problematically) the long-run perspective includes or follows from a *transformation* of the conflict, and not from any kind of 'victory' won by Western pressure. *A vague in-between position will not do.*

It has been said that the consensus on 'community of responsibility' was 'important because it meant that all parties accepted at least implicitly or passively, that the inter-German dialogue and the *Ostpolitik* are in one or another way linked with security matters'.[77] True. But that 'one or another way' begs all the questions. For the CDU, the concept seems to stand in for a link to overall East–West security politicy. By arguing from 'community of responsibility' one can defend a separate German–German détente *without* having to defend a European détente – rather as the Social Democrats in the early 1980s defended a separate European détente without arguing for superpower détente.

By this concept the CDU succeeds in establishing a rationale for their continuation of a Social–Liberal policy oriented towards improvements in German–German relations without having to link this to general East–West détente. The short-term policy is thus based on toughness and delinking. The long-term perspective is related to transformation, as the German problem, it is generally admitted, can only be solved in an all-European context. The CDU does not acknowledge (as the SPD more and more does) that the long-term perspective is just a further improvement in German–German relations to the point where relations across the border are natural. It is thus left open whether this all-European transformation is attained by some kind of annexation/liberation of Eastern Europe by Western Europe or through a mutual process of détente. At this point certain developments in the rhetoric of Genscher are also ambiguous, and perhaps bring him closer to the conservatives. His emphatic stress on all-European perspectives combined with emotional talk about European values *can* be seen as a criticism of narrow Western European thinking. However it might also suggest that his vision of future Europe is based on the values of Western Europe. And this would denote a change away from Social Democratic mutuality towards something more like overrunning Eastern Europe.

It is important to note that the CDU is to a certain extent bound to maintain the more traditional elements of its policy on Germany. In West German politics it is *necessary* to have a vision of 'Germany'. In this sense West German policy is not simply nationalist – that is, about reunification. And on the other hand, it is not true either that the national issue has long since lost its importance and reference to it become lip-service. It is an important issue in the sense that a conservative government in particular cannot do without *an answer* to the question: what are we doing about reunification? And then, as long as the said government can point to some kind of process or hope, the issue remains stable. But the situation might change in one of two ways: either a certain opportunity grows too inviting, or –

what is more likely – the policy is seen as *not* taking care of the national needs, and there follows the demand for more immediate and direct action towards the goal. For this reason, the national question and 'ordinary' foreign policy issues should not be weighed against each other – it is more important that they be integrated into a stable constellation. This, however, demands that a durable German policy be a component of an architectonic general policy; *especially at this point one can not just downgrade one logic without substituting another for it.*

The SPD seems, especially since 1984, to be shifting its policy on Germany. The logic of their original policy was to stabilise the status quo in order to overcome it; now it is more general East–West détente. The policy on Germany is now wholly to 'parcel the issue up' in a policy of détente.[78] The problem is not the *borders* but their dividing character. In some versions, this argument is taken further, in a general orientation away from a nation-state understanding of the world.[79] The main effect of this is to strengthen the absolute priority of détente.

5.3 Three Answers

In section 1.2, three questions were asked. The answers are:

1. The main line in the CDU has not become Genscherist. The CDU has not presented any *rationale* for participating in a process of détente and europeanisation. Thus, at present the CDU tentatively continues the process of détente but is extremely vulnerable to domestic and foreign criticism. In the absence of any explicit policy of détente, the CDU is exposed to the collapse of the consensus in favour of détente. Moreover, détente will in all probability throw up controversial issues, and the leadership cannot defend its present policy against its own right wing – or US criticism – because, to all intents and purposes, it has none. The conclusion must be that the CDU is a very mutable factor in the European political figuration.

   It could still be possible for the CDU to dissent on a limited number of single issues (like postponing the 'modernisation' of short range nuclear missiles) as long as this can be done by (more or less implicit) reference to the fear – shared with the allies – of the SPD winning the 1990-elections. This is different from proposing a concept of détente and *Ostpolitik* for the Western alliance. The latter would make it possible to back up specific stands with reference to a rationale actually competing for political influence in the allied capitals as well.

Furthermore, gradual change in Europe requires that many different states and social groups acquiesce in it. It will be difficult for the present German government to elicit any such consent until it defines itself more sharply. This means taking on its internal opposition. There are strong groups in the CDU with well-thought-out positions. But to date the party leadership has preferred to balance the different groups by imprecise policies and a political discourse that keeps all the options open.

The reason might be that the essential orientation of the CDU is domestic. Reinterpreting the Soviet Union obviously relates to the functions of ideology in domestic politics. There is a link between domestic interests and East–West ideological image-making. But détente and Germany are also very concrete issues. It is, therefore, possible for the conservatives to become much more active participants in détente. The present tendency is simply to fudge the issues, with all the dangers this implies.

2. The main controversies in the SPD at present are German–French relations and détente from above/below: these are important questions, and relate to prospective major changes in the European order. The SPD may well attain a realistic policy of stabilising *and* forwarding the change preferred. But this entails tough decisions and runs the danger of ending up as a policy of stabilising *simpliciter*. A certain drift to the centre is noticeable. It is thus likely that the principled, overall thinking will remain along the lines of 'common security' (etc.), whereas the specific questions, especially in relation to France, will be settled by the leadership – i.e., *Realpolitik*. This will make the SPD somewhat more capable of cooperation with the Right, but it does not at all constitute a consensus with the CDU. The Greens are not a possible ally either. The FDP and SPD have many principles in common. The likelihood of their reforming a coalition probably depends on other questions, in particular, the economic policy of either.
3. There are at least two main options:
   (a) The FRG keeps a rather low profile in European security – or at least in the *Western* formulation of a common policy. With an unchanged CDU in power, continuity will be the keynote under normal circumstances, and foreign policy will be defined by limited, individual goals (as in the *smaller* European countries – See Chapter 17, section 3.3).
   (b) Another possibility is a more activist line, where the FRG participates in the formulation of common Western positions,

> and even takes a role as one of the leading nations. This would require a decisive lead in the domestic debate. A strong architectonic policy would justify controversial positions. The CDU has hung back from such decisiveness. It could show decisiveness after a showdown with the right wing of the party. But such decisiveness might equally be shown by an FDP–SPD government after the 1990 elections.

The compromise between FDP and neo-SPD would be a whole-hearted but not intransigent commitment to transform the East–West Conflict in Europe. As shown above this is *at present* one way of giving a consistent rationale for Germany, Europe and Security policy.

Notes and References

1. *Die Zeit*, no. 44, 28 October 1988, front page.
2. Among the best descriptions of this interesting episode (the zero/double-zero debate in the FRG and especially in the government) is that of Berthold Meyer: 'Viel Lärm um Null und Doppel-Null. Eine *chronique scandaleuse*' ('Much Ado About Zero and Double Zero: A *chronique scandaleuse*') in *Vorgänge*, no. 5 (September 1987) 36–48. Details of the tricks and manoeuvres within the government parties were offered by *der Spiegel* throughout the period, and unflattering comments were heard from *die Zeit* and *Neue Zürcher Zeitung*.
3. See Egbert Jahn, Pierre Lemaitre and Ole Wæver, 'European Security: Problems of Research on Non-military Aspects', *Copenhagen Papers*, 1 (1987).
4. Action theory: Ole Karup Pedersen, *Udenrigsminister P. Munchs opfattelse af Danmarks stilling i International Politik* (Copenhagen: Gads Forlag, 1970). Inertia: Kjell Goldmann, *Change and Stability in Foreign Policy: The Problems and Possibilities of Détente* (Princeton University Press, forthcoming). Ideology: Walter Carlsnaes, *Ideology and Foreign Policy* (Oxford: Basil Blackwell, 1986); and Sasson Sofer, 'International Relations and the Invisibility of Ideology', *Millenium*, vol. 16(3) (1987) 489–521. 'Foreign Policy Eras' (a 'step-model' of regimes' mode of adaptation): Hans Mouritzen, *Finlandization: Towards a General Theory of Adaptive Politics* (Aldershot: Avebury, 1988). More generally on cognitive factors: Goldmann, *Change and Stability* and Mouritzen, *Finlandization*. (On the question whether this *is* a tendency in foreign policy theory, see my review of Goldmann and Carlsnaes, forthcoming in *Journal of Peace Research*.)
5. Josué V. Harari (ed.), *Textual Strategies: Perspectives in Post-Structuralist Criticism* (New York: Cornell University Press, 1979); Ernesto Laclau and Chantal Mouffe, *Hegemony and Socialist Strategy:*

Towards a Radical Democratic Politics (London: Verso, 1985); Jaques Derrida, *Writing and Difference* (Chicago: University of Chicago Press, 1978); and several other books by Derrida.

6. Laclau and Mouffe, *Hegemony and Socialist Strategy* (Note 5) especially 105–45.
7. Thomas C. Schelling, *The Strategy of Conflict* (New York: Harvard University Press, 1960) 34ff and 71. See also the 'bastion strategy' in Mouritzen, *Finlandization* (Note 4) 78ff.
8. That freedom is, for Willy Brandt, the fulcrum appears cogently from his '*wir sind nicht zu Helden geboren. Ein Gespräch über Deutschland mit Birgit Kraatz* (Zürich: Diogenes Verlag, 1986) for example 57ff, 107ff and 148ff. See also his *Menschenrechte misshandelt und missbraucht* (Reinbek bei Hamburg: Rowohlt, 1987) and *People and Politics* (London: Collins, 1978) 501ff. An example of the view that power is not necessarily productive is the reaction to President Reagan's actions and tone in the early 1980s, summed up in the (often-cited) words of then Chancellor Schmidt: 'We can afford no gestures of strength and no doughty demonstrations of steadfastness. We've had a noseful of that sort of thing'. Here quoted from G. Craig and A. George, *Force and Statecraft* (Oxford: Oxford University Press, 1983) 148.
9. It will be noted that these basic security political orientations are presented as sharing a basic structure. This I have tried previously to present in the form of some semi-semiotic *figures* ('Sikkerhedsfigurer i vesttysk debat, 1983–1987' ('Figures of security in West German debate, 1983–1987') in J. J. Jensen (ed.), *Europa i Opbrud* (The Break-up of Europe) (Esbjerg: Sydjysk Universitetsforlag, 1988) 189–221. However, I now consider this conception to be inadequately developed and prefer to circulate a draft to those interested in the possibility of working on the semiotic structure of *security* ('A Few – Somewhat Critical – Notes on the concept of Common Security: Part II', unpublished paper).
10. For an overview of the various elements of Deutschlandpolitik, see Rudolf Horst Brocke, *Deutschlandpolitische Positionen der Bundestagsparteien: Synopse* (Erlangen: Erlanger Beiträge zur Deutschlandpolitik, 1985). This book does not show the inner logic of the positions, but the specific arguments and positions. It is thus complementary to a project of the present type.
11. For example, Manfred Wörner in *Bulletin*, 5/2 (1987) 107. In the deployment debate, this was a crucial argument for Dregger (CDU) and Waigel (CSU) – *Die Nachrüstungdebatte im Deutschen Bundestag*, Hrsg. von Freimut Duve (Reinbek bei Hamburg: Rowohlt, 1984) 41 and 84.
12. *Die Nachrüstungdebatte* (Note 11), 84.
13. Christian Hacke, 'Die ost- und deutschlandpolitische Konzeption der parlamentarischen Opposition des 6. Deutschen Bundestages im Spannungsfeld zwischen Adaption und Alternative' in Egbert Jahn and Volker Rittberger (eds), *Die Ostpolitik der BRD* (Opladen: Westdeutscher Verlag, 1974) 29–52. Kjell Goldmann, *Détente. Domestic*

Politics as a Stabilizer of Foreign Policy (Stockholm: Department of Political Science Report no. 1, 1984) 60–7.

14. Richard von Weizsäcker, *Die deutsche Geschichte geht weiter* (München: dtv, 1985) (original version, 1983) 12.
15. 'Toward an Overall Western Strategy for Peace, Freedom and Progress', *Foreign Affairs* (Fall 1982) 42–66; here pp. 46ff. And in *Bulletin* 4/2 (1987) 94.
16. Gunter Holmann in *Die Zeit*. 27 February 1987, 5.
17. 'Toward an Overall Western Strategy' (Note 4) 48.
18. The lack of military détente is an established 'truth' in peace research circles, in Eastern Europe, and among the left wing in Western Europe. However, in strategic studies exactly the opposite is equally well-established: détente ran into trouble exactly because it tried to link the political aspects with arms control.
19. Brandt, *People and Politics* (Note 11) 495. Helmut Schmidt in *Die Nachrüstungsdebatte*, 92ff. Helga Haftendorn, *Sicherheit und Stabilität* (München: dtv, 1986) 20ff and 102.
20. Beer in the Bundestag, 4 June 1987; *Das Parlament*, 13 June.
21. The speech by Fred C. Iklé reprinted in *S+F* (1986/1) 48–51; quoted from p. 49.
22. *The NATO Report*, vol. 1, no. 24 (10 March 1986) 8.
23. For example, von Weizsäcker's: 'Die Deutsche Geschichte', (note 14) 58ff. Klaus Bölling quotes Genscher as follows: 'The FDP will have no part in the dangerous simplification that good and evil may be divided neatly by system', in *Bonn von aussen betrachtet* (Stuttgart: DVA, 1986) 137ff.
24. Wörner in *Bulletin*, 5 February (Note 11) 104.
25. See Egbert Jahn, 'The Tactical and Peacepolitical Concept of Détente', *Bulletin of Peace Proposals* (1981/1) 33–43; Johan Galtung, *There are Alternatives* (Nottingham, 1984) 40–8 and 69–80.
26. Bahr in the Bundestag, 7 May 1987, *Das Parlament*, 23 May. On 4 June Brandt characterised this – following Bahr word for word – as the second phase of détente policy (*Das Parlament*, 13 June, 3.) In Social Democratic terminology, this refers to a policy that could be implemented as of now.
27. 'Die Chance besteht', *Die Neue Gesellschaft* (1987/5) 412. This is developed at length in Bahr's small book, *Zum europäischen Frieden: Eine Antwort auf Gorbatschow* (Berlin: Corso bei Siedler, 1988).
28. See Jahn *et al.*, *European Security* (Note 3) Chapter 8, which expresses this view.
29. Wörner in *Bulletin*, 5 February 1987 (Note 11) 104.
30. This is forthcoming in V. Harle and P. Sivonen (eds), *TAPRI Yearbook, 1989* (London: Francis Pinter, 1989).
31. *TAPRI Yearbook 1989*, as well as Wæver, 'A Few – Somewhat Critical – Notes on the Concept of Common Security', working paper, forthcoming; and Jahn *et al.*, *European Security* (Note 11) 48–55.
32. The most thorough attempt to deal with this is Reinhard Mutz, 'Gemeinsame Sicherheit: Grundzüge einer Alternative zum Abschreck-

ungsfrieden', in Egon Bahr and Dieter Lutz (eds) *Gemeinsame Sicherheit. Idee und Koncept. Bd. 1.* (Baden-Baden: Nomos, 1986) 83–157.

33. An interesting meeting that took place before the drafting of the common paper is described by Carl-Christian Kaiser, 'Wandel durch Wettbewerb?' in *Die Zeit*, 7 March 1986; and by Peter Bender, 'Sicherheitspartnerschaft und friedliche Koexistenz' in *Die Neue Gesellschaft* (1986/4) 343–6. The common document was published among other places in *Frankfurter Rundschau*, 28 August 1987. Among the many interesting comments following, see *Die Zeit*, nos. 36 and 38, 28 August and 11 September – and especially *Der Spiegel* from 31 August 1987 with a most interesting interview of Eppler (SPD) and Reinhold (SED).

34. Erhard Eppler, 'Friedenspolitik und Ideologie' *Mediatus* (1986/4) 1, 9–13. This is included in his new book, *Wie Feuer und Wasser. Sind Ost und West friedensfähig?* (Hamburg: Rowohlt, 1988). The book does not add much to the article, but its existence does show that the issue of ideology can be presented as a general framework for understanding the situation. Thomas Meyer, 'Ein neuer Rahmen für den Ost–West-Dialog', *Die neue Gesellschaft* (1987/10) 870–7.

35. Eppler, 'Friedenspolitik und Ideologie' (Note 34) 11.

36. Eppler, 'Friedenspolitik und Ideologie' (Note 34). See also Christiane Rix, 'Ansätze für eine neue Sicherheitspolitik der DDR', *Hamburger Beiträge*, Heft 10 (December 1986).

37. Eppler, 'Friedenspolitik und Ideologie' (Note 34) 11. Less as an abstract exercise and more in terms of practical policy, ideas relating to responsible approaches to peace and democratisation in the East and West have been put forward by Karsten D. Voigt. ('Gesellschaftliche Reformen: gemeninsame Freiheit?', *Deutschland Archiv* (1988/6) 598–605; criticism by Klaus Leciejewski and a reply from Voigt followed in no. 10, 1051–7. He has presented similar ideas on many occasions.) He stresses that détente, the creation of a European peace order, and overcoming the division of Europe are all necessarily linked to domestic reforms on both side. This implies first that certain processes of domestic reform are necessary for this international change, and secondly that the international developments are important parameters for the attempts at domestic reform. The West should not try to decide developments on the Eastern side – but *should* be aware of the ways in which these developments set the conditions for processes of reform.

38. *Bulletin*, 14 December 1983, 1247.

39. *Bulletin*, 9 August 1984, 818.

40. *Bulletin*, 5 February 1987 (Note 11) 101 and 104. In one of his last speeches as minister, in which he adopted a more conciliatory line on several other questions, he made this point even more strongly (*Bulletin*, 24 November 1987, 1115).

41. *Bulletin*, 5 February 1987, 105 and in *Die Nachrüstungsdebatte* (Note 11) 147.

42. For example, *Bulletin*, 5 February 1987, 103. The rejection of 'security

partnership' appeared in the Ministry of Defence 'White Book' of 1983 (122) – but not in the 1985 one.

43. *Bulletin*, 4 February 1987 (Note 11) 96ff.
44. In Kohl's governmental address of 4 May 1983, the word 'détente' did not appear. In the 1983–5 period, Genscher, Geissler and von Weizsäcker (amongst others) presented broad, long-term détente as the aim, whereas Theo Waigel of the CSU said 'With us there is no continuation or "reprint" of a 1970s-style détente policy'. Kohl ended up in that position through his refusal to pronounce the word. See Mertes: 'Kontinuität und Wandel in der deutschen Aussenpolitik', *Bulletin*, 14 May 1983, 137–44; on Waigel and Geissler, see *Die Zeit*, 27 February 1987, 5.; von Weizsäcker in *Bulletin*, 1 March 1985; Genscher very clearly in *Bulletin*, 9 August 1984, 817.
45. Egon Bahr, 'Macht und Ohnmacht Europas in den Perspektiven der Allianz–Arbeitsteilung zwischen den USA und Westeuropa', in *Die neue Gesellschaft*, vol. 34/3, 1987, pp. 221–7, ref. to p. 225; 'Die Chance' (Note 27) 412.
46. As lately as the debate in the Bundestag on 4 June 1987: Theodor Waigel CSU; *Das Parlament*, 13 June, 5.
47. Rix, 'Ansätze für eine neue Sicherheitspolitik der DDR', (Note 36) especially 49ff.
48. *Bulletin*, 4 February 1987, 94f.
49. Wörner: 'Gemeinsame Werte – gemeinsame Schicksal', *Europäische Wehrkunde* (1987/1) 11, and 'Begrenzte Kooperation mit Moskau, aber keine "Sicherheitspartnerschaft"', *Europäische Wehrkunde* (1986/4) 195–200 (especially 196); General Hans Joachim Mack: 'Weichenstellung ins nächste Jahrtausend', *Europäische Wehrkunde*, 19–27 – see especially the figure on 22. See also Kohl in *Das Parlament*, 13 June 1987, 13; Genscher in *Bulletin*, 9 August 1984, 817 and 'Toward an Overall Western Strategy' (Note 15), 46; Karsten Voigt, 'Die Funktionen von NATO und Warschauer Pakt auf dem Weg zur Sicherheitspartnerschaft', *Die neue Gesellschaft* (1985/2) 134–9 (135); Reinhard Mutz 'Das Harmel-Princip. Fossil oder Wegweiser einer politischen Strategie der NATO?', *Die Neue Gesellschaft* (1985/2) 101–6; Peter Glotz, 'Mehr Sicherheit durch FOFA?' in *Europäische Wehrkunde* (1987/4) 195–9.
50. See, for example, Helga Haftendorn, *Sicherheit und Entspannung. Zur Aussenpolitik der Bundesrepublik Deutschland 1955–1982* (Baden-Baden: Nomos, 1983) 269ff.
51. On German television 25 February 1985, *Bulletin*, 25 (1 March 1985) 206.
52. The classic expression of this view is to be found in 'Referat des Leiters des Presse- und Informationsamtes des Landes Berlin vor der Evangelischen Akademie Tutzing am 15. Juli 1963' (Bahr's 'Wandel durch annäherung' speech), *Die deutsche Ostpolitik 1961–1970. Kontinuität und Wandel*, documentation published by Boris Meissner (Köln: Verlag Wissenschaft und Politik, 1970) 45–8.
53. 'We had to accept the *status quo* territorially in order to dislodge it politically', Willy Brandt, in *People and Politics* (Note 8) 498.
54. *Die Zeit*, 27 February 1987, 5. and *Bulletin*, 5 February 1987, 104.
55. Günter Gaus: 'we must sit tight with the fact that peace in Europe,

strengthened by relative detente, will for the foreseeable future be tied to the unconditional recognition of the status quo and the current political tenancy'. 'Western Europe needs a stable Eastern Europe to survive, and vice versa'. ('A Peace Policy for Germany', in R. Steinke and M. Vale (eds), *Germany Debates Defense* (New York and London, 1983) 97–116; quoted from 108 and 109). Klaus Bölling speaks out sharply against any form of destabilisation (*Bonn von aussen* (Note 23), especially 182–91). He even warns against spelling out, for example in speeches in the Bundestag, 'the insurmountable disparities between the systems' or the 'unjust character' of the DDR state (183ff). Gaus and Bölling are both influential social-democrats close to Schmidt, and both former leaders of the 'permanent representation' in East Berlin (the almost-embassy).

56. 'Toward an Overall Western Strategy' (Note 15) 57.
57. For instance in *Bulletin*, 1 July 1986, 661.
58. For example, *Bulletin*, 9 August 1984, 819: 'These contacts with our Eastern neighbours serve the cause of stability – they are not directed against anybody. They do not affect the relationship of the respective states with the Eastern alliance or to other alliance partners in that system'. Parts of this sentiment were repeated word for word by Kohl three months later, but without the explicit reference to the Eastern alliance and the role of the Soviet Union in Eastern Europe – *Bulletin*, 20 November 1984, 1242.
59. Kohl, *Bulletin*, 20 November 1984 (Note 44) 1244.
60. Reprinted in *Die Neue Gesellschaft* (1985/11) 1003–11, and in H. Ehmke, K. Koppe and H. Wehner (eds), *Zwanzig Jahre Ostpolitik* (Bonn: Verlag Neue Gesellschaft, 1986) 279–82. In the latter book – a Social Democratic compendium on détente and East policy – Ehmke's article, together with one by Hans-Adolf Jacobsen, constitute the section on 'Die humane Dimension'! Jacobsen's article is primarily a plea for contacts, confidence-building and especially the demolishing of enemy images ('Begegnungen in Osteuropa 1965–1985: Erfahrungen – Einsichten – Perspektiven', 293–308).
61. 'Entspannungspolitik in einer anderen Sicht. Eine Antwort' by the pseudonymous *** (spokesman for Solidarnosc) in *Die Neue Gesellschaft* (1986/6) 548–56.
62. This can be seen, for example, in the 'Memorandum to citizens, groups and governments in all CSCE countries' entitled 'Giving Real Life to the Helsinki Accords' and worked out by the so-called 'European network for East–West Dialogue' with the German, Green member of the European Parliament, Dieter Esche, as main coordinator. (The document is reprinted in *East European Reporter*, vol. 2, no. 2 (1986) 52–60). See also the articles and debates by and with Peter Brandt in, for example, *Deutschland Archiv*.
63. These could in classic diplomatic terminology be labelled 'détente', as this does not necessarily lead to basic change. (See Craig and George, *Force and Statecraft* (Note 8) 238ff.) The CDU prefers other terms.
64. The connection of the détente policy with reformism is spelled out by Voigt in 'Gesellschaftliche Reformen' (Note 38).
65. This is combined with adequate defence and thus with a measure of

self-help *security* too. Adequate defence is not part of the dynamic, but not to mention it at all would give a false picture. This distinguishes the new SPD view from that of the Greens, who would probably find little to quarrel with in the rest of the SPD scenario.

66. In particular in his widely noticed speech in Davos in February 1987 to the 'World Economic Forum'.
67. Hans-Dietrich Genscher, 'Wir müssen an der Brücke des Vertrauens mitbauen', in *Die Welt*, special section 'Welt Report', 21 October 1988.
68. Rupert Scholz, 'Plädoyer für ein Konzept gegenseitiger Sicherheit', *Die Welt*, 21 October 1988.
69. Here quoted from then minister of Defence Manfred Wörner, *Bulletin*, 24 November 1987, 1116.
70. 'Europa braucht eine neue Form der Toleranz', *Die Welt*, 21 October 1988.
71. *Das Parlament*, 23 May 1987, 7.
72. 'Ein Plan für ganz Europa', *Die Zeit*, no. 43, 21 October 1988, 3.
73. Christiane Rix, *'New' and 'Old' Thinking – Prospects and Limits of a New Security Policy in Europe. The Case of Both Germanies*, paper presented at the Symposium 'Central Problems of Peace and Conflict Research', Goethe Institute in collaboration with Centre for Peace and Conflict Research, Copenhagen, 7–8 November 1988, 9.
74. The underlying narrative is the 'strength' that has been a constant of CDU dealings with the East since Adenauer.
75. Ernst Martin, *Zwischenbalanz: Deutschlandpolitik der 80er Jahre* (Stuttgart, Bonn Aktuell, 1986). Similar claims were put forward, very shortly after the Kohl government came to power, by Pierre Hassner, as a theoretical possibility: 308 in his 'Zwei deutschen Staaten in Europa' in Werner Weidenfeld (ed.), *Die Identität der deutschen* (Münich: Hanser, 1983) 294–323. It is of course hotly debated whether the SPD would have achieved more or less in the same situation. See the debate in Parliament on 31 October 1987, where the SPD gave a positive evaluation to parts of the government policy but claimed they would have been able to do much more. *Das Parlament*, vol. 37, no. 44 (31 October 1987).
76. 'Community of responsibility' ('*Verantwortungsgemeinschaft*') is a very interesting concept. According to Rudolf von Thadden it is a concept he invented on 7 October 1981 – and even he himself has been surprised to see how fast the concept was taken up and how well it seemed to fit some needs. Rudolf von Thadden, 'Erbe und Verplichtung. Der Weg zur "Verantwortungsgemeinschaft" der Deutschen', *Das Parlament*, no. 23 (3 June 1988) 10.
77. Stephan Keukeleire, 'The second phase of the Ostpolitik: the changing attitudes of the West German political parties towards the security position of the FRG', paper presented at the ECPR Joint Session, Rimini, 5–10 April 1988, 10.
78. Wilfried von Bredow and Rudolf Horst Brocke, *Das deutschlandpolitische Konzept der SPD*, Erlanger Beiträge zur Deutschlandpolitik (1986) especially 12ff.
79. Von Bredow and Brocke, *Das deutschlandpolitische Konzept* (Note 78) 103.

13 The Debate on European Security in Bulgaria

Nansen Behar

1 INTRODUCTION

The debate on European security in Bulgaria has certain determining features. Bulgaria is a socialist state, and its military doctrines are determined by membership of the Warsaw Pact; it is also a Balkan state, with its own Balkan policy of peaceful and neighbourly relations. It has, for example, signed a treaty of friendship with Greece, which is a NATO member. The past few years have witnessed a transformation in the security debate in Bulgaria; interest in non-military aspects of security has grown as interest in military security has waned. Research institutes and public bodies such as the Bulgarian Academy of Sciences, the University of Sofia, the Committee for European Security, and the Ecoforum for Peace have been developing and discussing new models for general and regional security. Their debates have centred on two groups of problems:

1. First, the search for non-military structures of security: economic, ecological and other forms of security are discussed.
2. Second, the establishment of a nuclear weapon-free zone in the Balkans.

2 NON-MILITARY STRUCTURES OF SECURITY

The quickening of Bulgarian interest in non-military security may be ascribed to several factors. First, there is the tendency toward reform in the socialist countries exemplified by the *glasnost* and *perestroika* processes. These tend to create an atmosphere in which military thinking, as Gorbachev has said, tends to give way to more civilised forms of international relations. Secondly, the stance of some of the East European countries relative to the military aspects of security in

Europe and the world has been evolving. In his article in *Pravda* of 17 September 1987, Gorbachev stated that 'defensive strategy' and 'military sufficiency' were doctrines which, if accepted, would give a strong impetus to disarmament. These doctrines concern the limitation of armed forces to a level sufficient to ward off aggression but inadequate to initiating such aggression, and their implementation would enhance the mutual trust of contiguous countries. They are particularly applicable in regions where there are many small states belonging to different military and political blocs; the Balkan peninsula is a case in point.

A third factor relates to the economic development of the small socialist countries. The modernisation and restructuring of the economies of the small socialist countries has made them to a much greater extent dependent on the world market, and an increasing part of their revenue is derived from foreign trade and techno–scientific exchange. This has highlighted the need for a greater volume and a better balance of trade between countries of different social systems, a need which is itself one of the cornerstones of any system of non-military security.

Fourthly, processes within the Balkan peninsula have facilitated the development of new ideas, as conditions have begun to favour détente between countries belonging to different military and political blocs.

In recent years, experts at the Academy of Sciences and Sofia University have set out to define the elements of a stance on systems of common security appropriate to the needs of a small socialist country. The stance would include both military and non-military elements. This has not been easy. The opinion that security in the modern world inevitably means military security is widely held and deeply rooted, and it is unlikely to change in the immediate future. But discussion of these issues has begun.

Thus, in 1988 the Committee for Disarmament and Security of the Presidium of the Bulgarian Academy of Sciences published a book entitled *Peace – a Universal Value*, which focuses on aspects of non-military security, for the most part on economic security. The Institute for International Relations at the Bulgarian Academy of Sciences has organised publications and conferences on the subject of the relationship 'disarmament:development', 'development' being taken here as a prerequisite of security. A group of young scientists at Sofia University are working out mathematical models for a gradual decrease in the level of military confrontation between the blocs, and a gradual 'filling-in' of the security system with non-military factors. Naturally, though the common thread is non-military security, the approaches differ. Discussion has not yielded any common point of view on either the relation between the military and non-military components of a system of common security, or the relative importance of the different components of non-military security.

The Union of Scientific Workers has played a pioneering role in the Bulgarian security debate. In October 1987, in collaboration with the Berlin Regional Centre of the World Federation of Scientific Workers, it organised a symposium on the subject of 'European Security'. In Bulgaria, this subject was discussed at an open scientific forum attended by 42 scholars and scientists from fourteen countries including the USA. High-ranking officers also took part in the debate, which is a further indication of the new trends in the security debate.

Ecological security is a one concept of non-military security that has been much debated in Bulgaria in recent years. The problem of ecology is assuming ever greater importance in the East European countries.[1] Pollution is now a source of internal tension in certain countries and is detrimental to living standards. Since ecological problems transcend national boundaries, the search for a common solution gives rise to the notion of international ecological security. Some publications point out that in an age of trans-national ecological crises, it is not acceptable to regard ecological sovereignty as following from national sovereignty; every country should be obliged to comply with international norms restricting activities ecologically detrimental to their neighbour states. In the absence of such norms, there is a danger of pollution being exported to other countries, and the further danger that internal tension will follow within the neighbour state, with the repercussions this suggests for national and international security. Study of ecological security is still in an early phase in Bulgaria, but is expected to expand considerably over the next few years.

The international movement of scientists, 'Ecoforum for Peace', has played an essential part in the search for a commonly accepted concept of ecological security. This movement was organised on the initiative of scientists and of the magazine *Zashtita na prirodata* ('Protection of Nature'), and is based in Sofia. In the two years since its foundation, the movement has gained an international reputation in the scientific community. It was founded during the conference 'Ecology and Peace' in Varna in August 1986, which was attended by

88 scientists from 32 countries and observers from twelve international organisations. The main objectives of Ecoforum have been set out in the booklet of the same name published in Sofia in 1986, but the movement has also set out to promote and support studies in the field of alternative and in particular ecological security. In October 1988 Ecoforum for Peace organised a big international conference on the subject of the River Danube as a single economic and ecological entity. One of the major topics was the ecological security of the Danube basin, which forms part of eight different European countries, and how the ecological tensions related to the pollution of the river could be resolved. Ecoforum for Peace was invited to report on the conference's conclusions at the symposium on the problems of common security organised by the UN Economic Programme, the Peace Research Institute in Oslo and the Soviet Academy of Sciences.

The debate in Bulgaria on models of alternative security is not of merely national import. As such discussion becomes part of the all-European dialogue, it contributes to change the process of decision-making, to enhance confidence and to create a climate favourable to the solution of security problems in Europe.

3 A NUCLEAR WEAPON-FREE ZONE IN THE BALKANS: AN OUTLINE PROPOSAL

The creation of a Balkan nuclear weapon-free zone would have important political, strategic and economic aspects. It would contribute to regional security, and might create the impulse for new processes aiming at all-European security. Agreement between states which are members of the military alliances of the two blocs may help to establish more confident relationships between the alliances; it would also promote the goals of the Helsinki Process. If the Nordic countries and Central Europe became nuclear weapon-free zones, the Balkans would form a third and important link in a nuclear weapon-free belt traversing the areas of maximum tension in Europe. The task is the more urgent in the context of increasing fear of nuclear war in Europe.

In the Bulgarian view, the zone would take the following form. All Balkan states would participate; with the exception of Albania, they are all signatories of the Nuclear Non-Proliferation Treaty. The zone would be defined by political rather than geographical boundaries. It would be guaranteed by the nuclear powers. Membership of the zone would consist in the commitment not to manufacture, acquire or test nuclear weapons, nor support other countries in ways that would compromise the zone's status. The nuclear powers would undertake neither to provide nuclear weapons nor assist in their production; not to stockpile or deploy nuclear weapons or their delivery systems in the Balkan states, and finally not to threaten these states with the use of nuclear weapons. Verification procedures would be provided for.

Certain other considerations relate to this proposal. The creation of the zone would be consistent with the belief that armament – and, in particular, nuclear armament – contributes nothing to the security of nations, and that this is outstandingly true of small nations. The economic development of the region would be enhanced by the increased cooperation that would ensue, and this by contrast *does* contribute to security. The peaceful use of nuclear energy should not be ruled out, nor membership of defensive alliances be made incompatible with membership of the zone. Creation of the zone is favoured by the fact that no potential member has its own nuclear weapons, either indigenous or foreign. Members of the different alliances have declared their support for the project, and public opinion is also in its favour. In the Balkans, détente has remained a reality.[2]

Support is not, however, universal. NATO considers that the zone would tip the military balance in the area in favour of the Warsaw Pact, and is therefore applying pressure to Greece to reject the idea. There is no unanimity as to the nature or details of the zone, and the line dividing NATO and the Warsaw Pact passes through the area proposed. Clearly, the project is not susceptible of easy or immediate implementation, and the possibility of its realisation would depend on the climate of international relations.[3] But the proposal undoubtedly deserves the most serious consideration.

4 THE CONCEPT OF ECONOMIC SECURITY

Common general security in the contemporary world can be understood only in the following terms: as a policy of states and groups of states; as a mode of international relations; and as a process whose end product is a system of mutually advantageous rules and constraints which guarantee the prevention of both armed conflict and the build-up of tension.

The notion of economic security has been gaining ground in recent years as one of the possible components of such a system of non-military security; the relevance of the notion is clear in a world increasingly interconnected and interdependent not only in the economic field but in the fields of information and culture. Such interconnections do not necessarily follow the geo–military divisions of, for example, the European continent. Regional security and cooperation assume a particular importance in the light of this fact.

Of all the differences between the European states, the economic factor is that which has, till now, contributed most to the formation of a dual system of security. A feature of this system is that it is not a static one, and military parity may be maintained at ever lower levels while the complementarity of the European economies grows. The similar economic structures and levels of development of the different groups of European countries create the conditions for a rational and mutually beneficial interdependence. The differences in European economies merely enhance this potential for complementarity. Mutual benefit must of course govern these interactions, as 'interdependence' between countries of differing degrees of economic development – we may cite the relations of certain industrial countries with the Third World – does nothing to create a system of non-military security.

Economic interdependence in its turn gives rise to the problem of 'security limits'. Economic processes may trigger off national instability, and this may have repercussions for international security. Security is enhanced only where economic sovereignty is not threatened by interdependence. A distinction should be made between cooperation and interdependence: economic cooperation is a form of relationship out of which interdependence may grow. Interdependence then takes the form of permanent relations between the economies in question. It cannot exist where the potential for sanctions on the one side is greater than on the other, allowing one of the two economies to exercise excessive influence over the other. The main forms of economic interdependence between developed countries are the dependence of local production on imports, dependence on foreign energy resources, the dependence of internal growth on export revenue, and dependence on foreign credits. Threats to security are generated when imbalances are created, as has been shown by Poland's depending on foreign credit in the absence of any equivalent potential for generating export revenue. Politics of course counts for a great deal in these matters, and economic security cannot be judged in terms of the details of trade, but of the overall relations beween two countries or groups of countries. Self-interest must govern relations, in the sense that each country must seek to avoid the dangers inherent, for example, in imbalances of trade. But if bilateral interests are to develop into an international system of security, then it will be necessary to establish generally accepted norms for international economic relations, and by doing so, lay one of the foundation stones of the new world economic order.

Economic security as a policy contributes to international security. It is dynamic in character, and changes with shifts in the balance of power or new economic or scientific developments. It requires a quantum of political will, which is then reinforced by the economic security attained. The system of rules and agreements ensuring economic security could consist of: measures to limit economic policies discriminating against other countries; rules for achieving balanced mutual exchange; rules governing the credit policies of the two blocs; and agreements excluding the use of economic pressure for political ends. The purpose of these rules would be to prohibit the use of economic instruments against 'the other side'.

At a more practical level, a first step in this direction would be the improvement of East–West cooperation in Europe, and the development of new forms of cooperation such as scientific and technical cooperation, joint ventures, projects in third countries, and so on. The recent resumption of talks between Comecon and the EEC, which began in the 1970s and were subsequently broken off, is an excellent omen. The institutionalisation of the relationship between East and West can only benefit Europe and in the long term contribute to global security.

This is true not least because economic development in itself promotes security. Social tension and militarisation go hand in hand, and the satisfaction of basic human needs and higher level of social justice that characterise the developed countries inhibit the development of a militarist ideology.

A further step toward economic security might be increased scientific cooperation. The civilian orientation of scientific and technical research leads to intensified scientific exchanges at the international level. At present, the fewest exchanges occur in the most advanced fields of research, since these are generally connected to military research and production. Scientific cooperation among Third World countries is particularly well-suited to lead off this process, and would enhance their security by diminishing the dependence of the Third World on the industrialised nations. Such cooperation is obviously possible only after a certain threshold of development has been passed. In the more developed countries, moreover, the development of industry is not handicapped by the competition between military and civil institutions for scarce economic resources, with its concomitant of military influence exercised at governmental level.

After a five-year freeze in East–West economic relations, factors now emerging give some grounds for optimism in the search for non-military security in Europe. The resumption of talks between Comecon and the EEC is one such factor. Trade between the two systems has, during the past few years, tended away from the imbalances of the past. But time and tide wait for no man. The European resistance to stockpiling new nuclear weapons under the pretext of security is a first step towards the initiation of systems of non-military security, systems based not on mutual fear but on common interests. Only a system of this kind has the potential to develop into a system of genuine worldwide security.

Notes and References

1. N. Behar (ed.), *The Problem of Natural Resources and the Ecological Challenge in the East European Region*, sponsored by the UN University, Tokyo (Sofia, 1987).
2. Nicolae Ecobescu and Ioan Pascu, *Zone Denuclearizate* (Bucuresti: Editura Politica, 1985).
3. Study on 'The Question of Nuclear Weapon-free Zones', United Nations, New York (9 February 1985).

14 Finland and European Security: Traditions and Responses to Current Challenges

Pertti Joenniemi

1 SPECIFIC FEATURES

Although the European policies of Finland are in many ways similar to those of the other Euroneutrals, they are not identical. A different understanding of the term 'neutrality' prevails; it is not felt that war would be the ultimate test for Finnish neutrality, which is continuously at stake in the country's interaction with other states. The credibility of Finnish neutrality does not therefore depend upon the traditional appeal to international law. Nor has Finland adopted the critical approach sometimes associated with the small countries. The existing structures of power are accepted, and Finland has not sought to alter them. Finnish foreign policy is not about rebellion at the periphery.

European neutralism can be thought of as a reaction against the discipline exercised by the blocs in the name of unity and cohesion. In many cases, it can also be understood in terms of reactions against, and efforts to avoid, the subordination of European values to a form of East–West politics defined by the interests of the (more or less external) superpowers.[1] Neither of these considerations is relevant to Finland. There, the aim has been to support the established structures of power and the values they represent. Rather than adopt a critical stance, Finland has attempted to eliminate unnecessary conflicts, as these can jeopardise the stability of international relations. It has not made a habit of asserting unpleasant truths or spearheading exemplary initiatives. The approach has been pragmatic. Though Finland seeks concrete, realistic remedies for international instability, it keeps a low profile in issues which are ideologically sensitive or which stem from Utopian expectations.

Finnish foreign policy is not isolationist, and shows no signs of fortress mentality. 'Security is not about closing doors but about opening up', said President Kekkonen, in his opening speech at the exploratory phase of the European Conference on Peace and Security.[2] In general, Finnish neutrality is antithetical to the classic model, where the emphasis is on individualism, self-sufficiency and isolationism. Finland does not seek to opt out, but to score high on usefulness to the international system. Security is seen as a cooperative effort, as something that emerges from states adjusting to one another's requirements on a reciprocal basis.

At the heart of the Finnish outlook on security lies the desire for good and dependable relations with all essential powers, and in particular with the major powers and the neighbouring Nordic countries. The two alliances and the major powers are deemed to have considerable security interests in common. Though not always obvious, these are sufficient to avoid confrontation. Finnish foreign policy is not in the least idealistic, and is not underpinned by any expectation of international consensus. But it is widely thought that conflicts can be managed and security interests reconciled through cooperation and a skilful conduct of affairs. This belief is fundamental to Finland's attitude to European security.

For the uninitiated, it might seem that the Finnish attitude to security is related above all to its geopolitical position – that is, to the vicinity of one of the major powers. Circumstances rather than free choice might seem to have determined Finnish policy. This is partly true, but the current policies have deep historical, ideological, and cultural roots. The proximity of the Soviet Union influences Finnish policy less than is sometimes believed. To prove this point, a historical excursus is required.

2 PART OF TSARIST RUSSIA

The long period of Swedish rule in Finland came to an end with the Russo–Swedish war of 1808–9; Finland ceased to be a very peripheral part of Sweden and became instead a semi-peripheral part of Russia.

Sweden's Eastern buffer thus became the Russian Empire's Western buffer. The break with Sweden, however, was far from complete, and a part of the Finnish heritage stems from the period of Swedish rule. This meant, amongst other things, that certain traditions of popular participation could develop, and the country was spared a feudal system and an all-powerful aristocracy. The peasants established themselves as a fourth estate and had real, if limited, influence on the policies of the state. This influence was partly due to the fact that they owned their land and partly to the fact that the civil servants every now and then needed the support of the peasants to strengthen their own position. Another reason was that conscripted peasants were the mainstay of the army. Recruitment depended on the goodwill of the peasants, and they, in return, were granted some say in matters of state.

Finland under the Tsar had considerable autonomy. It was part of an all-European constellation in which the regional major powers were the most influential actors. It was in Russia's interest to make the border country a stable part of the Empire, as this helped to insulate Russia against the turmoils of the Napoleonic wars and exclude liberal trends at work in Europe. Since Sweden was now weaker, security from that quarter was no longer a major concern. Finland could be granted a special status, encouraged to prosper and permitted to develop its own culture to a greater extent than Russia's other Baltic possessions.

Finland was therefore allowed to possess all the institutions constitutive of nationhood with the exception of armed forces: a Senate, a civil service, a language (mainly Swedish among the elite) and its own religion. A long period of peace, with no real military obligations, imparted strong civilian and anti-war overtones to the Finnish self-image. The national identity was constructed within a community whose internal disparities were cultural and institutional, not military. Identity was defined in terms of belonging rather than exclusion, of being both within and without, and is not therefore bipolar in the usual way.

As careers opened up in the service of the Tsar and the Empire, the traditionally weak position of the Finnish nobility was further undermined. Among the peasants, a certain differentiation took place: those already wealthy prospered further, but the poor and landless became a rural labour force and sank to the lowest rung of society. This exacerbated inequality was later to prove catastrophic for the young nation.

Under the new conditions, the bourgeoisie had to adopt a consensual, hegemonic approach to politics. Its security depended on progress and competent management, on avoiding zero-sum types of conflict or a totalitarian, universalist approach to politics. What mattered was cultural development and national mobilisation, and not the acquisition of armaments or a policy of repression. Dissent had to be coped with, and the national church, for example, skilfully integrated into itself the various religious sects. Rivalries were mitigated, revolt was avoided. In 1905, after a period of somewhat tense relations with the Empire, universal suffrage was established by a far-reaching parliamentary reform. The labour movement, which developed fairly slowly in Finland, was tolerated and given a role in this national mobilisation, and a system of mass education was organised. As part of an Empire held together by traditions, Finland was loyal to the Tsar and his administrative apparatus, and this made ideological issues sensitive, not least for security reasons. The Russian Empire, like other European Empires, was particularly sensitive about the ideology of the French Revolution. The adoption of rather non-ideological positions was therefore in the national interest. For the smooth running of things it was advantageous to keep a low profile and to refrain from manifestations of sympathy towards Sweden or expressions of solidarity with the struggle of the Poles. Certain political currents, mostly left of centre, that combined ideology with populist, nationalist sentiment, had to be held in check. Under these conditions a bureaucratic tradition developed, which stressed the need for security issues to be left to the competent authorities.

3 LIBERALISM VERSUS REALISM

Although national consensus was the ideal, there were divergences of opinion on major issues of security.

A liberal school of thought took a constitutional position. It sought to minimise Finland's dependence on Russia, supported far-reaching reforms, and in general stressed the right to sovereignty of the small countries.[3] Its positions were often explicitly ideological, normative and legalistic. This line of thinking had largely Scandinavian and Western roots and found its support mainly among the Swedish-speaking elite.

A counterweight in the national debate was a realist school, 'realist' in the sense that its point of departure was the prevailing constellations of power. It did not seek radical changes, had no confidence in the force of law, and placed no reliance in international norms and universal solutions involving international organisations. In one respect, that it did not assert the primacy of military means, it deviated from realism as the term is understood today. For this school, national emancipation was a matter of development and cooperation within the existing pattern of power. It preferred to adopt a low profile on contentious issues and defined its position in terms of the national interest, rather than on ideological or normative grounds. The inspiration for these positions came from German thinkers, in particular Hegel; its spokesman was J. V. Snellman, a philosopher and a statesman.[4] Support came mainly from the Finnish-speaking rural areas.

The relationship to Russia was fundamental to the thinking of both schools. For a long time Finland remained a part of the periphery, with little security value for the Empire. Towards the end of the nineteenth century, however, this changed, and the Russian grip intermittently tightened. For the liberal school, this called for firm resistance, which at first took passive form – for example, the organising of appeals – but later issued in a general strike and efforts to acquire military power. Support was sought abroad in order to counteract the influence of Russia.

The realist school was confident that matters could be settled by skilful management of affairs and without recourse to external force. If developments generated fear and suspicion in Russia, the reason for this reaction should be understood and taken into account. The situation called not for protest, provocation, or revolt, but for demonstrations of loyalty. Issues could be settled by accommodation and cooperation; internal flexibility was stressed: the solution lay in resoluteness, in the ideological unity of the Finns, and in continued nation-building, which would take the form of further provision for the material and social welfare of the people. The realist school had little taste for dissenting political ideas or protesting individuals. It wanted the economically favourable relationship with the Empire to continue undisturbed.

Both schools were influential. The realist school was associated with the establishment and the liberal school with the opposition. The former may claim the credit for the fact that major clashes with the Empire were avoided and that independence was achieved without repression or armed struggle. Peaceful development, economic progress and a strengthening of Finland's culture continued without disruption. On the other hand, the liberal school could argue that its line had an impact on the final stage, the granting of independence by the Soviet Union in 1917. This was one of the effects of the First World War. Certainly the change of socioeconomic system in the Soviet Union fuelled aspirations for independence within both realist and liberal schools, and after the Russian Revolution, differences between the two schools were few.

4 BROKEN TRADITIONS

Soon after independence, the traditional Finnish approach to peace and security was set aside. The military training that the liberal, activist school had obtained from Germany came to serve a purpose quite other than that for which it had been sought; the victims of the civil war were not Russian, but Finnish. The divisions in Finnish society proved too deep to be bridged by social reforms and emancipation, and government became more repressive. The Soviet Union was fully occupied with its own internal problems, and there was no need for the bourgeoisie of an independent Finland to compromise. And though reformist rather than revolutionary in tendency, the workers were no longer prepared to wait peacefully for reforms.

A tragic contrast thus developed between the period of nation-building under Russian domination and the creation of the fully independent state. Consensual and hegemonic forms of government gave place to concepts of power based on arms and repression. In the Finnish Civil War of 1918 the Red Guards were defeated by the united forces of the Finnish White Guards and the German army. For later developments, it was important that the Soviet Union did not intervene, despite the fact that some Russian troops had remained in Finland after independence.

With the advent of independence, realist doctrines lost much of their attraction, and the liberal current of opinion prevailed in security matters. The political left, discredited by the Civil War, lost all legitimacy for some time to come. The emphasis was on liberal-democratic ideals, and Finland was perceived as something of a Western outpost against the East; the distinction between 'us' and 'them' became much stronger. Security was sought in the strengthening of international norms and in universal solutions, such as collective security within the framework of the League of Nations. One line of thinking favoured coexistence with the neighbouring great power despite its different socioeconomic system, and tried to avoid the impression that Finland was exploiting the difficulties of the Soviet Union. But activist ideas were also important. These were twofold: on the one hand, they sought to counterbalance the Soviet influence by recourse to political and military alliance. On the other, expansionist tendencies found expression in the aspiration to liberate various Finno–Ugrian peoples in the Karelian part of the Soviet Union. Finland's foreign policy was explicitly anti-communist.

In security policy, the doctrine of balance of power prevailed. Finland eschewed cooperation with the Soviet Union, and sought to counteract Soviet influence through alliances. At first, a common Baltic identity was stressed, under the protection of the Western powers whose supremacy had been established by the First World War. When conflict developed between these powers, this approach was abandoned in favour of a Nordic orientation, based on common neutrality.

This approach failed to convince the Soviet Union that no attack from Germany could take a Nordic route. The Soviet Union required guarantees that its security would not be threatened via Finland. Finland was, for its part, reluctant to give such guarantees, fearing that this would lead to loss of independence. At this juncture there was very little external or internal flexibility in Finnish security policies. Inability to come to terms with Moscow combined with the Molotov–Ribbentrop agreement between Moscow and Berlin to pave the way for the Winter War of 1939.

The losses suffered during this war did not change the Finnish outlook. On the contrary, an aggressive small-state ideology prevailed, acquiring chauvinist as well as pro-German characteristics in the early 1940s. Finland saw in alliance with Germany a solution to the Soviet threat. These hopes were unfounded, and after the 1941–4 war with the Soviet Union and the German defeat of 1945, it was time to draw the conclusions. Both the approach to security adopted by the 'irredenta' movement and the repressive internal policies had to be reconsidered, and reforms took place in both internal and external security policies.

5 THE POST-WAR PERIOD

Since reliance on international norms or organisations and attempts to predict the balance of power in Europe had proved catastrophic for Finland, Finnish policy had to be rethought. One option was to apply the approaches to security that had worked so well prior to independence. Flexibility became the key. This new line implied the restoration of good relations with the Soviet Union, freeing Finland from the vicissitudes of international relations, and opting out of balance of power politics.

Finland acknowledged the legitimate security interests of the Soviet Union – 'legitimacy' here meaning that these interests were and remain defensive in Northern Europe. The relationship between the two countries was regulated in 1948 by a Treaty of Friendship, Cooperation and Mutual Assistance. By this agreement, Finland guarantees that it will not engage in hostilities against the Soviet Union. This decreases the probability that an attack against the Soviet Union will come from a Nordic direction. Finland in this way succeeded in establishing trusting relations with its neighbour, something that has stabilised not only the security environment of Finland itself but the situation in Northern Europe more generally. A condition for the development of trust was that Finland very largely stay out of European post-war politics. As a country numbered among the defeated of the Second World War, it could, in any case, not expect to wield great influence. Relations between Finland and the Soviet Union are based on cooperation and the principle of non-interference in each other's internal affairs. Repressive models of power have again been replaced in Finnish security policy by notions of power stressing competence and progress.

After 1945, the realist school of thinking regained its influence. 'The pen has now to restore what the sword has destroyed' said President Paasikivi, the main guardian of the realist line during the immediate post-war period. In his words, wisdom in security policies started with recognition of the prevailing facts and realities. His policy was based on the understanding that the Soviet interest in Finland is a security interest and that, if this interest is taken into account, the relationship between the two countries is in every other respect normal. He assumed that, if Soviet security fears could be put to rest, the sovereignty of Finland was in no way endangered.

Throughout President Paasikivi's term of office, and until the late 1950s, Finnish foreign policy had isolationist features, as the priority was to establish trusting relations with the Soviet Union. It was thought that mutual trust could more easily be created if Finland did not take part in international politics. Prior to the Cold War, the United States and Great Britain also stressed that Finland should establish trustful relations with its neighbour.

The realist school also had considerable influence on the relations of internal and foreign policies. In general, the post-war years brought considerable democratisation in Finland. The labour movement and political left regained their legitimacy. This democratisation did not, however, reach as far as foreign affairs. Parliamentary influence, as well as the support of political parties and various non-governmental organisations, were needed in support of the new foreign policy line. But care was taken that these functions were confined to support. According to the realist school, the leadership has to be firmly in charge of foreign policy, otherwise ideological influences or moral currents may harm the national interest. President Paasikivi was himself a strong advocate of this rather elitist view. In his opinion, foreign policy was too complicated for the ordinary citizen to grasp, and public influence on his foreign policy was therefore insignificant.

The isolationist features of Finnish foreign policy have gradually disappeared, and Finland has become an active member of the international community. Internally, a broad consensus has emerged on foreign policy, and good relations with the Soviet Union have allowed Finland to pursue friendly relations with the West. A policy of neutrality has been articulated that defines Finland's position as outside the military alliances. A further reason for the adoption of a higher profile was the experience of the early 1960s, when Finnish relations with the Soviet Union deteriorated as a consequence of intensified East–West confrontation and events in Europe that ran counter to Soviet security interests. Since the Finnish–Soviet relationship had thus proved dependent on broader international developments, the conclusion was drawn that Finland could not remain passive. Efforts to preserve the stability of international relations were in the national interest. Disruption in superpower relations could have negative consequences for Finland, as the Berlin crises and the 1961 Soviet note to Finland (which requested consultations in the wake of increased Western activity in the Baltic) showed; clearly, a preemptive approach was needed. The line adopted has sometimes been characterised as 'status quo plus'. We might say that the notion of power defined in terms of progress and social competence has been expanded to international relations at large and is no longer confined to Finno–Soviet relations.

That Finnish policies have become active, while its isolationist features have gradually disappeared, does not signify a greater reliance on universal solutions, international norms, principles of collective security or policies of balance of power. In essence, the realist school of thought still prevails. The goal of international stability requires international activity, and sometimes changes are needed if nothing is really to change. This is the rationale behind Finland's active peace policy.

The adoption of such an approach has made Finland a diligent member of the United Nations and of many other international organisations. Nordic cooperation has developed and more generally Finland has acted as a bridge-builder between East and West. This has become one of its main foreign policy tasks. The European Security Conference has in many respects been the crowning glory of the new Finnish policy; Finland hosted one of the preparatory meetings, and the conference itself took place in Helsinki in 1975. In the words of the foreign policy leadership, Finland has become 'a constructive part' of the European security system.

6 THE CHANGING ENVIRONMENT

Though a more detailed analysis of Finnish post-war policy would be possible, the foregoing covers most of the essentials. Enough has been said to indicate that even among the small, neutral, European countries Finland is something of an odd man out.

What makes Finland difficult for many observers to categorise is that it has by and large rejected two lines of thinking: the ideas of balance of power and of spheres of influence maintained by force. These do not feature in Finnish foreign policy. It is felt that they place too much emphasis on the repressive aspects of power, and thus lead to a 'determinism' that restricts the options of small countries like Finland.

Both of these ideas have been tested, and found disastrously wanting. There is thus a broad awareness in Finland that balancing the threat of one Great Power against another is no answer to the country's security problems. A more scrupulous analysis is required. Rather than speculating on the vicissitudes of international relations, Finland has to opt out, to remove itself from balance of power calculations, and base its policy on commonality – that is, on the interdependence, heterogeneity and pluralism that characterise international relations.

Clearly, then, the period of détente was something of a heyday for Finnish foreign policy, and much attention has been devoted to the European Security Conference process. Détente seemed to prove beyond doubt that the basic assumptions of the Finnish foreign policy were valid. Against this background it is also clear that the decline of détente and the renewal of Cold War came not only as a profound disappointment, but as a fundamental challenge to the premisses underlying Finnish foreign policy, particularly in relation to Europe.

7 STRATEGIC PRESSURES

The dilemmas that Finland faced during the early 1980s related not only to deteriorating major power relations and international tensions in general, but to quite specific dangers.

Central Europe has for long been seen as the focal point of superpower tensions; the Nordic region has until recently remained peripheral, and has not, for a variety of reasons, been fully integrated into the system of blocs. But since the end of the 1970s it has been increasingly affected by the strategic rivalry of the superpowers. The overriding fear of the Nordic countries was – and to some extent still is – that the region might be drawn into this rivalry and the concomitant nuclear arms policies.

The increased emphasis on sea- and air-based cruise missiles was the first sign of these developments. It has since emerged that this emphasis derives not merely from the advent of a new weapons technology but from broader strategic trends. Much attention has been given to the naval developments in the High North, in the Norwegian and Barents Seas. The Nordic countries are inevitably exposed to the consequences of this strategic confrontation. There is no acute crisis but in structural terms the challenge is considerable.

These developments have been particularly confusing for Finland with its traditional allegiance to the post-war structures of international relations, and its assumption that the superpowers can prevent their confrontation from overflowing into the peripheral, Northern part of Europe. What mode of action is suitable for a small, neutral country like Finland under these new circumstances?

The issue has been taken up in presidential speeches. As early as 1978, President Kekkonen appealed to the major powers to restrict the development of cruise missiles.[5] President Koivisto extensively redrafted the security policy agenda in a speech at the Paasikivi Society in 1986.[6] Broaching the subject of maritime developments in northern waters, President Koivisto expressed his concern for the consequences for the Nordic region, and proposed that, in the Nordic region, particular consideration should be given to confidence-building measures relating to maritime areas, maritime air space, and naval operations.[7]

The speech of President Koivisto reflects growing Nordic concern. Finland has subsequently advocated naval confidence-building measures in several international forums, notably the United Nations. It has also proposed that the mandate of the European

Arms Control Talks in the context of the CSCE and the Stockholm Conference include naval arms control. The strategic pressures experienced by the Nordic countries have gone far toward legitimating the demand for a Nordic nuclear weapon-free zone, and it was agreed among the Nordic countries that a commission of inquiry should be established to study the matter. The task has been allotted to foreign ministry officials and a joint report is expected in due time. This is a significant step: the officials of three allied and two neutral countries are jointly studying the issues in preparation for a joint report.

Intensified strategic pressures have also led to some unilateral measures. In particular, Sweden and Finland have banned visits by ships avowedly or potentially equipped with nuclear weapons. Finland has recently passed a law on energy policy that forbids the entry of explosive nuclear materials on to Finnish soil. The foreign policy leadership has specified the Finnish position that nuclear weapons are unjustifiable under any conditions, peace or war. The President has expressed the more general view that nuclear weapons are not rational instruments of military policy but devices of senseless and uncontrollable destruction. This rather critical view, expressed from the early 1980s on, is a new feature in Finnish foreign policy, and not fully compatible with the traditional allegiance to the post-war structures of international relations, structures which have relied heavily on arsenals of nuclear weapons.

The late 1980s have shown that increased proximity to strategic confrontation was potentially rather than immediately problematic. The Soviet Union's response to new and more aggressive naval policies in the Northern waters has been cautious. It has scaled down rather than intensified its naval activities in these waters. On the US side, aggressive naval policies would seem to belong to the early period of the Reagan administration, when Lehman was in charge of naval affairs. Changes in senior personnel, scandals in acquisition policy, and budgetary restraint seem to have put an end to US naval adventurism. The issue will presumably remain high on the arms control agenda of the Nordic countries, and concern continues, but it is less acute than seemed likely during the mid-1980s. And as the superpowers are again on speaking terms after years of tension and confrontation, there are also fewer pressures for Finland to introduce unilateral measures or, more generally, seek out alternatives to its traditional role as a mediator between the Soviet Union and the United States. It can again be assumed that the superpowers will bilaterally control their strategic relations so that these do not adversely affect the security situation in Northern Europe.

But there is more to it than this. The Soviet Union seems to be willing to reduce naval armaments and limit maritime activity. The Western powers, including the United States, are clearly reluctant to follow suit. In his speech at Murmansk in October 1987, Secretary-General Gorbachev addressed security developments in the North, especially the naval dimension. Against a background of broader European arrangements for confidence-building and cooperation, he proposed various measures to reduce military build-up in the North. Some of the proposals were bloc-based, some directed specifically to the Nordic countries, inviting their cooperation on a sub-regional basis. Certain of these proposals were later detailed during the visit of Prime Minister Ryzhkov to Sweden and Norway in January 1988.

The Nordic countries have found it difficult to reply positively to the arms control proposals made by the Soviet leadership. Proposals on cooperation in matters of energy research, protection of the environment and the development of the Arctic region have proved easier to come to terms with. But even in these it is felt that comprehensive schemes of cooperation with the Soviet Union would imply some reappraisal of Nordic security policy traditions. This is perhaps less dramatic for Finland than for the other Nordic countries, but Finland too has chosen to keep a low profile and a 'wait-and-see' policy. No doubt all the Nordic countries are interested in the Soviet proposals and support the idea of reducing the naval build-up in the North, but at the same time they want the proposed measures to be more multilateral. To put it differently, the Nordic countries feel uneasy about cooperating with the Soviet Union without the consent of the USA. They would prefer a broader setting such as the follow-up to the Stockholm Conference. More generally the Nordic countries, Finland no less than the others, have to decide on security policies at the Nordic, European and East–West level. There are pressures to come up with new answers, but thus far traditional preferences have prevailed.

8 OTHER CONTENTIOUS ISSUES

Regarding more general security developments in Europe, Finland is at one with the trend toward a security built more on cooperation and interdependence than on balance of power and military confrontation.

In June 1988 President Koivisto stated that in Europe new forms of interaction seemed to be emerging. Developments were dictated less by the confrontation between the blocs. Power politics were still significant, but interdependence and cooperation were the best foundations for security.[8] In the view of the President, Europe would gain if its ideological and military division could be made less distinct. This view is not surprising in the context of Finnish foreign policy tradition. A European peace order, or 'European House' is quite acceptable to Finland, even if it means that the structures of power created during the post-war period, and upheld by military strength and block consolidation, are liable to change.

In this sense, Finland is perhaps less status quo oriented than it has been. It is increasingly recognised that forceful processes are at work, and that there is no way back to previous structures in Europe. The changes are gradual and probably peaceful in their essence and therefore also acceptable from the Finnish point of view. 'We hope that the changes in the international system will be positive for us but fear that the future implies growing difficulties', said President Koivisto. 'One has to do without the familiar enemy perceptions, that have created a sense of family and kept things in order. We have to be able to see far ahead'.

Most recent discussion in Finland has focused on European economic integration and the strengthened position of the European Communities. The EEC has not only become stronger in economic terms; it is also increasingly the centre of European political developments. Like other neutral European Free Trade Association members, Finland has to define a stance toward the EEC.

The discussion has been less intense than in Austria, Sweden or Switzerland but the conclusions are clear. Membership is out of the question as it would be incompatible with neutrality. However, with this proviso, Finland seeks close working relations with the European Communities. This endeavour is clearly facilitated by the fact that the EEC and Comecon have signed an outline agreement and that the Soviet Union has in recent years taken a fairly positive stand towards those EEC policies that aim to promote all-European cooperation and downgrade bloc-to-bloc confrontation. To that extent, the EEC has been a moderating force relative to the policies pursued by the United States during most of the Reagan presidency.

'It is important from our point of view that the perspective of all-European cooperation is taken into account, and reflected in the new patterns of economic cooperation emerging in our continent', said President Koivisto in his speech. This resistance to excessively narrow notions of Europe – Atlantic or Western Europe might be cited – is of long standing in Finnish foreign policy, and is still relevant today. In the long run, this also implies the scaling down of the bloc structures in Europe, a diminished role for military alliances, and a greater role for economic and political factors. Clearly, then, Finland sees no justification for intensified military cooperation among the EEC countries. The 'NATO pillar' perspective is seen as incompatible with developments in the context of the CSCE that stress political and cooperative solutions to European security. If bloc-based, militarily oriented efforts prevail, it will considerably narrow the options available for neutral countries like Finland. Such negative developments are, however, improbable, and there are good grounds for optimism. The Soviet emphasis on 'the European House' and the policies of *perestroika* would seem to derive from the conviction that an all-European system of cooperation will provide sufficient guarantees for Soviet security. This approach opens up considerable possibilities. Prospects will further improve if the dialogue between the superpowers continues, allowing a scaling down of the bloc system and of the military threat in Europe. In this regard, the contribution of the EEC is a vital one. Recent developments seem consonant with the Finnish perspective. If this favourable trend continues it will facilitate close relations with the EEC, and make it easier for Finland to contribute to the process of European integration.

9 CONCLUDING REMARKS

For a number of years there was some confusion in Finnish foreign policy as the traditional superpower emphases did not seem to yield results; the relations between the USA and the Soviet Union were tense, while the outlook for solutions that stressed the Europeanisation of security policies were bleak. This stalemate raised fundamental questions. 'If a policy that supports the endeavours of the major powers in reconstituting détente is not on the cards, what is Finland's role?' asked Prime Minister Kalevi Sorsa in 1986. 'What are the options? Passivity, protest, isolationism or perhaps new forms of cooperation?'[9] The implication was that the restoration of a favourable international environment might require something more than either policies aimed at promoting traditional stability, or good offices within the established, superpower-dominated structures. New policies might be needed that neither eschewed criticism nor sought to reinforce the status quo.

In fact the 'wait-and-see' policy continued, and no firm conclusion was reached in the debate. Finland, it seems, places equal stress on the Europeanisation of security developments and on its traditional role as mediator between the two superpowers. In this sense there has been something of a shift in Finnish policy. The concepts of progress and social competence are applied in a creative way in the current situation. Finland seems likely, for the foreseeable future, to continue to belong to a group of likeminded countries, mainly Euroneutrals, which seek positive changes in European politics by (i) downplaying the military dimension, and (ii) stressing both interdependence and cooperative approaches to peace and security.

Notes and References

1. This is the conclusion of a number of writers who have studied the situation of the neutrals. See, for example, Harto Hakovirta (ed.), *Fragmentation and Integration. Aspects of International System Change* (Tampere: Finnish Political Science Association, 1986) 31–5.
2. This was brought up by President Kekkonen in his address to the delegates during the opening days of the Helsinki Consultations, 22 November 1972; see *Ulkopoliittisia lausuntoja ja asiakirjoja. Ulkoasiainministeriön julkaisuja* (Helsinki: Ministry of Foreign Affairs, 1973) 98.
3. The labels 'liberal' and 'realist' schools have been used by Jan-Magnus Jansson, 'Suomalaisten ulkopoliittinen ajattelu ja sen kehitys', Suomalaiset ja turvallisuuspolitiikka. Maanpuolustustiedotuksen suunnittelukunta (Helsinki: Board for Defence Information, 1986) 25–35.
4. An in-depth analysis of this has been presented by Osmo Apunen and Helena Ryttöuori, 'Ideas of 'Survival' and 'Progress' in the Finnish Foreign Policy Tradition', *Journal of Peace Research*, no. 1 (Oslo: Prio, Norwegian University Press, 1982).
5. A speech by President Kekkonen at the Institute for Foreign Affairs, Stockholm, 8 May 1978. See *Ulkopoliittisia lausuntoja ja asiakirjoja 1978* (Helsinki: Ministry of Foreign Affairs, 1979) 20–6. For a detailed analysis of the main lines of the debate see Pertti Joenniemi, *Risteilyohjukset ja Suomen turvallisuuspolitiikka*. (Tampere, Rauhan-ja konfliktintutkimuslaitos. Tutkimuksia 28, 1984).
6. A speech by President Koivisto at Paasikivi Society in Helsinki, 15 October 1986. See *Ulkopoliittisia lausuntoja ja asiakirjoja 1986* (Helsinki: Ministry of Foreign Affairs, 1987).

7. A speech by President Koivisto to the Foreign Affairs Committee of the Hungarian Parliament, Budapest, 8 June 1988.
8. President Koivisto's Budapest speech (Note 7).
9. A speech given by Prime Minister Kalevi Sorsa at a seminar of journalists for peace, Helsinki, November 1986. *Ulkopoliittisia lausuntoja ja asiakirjoja 1986* (Helsinki: Ministry of Foreign Affairs, 1986) 3135.

15 Perspectives on the Swedish Debate: With Particular Reference to the New Cold War Debate Between Social Democrats and Conservatives in the Early 1980s

Erik Noreen

1 THE SWEDISH TRADITION

1.1 Two Perspectives

In his memoirs, Gunnar Hägglöf describes a meeting with his chief, Foreign Minister Östen Undén (Swedish foreign minister 1924–6, 1945–62), in late 1946. Hägglöf was at this time Ambassador in Moscow. Already, barely a year after the end of the Second World War, he was somewhat pessimistic about the willingness and capacity of the superpowers to cooperate within the framework of the new 'security organisation'.

After Hägglöf had painted a bleak picture of the world situation, Undén asked how he viewed the future. 'I answered', writes Hägglöf, 'that as I understood it, we must set our hopes on the emergence of a new balance of power'. 'Undén said, with a slight smile', continues Hägglöf, 'that he thought we had had more than enough of balances of power. The interplay of balances of power had always led to an arms race. Since the discovery of nuclear weapons, the world faced the possibility of total destruction. The only way out was cooperation between the great powers within the framework of the Charter of the United Nations'. 'But what if this cooperation does not occur?'

asked Hägglöf. 'All that we have hitherto seen of the debates in the Security Council suggests that the divergences between the superpowers are so great that there can be no hope of cooperation'. 'Maybe not right now', answered Unden. 'But we must see the whole problem in the long term. There is, quite simply, no other way than patiently to work to bring East and West closer.'[1]

The exchange that Hägglöf describes can be seen in terms of the clash of two conflicting perspectives. On the one hand, we have the pessimist or *realist*, Hägglöf, whose insight is that peace and security can be reached only if the superpowers hold each other in military and political check in the UN. On the other, the optimist or *idealist*, Undén, who conceives of peace and security in terms of cooperation, and more particularly in a form of common security for the superpowers within the framework of the UN.

It is customary to consider views on problems of peace and security as falling into a realist or an idealist (utopian) perspective.[2] For the realist, global politics is characterised by the striving of states after power; states aspire to maintain or expand their borders in competition with other states equally intent on expansion. The power of states, measured primarily in military terms, therefore becomes the dominating element in international politics. Military power is decisive for the individual country, and the *mot d'ordre* in security matters is: look after yourself, never rely on others.

According to the realist, security can also be achieved by alliance with other states of similar political and economic tendency. This is especially true for small countries. The international system tends in consequence to be split up into power blocs which deter one another by the strength of their military forces. The realist can consequently claim that the balance of terror between East and West is the primary reason for the almost half-century-old peace between the European states. According to the realists, the only security strategy of proven value is a balance of power.

The idealist has a more dynamic view of world politics, in the sense that he relies on untested ways – indeed, on changes in the international order. The idealist asserts that humanity draws conclusions from the horrors of war, and deduces that it is capable of influencing developments in the direction of a lasting peace. Ideas of this kind presided over the foundation of the League of Nations and the United Nations. The administration of Franklin D. Roosevelt – perhaps the most eager instigator of the UN – thus aspired to bury 'the obsolete system which was built on unilateral action, exclusive alliances, spheres of influence, balances of power and all the other egotistical considerations which had been tried for decades and always failed'.

The idealist, in short, believes that an international order characterised by national self-interest and balances of power can be replaced by a system in which cooperation and comparative advantages will be adequate to the creation of international security. In individual countries, security policies will stress confidence-enhancing political measures rather than military solutions.

For the idealist, a significant characteristic of the post-war European order is the fact that, despite the existence of different ideological systems, much is to be gained by cooperation in the economic, cultural and other fields. A common interest in defending peace can come into being in this way: much can be achieved through cooperation – everything can be lost through armed struggle.

The perspectives of realism and idealism, as they are used in the literature, are not unproblematic as analytical categories, mainly because they contain many different dimensions. In what follows, the concepts are used only when they refer to *adaptation* to the international system or *changes* of the international system. The realist recommends a security strategy adapted to an international order defined in terms of mistrust between the great power blocs, struggle, and balances of power. The idealist recommends a security strategy whose goal is structural change towards a security system based on trust and cooperation between the great power blocs. The latter is often termed 'common security', and is a concept to which we shall return.

It is Undén's views on the possibility of cooperation between the superpowers that mark him out as an idealist. Their clearest expression dates from mid-1945, just before Undén acceded to the post of Foreign Minister. Undén viewed the Swedish declaration of neutrality as illogical, and incompatible with the obligation of solidarity towards the UN.[3] He had been one of the sharpest critics of Swedish neutrality during the war (Sweden, he believed, had been far too compliant with Nazi Germany), and he considered neutrality a completely obsolete policy. It belonged to an order characterised by balances of power, 'which prior to 1914 were declared to be the only method for keeping the peace'.[4] The post-war order, with the UN as the collective organ, should instead be based on the cooperation of the great powers, in the context of a 'a rational organisation of the relations between states' whose purpose would be to 'lay a planned basis for peace'.[5]

Undén probably came to be a realist in the sense that, as Foreign Minister for a small country, he naturally adjusted to the realities of power politics, which came to prevail in the UN no less than in international affairs in general. The Cold War crept ever nearer, and in the spring of 1948 the contours of a Western alliance were discernible. The bloc division in Europe was thought to be unavoidable. Anxious that the Nordic countries avoid this division, Undén in May 1948 took the initiative of organising negotiations for a Scandinavian defence union.

As is well known, these negotiations, which involved Denmark, Norway and Sweden, broke down. It emerged that the Norwegians could not envisage a Scandinavian defence coalition without some form of connection with the West. A connection with the West was unthinkable for Sweden, *inter alia* because of Finland's sensitive relations with the Soviet Union. The regional context thus played a considerable role, but Sweden's foreign policy-makers were perfectly aware that national security or self-advantage could not be divorced from the international context. A wish not to contribute to heightened international dissension was a strong motive for remaining freed of alliances. The Swedish Foreign Minister gave clear expression to this motive in a secret memorandum just before the Berlin crisis: 'No task is greater or more important for a country like Sweden than to try to prevent our part of the world from being dragged into the general destruction. This task seems to be imposed on us partly so that, as long as peace survives, we should do everything that we, with our limited possibilities, are capable of, to promote a peaceful outcome, and above all, not to aggravate the situation... Surely no-one can fail to see that, in the present situation, Sweden should pursue a policy which promotes peace, and which in no way heightens international tension'.[6]

Strong military forces were naturally one consideration, which, in combination with the (all things considered) successful policy of neutrality during the Second World War, contributed to the option of non-alignment. When an independent Scandinavian defence union could not be realised, it remained to look to one's own capabilities – and, of course, to the UN.

1.2 An Active Foreign Policy

In his last official speech, on 4 July 1962, Undén declared: 'It is not difficult to establish that a fine mix of idealism on the one hand and a sense of reality on the other are the right recipe for [Swedish] foreign policy'. The second of these two *desiderata* refers to the policy of keeping the country out of armed conflict through a combination of neutrality and strong defence.[7]

But the official Swedish line during the post-war period has, as Undén pointed out, not been lacking in idealism. The *Undén Line* has been associated with a strong belief in collective solutions within the framework of the UN, and with the goal of a rationally organised international legal order. This policy is characterised by bridge-building tendencies within and without the ambit of the UN. For example, Sweden has taken several initiatives in the fields of disarmament and East–West relations.[8]

A further feature of the so-called *active* policy of neutrality, is the use of criticism as an instrument of foreign policy. Here bridge-building or mediating count for less than the adoption of a moral standpoint. The Swedish government has, on a number of occasions from the 1950s on, in the strongest terms condemned armed attacks, generally perpetrated by superpowers, on small states. Sweden may be said to identify with the small states attacked, considering itself obliged, as a small state, to react against such infringements of national and human rights.[9]

For most of the 1980s, Sweden has pursued an active foreign policy; untrammelled by alliance, it considers itself obliged to 'work externally for the reduction of international tensions and for peaceful development'.[10] This is a line we can trace from Hjalmar Branting's involvement with disarmament in the League of Nations during the 1920s, through Swedish initiatives in the UN in the 1960s, to proposals made at the CSCE and to the Six Nations and other international disarmament initiatives during the 1980s.

2 THE DEBATE

The overriding Swedish doctrine on security policy – freedom from alliances in times of peace leading to neutrality in war – has very seldom been questioned in public debate since the beginning of the 1950s, when the Riksdag dismissed a suggestion from the Conservative Party on cooperation between Sweden and Denmark over the defence of the island of Bornholm. There has, however, been a divergence of views during the post-war period as to *how* the policy of neutrality should be applied. An example of this is Sweden's relationship to the European Community. Since the early 1960s, the official Swedish line has been that membership is not compatible with neutrality. Foreign Minister Sten Andersson justified this line in a speech at Uppsala University on 10 September 1987: 'If we participated in a formalised foreign policy cooperation of this kind, it would imply a serious reduction of our freedom of action. It could give rise to apprehensions or expectations that we might, in time of crisis or war, deviate from the security policy we have chosen'.[11]

Some liberal and conservative currents, on the other hand, consider membership of the European Community perfectly compatible with neutrality. They argue that the issue of credibility has been overstated; the European Community is not regarded as an alliance,[12] and Sweden could therefore join without undermining international trust in Swedish neutrality.

That neutrality has the approval of the overwhelming majority of Swedish people does not mean that all participants in the security debate accord the same *meaning* to the word. This becomes clear when international tension rises, and clearer still when the vital security interests of the country are threatened. In this regard, the boundary violations detected during the early 1980s were exemplary. Critics of the government cite them as evidence that Swedish neutrality has failed. Nevertheless, there are few who question the policy of neutrality as such. It is only when we come to analyse the underlying perspectives of the debaters that the divergences come to light.

In what follows we shall plunge into the 1980s security debate in press and parliament at the moment of its greatest polarisation, after the stranding of U 137 in the Karlskrona archipelago in November 1981. Relations between the superpowers were tense. The cumulative effect of Afghanistan, Poland, the double track decision, and the Reagan administration's policies of embargo against the Soviet Union, had foreign policy commentators referring to a 'new Cold War'.

The debate in this account turns less on military threats and strategies than on the global environment by which they are determined. But here I have limited myself. North–South questions, and strife-torn regions outside Europe, are not considered, though they are not irrelevant to the formation of Swedish security policy. The focus here is thus on European security, and more particularly on the preconditions for averting military confrontation in Europe.

2.1 What the Debate is About

Having chosen to stand outside most international security systems, Sweden had, until the initiation in 1975 of the Helsinki Process, found itself on the sidelines of discussion of European security.

An illustration of this is the Swedish peace movement's choice of issues during the post-war period. These have been closely related to the *domestic* context – for example, to Swedish defence policy, though also to the credibility of Swedish neutrality in the light of successive international events. During the 1950s, the major issue was opposition to the acquisition and production of nuclear arms by the Swedish defence forces ('The Action Group Against Swedish Nuclear Weapons' contributed to halting the plans for Swedish nuclear armament). During the 1960s and 1970s, the peace movement played a marginal role in the Swedish security debate, but in the 1980s, it has returned to the forefront of political life. Through its initiatives in the 'Bofors Affair', it has undermined the very foundations of the Swedish arms export industry, and thus of the domestic arms industry. But on questions of European security, it has generally ended up in agreement with the government; we may cite its attitude to the double-track decision, and to proposals for a Nordic nuclear-free zone or a European 'corridor' free of tactical nuclear weapons.

In recent years, Swedish politics has seen a reawakening of interest in European security. The mass media have, for example, devoted some attention to the current debate in Europe on the future role of the USA in NATO (the decoupling process). And Sweden's relationship to the EEC is again being discussed, though in predominantly economic terms. But the debate on European security in parliament and press during the new Cold War period has centred on the Helsinki Process, the double-track decision and common security.

2.2 The CSCE Process

During the 1980s, a very broad consensus was reached on East–West relations and Sweden's role therein. As relations between the superpowers deteriorated, the whole spectrum of the press united to condemn the superpowers for the continued arms build-up in general and more particularly for their inability, or unwillingness, to agree on arms limitations in Europe. The latter referred primarily to the Geneva talks on intermediate range missiles, but the superpowers' intentions in relation to the follow-up Conference on Security and Cooperation in Europe (CSCE) also became the object of widespread suspicion.[13]

In early 1982, the Madrid Conference was on the point of breaking down over the military takeover in Poland, and the unwillingness of the Eastern states to discuss the Polish situation within the CSCE framework. Negotiations were adjourned, and after many informal sessions in which Spain, and the non-aligned states (including Sweden) were prominent, the Conference in autumn 1983 succeeded in agreeing on a final document. This presented, amongst other things, a scheme for a series of separate meetings in different locations, and thus obviated the difficulty of raising human rights issues at a conference where 'pure' security issues (such as confidence-building measures) were also discussed. One complex of problems could no longer stand in the way of another, as had happened in Madrid.

The official Swedish line during this critical period was that ideological conflicts between East and West should not be allowed to paralyse the CSCE process. The Foreign Minister of the time, Liberal Ola Ullsten, was unwilling to let Poland's misfortune serve as a pretext for bringing the CSCE process to an end.[14] But, in the spirit of Helsinki, it was also felt that crimes against liberties and human rights should be condemned.[15] On one point the Press was unanimous; the independent stance of Sweden and the 'non-aligned group' made them peculiarly apt to work for a fruitful dialogue within the Conference.[16]

Pessimism as to the superpowers' will and ability to cooperate was, as previously indicated, widespread, but not without nuances. Liberal and Social Democratic editorials claimed that the USA was exploiting the CSCE to excoriate the Soviet Union in connection with developments in Poland. The CSCE was a suitable forum for criticising offences against human rights, they said, but to use Poland as a stick to the Soviet back was going too far.[17] This, as we have seen, was also the government's line: ideological conflict between East and West should not be allowed to hamstring the CSCE process.

The Conservatives, by contrast, declared that criticism of the Soviet Union should be unbounded: 'all possibilities for international pressure must be exploited'.[18] The anti-Soviet line was pursued in the Swedish parliament with strong ideological overtones: the Soviet Union was painted as an expansionist, destructive dictatorship – a decadent empire which 'consciously exploits conflicts and crises in different parts of the world in order to reinforce its own position'.[19]

Soviet expansionism was, in the Conservative view, a consequence of the crisis of communist ideology. Military supremacy and threatening postures were attempts by the Soviet leaders to compensate for economic and political failure, and were a danger to peace. Peace in Europe was possible only if the social system in the Eastern Bloc was changed: 'peace without freedom is no true peace'.[20]

What we may describe as the 'ideologising' of security policy had, on the one hand, a moral aspect: Western democracy is the only true system (read: communism must be combatted). On the other hand, it can be interpreted as pragmatic. The Conservatives propounded the thesis that 'true peace' had a poor prognosis as long as antagonistic blocs based on widely different ideologies existed side by side. Thus far it was a thesis in the spirit of the realist school. But the Conservatives went further, and hinted at the possibility of a change in the international system. 'True peace' thus meant a change of system in the Eastern Bloc, resulting in a more homogenous Europe.

Olof Palme characterised 'true peace' doctrine as a 'crusade strategy', and deemed it inappropriate to Swedish foreign policy. It was, he felt, somewhat of a new departure to make the need for a change of system in the East a principal component of Swedish security policy. Questions of 'fundamental ideology' should not be confused with security policy. For Palme's party, the Social Democrats, and for the centre parties, it was essential for peace and the reduction of tension that a dialogue transcending bloc boundaries be kept alive – the responsibility lay no less with the East than the West.[21]

In the early 1980s, the realist 'security strategy' based on deterrence and balance of power, came under heavy attack, especially from the parties of the Swedish Left. In their polemic against the traditional '*Realpolitik*' security thinking, the Social Democrats developed a *common security* strategy, based on the work of the Palme Commission.

2.3 The Double Track Decision

Debate on security in Sweden has sometimes been quite fierce. The principal battle lines were drawn up between the Conservatives and the Social Democrats. The government of the centre parties, the Liberals and Agrarians, did not share the Conservatives' hard anti-Soviet line. On European security, it took a line which resembled the Social Democrats'. Thus, to the question whether the double track decision on Eurostrategic weapons was beneficial to European security, the centrist government replied in the negative. It was hopeless to attempt to attain a parity acceptable to both blocs.[22] Instead, it suggested freezing nuclear arsenals and delivery systems at the existing level, as a precondition for further arms reductions. Balance of power arguments could not, in the centrist view, justify the deployment of new intermediate range missiles in Western Europe. The balance of forces on either side was so complete that, from a security point of view, improved military capacity on either part was all but counterproductive.[23]

In the matter of Eurostrategic weapons, the Social Democratic government that came to power in 1982 held a view almost identical to that of their predecessors. Like the centrist government, the Social Democrats spoke of an approximate balance. They stressed the *total* equilibrium of strength – that is, of nuclear and conventional arms taken together. Initially loth to commit themselves on the issue of whether a regional balance in Europe was desirable, they later admitted that the proposal for a corridor free of tactical nuclear weapons required a balance of conventional forces in Europe. In short, for the Social Democratic and centrist parties, the existence of a very exact balance of strength between the blocs was largely irrelevant to European security. They assumed that the balance of power situation merely led to a continuing arms race. This argument was in the lineage of Östen Undén's fears of 1946: we had had more than enough of balances of power. Superpower rivalry had always led to an arms race, and was all the more dangerous in the nuclear age.

Alva Myrdal, in one of her last articles, articulated a view which expressed what many politicians doubtless thought:

> The deployment in Europe of the superpowers' new weapons . . . is governed by the fundamentally false notion of a 'balance of arms' between one bloc and the other. Both sides fear that the other side has 'got there first' and has a stronger position. These are the motives of an arms race which is now attaining insensate proportions. All this 'balance mentality' is basically wrong. . . the desire for effective deterrence does not imply balance. Anything beyond a minimum level of deterrence . . . has been promoted by armaments interests.[24]

In the Riksdag, two Conservative members staged a frontal assault on the official Swedish attitude to the Eurostrategic weapons. They claimed that the government's demands for a freeze on nuclear weapons failed to take into account the disparity of strength between the blocs, and was simply an attack on NATO's double track decision.[25] In contrast to the Swedish Left and the centrist parties, the Conservatives expressed emphatic support for deployment. In this context, Conservative representatives criticised the peace movement, which was alleged to condemn NATO's double track decision without taking an equivalent stand on Soviet deployment of SS-20 missiles.

The fundamental question in Swedish debate on East–West relations and European security can be summarised thus: should one, in the spirit of idealism, seek new paths toward the goal of peace and security, which go beyond the traditional machinery of military deterrence and balance of power? Or should one stick to the tried and tested '*Realpolitik*'? This question leads us into the more philosophical debate on the subject of national and international security. In Sweden, the early 1980s marked a renaissance in this field; this was partly the effect of the debate on the Eurostrategic weapons, and partly of the Palme Commission's report.

2.4 Common Security

In the spring of 1982, the *Independent Commission for Disarmament and Security Issues* (the Palme Commission) gave its final report. *Common Security: a Programme for Disarmament* presented a number of concrete disarmament and arms control proposals. The most notable was the suggestion of a corridor through Europe free of tactical nuclear weapons.

The proposal for a nuclear-free corridor became controversial not so much for its content as for the manner in which it was promoted by the Palme government. It was first aired in a speech to the UN General Assembly, and attracted little attention. Thereafter, all the European countries, together with the USA and Canada, were asked by the Swedish government in a diplomatic note for their views on the corridor suggestion. This procedure later caused a rumpus when the Swedish newspaper *Dagens Nyheter* (*DN*) revealed that large parts of the note had been adapted from a proposal by the West German SDP politician Egon Bahr, a member of the Palme Commission.

The debate on the corridor proposal came to be completely overshadowed by the 'Bahr Affair' – that is, by the presentation of the proposal. But on one point, the Bahr Affair touched on the central issue. *DN* noted, in a February 1983 editorial, that there was an 'obvious difference' between the Swedish note and the Palme

Commission's text. The Commission laid greater emphasis on the conventional balance of power than the Swedish government. Olof Palme afterwards stated that the Swedish government had deliberately left that question open. The note was to be regarded merely as a sounding-out, and the Commission itself has been divided as to the relevance of conventional balance to the 'corridor' proposal.[26] As *DN* pointed out in another context, ' "balance" seemed to be evoked throughout the debate on European security'.[27] The Palme Commission's report was no exception; it was a compromise intended to bring together politicians and researchers from East and West and small states and superpowers alike, and to attract not only 'idealists' but 'realists' too.

The Palme Commission's suggestion was based on a new concept, *common security*. The Commission asserted that it was time to launch a serious challenge to the philosophy of mutual deterrence, which in the last analysis was built on the traditional doctrine of wars that could be won or lost. But the nuclear age had stood this doctrine on its head. In a nuclear war, the Palme Commission claimed, there are no winners, only losers, and it went on to challenge the superpower blocs to 'achieve security not against the adversary but together with him. International security must rest on a commitment to joint survival rather than a threat of mutual destruction'.[28]

However, a strategy for common security should logically rest on a measure of trust between East and West. How should the decision-makers of two antagonistic politico–ideological systems transform their perspectives, or their perceptions of each others' views? Here, the Palme Commission was fairly pragmatic: 'given the ideological differences between East and West no meaningful convergence can be expected'. But the Commission thought that these differences could be excluded from the area of security policy, and continued: 'the task is only to ensure that these conflicts do not find an outlet in preparation for or acts of war. It means that the nations must come to understand that the maintenance of world peace must be given a higher priority than the assertion of their own ideological or political position'.[29]

The Social Democratic press and parliamentary party supported the principle of common security fairly unreservedly. And in September 1983, a conference was held to review the merits of common security at the Stockholm International Peace Research Institute (SIPRI). Prominent researchers and politicians, not least Social Democrats, were invited from all around the world. One of the conference's liveliest debates concerned the relation of deterrence to common security.

It was originally intended that 'common security' be promoted as an alternative to 'deterrence'. The latter, according to the Palme Commission, offered: 'very fragile protection indeed against the horrors of nuclear war. It is therefore of paramount importance to replace the doctrine of mutual deterrence. Our alternative is common security'. But several conference participants, amongst them the Palme Commission-connected researcher Emma Rotschild, saw no incompatibility between the two concepts. In certain cases, Rotschild held, common security could make deterrence more credible. The deterrence she referred to involved a much reduced level of nuclear arms, so that the threat was no longer of mutual destruction. This would be a more rational nuclear deterrent.[30]

The conference participants found it difficult to agree on a definition of 'common security'. The majority probably accepted the minimal definition which Rotschild suggested: common security was 'not a sort of encroaching confidence between blocs, but merely the political will to abstain from certain military measures or decisions in the common interest of making war less probable'. This definition does not exclude deterrence, nor is it, as Rotschild was at pains to point out, a new security doctrine.[31] Other conference participants went significantly further. Mary Kaldor's contribution had, for example, a clearer idealistic element; she spoke in terms of an alternative security *system*. This would be based on *confidence* between East and West, instead of *deterrence*; Soviet tanks would be interpreted in terms of their role as maintainers of order in Eastern Europe rather than as a threat to the West, and American nuclear weapons would be interpreted less as an answer to Soviet armoured vehicles, and more as a unifying force within NATO.[32]

2.5 Common Security and National Security

Common security and the problem of deterrence also became a theme for domestic forums. In parliament, the Conservatives criticised the Social Democrats because they wanted to replace the general philosophy of deterrence with a diffuse principle of common security. The Conservatives claimed that the Palme government had placed a question mark over the fundamental principles of Swedish defence policy: 'The doctrine of deterrence is implicit in every form of armed defence, including that of Sweden'.[33] In the debate, the

Conservatives tried to steer the discussion on deterrence away from the nuclear threat and global security towards more local security problems, such as the submarine incidents. The philosophy of deterrence was considered from the point of view of a national defence policy. With both feet firmly on realist ground, the Conservative expert on security policy (and subsequent Leader), Carl Bildt, stated that the doctrine of deterrence was 'the only sure, moral, defensible basis for our security policy'.[34]

The Conservative parliamentary group was not alone giving a hostile reception to the principle of common security, which the Palme Government had not scrupled to publicise. Leading Liberal, Conservative and independent newspapers published editorials expressing a sceptical view. *Dagens Nyheter*, which was not renowned for its hostility to idealist security policies, declared that common security focused far too much on superpower relations, and stood for a sort of superpower peace closing over the heads of the small states. *DN* also criticised the Palme government on the grounds that its campaign for common security was conducted at the expense of a more resolute management of its own security problems, in particular the submarine incursions: 'Without common security, no Swedish security – the opposite also applies'.[35] Palme drew a distinction here: 'vital security interests' were one thing, common security was another. This was taken to mean that they were not two sides of the same coin, but two quite different dimensions of security.[36]

Allowance once made for the distinction between common and national security, it did not seem illogical to promote an active foreign policy in the spirit of détente while *at the same time* giving a strong profile to national defence. This meant that the government desired to 'contribute to a development which reduces the antagonisms in Europe', while maintaining a '*Realpolitik*' conditioned by 'vital Swedish security interests' in and around the Swedish territory.[37] This security policy *dualism* was profitably applied by the Palme government throughout the 'submarine crisis'.

The government had declared in November 1982, during the submarine hunt in the Stockholm archipelago, that it would not hesitate to sink foreign submarines in Swedish waters. Similar statements were made after the report of the submarine commission. And submarine defences were afterwards reinforced.[38] As regards diplomatic ripostes, a certain caution was observable. The Swedish government certainly protested forcefully against the Soviet incursions, and exchange visits at ministerial level were, for a time, discontinued. But the government was also anxious to reassure the alarmists; there were those who suggested that Sweden should look for alternative security arrangements, for example a mutual assistance agreement with NATO.[39] The Prime Minister insisted that there was no reason for panic; the government did not see the submarine incursions as a prelude to war, and it was still important to have good and stable relations with the Soviet Union. The Palme government's campaign in favour of common security thus continued unabated.[40]

But the new Cold War, whose onset during the early 1980s had been widely remarked on, came to an end. It reached a peak during 1983–4, after which East–West relations improved significantly. The atmosphere of superpower negotiations has distinctly improved, as witness the Stockholm Conference and the INF agreement. The debate in Sweden is no longer exacerbated by international tensions as it was in 1982 and 1983.

Parliamentary debate illustrates this point; there has been a reversion to the Swedish norm, and calm reigns. The conflicting perspectives of the participants in the debate have scarcely been obvious during the second half of the 1980s. And in consequence, some of the more philosophical aspects of the debate on 'common security' or 'balances of power' have faded from the political agenda.[41]

True, Communists and Conservatives alike support *glasnost* and the more conciliatory attitude of the second Reagan administration toward the Soviet Union. The INF agreement, and the 1988 Swedish–Soviet Union agreement on boundaries in the Baltic were thus widely approved. In the latter case, the bone of contention had existed since the 1960s, and Swedish Foreign Minister Andersson stated in an interview with the magazine *Tempus*: 'We could not have come to this agreement without the new Soviet leadership'.

To sum up the debate of the later 1980s, there is a tacit consensus on the benefit of some sort of mild common security, of a kind that is compatible with a balance of power in Europe at a lower level of deterrence. The mainstream of the debate has moved away from the more extreme positions of realism and idealism towards a central 'grey-zone' of moderation.

2.6 The Academic Debate

The academic debate in Sweden has had several different focal points. The EEC is at present much discussed, in particular in the context of the compatibility of membership with the policy of neutrality. Views diverge. Rolf Lindholm has argued in his dissertation that membership is not thus compatible, as the EEC has developed into a dynamic and supranational organisation.[42] In this he sides with the official view, that membership would severely constrain Sweden's freedom of action.[43] In connection with the 'submarine crisis', the courses open to Sweden in relation to the strategic tensions in Northern Europe have been widely discussed. The central topics of that debate, military strategies and national defence, fall outside the scope of this study.[44]

Security matters, with particular reference to regional policy and tension prevention, have also been discussed. Nuclear weapon-free zones in the Nordic region and Europe (the 'corridor') were assiduously debated in the early 1980s. These themes have been central to the research at SIPRI, which is oriented toward policy-making;[45] its starting point was the Palme Commission's proposal for a nuclear weapon-free corridor in Europe.

Another development in the field of 'non-military' security research is regional integration studies, dealing mainly with the Nordic countries.[46] The central question here is whether the process of creating a 'security community' in the Nordic countries may serve as an example for other regions or sub-regions, such as the Balkans.

A third type of 'non-military' security research is studies on the mechanism of and preconditions for détente policies.[47] A group around Kjell Goldmann at the University of Stockholm has been working in this field since the 1970s. Among the questions considered have been the following: Are attempts to reduce tensions inevitably ephemeral in effect? Are enduring improvements in superpower relations possible? Can the newly improved international climate be maintained?

The Stockholm scholars in international politics naturally have no categorical answers to these questions. But by comparing détente policies between the USA and the Soviet Union on the one hand, and between the Federal Republic of Germany (FRG) and the Soviet Union on the other, they have been able to show that the greater stability of the latter was a product of these factors: (i) A higher level of mutual economic dependence, (ii) détente was more central to the outlook of both politicians and electorate in the FRG than in the USA. (iii) The problem of consistency (how can we contemplate amicable relations with an 'evil empire'?) was not considered as important in the FRG as in the USA. (iv) The anchoring of détente policy in domestic politics was stronger in the FRG than in the USA.

Kjell Goldmann considers the connection between international and domestic politics especially significant for the process of détente. 'Exerting a favourable influence on another state's foreign relations through dependence-creating cooperation rather than intervention and oppression seems to be a serious possibility',[48] he claims.

This conclusion is hardly challenging, but does suggest the way forward to a European security order placing more emphasis on non-military means. Here the common security debate of 1983 comes into focus again. Can one really speak of a non-military security order as an alternative to a balance of deterrence? Or is it more relevant to talk about a *combination* of détente and deterrent policies? Goldmann articulates the latter question thus: 'How combine greater East–West integration, which would stabilise détente, with stability in Eastern Europe . . . while preserving the balance of deterrence [between East and West]?'[49]

These questions cannot be answered without reference to the time perspective in which they are considered. The problem formulated by Goldmann relates to current policy concerns such as the CSCE Process, while the goals of the Palme Report are longer term. The Palme Report has accordingly been criticised as premature; replacing the balance of deterrence between East and West is not yet on the agenda. Many problems – ideological, economic, and ethnic – will have to be solved before preparations can begin for a non-military security order embracing Europe from the Urals to the Atlantic, and involving such 'security community' that there will be no further need for deterrence between European countries.[50]

Notes and References

1. Gunnar Hägglöf, *Fredens vägar 1945–1950* (Stockholm: Nerstedt, 1973) 83ff.
2. See, amongst others, Ian Clark, *Reform and Resistance in the International Order* (Cambridge: Cambridge University Press, 1980), and Barry Buzan, *People, States and Fear: The National Security problem in International Relations* (Brighton: Wheatsheaf, 1983). A Swedish study structured along these lines is Thorsten Nybom's *Motstånd anpassning uppslutning linier i svensk debatt om utrikespolitik och internationell politik 1940–43* (Stockholm, 1978).
3. Speech in Koppom 22 July 1945, quoted in *Dagens Nyheter*, 23 July 1945.

4. Östen Undén in *Tiden 1/1945*, 12.
5. Undén, *Tiden 1/1945* (Note 4).
6. *Strängt förtroligt PM*, by Östen Undén, 2 April 1948, Foreign Affairs Department archives (Stockholm).
7. *Documents on Swedish Foreign Policy, 1962*, Ministry of Foreign Affairs (Stockholm, 1963) 32.
8. See, for example, Bo Huldt, 'Swedish Disarmament and Security Policy from the 1920s to the 1980s', in *Neutrality and Defence: the Swedish Experience*, special edition of *Revue Internationale D'Histoire Militaire*, No. 57 (Stockholm, 1984) 35–59.
9. Elgström, Ole, 'Active Foreign Policy as a Preventive Strategy Against Dependence', in Otmar Höll (ed.), *Small States in Europe and Dependence* (Vienna: Braumueler, 1983) 247.
10. *Svensk säkerhetspolitik inför 90-talet: SOU 1985:23,* report from the 1984 Defence Committee (Stockholm, 1985) 7.
11. *Sverige i Europa*, speech of Foreign Minister Sten Andersson, 10 September 1987 (Stockholm, 1987) 19.
12. Mats Bergqvist, *Sverige och EEC: en statsvetenskaplig studie av fyra åsiktsriktingars syn på svensk marknadspolitik 1961–1962* (Stockholm: Nerstedt, 1970) 138ff.
13. See, for example, *Dagens nyheter* (indep.), 2 January 1982, *Falu-Kuriren* (Lib.), 7 January 1982, *Borås Tidning* (Cons.), 15 January 1982, *Svenska Dagbladet* (Cons.), 28 January 1982, *Stockholmstidningen* (Soc. Dem.), 27 January 1982, *Arbetet* (Soc. Dem,), 10 February 1982, *Göteborgstidningen* (Lib.), 9 March 1982.
14. *Utrikesfrågor. Aktstycken från Kungliga Utrikesdepartementet*, 1982 (Stockholm, 1983) 101.
15. *Utrikesfrågor* 15.
16. *Svenska Dagbladet* (Cons.), 9 February 1982, *Expressen* (Lib.), 10 February 1982, *Dagens Nyheter* (Indep.), 31 August 1982.
17. *Dagens Nyheter*, 10 and 13 February 1982, *Arbetet*, 10 February 1982, *Expressen*, 10 February 1982.
18. *Svenska Dagbladet*, 11 February 1982, 14 March 1982.
19. *Riksdagens protokoll* (*Rd. prt.*), 17 March 1982, 20ff.
20. *Rd. prt.*, 16 March 1983, 11ff.
21. *Rd. prt.*, 75; *Utrikesfrågor*, 1982 (Note 14) 47ff.
22. The coalition formed by the so-called 'middle parties' – i.e., the Agrarians (Centerpartiet) and Liberals (Folkpartiet).
23. *Utrikesfrågor* 1982 (Note 14) 46, 98.
24. *Dagens Nyheter*, 30 December 1983.
25. *Rd. prt.*, 22 November 1982 (Note 19) 9.
26. *Dagens Nyheter*, 3 March 1983.
27. *Dagens Nyheter*, 28 January 1983.
28. *Common Security: A Programme for Disarmament. The Report of the Independent Commission on Disarmament and Security issues under the Chairmanship of Olof Palme* (London, 1982) ix, 28.
29. *Common Security* (Note 28) 8.
30. *Policies for Common Security*, SIPRI (London: Taylor & Francis, 1985) 99.

31. Interview in *Dagens Nyheter*, 5 September 1983.
32. *Policies for Common Security* (Note 30) 49.
33. *Rd. prt.*, 22 November 1982 (Note 19) 16.
34. *Rd. prt.* (Note 19) 35.
35. *Dagens Nyheter*, 2 September 1983.
36. *Dagens Nyheter*, 9 October 1983.
37. For example, Olof Palme, *Sveriges utrikespolitik* (Stockholm, 1984) 7ff, interview in *Dagens Nyheter*, 9 October 1983.
38. *Svenska Dagbladet*, 27 April 1983.
39. *Svenska Dagbladet*, 1 June 1983, K. Goldmann 'Blir neutraliteten omöjlig?' (Will neutrality become impossible?).
40. *Dagens Nyheter*, 28 April 1983. For example, Palme's speech to NATO's parliamentary assembly meeting in Copenhagen, 13 June 1983, *Utrikesfrågor*, 1983, 42f.
41. Nils Andrén, 'Säkerhetspolitikens grunder och enighetens gränser', *Fred och säkerhet. Debatt och analys 1984–85* (Stockholm: Swedish Institute of Foreign Affairs, 1985) 158.
42. Rolf H. Lindholm; *Swedish Neutrality* (Lund, 1987) 46.
43. See above (Note 11).
44. Amongst others, Wilhelm Agrell, 'Behind the Submarine Crisis: Evolution of the Swedish Defence Doctrine and Soviet War Planning', *Cooperation and Conflict*, 4 (1986) 197–219, and Gunnar Jervas, 'Sweden in a Less Benign Environment', in Bengt Sundelius (ed.) *The Neutral Democracies and the New Cold War* (Boulder, Col.: Westview Press, 1987) 57–75.
45. For example, Sverre Lodgaard and Marek Thee (eds), *Nuclear Disengagement in Europe*, SIPRI, PUGWASH (London: Taylor & Francis, 1983).
46. Bengt Sundelius (ed.), *Foreign Policies of Northern Europe* (Boulder, Col.: Westview Press, 1982) 177–95. Also Håkan Wiberg, 'The Nordic Countries: A Special Kind of System', *Current Research on Peace and Violence*, 1–2 (1986).
47. Kjell Goldmann, *Tension and Detente in Bipolar Europe* (Stockholm: Esselte, 1974). Several works have since been published around this problem, lately Kjell Goldmann and Håkan Karlsson, *Rivalitet och samexistens. Fem uppsatser om supermakterna* (Lund: Studentlitteratur, 1987), *Change and Stability in Foreign Policy: The Problem and Possibilities of Detente* (Princeton: Princeton University Press, forthcoming). Also *European Neutrals and the Soviet Union*, Swedish Institute of International Affairs, Conference Papers, 6 (Stockholm, 1986), Peter Wallensteen, 'American–Soviet Detente: What went Wrong?', *Journal of Peace Research*, no. 1 (1985).
48. *Rivalitet och samexistens* (Note 17) 169.
49. Kjell Goldmann, 'Sverige och den internationella säkerheten', *Tio debattinlägg om svensk säkerhetspolitik* (Stockholm: Centralförlbundet Folk och Försrar, 1985) 105.
50. For a definition of 'security community', see Karl W. Deutsch, *Political Community and the Atlantic Area* (New York: Greenwood Press, 1957).

16 The Debate on European Security in Denmark

Ole Karup Pedersen

1 INTRODUCTION

In August 1987, the Danish Minister of Defence, Hans Engell published a book entitled: 'Ja, var der ingen fare. . .' (If there were no danger).[1] The words are taken from a Danish national song written during the First Schleswig-Holstein War (1848–50). The Minister no doubt chose his title carefully; the burden of the song is that if only people outside Denmark were more peaceful, Danish soldiers would prefer to stay at home with their farms, wives and children. Denmark was and is a peace-loving country, with no political ambition other than that of being allowed to live a pleasant life without too much outside interference. It is significant that a right-wing Minister finds it politically advantageous to illustrate the fundamentally peace-loving nature of Danish society; indeed, the publication of his book is an indication of the scale and intensity of the Danish debate on European security.

2 THE DANISH TRADITION

The current debate about security in Denmark is best understood in the context of Danish history. The debate goes back a long way, and is, of course, closely related to the 'core values' of Danish society. Even before the Danish defeat in the Second Schleswig-Holstein War in 1864, discussion had been aroused, in particular by the introduction of conscription, about the extent to which military means promoted Danish security.[2] In the last thirty years of the nineteenth century, pacifism gained ground rapidly, and the issue became one over which right-wing governments and the liberal opposition traditionally skirmished. It has been clearly shown that the views of the two parties were not very far apart, but the issue served to highlight differing views about the core values appropriate to Danish society, and was tactically useful for the government.

In this way, a tradition of discussion as to the proper dimensions and function of the Danish military apparatus was founded. It again came to the fore in the aftermath of the First World War, and was one of the nubs of disagreement between the 'bourgeois' political parties and the Social Democrat and Radical Left coalition government of the 1930s[3] (despite its name, the Radical Left party is to the right of the Social Democrats). Until 1932, the government maintained its proposal for drastic reductions in the Danish armed forces, but the bourgeois majority in the Second Chamber ensured that these were never implemented. In this connection, the question was raised whether Denmark should adopt 'permanent neutrality' or ally itself with one of the great powers, but debate was normally short-lived. There was a broad consensus of opinion against overt connection with any of the world powers, which would have ruled out neutrality in any conflict involving them. In the 1930s, a Scandinavian defence alliance was considered and rejected; Norway and Sweden also opposed this. Arrangements limiting Danish freedom of manoeuvre in case of war were looked on with suspicion. That it was the responsibility of the government to protect the Danish population against the disaster of war was a very widely held view, and it has been said that Denmark and other similar states attempted both to remove themselves from the European cycles of war and also to make war criminal.[4]

During the German occupation which began in April 1940, all such discussion was laid aside in the effort to make the best of a bad situation. On the whole, these efforts were successful, and the Danish population was spared the worst horrors of war. But the Danish resistance demonstrated the will and the capacity to use arms against the enemy, and thus gained admission to the club of the victorious nations in San Francisco in 1945, where Denmark became one of the founding members of the UN.

The experience of the Second World War greatly influenced opinions of security. A consensus was established as to the need for armed forces to protect the country, but disagreement remained as to the size and composition of such forces. It was assumed that they would figure in the collective security system which was expected to emerge from the embryonic United Nations. But the traditional scepticism concerning alliances remained.[5]

As the animosity between the Western powers and the Soviet

Union grew during the late 1940s, the Danish government first resorted to a 'Scandinavian solution' in combination with Norway and Sweden. Though still anxious to avoid connection with either superpower, Denmark was willing to entertain the prospect of military commitments and abandon its hitherto untramelled freedom of manoeuvre. As the Scandinavian project aborted, the Danish government (and parliament) chose to join NATO,[6] thus also abandoning its principle of non-alignment. But it was from the beginning a reluctant member of the alliance, and even strong supporters of membership were nervous of the consequences.[7]

It is well known that Denmark has maintained a rather special role within NATO. Successive Danish governments have stressed the non-military aspects of NATO, and its defensive character. For some twenty years after 1949 NATO membership remained uncontroversial. But doubts remained; they were particularly strong in the Radical Left party, and were given an institutional platform by the bourgeois government's creation, in 1969, of a commission of inquiry into Danish security.[8] The commission found conclusively in favour of membership but, again, concern remained, and in 1980 the government set up a Committee for Security and Disarmament to follow and evaluate developments in the field.[9] The work of this committee, which is still active, has been central to the debate, and I shall return to it.

The importance of the tradition may be summarised under the following heads: (i) the habit of using security and defence problems as a platform for domestic political controversy, (ii) a deeprooted scepticism concerning the intentions of the great powers, and (iii) widespread doubts about the viability of safeguarding Danish security by military means. These three tendencies recur throughout the current debate.

3 THE PARTICIPANTS IN THE DEBATE

Questions of security and foreign policy have tended in Denmark to remain the province of professionals, not to say experts. But there has been a 'democratisation' of the issue that goes beyond the citizen's right to make political comment. Parliament's role in foreign policy has grown, and the constitution of 1953 made it obligatory for the government to inform parliament of any important foreign policy decision, though another effect of this measure is, in keeping with the tradition, to make foreign policy still more an issue for domestic politics.[10]

The debate reached successive peaks of intensity in connection with German membership of NATO in 1955, with the anti-nuclear campaign in the early 1960s, and during the Vietnam War. But the consensus on NATO held strong, and there was little debate during the early 1970s; only during the late 1970s and the 1980s did the debate gain real momentum. The momentum has gained from and attracted new participants, but its salient feature today is the virulence with which it is conducted within the establishment. The government's disagreements with the parliamentary majority on important security issues, on Danish participation in international debates, and on questions of European and world security have been very public. The most important participants have thus been the political parties, and parliament their theatre; the parliamentary majority has been able to tie the hands of the government over certain issues arising in international forums.[11]

The participation of the establishment has not been confined to parliamentary activity. The staff of the Foreign Ministry are bound by their duty of confidentiality, but certain Danish diplomats, aware of the controversy concerning aspects of foreign policy, have participated in open discussion. The Danish military establishment has a long tradition of participation in public debate, not only on military matters but also on the political implications thereof, and widely differing views have been revealed as to the political import of the Danish armed forces and their position within the European and Atlantic axes.[12] Also close to the establishment are the various independent institutions for the study of foreign and security policy. Their members may be politicians, but they offer open forums, and certain of them have gained a reputation as meeting places for enlightened citizens.[13] Journalists and political scientists also frequent these institutions.

The institutions were till 1980 rather closed circles exhibiting a broad consensus on Danish security. Since 1980 new institutions have grown up, notably the aforementioned Committee on Security and Disarmament. Though financed by the state, it is independent and can choose its own subject matter within the terms of its competence. It is not a policy-making institution, and its main purpose is to stimulate and inform debate in the field; it has access to generous state funds which can be allocated to private organisations for the same purpose. Another important such institution is the Centre for

Peace and Conflict Research, which arranged the 1987 conference at which the studies in this volume were presented.[14] All these institutions belong in different degree to the establishment, but no consensus has resulted, and open controversy – and sometimes fierce divergences – are the rule today. The experts no longer agree.

In recent times, the peace movement in Denmark has often been identified in the public eye with anti-US sentiments and thus with a leaning toward the Soviet Union.[15] But from 1980 on, a new peace movement has grown up, often but not always at odds with the old movement, and has focused attention on the negative effects of *bilateral* military build-up. Its impact has been considerable, less in terms of its organisation – certain of its members are more or less part of the establishment – than of its redefinition of the security agenda.[16]

Both old and new organisations are grassroots movements, and alongside them there are countless other peace organisations at local or professional level. The impact of the smaller groups is difficult to assess – the importance of broad popular discussion, however critical, is in any case a widely valued constant in Danish political culture. Organisations supporting adherence to NATO, or of strengthening Danish defence in this context, have also appeared or re-emerged. Their impact on Danish opinion is unclear, and the formulation of new problems is more difficult from their perspective.[17]

4 THE SUBSTANCE OF THE DEBATE

As in other NATO member states, the start of the current controversy was the (conditional) missile deployment decision of 1979. The government of the time was a Social Democrat minority; it tried unsuccessfully to argue for a postponement of the decision within NATO. Subsequently the Danish government argued that the deployment of the missiles after four years would have to be made conditional on the 'seriousness' of negotiations between the USA and the Soviet Union, a seriousness required of both partners. At the same time both the government and the Social Democratic Party began to reconsider the possibility of a nuclear weapon-free zone in Norden (Norway, Sweden, Denmark, Finland and Iceland). In October 1982, a coalition of four bourgeois parties under the premiership of the Conservative party formed a new government. From then on, the divergence of government and parliamentary majority became increasingly obvious. It took place because the Radical Left party, which supported the government on domestic issues, supported the Social Democrats in their criticism of the government's security policies.[18] The two parties to the left of the Social Democrats, the Socialist Folksparty and the Left Socialist Party, were only too happy to find the Social Democrats alive to this issue. It was no accident that the issue which triggered off this controversy was nuclear weapons; successive governments had, since 1959, adhered to the principle that no nuclear arms should enter Danish territory in time of peace. But the build-up of nuclear arms within both NATO and the Warsaw Pact seemed likely to become so overwhelming that Denmark would be forced to accommodate them on Danish soil. The majority parties also felt that Denmark should do what it could to rid Europe of nuclear arms. The gap between the government and the majority on these issues was not wide, and mostly concerned the timing, tactics and the channels through which the Danish government should present its views to the NATO allies. On the nuclear-free zone in Norden, however, there was complete disagreement, as the government considered the very notion incompatible with membership of NATO. The disagreement has continued, and the government was very angry that the majority forced it to cancel Danish financial contributions to the NATO missile programme after the 1983 deployment decision.[19] The government, too, is worried by the proliferation of nuclear weapons in Europe, but feels that Denmark must respect NATO decisions, even those it has opposed, and must use diplomatic channels to indicate its concern at the nuclearisation of Europe, for which it considers the Soviet Union rather than the USA or NATO to blame.

An analysis of this stormy disagreement suggests that the issues are fairly simple; they represent in a new form the question whether Denmark should follow the lead of the majority in NATO (and more particularly the USA), or attempt to formulate its own policy in accordance with the non-military traditions of Danish foreign policy.[20] A similar divergence has occurred over the different strategies formulated within NATO, which is rooted in a slightly different appreciation of when and to what extent military security arrangements assist the non-military process so much preferred by all Danish political parties. The present government emphasises the contribution made to security by military power, while the parliamentary majority fears that arms may become an obstacle to negotiations. A similar division manifests itself in attitudes to the Soviet Union.

The government is closer to the present outlook of the USA, and identifies the Soviet Union as the main threat to world security, whereas the parliamentary majority see in the Soviet Union not an adversary but a negotiating partner, who must be treated firmly but not inflexibly if the goal of a demilitarised or less militarised Europe is to be attained. In this, it makes little distinction between the USSR and the USA.

From this divergence relative to the intentions of the superpowers, others necessarily follow concerning the movement toward 'europeanised' and non-military security in Europe. Here the main issue is the extent to which Western Europe needs the US presence to be able to withstand pressure from the superpower on its own continent. It is taken for granted that superpowers will attempt to mould their environment and neighbours to suit their own convenience. The question that follows thus relates to the means open to Europe to put pressure on the Soviet Union so that the latter becomes less liable to underline its superpower status with demonstrations of military prowess, at least in Europe. The government regards the American presence as indispensable and has less confidence than the majority in the adequacy of non-military means; it is unwilling, in terms of Barry Buzan's distinction, to allow its strength as a state – in which it has great confidence – to be put to the test against its weakness as a power.[21]

Government and majority alike are anxious to see Europe assume greater responsibility for security in Europe, but argue this point from different perspectives. For the government, Europe could free the USA of the burden of European security, allowing it to concentrate more on other and more dangerous parts of the world. The weight upon the shoulders of an overworked ally could be lightened. For the majority, Europe should free itself of its dependence on the superpowers, freeing itself in this way from entanglement in non-European superpower controversies and allowing it to determine its own security interests in purely European terms. A further difference concerns the consequences of European autonomy in matters of security. Would this necessarily require heavy military spending on the part of the European states? While no clear indications have been given on this point, the government would probably favour the West European Union concept or some similar arrangement; this is less evidently true of the majority.

But the most heated discussions have concerned the size and structure of the Danish armed forces. The main points are: how much money the Danish taxpayer is willing to contribute to military expenditure, to what extent membership of NATO confers an obligation to maintain certain levels of military expenditure, the degree to which the level of the Danish military contribution affects the readiness of its allies to come to its aid, and how a purely defensive configuration of the Danish armed forces could be convincingly adopted.[22] Though such questions have their international implications, they largely relate to Danish security taken in isolation, and it would be superfluous to go into them in depth. They are of most interest in relation to their implications for the core values of Danish society. Particularly controversial has been the notion of 'non-offensive defence'. Two reasons may be given for this: on the one hand, the notion is taken to have pacifist connotations, and these evoke the pacifist movements of the Danish past, notably those that existed before the Second World War.[23] But this is unfair, and the proponents of non-offensive defence are by no means pacifists in that sense. On the other, the theory is clearly at odds with established strategic thinking and indeed with the core values of those for whom national autonomy is unthinkable in the absence of a powerful force of national defence.

What do Danes agree about? The consensus on NATO has survived the vicissitudes recorded above, despite the lack of enthusiasm with which the necessity of membership was acknowledged. For most political parties – and, if we are to judge by the polls, for the nation at large – the necessity remains. By contrast, the consensus in all parties to the left of the Social Democrats, for which NATO was an imperialist conspiracy against not only the Soviet Union but the poor and oppressed of the entire world, has collapsed. The consensus on NATO now covers almost the entire political spectrum, and would be abandoned only if better security arrangements within Europe should come into being.[24] A tactical consideration may govern the attitude of the left in this regard. NATO membership is now of long standing, and the political gains the left might derive from Denmark's leaving NATO might be offset by the repercussions for the security debate; the left seeks to establish the claims both of non-military security and a more autonomous Europe, and since these are issues with which the public has been familiarised largely by the security debate, it is not anxious to rock the boat. And so, paradoxically, the establishment has its way.

5 WHAT NEXT?

Danish governments have consistently stressed the 'political' aspect of NATO, as this was formulated in the Harmel report of 1967. In this perspective, the main function of NATO is to promote the demilitarisation of Europe. Denmark is not alone in viewing NATO in this light. But NATO is not the only forum for the promotion of Danish views on and Danish security *simpliciter*. The UN is rarely mentioned in this context, though Denmark is an active member, and the UN may in the long term prove a useful forum for European security interests. More important for the immediate future is the increasingly institutionalised political cooperation within Western Europe, with its potential for the 'europeanisation' of security in Europe. Differing evaluations of the military aspect of this cooperation arise for the most part from fundamentally different evaluations of the worth of military contributions to security.[25]

Denmark has been fully committed to the Helsinki Process from the outset, and more particularly to the '3rd basket' dealing with 'human aspects'. Whereas there are conflicting opinions about the value of the Process at large, the Danish focus on human aspects is widely accepted in Denmark. The Process also challenges the definitions of Europe current in Denmark, and the last five–ten years have seen an awakening consciousness of the country's historical connections with Eastern Europe.[26]

Though bilateral contacts do not always have an institutional framework, they are important. Nordic cooperation is partly multi-partly bilateral, and its long-standing traditions and popularity make it useful for common efforts in international forums. The proposal for a nuclear-free Norden serves to illustrate how Nordic cooperation can or could influence European – and, indeed, global – security.[27] Many other bilateral contacts could be mentioned. With Norway, another member of NATO, a special relation exists, though Norway is more Atlantic orientated. Denmark's geographical position and historical roots draw her rather towards the continent, and account for the influence exercised in Denmark by events in West Germany, with which Denmark shares its only land border. Relations with West Germany have been strengthened in the post-war period, and the relations with Britain that served in the past as a counterweight to excessive dependence on Germany have somewhat declined over the same period. In this way, Denmark has tended to be involved in the processes that concern the Federal Republic and its security aspirations, and to be influenced by its views on European security. This is as true for the current Federal government as for the views of the German Social Democrats.[28] Discussions about 'common security' and 'non-offensive defence' are common to the security debate in both countries. All of these areas complement the dependence on NATO while simultaneously offering the perspective of a better solution to Danish security problems. Their relative importance varies with time, and none can be discounted.

To sum up, it appears that Denmark favours all efforts to promote European security through the demilitarisation of Europe, on condition that no turbulence arises from this process. A further condition is that the core values of the Danish and other West European states should not be sacrificed, indeed, that they should rather take root in the East European societies. The latter concern is obviously reflected in the Danish preoccupation with the human aspects of the Helsinki Process. But Denmark on its own cannot make much headway in this regard, and will therefore try to coordinate its efforts with those of other likeminded countries, compromising the specificity of its own preoccupations as little as possible in so doing. Such efforts are in any case preferable to the existing situation on European demilitarisation, which has been in stalemate for some years now. No one in Denmark likes the status quo, but there is no consensus on the way forward.[29]

6 HOW IMPORTANT IS A UNIFIED VIEW?

The overt conflict between government and majority over foreign policy is one of the most significant facts about security and approaches to security in Denmark. Since 1982, politicians have united in condemning this situation, without the situation changing on that account. In 1984, a commission of civil servants was set up to inquire into the nature of the disagreements,[30] but though their report was an excellent one, the disagreements remained. Since 1985, a parliamentary committee has been working to overcome the discords, again without success.

How influential can Danish foreign policy hope to be, where the nation's own institutions are at variance? Is it not possible that such internal disagreements – obvious as they are to all Denmark's international interlocutors, and confined as they are to a narrow range of issues – enable Denmark to have a greater impact on international debate than it could if its policy derived from a firm and coherent set of views? The Danish acknowledgement of the diversity of possible solutions may itself be productive. Openness, flexibility and patience are of the essence in these matters. And though institutional discord such as occurs in Denmark is unusual, disagreement in matters of foreign and security policy is universal; the unity of policy of any particular government is generally an expedient that does not represent the diversity of opinion to be found in that society. The guiding principles of diplomacy: secrecy, unity, and obedience are no longer acceptable today, when security has become a matter that concerns everyone, and is much too important to be left to the specialists.

7 *POST SCRIPTUM*

In the year following the initial presentation of this study, events have shown that the Danish establishment does not altogether appreciate the existence of open disagreement between majority and government, however 'healthy' such debate might in principle be.

Denmark has a long standing policy of refusing to allow nuclear weapons on its territory in time of peace. In April 1988, the Danish Parliament (Folketing) debated the issue of foreign naval vessels visiting Danish harbours and territorial waters. Should the Danish authorities seek a guarantee that such ships did not carry nuclear weapons or ammunition? Though the differences between government and majority were very slight, procedural tactics caused the government to be voted down yet again. The Prime Minister shortly afterwards declared that the government could not accept defeat on this issue, and called an election for the middle of May.

It was a peculiar reason for such a decision. Though they often serve as stalking horses for domestic issues, foreign and security policy are seldom the central themes of an election. And during the very short election campaign, it was clear that domestic issues, notably economic policy, were the main topics of debate. One of the parties of the former coalition did attempt to keep the security issue at the forefront of the election, and the campaign elicited a great deal of foreign comment on the subject of visiting naval vessels, most of which was directed against the former opposition majority. The election was typical in that it did not result in any clear mandate, and the negotiations about the composition of the government were very long drawn-out. In early June a coalition was formed under the outgoing Prime Minister, but the (three-party) coalition this time included the Radical Left, who had been part of the majority which had voted the government down in April. The formation of this coalition put an end to the discord between government and majority by unifying those two entities. The Radical Left cannot at one and the same time be a partner in government and vote with an alternative security policy majority in Parliament.

The outgoing Foreign Minister retained his post in the new government, and in a recent interview, declared that for him and his party, the elimination of discord on foreign and security policy had been one of the main reasons for accepting the new coalition partner.[31] This may not be the whole truth of the matter, but disappearance of open disagreement between government and majority will undoubtedly result. 'In place of strife', several new parliamentary commissions will be established, within which disagreements will be discussed, and some sort of common denominator be arrived at. A commission on defence has already been established, and another on broader security issues has been revitalised.

The opposition parties, the Social Democrats and the Socialist Folksparty, support this procedure. Of course, they lose an opportunity to influence policy-making on the commissions if they boycott them, and to this extent their hand is forced. But it may be that they too are content to see the end of the dissension between majority and government. Under the previous arrangement, Parliament could not control, even if it could intermittently affect, government policy, and it may be that the political cost of these small inflections of government policy was too high. Institutionalised dissent did nothing for Denmark's image in the eyes of its most important security partners, and since it did not advance the opposition's security agenda either, the opportunity to affect policy through cooperation may have been welcome.

It is, of course, difficult to give a complete explanation of this change in the conditions of the security debate in Denmark. But certain points should be emphasised. The period of institutional dissent lasted from 1982 to 1988, and was without precedent in the previous forty years. And the international situation has evolved during these years in a way that enhances the likelihood of consensus. With the INF agreement ratified, and preparations under way for further all-European negotiations on arms reductions, the subject of foreign and security policy has lost some of its attractions.

No party has won any very significant victories. Skirmishing was continuous, and all the parties have had to alter their stances in some degree. Paradoxically, an election ostensibly fought on a security issue may mark the end of foreign and security policy as live political issues. The perception of the electorate, that Denmark's domestic (for which read: economic) problems are of greater urgency, cannot long be resisted by the political class. And the question also arises, whether there is sufficient political will and energy to keep so complex and long-term an issue as European security on the political agenda.

But the period of dissension and open debate has not been a waste of time, if, as we may suspect, it has encouraged awareness in the Danish public of the complexity of European security questions in general – and, more particularly, of the degree in which their own security depends on that of Europe as a whole.

Notes and References

1. Hans Engell, *Ja, var der ingen fare...* (Varløse: Forlaget Kontrast, 1987).
2. Kristian Hvidt, *Venstre og forsvarssagen 1870–1901* (Århus: Jysk Selskab for Historie, 1960). 'Det fredssyge Danmark'. 100 års dansk fredsarbejde (Copenhagen: Komm. S. Historie, 1982).
3. Viggo Sjøqvist, *Danmarks udenrigspolitik 1933–1940* (Copenhagen: Gyldendal: 1966). Ole Karup Pedersen, *Udenrigsminister P. Munchs opfattelse af Danmarks stilling i international politik* (Copenhagen: Gads Forlag, 1970).
4. Georg Cohn, *Neo-Neutralitet* (Copenhagen: Gads Forlag, 1937).
5. Nikolaj Petersen, 'Abandonment *vs.* Entrapment: Denmark and Military Integration in Europe 1848–1951', *Cooperation and Conflict*, 21 (1986) 169–86.
6. Geir Lundestad, *America, Scandinavia, and the Cold War 1945–1949* (Oslo: Universitets-forlaget, 1980).
7. Thomas Clausen, *Ørnen og spurven* (Århus: Historisk Revy, 1984). Poul Villaume, *Danmarks stilling i den atlantiske alliances politiske og militære strategi 1949–1954*, (Thesis, University of Copenhagen, 1986).
8. *Problemer omkring dansk sikkerhedspolitik* (Copenhagen, 1970).
9. Det sikkerheds- og nedrustningspolitiske udvalg. Årsberetning (Copenhagen: Forlaget Europa, 1982–7).
10. Ib Faurby, Hans-Henrik Holm og Nikolaj Petersen, *Kampen om sikkerheden* (Århus Politica, 1986).

11. Per Voetmann, *Dobbeltbeslutsom. En analyse af Socialdemokratiets kernevåbenpolitik 1979–1984* (Århus: Århus Universitetsforlag, 1986).
12. *Danmark og NATO's strategi*. Rapport fra et seminar (Copenhagen: Det Krigsvidenskabelige Selskab, 1986).
13. Det udenrigspolitiske Selskab (Copenhagen).
14. Center for Freds- og Konfliktforskning. Beretning (1986).
15. 'Det fredssyge Danmark' (Note 2).
16. Nej til Atomvåben (Copenhagen).
17. Atlantsammenslutningen, Værn om Danmark.
18. Per Voetmann, *Dobbeltbeslutsom* (Note 11). Det sikkerheds-og nedrustningspolitiske udvalg: *Dansk sikkerhedspolitik og forslagene om Norden som kernevåbenfri zone* (Copenhagen:, Forlaget Europa, 1982).
19. Søren Møller Christensen (ed.), *Man har et standpunkt . . . Socialdemokratiet og sikkerhedspolitikken i 80'erne* (Copenhagen: Eirene, 1984).
20. Poul Villaume (Note 7).
21. Barry Buzan: *People, States and Fear* (Brighton: Wheatsheaf, 1983).
22. Hans Engell (Note 1).
23. Mogens Godballe, *Selvforsvar i atomalderen. En debatbog om defensivt forsvar* (Copenhagen: Politisk Revy, 1987).
24. Klavs Birkholm, 'Rød realisme', in *Information* (1986).
25. Peter Dyvig, 'Det europæiske politiske samarbejde (EPS): status og fremtid' in C. Tune and N. Petersen (eds), *Dansk udenrigspolitisk årbog 1983* (Copenhagen: Jurist og økonomforbundets Forlag 1984).
26. Det sikkerheds- og nedrustningspolitiske udvalg. *Øst–Vest forholdet. Vestlige alternativer i østpolitikken* (Copenhagen: Forlaget Europa, 1984).
27. (Note 18.) Erik Boel, *Socialdemokratiets atomvåbenpolitik 1945–88* (Copenhagen: Akademisk Forlag, 1988).
28. Det sikkerheds- og nedrustningspolitiske udvalg. *Det tyske spørgsmål* (Copenhagen, 1986).
29. Det sikkerheds- og nedrustningspolitiske udvalg: *Dyvig-rapporten*. Danmarks sikkerhedspolitiske situation i 1980'erne med kommentarer og debat (Copenhagen, 1985).
30. (Note 29.) For a very sophisticated and penetrating analysis of the Danish debate, see Georg Sørensen, 'Peace and Security in Europe: The Context for Denmark's Choices' *Cooperation and Conflict*, 21 (1986) 219–40.
31. *Udenrigs*, 1.3 (1988) 1–11.

17 Conflicts of Vision: Visions of Conflict

Ole Wæver

The preceding sixteen chapters have opened up a lot of perspectives and introduced a number of elements necessary to a general analysis of European security. Some of these will now be integrated into a common framework. This chapter will also try to sketch some guidelines for future research; it will be argued that an approach based on national analyses is necessary, but it will also be suggested that the *next phase* must necessarily involve a more consistent development and employment of analytical concepts and theories. This is the more necessary if the aim is a perspective which permits the transformation of the East–West conflict into a security community or non-violent conflict culture – that is, a community where war is no longer a possibility but conflict is continued in a constructive manner. The *direction* of thinking in the individual studies will be noted. Potential for common terminology will be evaluated, with the aim of furthering the next step in the analytical process. This final chapter also contains a brief presentation of some of the essential ideas of the Copenhagen project 'Non-military Aspects of European Security'.[1]

1 NEW OPENINGS IN EUROPE

1.1 'New'?

'For the first time since the end of the Second World War'. Few expressions create such a strong sense of *déja vu*; it just asks for the cynic's riposte 'That is just what everyone said in 1956, in the 1960s – and in Europe even a long way into the 1970s. Today, we are again told that the world is becoming multipolar, that the Cold War has ended, and so on. These events are of course irreversible, and they are happening for the first time – again.

Still – sobering as this criticism might be – its logic is flawed. We must examine the situation in hand. Changes occur, crying wolf doesn't prevent the beast showing up some day.

Also, the present situation *does* present some new features:

1. During the late 1980s, it has been a common perception in world politics that the USA and the Soviet Union are in decline.[2] A somewhat similar impression existed at the time of the first détente. On the basis of the ambivalence Galtung notes in 'final act',[3] we might give the '*floruit*' of the first détente as *1969* (with the important changes of governments in Britain, France, the USA and the Federal Republic)[4] *to 1975* with Helsinki as its *final act*. The détente of the 1970s also featured a threatened or declining USA, as Kissinger has stated. Nixon, in this context, went so far as to mention multipolarity. But the Soviet Union was then perceived as stable at very least.

   Happily, the two superpowers might this time be hitting a trough *in synch*.[5] Phases of decline are destabilising when they combine with the expansion of other powers seen by the declining power as threatening. This has previously been the case in US–Soviet relations – not least in Europe. Now both superpowers seem in parallel manner to be turning inwards, to have given up all 'imperial' expansionism, and to have little taste for pursuing gains on the chessboard of Europe. This is not altogether reassuring; decline implies weakness, and weakness incites to conflict.
2. The European identity seems in many respects much stronger and more *self-centred* this time. During the 1980s the new European awareness has grown not only in the more relaxed atmosphere of 1987 and after ('second détente'),[6] but also during the period of tension ('new Cold War').

   The European identity this time seems different, more self-assured. Of course, Europe counted for something during the 'first détente' too, as witness the CSCE conference and process. However, the focus of interest in Europe then was security and East–West conflict, with particular reference to the German problem.

   Nowadays, talk of 'Europe' has become quite intellectually respectable.[7] It has even begun to seem intellectually irresponsible *not* to talk about Europe.[8] The talk borders at times on Euro-patriotism: remarks that would savour of chauvinism and worse if made about a nation-state, are quite acceptable about 'Europe'. All things European now sound 'progressive' or liberating by definition – the specific reference is immaterial. Moralising about superpower domination or dressing up partisan projects in neutral colours are just some of the new functions of 'Europe'.[9] This seems to constitute a basis for European intellectual constructs with a higher degree of independence of 'East' and 'West' – Europe is now seen as a value in itself. Projects can, it is widely felt, be grounded in 'Europe', despite the many versions in circulation of what or where that entity is.

Examples of this Euro-patriotism? Well, consider the sentimental tone adopted of late by that rather matter-of-fact politician Genscher, in speeches entitled 'Responsibility for the Future of Europe', 'Europe – our Future', 'Shaping the Future according to the European Spirit' or 'A Plan for All of Europe'.[10]

Books on Europe stream from the presses. Many are structured around European journeys, like the travel books of the Grand tour – and have a direct political slant of the kind fashionable in the inter-war period and immediately after the Second World War. Rediscovery of European *forms* and genres go hand in hand with the ubiquity of Europe as *theme*.

French interests related to economy, technology and civilisation; West German '*Deutschlandpolitik*'; the Soviet interest in a 'Common European House'; East Central European attempts to link up with Western Europe and 'catch the eye of the Western Europeans'; all tend to converge on the theme of 'Europe'.

3. The most important prospect is this: that social changes might go so far as to become *irreversible*. Détente has a disintegrative effect not only on the alliances (at the state level)[11] but in the political life of each society: there is more room for social forces that do not define themselves in relation to the two poles of the ideological *mêlée*.[12] Moreover, the reintegrative efforts of the early 1980s had only limited success, and the present period therefore to some extent starts where the first détente left off. So it seems likely that social change – especially in the East – will have repercussions for domestic balances of power and institutions. Europe will alter. It is more than a change of policy. One change affects political culture and expectations; it changes the self-images of social forces, enhancing in their own eyes the legitimacy of their claim to participate in national and trans-national politics. Another affects the pattern of East–West politics: the sequence first détente, increased tension, new détente, may have effaced those 'diagonal alliances', so characteristic of Europe, in which the opposition of the one system/elite was the natural (or dedicated) ally of the other.[13] The communist parties present no serious threat in the

West and the East is interested in controlled learning from the West – influence from the West is no longer seen as subversion.

Networks of economic and technical *interdependence* tend to raise the *price* of renewed isolation, but the irreversible aspect of the process is the formation of new domestic *political* constellations during the period of détente.

4. Even supposing first and second détentes are identical, the situation is interesting, and like the first détente means a marked opening of horizons, the loosening of bloc ties, the liberation of forces not always reassuring – and a proliferation of *visions* of future dispensations.

1.2 'Europeanisation'

The process leading to 'second détente' began in the mid-1980s. Disarmament and the expectation of more was part of it. It is closely related to the 'New Thinking' in Soviet foreign policy and the spontaneous influence on both generated by the domestic reform policy. But it is also generally seen as implying some kind of *Europeanisation*. What does this mean?

What we have seen since the INF agreement (with all that it implies about superpower relations) is a *removal* of previous constraints on the European order. It is a manifold development. There is no new system awaiting intronisation. 'Europeanisation' is a fact – if it is taken to mean a Europe that is gradually being defined more from the inside, and less from the outside – less, in short, by the superpowers.[14] What is then of interest is not 'Europeanisation' as such, but the question: *which* Europeanisation is going to win out?[15]

1.3 The Role of Vision: The Analysis of Politics

It is at such moments in history that the influence of schemata and organising concepts is at its highest. How can we analyse events of this kind? We need to examine the sources of concepts, and the processes of national politics whence they arose. Then we can analyse the interplay of the different organising principles. Hence a conference principally devoted to papers investigating: 'The Debate on European Security in ....'. To many this seems the least theoretical of approaches. Wrong.

Power lies not with any one actor but in the figuration, the relationship, *in between* the actors. Therefore an analysis of the situation should not try to find the actor able to get his model implemented, or the model that all actors will adopt. First it is necessary to understand the present situation as a complex figuration of policies pointing in many directions. And we must not, in this process, dismiss 'official' policies, since they are clearly important parts of the political process. Analysis of European security therefore begins with an analysis of the interplay of the different concepts, visions and programmes of European security.[16]

2 THE GEOGRAPHICAL IMAGERY: VARIOUS EUROPES, VARIOUS THREATS PERCEIVED

First, a presentation of the implications of various concepts of 'Europe'. It will be shown that Europeanisation does not mean an absence of conflict, that it *can*, indeed, mean the continuation of (security) conflict by different means.

2.1 4 × Europe

In the security debate the four most important visions or frames of 'Europe' are: (i) Europe from the Atlantic to the Urals; (ii) Europe from Poland to Portugal; (iii) Western Europe as Europe; (iv) The European Security Area ('CSCE Europe'). The first includes (parts of) the Soviet Union – and not the USA, whereas the second places the divide between the Soviet Union and the smaller Eastern European countries, which are thus grouped with Western Europe. In the third the Eastern dimension is wholly omitted, and in the fourth both global powers are included.

1. *The 'Common European House'* is the latest form taken by the Soviet/(Russian) attempt to picture 'Europe' as a unit naturally including Moscow; traditionally this involves excluding or confronting (the threat from) the extra-European Washington.[17]

   This European project is at odds with other of the orientations or self-images of the Soviet Union:

   There is, first and foremost, a structural pressure toward bilateralism, toward definition 'against' the US; this is the 'two-superpower relation', and the self-image of the global power.[18] In Europe, the Soviet Union presents itself as a regional power. And in Vladivostok Gorbachev launched the Soviet Union as a (regional) Asian power.

The attempt to be seen as 'European' is controversial from a Soviet perspective too. At one level this is because the Soviet Union comprises large areas that are definitely not European (and do not want to be). At another, we find some deeper-lying tensions in the Russian 'geo-self-image': More European than Europe versus Anti-European (Slavonic) – or both. There is a Russian tradition of seeing itself – its mission – as saving a decadent Europe from itself – the true civilisation will be brought back from Russia to a Western Europe that is no longer truly 'European'. In relation to Christianity, this was the idea of Moscow as the 'third Rome'.

This inferiority–superiority complex towards Europe makes Russia's position in the 'Common European House' just as problematic from the East as from the West. One of the purposes of the 'House' might currently be domestic: to help the Soviet Union identify itself *into* Europe and obtain the economic, technological and political impulses needed for the process of reform.

The immediate foreign policy thrust of the Common House seems to be against *Western European* security integration – and not against transatlantic community. The Soviet Union's objections to Western European economic integration are fading. But it is emphatic on the point that new defence cooperation in Western Europe is detrimental to détente and the common house.[19]

Another – and related – tendency of the late 1980s is a new optimism of the liberal and conservative right in Western Europe. The latter now tends to define the Western European integration project (see below) in an all-European perspective – and the other way round.[20]

The basic purpose of the 'Common European House' seems to be that of creating an image of closer relations between Western Europe and Eastern Europe – especially the Soviet Union, with no obvious role for the North Americans. Western European opposition to the term therefore seems to emanate principally from the Right, which argues that it would mean Soviet hegemony ('just look at a map'). At the same time, the response often takes the form of: 'we accept the metaphor on condition that in the Common House there is free passage between the rooms', etc. It seems that Gorbachev came up with a too vivid a metaphor – it just asks for elaboration in figural language. And thus the metaphor itself becomes a figurative battlefield.

So for 'Europe (i)' we should keep the label 'Europe from the Atlantic to the Urals', as this is an attempt at structuration, whereas the Common House is a more lively, but consequently less predictable, (linguistic) phenomenon.

2. *Europe from Poland to Portugal.* Milan Kundera, Gyorgy Konrad and others, notably from Czechoslovakia, Poland, and Hungary, argue roughly as follows: 'Our East-Central European countries belong to Europe, in fact, they are culturally and historically among the most important parts of Europe'. 'Central Europe' is, in short, central to Europe. And now this area is placed outside Europe – or controlled by a non-European power: Asiatic Russia.

   This sentiment has been reoriented in several directions. It has been used by peace movements and like-minded groups to support the idea of détente from below. This is the idea that people from East and West have something to meet about: Europe. Obviously the perspective of the lost Eastern Europe also fits into a more or less 'revanchist' right-wing programme. 'Justice' and 'Peace' are, in this view, unattainable unless and until Eastern Europe is free to join Europe. This tendency is especially strong in the Federal Republic of Germany, as it serves to keep the German question open.

   The view that Eastern Europe needs liberating from the Soviets is frequently implicit in cultural input into the security debate. 'Eastern Europe' here means the Warsaw Pact nations with the exception of the Soviet Union – a terminology that is itself linked to our second perspective. (In the first, Eastern Europe would be Russia.)[21]

   The basic figure of 'creating Europe' by extending Western European principles to Eastern Europe assumes the most various guises. They range from conservatives who see this as a necessary task of the EEC,[22] to peace movement visions of 'Europe from Poland to Portugal'. This purview would remove the distinction between East and West. No give and take is envisaged. It is simple irredentism. It is clearly both anti-Soviet and anti-communist, given that only the contiguity of the Soviet Union saves the communist elite in Poland.

   Arguments in favour of this 'not quite all-Europe' are mainly of two kinds:

   (a) Arguments from religion, culture and history, which present Russia as non-European. Russia has made important contributions to European culture mainly by being *different*, it is often argued.[23] This is linked to traditional anti-Russian and anti-Slav prejudices and policies.[24]

(b) A military–political argument runs as follows: the Soviet Union is one of the two dominant world powers and cannot therefore form part of any regional security complex.[25]

Events in the East which they interpret as the 'surrender' of communism elicit such optimism in some conservatives that they move from Europe (ii) to Europe (i) (European Common House). They expect Western Europe to be strong enough to enter a construction covering Western Europe, Eastern Europe, and the Soviet Union. A diminished role is accorded to the USA. Traditionally the conservative establishment rejects this model; it fears the geopolitical weight of the Soviet Union and conceives that, in this European house, the Russian leader would sit at the head of the table. However, a belief in the weakness of the socialist system tends to convince some conservatives that an 'all-European' integration of this kind would result in the victory of Western ('European') values. In this case, the logic of Europe (ii) becomes so energetic that it takes on the task of dealing with the larger Europe (i) – but in the form of Europe (ii).

3. A third 'Europe' is the Europe of the *European Community*. This *can* be linked to any of the other concepts of Europe (the Western European integration process being a component of any Europeanisation). However, it often functions as a full image of Europe. To many people – policy-makers as well as general public – Europe is the European Community.

   Here there has been a small revolution. 'EC people' have started to show a surprising interest in Eastern Europe. The new focus on *value, culture* and *tradition* as integral to the 'European' project (EC) has attracted to the 'liberation of East-Central Europe' those whose basic interest is Western European integration, but who realise that they need an All-European discourse if they are to revive the sometimes jaded enthusiasm for integration.

4. Europe (iv) is the *European Security Area*; it can also be labelled the 'CSCE Europe'. Basically this concept is pragmatic. Instead of seeking values *prior* to the current political nexus (history, culture, geography, religion), it takes its starting point in the present European security figuration. Transformations must start *from* this point.

The 'security Europe' includes states that do not form part of the geographic Europe. The Soviet Union is partly *in* because it is part-located on European soil, and because it has a 'real-political' role in Europe. The USA and Canada are *in* due to their role in European affairs. Of course, it can be added that USA and Canada as well as the Soviet Union have strong European roots culturally and historically. But that is not a satisfactory criterion. On that basis, Australia and New Zealand should join. And what about South Africa, etc.? The USA and Canada are defined into the European Security Area because of the *role* they play in European security, whether or not this derives from the common roots. In general, no absolute link can be established from cultural to security fellowship, as Kundera will tell us. There is a sense (colonisation) in which the whole earth has been Europeanised, and subsequent efforts been made (by recently created, European-model states) to reverse the process. The distinction European – non-European is extremely complex, especially in the cultural sphere.

Much of the debate on peace and security is a disguised debate on the problem of political identity. Studying non-military aspects of European security involves particular attention to political identities in Europe that influence the definition of friends and enemies, allies and adversaries. This is often decisive for the perceptions of security or insecurity, and determines whether weapons are perceived as a protection or a threat.

Parts of this debate deal with variants of national identity. But even these are liable to adduce the competing conceptions of 'Europe'. For the intellectual structures seeking primacy in the *mêlée* that détente has allowed, the prime question is 'what' or 'which' Europe. That question is not always explicit. Europe is the ideological stalking horse of our day.

2.2 'Euro-national' versus 'Regional International' Security

These different conceptions of Europe relate to different conceptions of 'the threat'. And the geopolitical structurations to which either gives rise will, to a large extent, define the future of Europe. They are *competing organising principles*. The relations of influence, the capacity to mould political developments; this is what they organise. Their socio–political effects are the name of the game. This has already been partly shown in section 2.1. But the different Europes also imply different *types* of security arrangement.

Europe (i): This vision of Europe has an anti-USA slant. It is not presented as a way of *handling* the existing East–West conflict because then the USA obviously should be in. It is presented as an area of natural harmony: We could fence off this area from global politics, and it would then be secure. 'The threat', it is implied, comes from outside (this) Europe.

That is why many in Western Europe fear that this arrangement would – one way or the other – lead to a dominant position for the Soviet Union. The Soviet Union casts a long 'geopolitical shadow', one which might cover 'Europe from the Atlantic to the Urals'. The relations of some of the Warsaw Pact countries to the Soviet Union show how difficult is a suppositious 'friendship' where this maps onto a traditional 'enemy image'. The reversion to the latter is the more explosively shocking.

Europe (ii): This has the opposite orientation. Excluding the Soviet Union and pulling the smaller Eastern European nations closer into a Western European orbit, it will necessarily *in Eastern Europe* mean more influence from the West, less from the Soviet Union. This is unlikely to meet with Soviet approval unless it happens *inside* a larger framework, which would define the limits of Western European 'attraction'. This form of European dynamic is not therefore an unrealistic one, and may even be unavoidable, on condition it coincides with an all-European arrangement involving the Soviets.

This image of security is 'Euro-National' in the further sense that no security conflicts between West Europe and the smaller countries of Eastern Europe are expected; threats are, by definition, external. Yet it seems clear that Eastern Europe *is* threatened, to the extent that all the changes that this image implies will occur in the East. For it is logically implicit in this conception that 'security' in Eastern Europe is not defined by or with the *state/elite* but by the people. So the East–West harmony in this Europe is between the *existing* power-holders/establishments in the West and some *future/ideal* power-holders/establishments in the East. If *national* security is taken (in its traditional sense) to mean security as defined by the state government, this Europe is a clear threat to the security not only of the Soviet Union but of Eastern Europe. The 'dialectic of security' in its turn implies that the threat to the security of this Europe is the Soviet Union, especially in the form in which it is present outside its own borders.

Europe (iii): This Europe does not seem to be threatening any one directly – nor is its construction motivated by the perception of a threat. But it is hard to evaluate this point, as Europe (iii) is often integrated into a larger project. It can be so closely linked to an Atlanticist model as to seem simply a more effective West – and therefore elicit no great enthusiasm in the Soviet Union. It can signal a break with the USA – thus entering the perspective of Europe (i) (eliciting fear in the West among Atlanticists and Establishment circles) or be linked with an attractive 'third way': a perspective like Europe (ii), whose principal significance would be greater pressure in East–East relations towards more independence for the smaller Eastern European countries. Lastly it can be a fortress 'Europe' (fortress Western Europe) with no active foreign policy and no increased vulnerability to overtures from the East. This might itself be a threat to the smaller Eastern European countries as implying a more definite division of Europe. It would limit the possibilities for integration of the two parts if the Western part, upon leaving the era of Atlantic organisation, immediately started creating a new, purely *Western* structure. Criticism of this last project is heard in both the East and the West (in the West largely from the Left); its critics fear the creation of a Western European Superpower – usually presented as 'Nuclear France' writ large.[26]

But the realisation of Europe (iii) as such is not likely; the security complex *is* all-European. The *interdependence of security dynamics* is so high that any process of Europeanisation has to be conceived in all-European terms.[27]

Europe (iv): This represents an attempt to integrate all the main actors and organise security *among them*. It is therefore *regional international security*.

Summing up: We see here two kinds of threat perception: from powers external to the region – (Euronational) – or from conflicts within the region – Regional International Security. Euronational versus Regional International Security is one of the most basic questions in European Security: does 'European Security' secure Europe from something Non-European or is it a way of organising security among Europeans, and controlling the threats Europeans pose one to another?[28]

Traditional thinking on security tends to identify in-group and out-group, and to organise peace among 'us' by fencing off *the other*.[29] Political philosophy is to a large extent built on the dichotomy of inside/outside: the ideas of 'community' on the one hand, with order, harmony, rules and progress, and on the other, the domain of international politics, where power rules, and the structures of the past repeat themselves without cease. These ideas are mutually supportive.[30] It is therefore likely that 'European security' will first and foremost evoke a 'nation-state' image of security. On the other hand, the tradition of 'international security' considers international *arrangements*, international codes of law, and so on. 'European security' will also have to draw on this tradition, and the sooner the better. It is, after all, a largely European tradition.

Among the non-military dimensions the political is the primary one.[31] And it even has a focus:

2.3 The Importance of the East–West Conflict

1. In discussion of Europe, there is a danger of the sub-continent fragmenting into an indecipherable debris of aspects, projects and purviews. The East–West conflict is for the time being the major issue and thereby the focus for questions of European security. Other conflicts are mainly to be analysed in their interplay with this.

   The East–West conflict is not a simple conflict between two 'parties'. But it is the unifying name of the conflict formation that focuses the thinking of Europeans on security.
2. The East–West conflict is not a conflict to be solved: conflict management means setting out and delimiting the various possible forms of enacting the conflict. 'Form' signifies, in the first instance, 'means', and 'management' here signifies excluding military force as a means. 'Form' is also a wider question of 'rules of the game', of achieving some agreement on norms and procedures for interaction and competition. The aim is a *non-violent conflict culture*.[32]
3. For individual nations (especially the smaller ones), day-to-day variations in national security are to a large extent the product of changes in East–West relations.[33] An awareness of this characterises international in contradistinction with national security strategy. The narrow national strategy focuses on direct threats against the national territory. International strategy will, for the smaller and medium-sized countries, imply attempts to influence the international climate, as this is of decisive importance for their local interests.

   Therefore the smaller countries will tend to be pragmatists in the sense that they do not see the ideological cause as something they can contribute much to. Security policy consequently becomes a balancing act between the necessary symbolic acts towards the major ally(ies) on the one hand and on the other attempts to create a relaxed atmosphere around the area for the sake of more tangible aims.[34]

This position differs from that of the medium-sized nations in that countries like France, West Germany, Poland, Italy and Great Britain manoeuvre in European politics with an eye to their own position in the power structure – their future role in European politics.

2.4 The East–West Conflict and/in Europe: Conflict Formation versus Security Complex

How are we to conceive the East–West conflict at the theoretical level? Politically, it serves as a litmus test.[35] The non-communist left in Western (and Eastern?) Europe present the East–West conflict as simply a power struggle between the USA and the Soviet Union – a contest for *hegemony*. The right and centre (the extreme, nationalist right excepted) tend to see the conflict as an important struggle between two *social systems*, the upshot of which will determine the domestic social and political order.

Serious research involves an understanding of both perspectives. Werner Link argues that 'the East–West Conflict' is constituted by the convergence of these two conflicts (Figure 17.1).[36] This happened in 1917–18 with the establishment of the socialist, revolutionary programme in state form and with the USA entering the First World War as the champion of democratic *principles*. The two states launched the two major programmes for both *international politics*

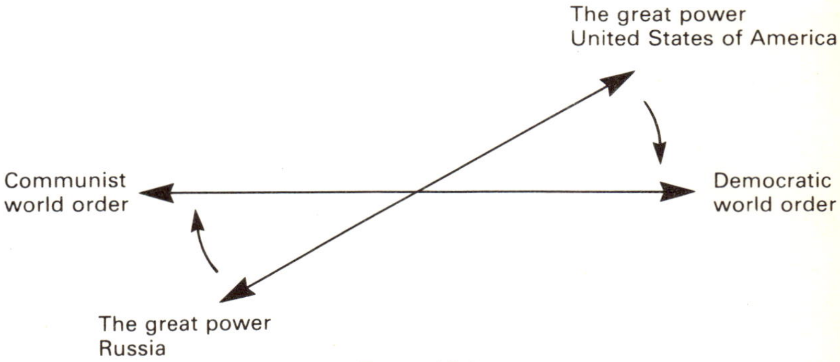

Figure 17.1

and domestic politics – Lenin versus Wilson.[37] The dominance of this combined structure did not become apparent till the late 1940s but since then it has been the major organising principle of international politics.

What is happening now? Are the two axes in Figure 17.1 separating? In a way 'no', and in a way, 'yes'. The superpower conflict remains a combined power and order conflict. There may be a certain deideologisation taking place especially in the Soviet Union[38] and perhaps too in the USA of President Bush. The major change in the East–West conflict is in the role of the central arena, Europe.

The role of an arena is of course a passive one. It is said that Europe will take less and less part in the superpower conflict.[39] One conclusion drawn from this, even by those who recognise the dual nature of the conflict, is that Europe will thus leave the East–West conflict. The conflict came with the superpowers, it will be left behind if Europe leaves the superpower conflict. This is to overstate. The second conclusion is that the East–West conflict will continue within Europe. The hegemonical aspect of East–West conflict can be neutralised by a European decision made in common with the superpowers to declare the European arena out of bounds to hegemonical conflict. But such an agreement could be arrived at only on condition the ideological conflict retained the geopolitical form it now has. To return this to its theoretical framework, we can simply say that if the hegemonical axes are no longer superimposed on the ideological axes, the conflict or intersection of the ideological axes will remain. European security, even if Europe should cease to participate in the superpower conflict, will thus still depend on the forms taken by the competition of political interests.

'Europeanisation' means removing overlay; what is to be found beneath? In non-overlaid regions there is a distinctive and relatively stable regional security pattern. The stability of a *security complex* is defined in terms of the temporal continuity of the security fears and goals within the area considered. It does not imply that wars do not occur, only that they do not change the complex of security interests. In this sense, there was a relatively stable regional security complex in Europe prior to 1945; it was, however, an untypical example of one, in that it was *folded out* on the world (especially during the period of colonialism). After 1945 (1943) the European security complex was *folded in* – its own dynamic was suppressed by the conflict of the superpowers. There is thus no longer a continuous distinct European complex, and it is unclear what would be 'discovered', were the overlay removed. It would be a mixture of three factors:

1. old conflicts ('German problem', Hungary–Romania, Greek–Turkish conflict, etc.);
2. the continuation of the conflict introduced by overlay (East–West);
3. specific effects of the *way* overlay is removed – it makes a difference whether there is a sudden unilateral withdrawal of American troops or negotiated arrangements or a continued military presence of the superpowers combined with a military and political *stabilisation* of Europe that withdraws it from the operations board of the superpower game.

Because of this complex situation, the key issue in Europe relates to the interplay of Europe as a *local version* of the East–West conflict and Europe as a *region*.

This book has presented an overview of concepts, programmes, and visions in European security. The next task is to analyse the dynamics at the aggregate level. For this we require a *structured* analysis.

Two concepts seem essential: 'The East–West Conflict Formation' (Senghaas) and 'Regional Security Complex' (Buzan). Elements of the latter have already been introduced. These concepts overlap, but their proximity and differences are precisely what makes their combined use illuminating.

Security Complex is a concept aimed at 'identifying durable, and relatively self-contained, patterns of security relations generated by the local states themselves'.[40]

The premiss is that mutual security awareness is not equally distributed across the globe (therefore a general international analysis is not necessarily the best): (national) security relations combine as regional formations. Inside these it is not possible to analyse the security of one state in isolation (the national level in isolation is insufficient). The complex is identifiable by stable patterns of amity and enmity *inside it*, and by its difference from surrounding patterns, which takes the form of a 'boundary of relative indifference' in relation to states outside the complex:

> we can attempt to define regional security subsystems in terms of patterns of amity and enmity that are substantially confined within some particular geographical area. The assumption is that local sets

> of states exist whose major security perceptions and concerns link together sufficiently closely that their national security problems cannot realistically be considered apart from one another ... Unlike most other attempts to define regional subsystems, security complexes rest, for the most part, on the interdependence of rivalry rather than on the interdependence of shared interests ... Security complexes are an empirical phenomenon with historical and geopolitical roots. They are characteristic products of an anarchic international system, and represent durable rather than permanent substructures within such a system.[41]

The method is then to analyse four levels: (i) domestic factors in the relevant states (especially sources of strength or weakness as states-vulnerabilities); (ii) the operations of the security complex as such – the interaction of the perceptions and policies of security of the various states; (iii) the interplay with neighbouring complexes; (iv) the involvement of the global powers – degrees of overlay.

Conflict formation is a concept mainly developed by Dieter Senghaas.[42]

Conflict formations are 'action sets' (*Handlungszusammenhänge*). These are the macropolitical, macromilitary and macroeconomic axes that structure international politics. Conflict formations are identified within the complex of international politics, of which they do not constitute an exhaustive description.

Senghaas uses them to build a global analysis without postulating uniformity of relations. This approach helps the analyst to respect the very different content, form and intensity of the individual conflicts. The five conflict formations are: East–West, conflicts within the West, conflicts inside the socialist system, the North–South conflict, and regional conflicts in the third world.

Neither concept has any teleological implication. Both are defined by *in*-security: the common conflict or the mutual interrelationship of security *fears*. Neither postulates 'universal' or 'natural' goals. (In contrast, security often seems to be defined as the fulfilment of human needs – international security then becomes the aggregate parameter of the success of the human race.) Senghaas focuses on the content or character of the conflict, and this enables him to make general statements about structural changes affecting, for instance, all cases of North–South conflict. This is possible by working with categories that imply relations of a single *kind*. The relations are *not* regionally (geographically) grouped in the manner of Buzan's security complexes.

One could say Senghaas's analysis is 'top down' (logic first) and Buzan's the contrary. In this volume, we have concentrated on the way the various states perceive and define their security problems and security needs – and the interactions of these. This is closer in methodology to Buzan than to Senghaas. It allows us to ask a simple but essential question: to what extent do decisions on *national* security take *international dynamics* into account?

In the approach outlined here for the further anlysis of European security we therefore propose as the general, analytical framework: security complex. Of the important dynamics, the first is the East–West conflict formation. It is the essence of level (iv) in the security complex – the dynamics of global rivalry of the superpowers. In the European case, the focus of analysis must be on the interplay of this and the dynamics 'generated by the local states themselves'.

2.5 Many Europes as One Europe

Maybe the best hope for Europe is an inconsistent, indecisive outcome of the struggle of the Europes. An illogical mixture of all the models will limit the threats contained in each.

A European superpower is not a likely prospect. But steps in that direction might be necessary: a strong Western Europe is probably necessary in order to maintain a dynamic equilibrium with an all-European structure that includes a strong role for the Soviets; this would allow interdependence and interaction between Western Europe and the smaller Eastern European countries to grow. And the USA continues to be part of the overall CSCE process.

A likely perspective for Europe is a pattern of '*interference*', defined in physics as the dynamic co-ordination that results when different wavelengths (ordering principles, in our metaphor) collide.

Section 2 has shown that 'Europeanisation' is not necessarily convergence or harmony. There are conflicting 'Europes' in the making. Different threat perceptions will be set off by different vulnerabilities. This is natural if, as can be argued, different nations and different social groups have different *concepts of security*.

Section 3.1 will first delineate the basic understanding of security in use here, and more especially of the curious term or concept 'Non-military aspects of European Security'. The larger section 3.2 will then outline the main variations in security concepts in Europe and thereby map some basic traits of the European security figuration.

3 'NON-MILITARY' ASPECTS OF SECURITY?

3.1 'Security': In Defence of the Classical Approach

The study of non-military aspects of security takes its starting point in the traditional acceptation of *security*.[43]

Security is structured around the *problématique* of war. And war is basically an inter-state phenomenon operating in a world where the core concepts are sovereignty, defence and borders. 'War is not, therefore, a relation of man to man but a relation of state to state, in which individuals are enemies only by accident, not as men or even as citizens, but as soldiers, not as members of the homeland, but as its defenders.'[44]

The security to be found in the term 'Non-military aspects of security' is the same old security; 'real' security, 'realist' security. 'Non-military aspects' of security does not aim to replace the pursuit of classical security with some airy-fairy aim – individual security instead of national security; civil interests instead of integrity or sovereignty; security of energy supply more important than integrity of borders; etc. Some of these issues might be relevant. But it is illogical to attempt to define the internal hierarchy of a concept as situation-related as security.

Moreover, the 'alternativistic' redefinition tends to obscure the relationship of ends and means. 'Security' in its traditional sense relates to the concept of sovereignty and the capacity to avert outside interference *if it is deemed unwanted*. Thus a basic structural quality of 'security' is the capacity to avoid being *put at the mercy of others*: 'security' means to have at one's disposition means of identifying unwanted developments, labelling them security problems and then handling them – if necessary, by politically unconventional methods. The nature of the fears is no more a given of the situation than the nature of the reaction; both are political decisions.

Non-military dimensions of security are not at the margins of 'real' (national) security: they are the non-military links in the chains of thinking, deciding and enacting security policies. In a sense, the study of 'non-military aspects of security' is contemporary history and future studies, conducted from the perspective of diplomatic and political history: it treats of international politics, 'European politics of the XY century', power politics, states and ideas, domestic political conflict and international structures. These subjects are not fundamentally military subjects, though their enactment in history often takes military form.

When the book of history is written, the military aspects are like the colours on a picture – the logic of the narrative hinges on non-military decisions and orientations. In these processes, conceptions of international organisation are crucial to the interplay of national policies aimed at regional and international security.

It is important to set out in detail the different *categories* of non-military aspects (economic, political, etc.), and comprehend *each* of these sectors in its own right. Several chapters here contribute significantly to this goal. The typology itself – both the *sectors* of security and the *modes of influence* – need careful consideration.[45] This will be an essential future task – not least for the project in Copenhagen.[46]

3.2 Home-bred Concepts of Security

As Barry Buzan has pointed out, security is one of those 'essentially contested concepts' that, given their inherently political character, cannot be precisely defined.[47]

The core fears of each nation are unique; they relate to its vulnerabilities[48] and historical experience.[49] Security thus *means* different things to different nations.

Is it possible to adumbrate a general pattern for the late 1980s and early 1990s, a situation characterised by post-INF dynamism and general expectations of some kind of 'Europeanisation'?

The contributions here have called attention to the difference in emphasis between East and West on non-military dimensions of security. Among the most urgent priorities for the East is *economic security*, whereas the West tends to focus on the *political (military–political)*. To use these facts to outline the transnational figuration, we must structurally locate the relevant fears.

Western fears focus on the 'high level' related to diplomacy and disarmament policy: the image of Gorbachev being the most 'able' player on the diplomatic scene – and especially on the trans-national media screen. (This fear is probably not lessened by the change of American President in 1988–9!)

For *the East*, the perceived threat is developments coming from below, developments whose goals are not necessarily clear. But social interaction with the West, the need to react to human rights campaigns or 'intervention in domestic affairs', does pose a challenge. So do the processes of economic integration, which happen pretty much on the terms set by the West – or, more particularly, the EEC. The

West is acquiring increasing possibilities of leverage in the East through economic linkage. But it may well be that the *political* effects of *not* linking up to the world market are more threatening and, paradoxically, take similar forms: destabilisation and popular discontent.[50]

It is thus very understandable that *Eastern* security concepts in the 1980s involve a 'broad understanding' of the term, and considerable interest in 'non-military aspects'. This (awkward) term is very frequently encountered in the 1988 special issue of *Külpolitika* (the Hungarian quarterly 'Foreign Policy'), on 'International Security'.[51]

Eastern diplomacy has always stressed the need for non-intervention, respect for borders, and so on. In the new security debates, this has evolved into a broader notion of security, including social, political and especially economic security.[52] The sensitivity generated in the East by the 'German problem' relates partly to military matters, but also to the fear of social destabilisation. The Federal Republic is, after all, the only state in Europe to avow what we might call a 'revisionist' outlook in the matter of nation states – though not, pray, at the level of borders. The more *general* 'revisionism' of East and West, their tendency to 'correct', adjust, or reject each other's ideologies and social systems, is more difficult to calibrate in so far as it affects nation states.[53] But clearly the level of interaction that takes place amounts to trans-national politics. And a core question for European security is the politically decided one of where to place the limit to what is ordinary interaction (trans-national politics) and what is a *security* problem. The 'security problem' status can be asserted by appeal to the category of interference. This the East generally did until the mid-1980s when criticism of human rights was accepted as in principle legitimate. The pretext now heard invokes a different aspect of security; lack of human rights is justified in terms of internal security, and sovereignty is thus at risk from within rather than from the objections raised from without (interference). 'Vulnerabilities' may be confessed. Order has to be maintained. In these cases, the East has to mobilise a logic of security and international politics to combat phenomena that are seen by the West as natural parts of civil and civilised interaction. The problems of the East in this regard are unlikely to be alleviated by the process of Europeanisation and normalisation of East–West relations.

For the East, there is direct, defensive action to be taken by a nation which forms the object of such criticism; the question whether and how to label these interactions as security problems or violations of international law – how to take them out of the area of trans-national politics, which are supposed to function according to the rules of domestic politics. Then at the institutional level there is the task of designing a European security system able to handle these problems. Marek Grela (Chapter 7), amongst others, points to some of the dilemmas involved in setting up a European security system that both allows the necessary processes of change and at the same time provides for a degree of stability. The question of how to deal with this issue constitutes a major issue for Western *Ostpolitik.*

The *Western* concept of security focuses more on the *military* dimension, on the security problem arising if one is to face an opponent superior in *power.*

Basically this is due to the difference between what Buzan labels 'strong' and 'weak' states. He distinguishes between strong and weak *powers* – the classic question of power to influence others – and strong and weak *states*, referring to the strength of the state as state, its coherence, the degree of harmony between state and nation, and between its different components: physical base, institutions and ideas. In this sense the states in Eastern Europe are much weaker states. They are thus much more vulnerable at the level of institutions and ideas – whereas the Western states are so coherent that they are mainly to be threatened through physical power. This does not necessarily mean *use* of physical power, but the main fear is that in the *shadow* of Eastern power the West will be vulnerable to coercive diplomacy. On further investigation, it becomes clear that the right wing in the West *does* in fact doubt the capacity of Western society to withstand pressure. For the Right in particular, Western European states have been sapped by decadence, the welfare state, post-material values, etc.[54]

So in reality the West is also rather ambivalent towards enhanced political and societal interaction with the East. The patterns of reciprocal fear can be modelled (Figure 17.2). The fear in the West is not that 'Eastern values' may somehow prevail, but rather of the 'softness' of the Western population being somehow part and parcel of the spreading ignorance regarding the motives of the East and the rules of the power-politics game. The Western security establishment fears that the characteristic weaknesses of democracies can be exploited by diplomatic manoeuvres, and the 'breakthrough' feared is supposed to happen at the level of 'high politics'.

The context of the model in Figure 17.2, we remember, is the withdrawal of the overlay which has for forty years limited interaction

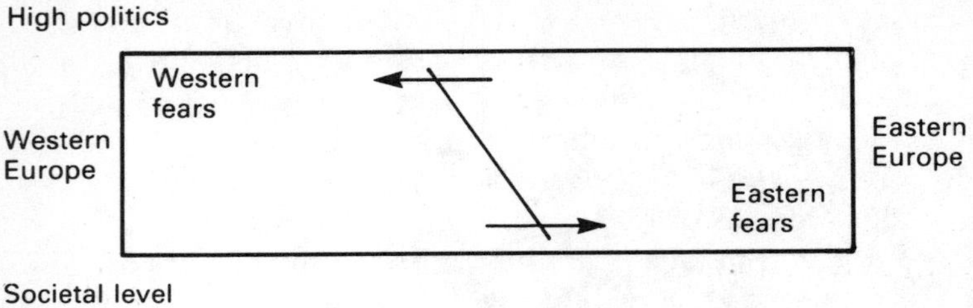

Figure 17.2

between the blocs, and structured it on the lines of the superpower conflict.[55] The overlay is now 'retreating', and Europe is consequently less stable. One way or another, the two parts of Europe are tending to drift towards each other. This necessarily entails more contacts and mutual influence. It means new options, and maybe perspectives for transformation of the regional system, but it also means – for the professionally pessimistic, and all societies have, and have to have, a security establishment – a higher level of fears of breakthrough in the non-military East–West war. So we start to worry more about breakthroughs. And breakdowns. At a time when the level of hope in society at large is rising.

As the fears are *asymmetrical* (Figure 17.2), to understand the situation is not simply to establish whether it is the one *or* the other side that is gaining ground. It is not possible to say who should feel secure, and who insecure. There are fears on both sides, but different ones. The fears of both sides may very well be founded. And for those who favour a continuation of the process of détente and Europeanisation, the fears of both sides should be taken into account by both sides because if any of the elite groups threatened feels *too* threatened there is a risk of the whole process being paralysed.[56]

So to dabble in politics a bit: the main task at present might be to stabilise both West–West relations[57] and the basic political/social system in the East – within the overall framework of change.

What is threatened is what peace researchers have traditionally seen as relations of domination. The pressure is mostly on the inter-state dimension in the West (superpower dominance), and on the political–societal dimension in the East (domestic relations of power and control). In the present situation the paradoxical task of peace politics might be to stabilise exactly these two relations of 'domination'; the reactions from these quarters are the most likely stumbling blocks for a process of détente.

The reason why this is a task for peace researchers is that they take détente seriously as a *principled* project, trying to work in a long-term perspective of *transformation*; including transformation of the two threatened relations of domination, which are more likely to change when imbedded in a steadily-moving, integrated process.

This interest in specific groups and interests points to the classic question of *actors*, often presented as states *or* sub-state actors. The approach presented in this study analyses by disaggregating the state, but at the sub-state level one of the main groups sees itself as being the true guardian of the national interest – the security establishment. In this way the state-as-actor is present as actor in the state.

3.3 Actors (Figuration Domestically and Internationally)

The figuration of power is *trans-national*. This book offers several convincing cases for this: most direct is probably the analysis by P. Lemaitre (Chapter 10) of Hungarian security thinking, where a crucial motive behind the Western oriented economic strategy of the reform forces is a search abroad for allies for the process of reform. The reform group knows there will be situations when it will be incapable of enforcing its policy against domestic opposition, but it does have the power to make trans-national 'linkages' that may change the balance of forces at the later critical moment. This is to operate consciously at the level of the trans-national figuration of power.

'Trans-national'? Is this one more version of the 'liberalist' attempt to deny the specificity of international politics? No. National politics *are* different from international politics. But the interplay of power and domestic politics is such that, though the form of power changes when the borders are crossed, the figuration of power is in a sense *one*.[58]

Let us take the relationship between 'fractions' in the Soviet Union and New Thinking. A policy can be upheld for its appeal to groups whose views are incompatible; in the Soviet Union, correlation-of-forces thinking *and* 'new thinking' can at present be the basis for the same conclusion: the necessity of *perestroika* and *uskorenije* (acceleration). Therefore for the West, to avoid destabilising this new Soviet policy does not only mean respecting the key fears of the *major* policy formulating groups (who, for example, deny the validity of the Brezhnev doctrine). It is also necessary to be aware of the calculations that make supporters (or non-opponents) out of other groups (who, for example, definitely see it as *unacceptable* to 'lose Eastern Europe').

Another example: if a new détente is to be acceptable to 'NATO circles' in the West, the latter must not feel outmanoeuvred by Gorbachev.[59]

The kind of awareness prescribed here is often limited to a discussion of whether this or that policy brings this or that group into power on the other side – and *then* of the foreign policy this group will conduct. (The classic theme: does dovish policy strengthen 'their' doves – or their hawks?) It is rarely perceived that no single group 'has' power – power lies *in between* several groups. And this unstable domestic figuration is in constant interplay with the international figuration.

More schematically we could point out the different roles of actors at different levels:

1. The logic of the international system, and the role it allocates to the superpowers, limits the superpower's policy choice.[60]

   (In Europe, there are different roles for government, opposition parties and critical movements.[61])
2. Basically governments have the responsibility for day-to-day politics – and a limited possibility for formulating visions. Research on parties in power therefore tends to focus on the interplay of the policies of states – how they reinforce or hinder each other.
3. It is in parties that are at present in opposition that we find most of the 'new security concepts'. 'Actors' in opposition will feel the need to present images of *how the present or future could be different* if another party had gained power. Therefore the alternatives will often be in a short- to medium-term perspective, and deal with security, a more benign East–West interaction, etc.
4. The real *visions* about a different situation will usually originate from social movements. As the ideas are not 'realistic' they will be viewed as 'unpolitical', or irrelevant and irresponsible.[62] Established parties will always be hesitant to present this kind of thinking.

This scheme should not, of course, be taken as absolute – peace movements play a role here and now, and governments sometimes present visionary plans. But it points to a certain complementarity of perspectives even when the programs are synchronically incompatible. The domestic interplay might constitute a kind of informal compromise process *over a certain period of time*.

The argument against 'alternativistic' definitions of security (section 3.1) is reinforced if we note that genuinely alternative security can originate only with certain actors.[63] It is not thought of as future state policy (because then it would have to relate to the tradition and would inevitably get involved with the traditional meaning of security either by taking it over or by denying it and thus mirroring it). The interesting 'alternative security' of the social movements is that which does not define itself in relation to the state, but defines its own independent tasks. It can in this way create a *détente from below* that is compatible but not identical with, nor unproblematic for, the traditional détente from above. (This compatibility is not necessarily any part of the originating intention. As soon as the movement stops defining itself *in relation to* state policy – and thus reactively in a basic sense[64] there is a good chance that its activities, now defined in independent self-confidence, will operate at a different level and thence acquire the respect of the pragmatists in due course.)

The 'size' (importance) of a state is also likely to be decisive for its security considerations. The contributions here suggest a certain identity of outlook between the Nordic countries and Hungary and Bulgaria: a policy of small-scale but coherent measures intended to secure specific advantages and make space within a system they cannot hope to influence. The policy will directly relate to national core values. Medium-size nations work to secure or improve their own position in the international figuration. This category includes France, the FRG, Poland, the UK, and Italy.[65]

4 DICTIONARY OF 'SUPRA-CONCEPTS' AND 'CONCEPTS OF SECURITY'

'Concepts of security' are intended to describe 'how we should understand our *true* security interests' in relation to the other(s). (They define *what* security is and *how* it is to be realised – by what kind of international strategy.) 'Supra Concepts' are the analytical concepts that describe the dynamics of regional figurations.

4.1 Dictionary of 'Supra-concepts'

The aim in the long run is a *security community*. 'A SECURITY-COMMUNITY . . . is one in which there is real assurance that the members of the community will not fight each other physically, but will settle their disputes in some other way'.[66] War is ruled out; this links up to a possible definition of Peace.[67] Peace is when the institution of war is removed – when war is no longer a possibility. A security community is this realised at the regional level. (Security communities now exist only in some *sub*-regions, for example, Scandinavia, and (probably) *inside* the Western alliance.)

The possibilities on the road towards security community are:

1. Security built on alliances and balance of power/deterrence, that is: self-help security. When this system is stable – it is a security system, but with clear drawbacks.
2. Mutual security regime (Jervis, MccGwire). For our purposes, this is given the minimum definition implied in Jervis's work on security regimes:

   '*those principles, rules and norms that permit nations to be restrained in their behavior in the belief that others will reciprocate*'. This implies 'not only norms and expectations that facilitate cooperation, but a form of cooperation that is *more than the following of short run self-interest*'[68]

   A security regime has come into existence when possible short-term gains are *not* cashed in, as each member prefers to 'invest' in the positive development of the relationship. There is thus a *threshold* – defining the emergence of a security regime – a threshold where the actors start to exhibit self-restraint in the expectation of reciprocation.[69] These are the first limits to the traditional competition for relative gains.[70]
3. A different *system*, where there are *rules* and some kind of central organisation of European security. This relates to the concept of *regime* in the meaning of general regime theory: 'norms, rules and decision making procedures around which actors' expectations converge in a given issue area of international relations'.[71] Regime thinking of this type is related to approaches focusing on international institutions and growing interdependence. This step is reached when there is a principled and basic agreement on a definition of principles, norms, rules and decision making procedures.[72] To what extent this takes the form of international *organisations* or legally binding security orders is largely a pragmatic question in this perspective. The decisive point is the convergence around common 'rules of the game' (implicit or

explicit) and thus a high level of regulation – more or less formalised.[73]

4. Conflict transformation to a 'non-violent conflict culture'. At the regional level this is identical to a 'security community' – but it implies a stress on the continuation of conflict as a dynamic factor.[74] The realisation of conflict culture involves retaining or increasing the positive role of conflict. An example of this might be the impetus imparted by the continuing conflict among catholics and protestants in i.a. Germany of today.[75]

These 4 concepts constitute a *ladder of analytical concepts*. The analysis of such levels should be taken further so that the concepts more precisely designate qualitatively different stages, allowing the situation to be regularly monitored. It would also help to illuminate the crucial difficulties involved at any juncture, and to set feasible goals – e.g., when to set the aim of 'collective security', and when this would be counterproductive.

The concept of 'security complex' is of a different kind, as it is a unifying framework for analysing the processes and explaining the dynamics of security in an area. This it can do *across* the various steps. But it says very little about *aims* or practical *measures*. It is implicit in the idea that the concept is a tool for *conflict management* (and not conflict solution). It can 'teach' the participants about unfavourable interactions, in particular security dilemmas. Generally by shifting the *level* of analyses from national and/or global to regional dynamics it should breed an understanding of the *interactive* character of security. However, it still does not contain standards for change – except for that moment when the complex changes to a new one, by actors joining or leaving or by basic shifts in patterns of opposition or alliance. There is therefore a complementarity between the concept of security complex as an ahistorical explanatory structure and the list of supra-concepts that (i) show the quality of the relationships at a given time, (ii) point out the particular dynamics and dangers of that kind of constellation. All the listed concepts are 'mixed-motive' – cooperation and conflict – and therefore they all contain the possibility of the next move being up *or* down.[76]

'Conflict formation', too, is essentially a dynamic concept for the analysis of structures (or 'structuration'). It is one of the main dynamics at work within or 'across' the security complex (see Figure 17.3 over leaf).

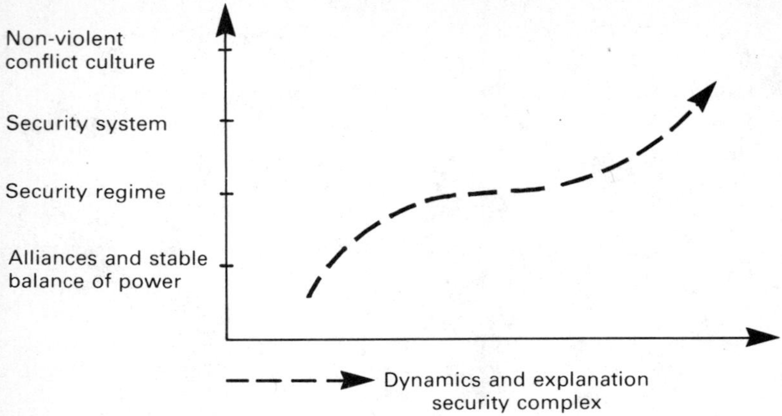

Figure 17.3

4.2 Dictionary of 'Concepts of Security'

'*Collective Security*'
This system is basically an organised balance of power: all against the aggressor.

According to West German Social Democrats like Egon Bahr and Erhard Eppler, the international legal structure for a 'European Peace Order' should be '*a system of collective security*' (a European peace treaty).[77] This is, as Bahr puts it, a system where 'every state has its borders guaranteed by all the others'.[78] However, this raises two categories of problems: (i) It is a system building on the possibility of war. (Will we all threaten to set off a possible world war to guarantee the borders of Romania or Greece?[79]) It is an enlarged system of deterrence; this is against the logic of Common Security out of which the proposal is stated to grow. (ii) It says nothing about the regulation of *non-military* threats. Should all states join together in a holy alliance upholding the existing systems? Or should they support 'natural' change? When power is centralised in an all-European security organisation, it is hard to imagine completely sovereign national decisions on the regulation of trans-border flows. Related to the latter is the problem that all *orders* imply a structuration of patterns of influence, thus they are inherently *political* (include domestic effects).[80] It is therefore very hard to imagine a system of collective security combining with the existing ideologically and socioeconomically competing systems, unless it were built *over* the alliances – an improved CSCE regime.[81]

Peaceful Coexistence
In the late 1980s this term ceased to have a very precise sense. Now it seems to mean the free and peaceful competition of the systems. Previously the notion had the dual characteristic of non-state class struggle and state-to-state peace. This derived from the belief that the 'peace' that resulted from arms parity was in a sense 'forced' on the warmongering imperialists, and in the long run served the cause of socialism. In this sense, it was unacceptable to most Western political groups. The 'new' concept stresses interdependence and 'peaceful coexistence' as a *necessary* condition of equal opportunities in peaceful competition. On this, see the chapters by Podlesnyi and Lemaitre (Chapters 4 and 10).

Détente
Many questions attend the use of this term (see Wæver's Chapter 12). It seems to imply something more than just 'relaxation of tension' (the literal meaning of the term). It is thus generally used to designate a relatively enduring process with an unspecified perspective of conflict transformation.

'Common Security'
This is a concept based on the perception of the negative sum dynamics of the security dilemma and of the impossibility in the nuclear era of settling the East–West conflict by a 'victory'.

In order not to diminish the security of the other, certain self-limitations are to be respected in the effort to achieve security. And together the two sides are to develop models for mutually non-threatening means of security – military as well as non-military. The concept has, at least as regards the first step, a meaning very similar to 'Security Regime' (*à la* Jervis).

However, it is claimed by the adherents of the concept – especially researchers and social democratic politicians in the FRG – that it also contains long-range perspectives. It is generally acknowledged that the concept does not set out a *process*, regarding (for example) the means by which short-term stabilisation of mutual deterrence will in the long term lead to the overcoming of deterrence.

Another – in this context more problematic – ambiguity is this: it is said that there can be no security that does not take into account the security of the adversary, and to that extent all security is necessarily common. On the other hand, the same notion is presented as something to be created – a *political* project, a *choice*, and maybe even a *model* for the future organisation of European security.[82]

Comprehensive Security

Since the advent in power of Gorbachev, the Soviet Union has been elaborating a series of new concepts of international relations. Among these is comprehensive security. It is at the top of the hierarchy of the 'New Thinking', and its particular merit is to include all forms of security, including the non-military. It was first proposed at the XXVIIth Congress of the CPSU. It has four components, military, political, economic and humanitarian. The military components calls upon the superpowers to renounce war conventional and nuclear. It also calls for disarmament to be promoted, and includes the concepts of 'reasonable sufficiency' (see Chapter 4 by Podlesnyi) and non-offensive defence. In the political field, it stresses the right to national self-determination. In the economic field it calls for an end to all politically determined embargoes, and for a new international economic order. In the humanitarian field, human rights are stressed, and reference is made to freedom of emigration. It has three levels, global, regional and national.[83] It is a sort of umbrella concept among security concepts, and it 'aims to make "peaceful coexistence" the supreme universal principle of interstate relations'.[84]

When talking about a '*System* of Comprehensive Security', the reference seems to be especially to an upgrading of the role of the United Nations; this institution is in principle assigned 'the decisive role'.[85] At the 42nd session of the United Nations General Assembly (September 1987), Gorbachev launched an appeal for turning the UN into 'a mechanism capable of discussing common problems in a responsible fashion and at a representative level and mutually searching for a balance of differing, contradictory, yet real, interests of the contemporary community of states and nations' (*Pravda*, 17 September 1987[86]). On this occasion, he stressed 'the idea of a "*comprehensive system of international security*" – the idea advanced at the 27th CPSU Congress' eighteen months earlier.[87]

Except for a very general notion of interdependence (almost of the 'everything is related to everything' type) the concept of 'comprehensive security' seems to imply mainly a proposal for institutional arrangements. Disarmament seems to be essential to this. It is less clear what, if any, are the innovations in this concept which are expected to prevent its sharing the fate of previous proposals of this kind.[88]

Reasonable Sufficiency

This is defined in Chapter 4.

'Mutual Security'
This is now used energetically by, for example, the West German Minister of Defence Scholz. There it seems to be close to the minimum meaning of 'security regime' (Jervis).

*****

If we compare the two lists, we will see that most of the political terms are close to step (iii) in the first list – the alternative security *system*. There is a lack in the political debate of terms for processes and steps. (Maybe détente does invoke this image in many quarters but the term is controversial and directly linked to a specific period.) This facilitates tergiversation and evasion. The scientific literature on common security makes some attempt to fill in this lacuna.

It seems that the political concepts are generally too high up the ladder. Concepts such as common security that cover the full extent of the ladder are insufficiently explicit, and tend to fudge the problem of process.

This might indicate something general about the debate on European security: the difficulty of coming up with political projects whose effects are far-reaching, but which take their starting point in present reality and secure stability by a combination of continuity and change. Referring back to the 'division of labour' between different actors (section 3.3.), this might indicate that the opposition parties find it difficult to fulfil their role; their ideas are either alternativistic or short-term.[89]

5 COMMON INTERESTS?

'Is there a security interest common to both Eastern and Western Europe? If so, is it compatible with national and alliance security interests?'

Yes, the European states have a major common interest in managing their common conflict, their common security complex, so that it can climb to qualitatively higher steps on the ladder of benign interaction.

To the second part of the question, one could answer – with only a slightly rhetorical twist – 'yes, because if they were not compatible with alliance and national security they would not be common interests, because they would not be *interests*'. The alliances are necessary building blocs for what ever all-European structures might be considered. And basically security *is* national security. Regional arrangements work to the extent that they can enhance national security.[90] The essential question for European security should therefore be: can the European states create benign security dynamics in the regional complex – can they tame the security dilemma? In the longer run, this means channelling the East–West conflict into forms of competition which are not only *non-violent* but also *non-security*. The task is to 'push back' the use of the emergency right to label challenges as 'security interests'. 'Security' is a label used by a regime when it needs or wants to claim a special 'state' right to use all means necessary to hinder a particular development that allegedly threatens 'security interests'. More and more trans-national activities should become purely 'economic', 'social' and 'political'.

The military structure should therefore become stable, undynamic, and not raise political issues. Security problems would then not arise – and 'security' would not be something we all walked about 'enjoying'; it would be something taken for granted. In the non-military fields, trans-national activities that would be labelled security problems today would probably multiply in a 'europeanised' Europe. In a non-violent conflict culture, social problems would be dealt with as social problems, economic problems treated by economic means and political problems would have to be faced as such.[91]

Creating clear rules of the game for legitimate interaction across the East–West border means – in the language of international law – a more precise formulation of the rule of non-intervention and especially its *limits*: what is only a challenge and not a threat, what is to be met by politics and not by security politics.

The discussion of common interest between East and West often focuses on the high level of commonality of *some* European countries – 'Central Europe' for example, or the two Germanies. We will first discuss this issue and then – finally – conceptualise the character of communality in Europe at large.

Do the countries closest to the dividing line have some special common interests? This seems to be the basic idea of (for example) the German version of the Central-Europe debate. One of the most important contributions to this debate is an article by Peter Bender (a Social Democratic journalist) on '*Mitteleuropa*: Mode, Model or Motive?'.[92] He argues convincingly that there can be no special solutions for Central Europe – no model. True, people in Central Europe feel the division more intensely and therefore form a community of interest to promote more détente than communities less immediately affected.[93] But, these are not really special *interests*. People close to the line are just more sensitive to the problems caused by the division. Most of the problems will be all-European. The logic of the security debate, the problems and approaches will be the same in the centre as at the periphery of Europe. The security interests of both are connected in the longer run (cf. 'security complex'). The difference between Central Europe and the other areas is mainly one of *time*; of when the various debates and arguments arrive – (or not arrive) – see Michael Clarke's Chapter). Pierre Hassner asks:

> 'Does the concept of common interests make the two German states closer to their neighbours or does it estrange them? In other words: are the interests they support common to all mankind, or merely to all-Europe, or exclusively to the greater Germany, or unique to themselves?' Expressions such as 'No more war must start from German soil' or the idea of a 'community of destiny', these are – as Pierre Hassner points out – 'extremely unclear. A nuclear war that started on Belgian or Bulgarian territory would be just as culpable and disastrous as one that started on German soil. It is probably illusory to suppose that a nuclear war that broke out in Germany could fail to extend to American and Soviet territory; it is undoubtedly an illusion to believe it would not reach Poland or France . . . The same is true of the harm that can result from the civil use of nuclear energy or from modern technology dangerous to the other highly developed states. If the awareness of these things is greater in the two German states than elsewhere, this is the result of a cast of mind influenced more by a specific cultural and religious tradition than by interests'.[94]

Not for immediate survival, not for direct security, but for improving the workings of the regional security system and thereby improving their security, all European states depend on a *process* that has to be *common* because it is a very delicate process that could be blocked by a lot of different actors. The process of détente and Europeanisation is a kind of multi-veto project, and there is a high degree of interdependence in all projects implying considerable change.[95]

That which is common is something missing – it is that which is not there. There *are* common interests but it cannot scientifically be decided that this or that specific development is something that all ought to see as part of the 'common interests' – i.e., as *their* interest. *What is common is a possible political project*, which can take very many different forms, and the more concrete common interests will therefore be defined by mutual interaction, that is: politically.[96]

The common security interest is first of all the possibility of improving the operations of the regional dynamics – cutting down on vicious circles. This requires first and foremost that a real *dialogue* be created in which it is possible to put forward political and not only peace-political views and the first step consists of *raising one's voice*.[97]

It will not be enough to talk about 'the common interests' and what should *not* be allowed. A dynamic process also requires that the visions enter the process even though they contain threatening elements. There has to be give and take in a process limiting destabilisation, and a higher tolerance of criticism and *politics*. The actors must present their *own* visions – not something that is already a compromise. To quote Pope John Paul II: 'If, in a dialogue, one relinquish one's own understanding of the truth, what is lost is not only one's own values; the purpose of the dialogue is also lost'.[98]

In one's own interest, certain limitations to the *form* taken by the competition of ideas and visions – some rules of the game, a conflict culture – must be worked out. These must however be an adequate channel for the ideas of the different parties. We could end with William Blake's words:

> If the sun or moon should doubt,
> They'd immediately go out

The task is to reconcile this with Nietzsche's view, that the main human weakness is hatred and revenge, forms taken by the drive toward uniformity and identity. The superior attitude is to reconcile oneself with the existence of that which is different. Thereby one avoids becoming merely reactive and can instead concentrate energy on *creative power*, and look well on that which one proposes.[99]

Notes and References

Generally this chapter benefited from being exposed at different stages to criticism and suggestions from the present project group: Barry Buzan, Ulla Holm, Pierre Lemaitre and Elzbieta Tromer. The responsibility for all the remaining errors is definitely mine.

1. For the present the most extensive presentation of the theoretical part of this project is Egbert Jahn, Pierre Lemaitre and Ole Wæver,

'European Security: Problems of Research on Non-Military aspects', *Copenhagen Papers* 1 (August 1987). A later and shorter version – by the same authors – appeared as 'Conflict Analysis and Conflict Continuation: Understanding the European Security Configuration through Concepts of Security', in Chadwick Alger and Michael Stohl (eds), *A Just Peace Through Transformation: Proceedings of the XIth General Conference of IPRA* (Boulder, Col. and London: Westview Press, 1988) 573–91. The latter version condenses some parts of the first publication and expands on other issues. Section 2 of the present chapter draws directly on these publications.

2. There exist numerous analyses of each of the two powers as well as quite a lot of looser remarks on both – especially from a European perspective. (The same evidence has been taken to show a reorientation of their *interests* rather than a decline.) Two general analyses that try to present the decline of *both* powers in some perspective are: Dieter Senghaas, *Die Zukunft Europas: Probleme der Friedensgestaltung* (Frankfurt/M: Suhrkamp Verlag, 1986); Paul Kennedy, *The Rise and Fall of the Great Powers: Economic Change and Military Conflict from 1500 to 2000* (New York: Random House, 1987).
3. Johan Galtung, *There are Alternatives* (Nottingham: Spokesman, 1984) 64.
4. See Pierre Hassner, 'The Politics of Western Europe and East-West Relations', in N. Andren and K. Birnbaum (eds), *Beyond Détente* (Leyden: A. W. Sijthoff, 1976) 5–37; 'Postwar Western Europe: The Cradle of Eurocommunism', in R. L. Tökes (ed.) *Eurocommunism and Détente* (Oxford: Martin Robertson, 1979) 19–67.
5. See Arnold L. Horelick, 'Détente by any other name', in *Bulletin of the Atomic Scientists* (October 1988) 5–6. He argues that the new phase we are entering 'rests on a shared premise about the correlation of forces . . . that in almost all components of the global competition the tide is running against the Soviet Union . . . If George Schultz were more given to Kissinger conceptualising, he might describe the strategy . . . required by the West as one for managing the decline of the Soviet Union.' (Kissinger defined détente as a strategy for managing the emergence of Soviet power.) But, both superpowers are in a difficult phase. And it is difficult to make long range projections. What is essential is Horelick's argument that both the global powers 'are more or less in synchrony with respect to the balance between their internal and external preoccupations. In almost all previous periods, one or the other superpower was in an inward-looking phase of its development while its counterpart was playing a more outwardly oriented, assertive foreign policy role'.
6. It has often been pointed out that Europeans react to both highs and lows in the superpower relationship (cf. Kissinger's famous remark in the *Memoirs*). But this analysis highlights superpower relations and thus reinforces the East–West structuration of Europe. In the 1980s the tendency has been for autonomous structures to emerge, which do not define themselves by relation to the superpowers either positively or negatively.

7. For an explanation of this historical change. See Jahn *et al.*, 'European Security' (Note 1) 25ff.
8. Klaus Rifbjerg, 'Min Drøm om Europa', *Weekendavisen*, 11 November 1988.
9. Most interesting regarding the late 1980s is probably the (different) ways this happens in the core countries France and FRG. See Werner Weidenfeld, 'Land im Brennpunkt Europas: Die europäische Qualität der Deutschen Frage', in P. von Bismarck *et al.*, *Die Teilung Deutschlands und Europas* (Bonn: Europa Union Verlag, 1984) 21–32; Klaus Schubert, '"Abschied" vom Nationalstaat – "Flucht" nach Europa? Anmerkungen zum neuen französischen Europa-Diskurs', in *Dokumente*, 1988/5, 341–50; Edgar Morin, *Penser l'Europe* (Paris: Editions Gallimard, 1987). See also Special Issue of *Current Research on Peace and Violence* on 'European Identity' (forthcoming).
10. *Bulletin Presse- und Informationsamt der Bundesregierung*, No. 92 (5 July 1988); Address in Memory of Knut Frydenlund (Oslo, September 1988); *Bulletin*, No. 44 (30 March 1988); *die Zeit*, No. 43 (21 October 1988) 3.
11. Kjell Goldmann, *Tension and Détente in Europe* (Stockholm: Esselte, 1974).
12. Hassner, 'Postwar Western Europe' (Note 4) and Egbert Jahn 'Social Reform Policy and Détente Policy in Eastern and Western Europe' in E. Jahn and Y. Sakamoto (eds), *Elements of World Instability: Proceedings of the IPRA Eighth General Conference* (Frankfurt and New York: Campus Verlag, 1981) 332ff.
13. Galtung, *There are Alternatives* (Note 3) 69–80; Jahn, 'Social Reform Policy' (Note 2) and especially Egbert Jahn, 'Elemente eines friedenswissenschaftlichen Entspannungsbegriffes', in P. Schlotter (ed.) *Europa Zwischen Konfrontation und Kooperation* (New York and Frankfurt: Campus Verlag, 1982) 15–36.
14. In the terminology of Buzan this is 'diminishing overlay'. See especially B. Buzan, G. Rizvi *et al.*, *South East Asian Insecurity and the Great Powers* (London: Macmillan, 1986).
15. If any! The method of figuration analysis in fact points to the likelihood of the result being different from *all* of the projects (see Norbert Elias, Michel Foucault, Hannah Arendt). On this see Ole Wæver, 'Politics of Movement. A contribution to political theory in and on peace movements', forthcoming in K. Kodama and U. Vesa (eds), *Towards a Comparative Analysis of Peace Movements* (London: Gower, 1989).
16. See Jahn *et al.*, especially 'Conflict Analysis' (Note 1) 574–8.
17. Soviet scholars and politicians occasionally take the trouble to argue that the concept is *not* aimed against anyone – and in particular not at the USA! This, however, is not the issue in the present analysis. We are not attempting to set up new 'enemy images', or conclude that the 'Common European House' is a Soviet plot. The aim is to investigate the effect of such organising principles. Creating international frameworks necessarily implies a topological *structuration* of politics. These competing Europes will mean different *spatial organisations of flows of*

information, goods and political influence. In each case, the motives ascribed to the creation of a geopolitical structuration are no less relevant than those that 'in fact' inspired it. H.-D. Genscher, for example, also takes the trouble to underline that Western European security cooperation (and the Franco–German partnership in particular) is not directed *against* anyone. This does not endear it to the Soviets.

18. See Kenneth N. Waltz, *Theory of International Politics* (Reading, Mass.: Addison-Wesley, 1979).
19. Cf. Gorbachev on the occasion of Kohl's visit to Moscow in November 1988, *Tass* (24 October 1988).
20. For example, Parl. Staatssekretär in the Ministry of Inner-German Relations, Dr Ottfried Hennig in *Bulletin*, 16 September 1987, 764.
21. See in Egbert Jahn, 'Die Beziehungen Westeuropas zu Osteuropa (Einschliesslich der Sowjetunion)', paper from June 1985. Published (in Dutch) in E. Boeker, M. v. Ophuijsen and M. Tulp (eds), *Oost-West. Mogelijkjeden voor een Nederlandse vredespolitiek* (Amsterdam, 1985) 45–57.
22. Lord Young, the British Minister for Trade and Industry, declared in October 1988 at the annual conference of the Conservative Party, that the EEC would not be complete until it included the Eastern European countries. On the divisions within the West German liberal–conservative coalition, see Chapter 12 of this volume. Most of the CDU politicians present the EEC as *the* European organisation. Foreign Minister Genscher did not at first subscribe to this model. But he seems now, when stressing the cultural dimension, to suggest that 'All-Europe' would merely be an enlarged Western Europe – that the whole of Europe will find its way back to the true European tradition represented by the West.
23. See the debate among Kundera, Brodsky, Mifosz and others on 'Russia and the West', centred on the evaluation and interpretations of Dostoyevsky and his picture of man. See *Cross Currents. A Yearbook of Central European Culture*, no. 5 (Michigan, 1986) 455–505.
24. See Dietrich Geyer, 'Ostpolitik und Geschichtsbewusstsein in Deutschland', in *Vierteljahrshefte für Zeitgeschichte*, vol. 34 (2) (1986) 147–59.
25. This can be combined with the argument that both global powers are part of most of the world's regional security complexes – both are clearly part and parcel of European security. The argument leads towards Europe (iv), and enables us to avoid deciding whether Europe does or does not include the Soviet Union (or Russia *simpliciter*). It seems analytically advantageous to *avoid* this kind of decision. The choices Europe (i) and Europe (ii) involve taking sides in the conflicts. Europe (iv) is both *one* of the competing Europes *and* an analytical concept that keeps open the possibility of investigating the other three.
26. See, for example Johan Galtung, *Europe, the contradictory* (forthcoming).
27. This point is at odds with the perspective of Barry Buzan in Chapter 1 of this volume, and his two-step model of Western Europeanisation

first, Common Security second. The question is whether the level of interdependence is so high that Western Europeanisation *also* depends on all-Europeanisation. This could be so because détente would be needed in relations with the Soviet Union, both in order to limit the military expenditure of Western Europe's going it alone, and to avoid interaction with Eastern Europe causing destabilisation and/or excluding any prospect of German reunification. Such détente would inhibit the construction of an independent Western European defence force. This criticism takes the present situation in Europe as constituting a security complex. Buzan argues that Europe becomes a security complex only after the superpower overlay has been removed.

28. In the terminology of international relations, we might say that the former is the *idealist*, the latter the *realist* approach. Regional International Security is based on the assumption that there will always be security problems, security dilemmas and a danger of *mistakes*. Euronational security is based on the idea of (only) a specific state (or a specific group of states) being *the problem*.
29. See, for example, Johan Galtung, 'Social Cosmology and the Concept of Peace', in his *Essays in Peace Research*, vol. V (Copenhagen: Chr. Ejlers Forlag, 1980) 415–31.
30. See Richard K. Ashley, 'The Geopolitics of Geopolitical Space: Toward a Critical Social Theory of International Politics', *Alternatives*, vol. XII (4) (October 1987) 403–34.
31. Jahn *et al.*, 'European Security' (Note 1) 17ff.
32. See Jahn *et al.*, 'European Security' (Note 1), Wæver 'New Non-military East–West Controversies in a De-nuclearizing Europe', paper for TAPRI workshop on 'Political Consequences of Nuclear Disarmament in Europe' (Tampere Finland, June 1986); 'Der Streit der Ideologien und die Gemeinsame Sicherheit', common paper from SPD and SED published in *Frankfurter Rundschau* (28 August 1988) (and many other places); Thomas Meyer, 'Ein neuer Rahmen für den Ost–West-Dialog', *Die neue Gesellschaft* (1987/10) 870–7.
33. Nordic security in the 1980s constitute a clear example of this; see Chapter 14 by Pertti Joenniemi in this volume.
34. See Glenn H. Snyder, 'The Security Dilemma in Alliance Politics', *World Politics* (July 1984) 461–95.
35. See Wilfried von Bredow and Rudolf Horst Brocke, *Das deutschland-politische Konzept der SPD*, Erlanger Beiträge zur Deutschlandpolitik 1986, especially 95.
36. Link, 'Internationale Politik: der Ost-West-Konflikt', in K. von Beyme *et al.*, *Funk-Kolleg Politik* (Frankfurt: Fischer, 1987) 334–60. In English: Werner Link, *The East–West Conflict* (Leamington Spa, 1986). For a good discussion of the East–West conflict: (i) conflict about hegemony or social systems?, (ii) as reality or 'a wall in our head', (iii) possibilities of overcoming it, see C. Rix (ed.), *Ost–West-Konflikt: Wissen wir, wovon wir sprechen?* (Baden-Baden: Nomos Verlag, 1987).
37. See also Jahn *et al.* 'European Security' (Note 1) 24ff.
38. See Chapter 4 by Pavel Podlesny in this volume; and Egbert Jahn,

'Der Einfluss der Ideologie auf die sowjetische Aussen- und Rüstungspolitik', *Osteuropa* (May, June and July 1986).

39. A thesis shared by, for example, Zbiegniew Brzezinski, *Game Plan: A Geostrategic Framework for the Conduct of the U.S. Soviet Contest* (Boston: Atlantic Monthly Press, 1986).
40. Barry Buzan, 'The Southeast Asian Security Complex', *Contemporary Southeast Asia* (forthcoming).
41. B. Buzan, G. Rizvi *et al.*, *South East Asian Insecurity* (Note 14) 7–8.
42. *Konfliktformationen im internationalen System* (Frankfurt: Suhrkamp Verlag, 1988). This includes a reprint of his first (1973) attempt at global analysis in terms of conflict formations.
43. To 'dump' the old concept, it is not sufficient to subject it to a sustained critique and then redefine. If it is an essential, metaphysical concept – as 'security' is – it will just follow in our pioneering footsteps. It will reappear in mirrored form, as that in relation to which the new is defined. Such concepts have to be treated more 'respectfully' if they are to be caught napping. The aim should be to make them slide: to go on dealing with the classical core but create a new circumscription. In this way the meaning *does* change. See Jacques Derrida, *Positions* (Chicago: University of Chicago Press, 1981) and *Margins of Philosophy* (Brighton: Harvester, 1982).
44. Jean-Jacques Rousseau, 'On Social Contract or Principles of Political Right', in A. Ritter and J.C. Bondanella, *Rousseau's Political Writings* (New York and London: Norton, 1988) 90.
45. Johan Galtung, '25 years of Peace Research: Ten Challenges and Some Responses', *Journal of Peace Research*, 2 (1985) 141–58; J. David Singer, 'Inter-nation Influence: A Formal Model', *The American Political Science Review* (June 1963) 420–30; Gunnar Sjöstedt, *The Non-Military Power Structure: Dispersion or Concentration?*, forthcoming; and a special issue on 'International Security' of *Külpolitika* (Zalka Press: Budapest, 1988).
46. A collective publication by Buzan, Tromer, Lemaitre and Wæver is scheduled for 1990.
47. Barry Buzan, *People, States and Fear* (Brighton: Wheatsheaf, 1983) 6ff.
48. Buzan, *People, States and Fear* (Note 47) 36–93; and Henry Kissinger, *A World Restored* (Boston: Houghton Mifflin, 1957) 29ff, 82ff, 207ff, 305ff, and 324ff.
49. Richard E. Neustadt and Ernest R. May, *Thinking in Time: The Uses of History for Decision Makers* (New York and London: Free Press, 1986); Robert Jervis, *Perception and Misperception in International Politics* (Princeton: Princeton University Press, 1976) especially 58ff and 217ff.
50. For a typology of economic effects on security, see Hanns Maull, 'Trade, Technology and Security: Implications for East Asia and the West: Part I', *Adelphi Papers*, 218 (Spring 1987) 23–38. The effects of economic performance have to be weighed against the risks of increased vulnerability to foreign leverage made possible by dependence. On the rationale of linking up to the world market, see the chapters by Kiss (Chapter 9), Grela (Chapter 7) and especially Lemaitre (Chapter 10) in this volume.

51. *Külpolitika*, 'International Security' (Note 45).
52. As we shall see below, 'economic security' has here a double meaning: (i) securing the economic *system* – and thereby the social status quo (state) – and (ii) securing the performance of the economic system, that is welfare in *society*.
53. A good discussion of Eastern as well as Western 'offensive ideology' is found in Erhard Eppler, *Wie Feuer und Wasser: Sind Ost und West friedensfähig?* (Hamburg, Rowohlt, 1988). A more formal and concise presentation of a very similar analysis is Egbert Jahn, 'The Tactical and Peace Political Concept of Détente' in *Bulletin of Peace Proposals* (1981/1) 33–43.
54. For example, Werner Kaltefleiter and Robert L. Pfaltzgraff, *The Peace Movements in Europe and the United States* (London and Sydney: Croom Helm, 1985) (especially the introduction by Kaltefleiter and the chapter by N. H. Serry); Andreas Windel, 'The Case of the Federal Republic of Germany', in Sverre Lodgaard and Karl Birnbaum (eds), *Overcoming Threats to Europe: A New Deal for Confidence and Security*, SIPRI (Oxford: Oxford University Press, 1987) 90–193. For some penetrating comments on the way, for example, *The Economist* turns Gorbachev into a threatening figure who can outsmart the West, see Rüdiger Zimmermann, 'Adversary Images in East–West Perception: Integrating Gorbachev', *Current Research on Peace and Violence* (1987/1) 44–9.
55. As is argued in section 2.4, this conflict is (in Europe) not to be seen as merely exterior and imposed – it is very real *in* and *among* the societies in Europe. Luckily it is not necessary here to settle the historical hierarchy of causation in the mutual interplay of domestic and extra-European conflicts. The convergence of the social conflict and a geopolitical structure created a stable format for European security. For internal as well as international reasons this format is 'losing its grip'.
56. Note that the present analysis does not apply to social groups threatened in their *personal* area by the process – this is not likely to cause a veto on détente. On the other hand, we are not talking about the national security debate or popular opinion either. It is a question of crucial elite perspectives on 'national security'.
57. See Christoph Bertram, 'Aufgaben und Perspektiven, der Sicherheitspolitik Westeuropas in den neunziger Jahren', *Aus Politik und Zeitgeschichte*, B 18/88 (29 April 1988) 3–11; especially 8.
58. This could also be formulated as the interplay of national and international figurations.
59. Another important example and a similar mode of understanding can be found in Sverre Lodgaard, 'Threats to European Security: the main elements', in Lodgaard and Birnbaum (eds), *Overcoming Threats to Europe* (note 54), 3–36. Lodgaard points to the coexistence of 'World War I' and 'World War II' images of the current war-danger: both groups have to feel secure.
60. See Waltz, *Theory of International Politics* (Note 18) and especially Snyder, 'The Security Dilemma' (Note 34).

61. This is dealt with more extensively in Jahn *et al.* 'European Security' (Note 1) Chapter 10.
62. And this is exactly what is necessary for a social movement to gain the initial *attention* required to *become* a political fact and force; see Ole Wæver, 'Politics of Movement' (Note 15).
63. Zsuzsa Hegedüs, 'The Challenge of the Peace Movement: Civilian Security and Civilian Emancipation', *Alternatives* (1987/1) 197–216; and the chapter by Mary Kaldor (Chapter 3) in the present volume.
64. See F. Nietzsche, *Zur Genealogie der Moral*, II, 12.
65. The GDR is in a peculiarly complicated situation with a role on the main axis (Paris, Bonn, Berlin, Warsaw, Moscow). It has to balance its own interests in a high-profile environment more like a stronger power – and a stronger state. The policy is to a very large extent built not on the basis of its own interests but on balancing the interests of others, mainly the FRG and Soviet Union – with some consideration for France and Poland. A uniquely dangerous position.
66. Karl W. Deutsch *et al., Political Community in the North Atlantic Area* (Princeton: Princeton University Press, 1957) 5.
67. Jahn *et al.*, 'European Security' (Note 1) 44–6.
68. Robert Jervis, 'Security Regimes', *International Organization*, vol. 362 (Spring 1982) 357–78; quote from 357.
69. See Ole Wæver, *The Interplay of Some Regional and Sub-regional Dynamics of Security*, paper presented at a conference at Uniwersytet Szczeciński, Poland (November 1987).
70. A clarification might be needed regarding 'security regime'. There is a tendency to use the term for reciprocal arrangements similar to those described by *general* regime theory (not Jervis's security regimes). In this broader sense, the term 'regime' is defined only by a high level of communality; those who enter upon a more or less formal arrangement. In this meaning, the main security regimes in Europe would be NATO and the WTO. Of course these also have the function of regulating security and conflicts among members. But that goes for classic alliances as well. So from this sense of 'security regime' not much would be gained. If one follows Jervis, it must be an implicit premiss that a security regime includes the central conflict. On the other hand, the protested usage seems already so common that it might be necessary to clarify by using Michael MccGwire's formulation 'Mutual Security Regime'. ('A mutual security regime for Europe?', *International Affairs* (1988/3) 361–79.)
71. Stephen D. Krasner, 'Structural Causes and Regime Consequences: regimes as intervening variable', *International Organization*, vol. 36 (2) (Spring 1982) 185–206; quote from 186.
72. See Peter Michael Nielsen, *CSCE-processen set i et regimeteoretisk perspektiv* ('The CSCE process in the perspective of regime theory', in Danish) MA thesis (Copenhagen, 1988).
73. Conceptually, one could also distinguish between mature and immature security regimes (parallel to Buzan's mature and immature anarchy). Immature security regimes have just passed the minimum threshold implied in Jervis's definition (self-restraint). Mature security

regimes have a more developed set of common norms (see the regime definition of Krasner and Nielsen, Notes 71 and 72).

74. An advantage of this concept is that the conflict culture (the behaviour and the development of the rules of the game) is something that needs to be practised from an early stage – and this is possible. Conflict cannot immediately assume the *form* of conflict culture; this is a longer-term goal, which is possible only after step (ii) at best.
75. See Wæver, 'New Non-military East–West Controversies' (Note 32).
76. See Glenn H. Snyder and Paul Diesing, *Conflict Among Nations; Bargaining, Decision Making and System Structure in International Crisis* (Princeton: Princeton University Press, 1977) 152–82, and especially the diagrams of a supergame on 168ff.
77. Bahr, *Zum europäischen Frieden* (Berlin: Corso bei Siedler, 1988) especially 90; Eppler, *Wie Feuer und Wasser* (Note 53) 41.
78. *Zum europäischen Frieden* (note 77) 90.
79. See Jahn *et al.*, 'European Security' (Note 1) 48.
80. See section 2 of the present chapter as well as my 'New Non-military East–West Controversies' (Note 32).
81. E. Bahr talks about 'collective security' as a system replacing the alliances. And rather soon! As soon as we have conventional stability guaranteed by treaty and of proven effectiveness, so that no state can attack another. (How they are then to enforce the system of collective security remains unclear to the present author.)
82. To this could be added a *political* criticism – that the perspective has a tendency to be socially status quo oriented by wanting (both sides) to respect the 'security interests' of the power holders on the other side, not least in non-military matters.
83. 'New political thinking views humanity and the world as a multicoloured and multifaced yet single whole indivisible primarily as to security. And security itself has numerous facets: military, political, economic, humanitarian, cultural, ecological. Any state which accepts the idea that the world is an integral whole will come to realise sooner or later that it cannot uphold and guarantee its interests outside the context of global, universal objectives', Soviet Foreign Minister Eduard Shevardnadze, 'Towards a Safe World', *International Affairs* (Moscow) (1988/9) 3–14, quotation from 5. See also László Kiss, 'Interpretation of Security in the Eighties' in *Külpolitika* (Note 45) 20ff.
84. *What's What in World Politics. A Reference Book* (Moscow: Progress Publishers, 1986) 96.
85. Minister of Foreign Affairs of the USSR, Eduard Shevardnadze, 'Foreign Policy and Diplomacy. Report at the Scientific and Practical Conference of the USSR Ministry of Foreign Affairs', in *International Affairs* (Moscow) (1988/10) 3–34 here 17. See Gorbachev's article in *Pravda*, 17 September 1987. This concept has been promoted through the United Nations – with some success according to Foreign Minister Shevardnadze, 'Closing Speech' on 27 July 1988, *International Affairs* (Moscow) (1988/10) 58–64; reference is to 59. It is sometimes also referred to as 'a system of all-embracing security'.

86. Translated as 'Reality and Guarantees for a Secure World', *International Security* (1987/11) 3–11.
87. 'Reality and Guarantees' (Note 86) 3.
88. There is also a specifically *Japanese* use of the term 'comprehensive security' which integrates economic security. This will not be included in the discussion here, as we are dealing with European security.
89. See Barry Buzan, 'Common Security, Non-provocative Defence, and the future of Western Europe', *Review of International Studies* (1987/4) 265–79.
90. 'National security policy, except when directed against a country unalterably committed to attack, is the more rational the more it succeeds in taking into consideration the interests, including the security interests, of the other side', Arnold Wolfers, *Discord and Collaboration* (Baltimore: Johns Hopkins University Press, 1962) 161. (The essay originally appeared in *Political Science Quarterly* (December 1952).)
91. The absolute opposite of 'in-security' is not security, but non-security. Security is the necessary concomitant of a security problem – a feeling of 'in-security'. Transcending this dialectic of 'in-security' and security leads to non-security.
92. Peter Bender, 'Mitteleuropa. Mode, Modell oder Motiv?', *Die neue Gesellschaft* (1987/4) 297–304.
93. There is a danger relating to the quantitative argument, 'more' détente, if the form or 'type' or conditions of détente are not considered (see my own chapter on the FRG (Chapter 12) in this volume). This might raise problems similar to those of the concept of common security, see Jahn *et al.*, 'European Security' (Note 1) 48–55.
94. Pierre Hassner, 'Zwei deutsche Staaten in Europa. Gibt es gemeinsame Interessen in der internationalen politik?', in W. Weidenfeld (ed.), *Die Identität der Deutschen* (Munich: Hans Hauser, 1983) 294–323; quotations from 297f (my translation).
95. Stabilisation does not in principle require the same degree of coordination, but in the longer run: 'The search for an immutable status quo is as sterile as the search for perfect security, and for the same reasons. Which is just another way of formulating the well-worn notion of peaceful change as the only alternative to war and revolution'. Pierre Hassner, 'Change and security in Europe, part I', *Adelphi Paper* 45 (1968) 10.
96. 'The search for a new system can be based only on political objectives', Hassner, 'Change and security' (Note 95) 4.
97. See John Paul II, 'Peace Dynamics', *The Atlantic Community Quarterly* (Summer 1985) 115–88; especially 116.
98. John Paull II quoted from *** (pseudonym for a representative of Solidarnosc), in *Die neue Gesellschaft* (1986/6) 548–56; quote from 554.
99. Especially (Frankfurt/M, Berlin, Wien: *Also Sprach Zarathustra*, and *Ecce Homo*, in *Werke* vols. II and III, Karl Schlechta (Hrsg.) Nietzsche's Ullstein Materialen). For the more specific explanation of how the attitude of giving – bestowing virtue, will to power – is able to 'make peace between moon and sun', see 'Of the Bestowing Virtue' the last chapter in part I of *Thus Spoke Zarathustra*.

Index